RECORDS

OF THE

TOWN OF BROOKHAVEN

SUFFOLK COUNTY
NEW YORK

THIS VOLUME CONTAINS THE ENTIRE RECORDS FROM 1798 TO MARCH, 1856, INCLUSIVE, COPIED FROM THE ORIGINAL RECORDS, IN THEIR ORDER, UNDER THE DIRECTION OF THE SUPERVISOR AND JUSTICES OF THE PEACE, AND PUBLISHED BY THE AUTHORITY OF THE TOWN

HERITAGE BOOKS
2012

HERITAGE BOOKS
AN IMPRINT OF HERITAGE BOOKS, INC.

Books, CDs, and more—Worldwide

For our listing of thousands of titles see our website
at
www.HeritageBooks.com

A Facsimile Reprint
Published 2012 by
HERITAGE BOOKS, INC.
Publishing Division
100 Railroad Ave. #104
Westminster, Maryland 21157

Originally published:
Port Jefferson, New York
Times Steam Job Print
1888

— Publisher's Notice —

In reprints such as this, it is often not possible to remove blemishes from the original. We feel the contents of this book warrant its reissue despite these blemishes and hope you will agree and read it with pleasure.

Pages 107–108 are missing from the original edition of this book.

International Standard Book Numbers
Paperbound: 978-0-7884-2849-4
Clothbound: 978-0-7884-9286-0

CERTIFICATE OF THE TOWN CLERK.

Suffolk County, } ss.
Town of Brookhaven.

I hereby certify that I have compared the printed records in this volume, with the original records in my office and found them to be literal and accurate transcripts thereof.

HENRY P. HUTCHINSON,
Town Clerk.

Middle Island, August 4, 1888.

CORRECTIONS OF MISPRINT.

Page 34.—May 1800.
" 34.—first Obtain.
" 46.—Phillops Roe.

PREFACE.

At a meeting of the following town officers, to wit : Supervisor, James E. Bayles ; Town Clerk, Henry P. Hutchinson and Justices, D. H. Buckingham, George W. Hopkins, Timothy Ketchum, A. H. Mills, George T. Osborn, D. H. Raynor, Charles R. Smith, and Wm. J. Weeks—at the Clerk's office, on Tuesday, March 3d. 1885, among the resolutions adopted and to be submitted to the electors of the town at the ensuing annual town meeting, was the following :

" Resolved, that the copying and publication of the Records of the town of Brookhaven now in the clerk's office, be continued from the close of the present published volume under the direction of the Supervisor and Justices of the Peace."

At the ensuing annual town meeting, the whole number of ballots cast, in reference to the above resolution, was two hundred and seventy-two, of which two hundred and fifty-two were in favor of it, and twenty against it.

At a meeting of the Supervisor, Town Clerk and Justices, held in Patchogue, May first, 1885, the following resolution was adopted :

" Resolved, that the Supervisor, James E. Bayles Geo. T. Osborn Esq. and William J. Weeks Esq. be and hereby are appointed and authorized to take charge of the copying and publication of the " Records" of the Town of Brookhaven, in accordance with Resolution, No. 2, passed at Town Meeting, April 7, 1885."

In executing the trust comprised in the foregoing resolutions, the committee first met at the town clerk's office, June 16th. 1885 and engaged Miss Cynthia Hutchinson—who had convenient access to the records and experience in copying—to prepare a manuscript copy of the records, and whenever a supply of this manuscript was ready, the committee has met from time to time to compare the copy with the original records and correct any errors which might appear in the copy. In doing this work, the records have been followed in their order as they appear, and the copy has been carefully and diligently compared with the originals, exhibiting the capital letters, the spelling, the abbreviations, the punctuation and the OMISSION to punctuate, in fact omitting nothing which seemed to be an authentic part of the records.

The undersigned believe that to all intents and purposes, the present volume is an accurate transcript of the entire records within the dates specified.

A few notes have been introduced here and there, which might be useful for reference or explanation.

Owing to the greater amount of recorded material of late years, it is possible another volume, equal to or larger than the present one, may be required to include the records down to the year 1885.

January 6th, 1886.

James E Bayles

George S. Osborn

W. J. Weeks

TABLE OF CONTENTS.

COMPILED AND ARRANGED BY W. J. WEEKS.

	PAGE
A, Book, Introduction	5
Amendments to Constitution, votes upon, 1826	283
Appeal of Christopher Robinson, alteration of district	306
" " Wm. Sidney Smith, boundary between school districts 18 & 19	535
Application, Vincent & M. Dickerson, ship yard	456
" E. Darling, to purchase land, denied	491
" of several Gentlemen from Stony Brook for liberty to set an Academy	545
Arbitration, boundary line between B'haven and Smithtown, at Stony Brook	388
Articles of agreement, John Wade, Water Mill in Setauket	260
" first Presbyterian Church	151-2
Assembly & Senate, Election for, 1799	18, 19
" " " " 1800	33

"	1801, pp.	43, 44	1802, p. 54		1803, p.	65
"	'04,	76, 77	'05,	96	'06,	103-4
"	'07,	112-13	'08,	121-2	'09,	128-9
"	'10,	139-40	'11,	147-8	'12,	160-1
"	'13,	176-7	'14,	183-4	'15,	192
"	'16,	200-1	'17,	205	'18,	209-10
"	'19,	216-7	'20,	224	'21,	230-1
"	'22,	243-4	'23,	253	'24,	264-5
"	'25,	270-1	'26,	282	'27,	286-7
"	'28,	291-2	'29,	300	'30,	306
					'31,	316

Bank, application to establish, in the town	188
Bass, toleration for selling, to any foreign market	148
Bay, (See East, South and West Bay)	
Beaver Dam Swamp (see Distance)	

TABLE OF CONTENTS.

	PAGE
Barney O Goram, Tho's S. Strong to take care of	57
Bound, Phebe Smith, to David Cole	57
" Indian Boy, James, to James Foster	94
" Wm. Arch, to David Day	30
" Sonney " Capt. John Havens	30
" Hannah " Wm. Scidmore	30
" Shadrick Bur, to Gabraell Mills	104
" James Bur " " "	104
" Isaac " Cephas Foster	110
" Henry Smith, colored boy, to Wm. Hawkins	432
Boundary Line between B'haven & Islip, inquiry	480
" " Supervisors to cause a true survey of	481
Brant, penalty for killing and marketing, except	107
" " " " or taking out of town	126
Burying ground, negro, at Laurel Hill	496
Baileys Hallow, Certain Road	205
Bay in Partnership with Gen'l John Smith	66
" " " "	68
" " " "	107
" " " "	126
" in Company with "	141
" " " "	142
" " " "	163
" belongs to "	194
" belonging to "	174

Cattle, not to run at large, West Meadow Beach	7
Census, 1801, Electors possessing freeholds	46
Charles's pond, privilege to Rich'd Hudson	27
Church, first Presbyterian, Meeting	150-1
" " " Grant of land to	152
Clambs, or Other Shellfish East of Woodhull point, not to be carried out, except by permission, & 3 cts. per bushel	34
" not to be carried out of the Town	58
" Toleration for taking out of "	97
" voted not to be "Catched by fouringers"	103
" penalty for removing without liberty	106
" law respecting, confirmed	114
" Act concerning, revised	124
" " " confirmed	131
" Toleration for taking out	131
" Tolerating Masters appointed to tolerate to Catch	131

TABLE OF CONTENTS.

	PAGE
Clambs not to be taken away without toleration	159
" Act to prevent catching	173
Clambing in Flax pond reserved to inhabitants	219
Chattel mortgage, Walter F. Smith, to Geo. W. Smith	520
Commiss'rs to locate boundary between B'haven & Smithtown	387
Commissioners fix the western line of the fisheries	339
" set up monuments of Stone "	341
Comm'rs of highways (see also Road)	
" " appeal of Warden Toby, decided	234
" " determine certain encroachments	246–7
" " divide a division fence bet. Hawkins & Ruland	303
" " 1830, number and define districts	308–9
" " permission to Smith and Gillett, to build dam	328
" " stake out a tract of land in Setauket	330
" " appoint to fill vacancies in Overseers of h.	351
" " Agreement with Dan'l Hawkins for damages	397
" " grant private R. District to Sam'l Hopkins	431
" " assign " " " Wm. Sidney Smith	516
" " divide District 21, Robinson Mill Stream	482
" " " " No. 1. in Stony Brook	507
" " " " " 22 " "	511
" " alter " " 20 " "	511
" " to remove obstructions around Setauket harbor	500
" " 1854, dividing line of Dist. 4 & 49 altered	517
" " Appeal of D. Robinson from order of	531–2
Commis'rs of Schools, special town meeting to vote in, 1799	20
" " divide the town into school districts, 1813	178
" " set off a district in Bald Hills	189
" " " " Westfield	189
" " divide first District	252
" " part of district 15, annexed to, in Southampton	276
" " divide 21st school dist. from Islip line	283
" " part of dist. 20 annexed to 21	297
" " resolution to extend dist. 14 to M. Robinsons.	301
" " form a new dist. Daytons Creek	320
" " in relation to division of districts 11 & 12	334
" " division of 3d dist. Setauket	338

TABLE OF CONTENTS.

	PAGE
Commis'rs of Schools, define boundaries of district 4	345
" " of Riverhead & B'haven form a new dist	357
" " define district 35	358
" " Change site of school house in dist. 15	359
" " alter No. 20 and form a new district	366
" " districts in the town renumbered	525
" " Boundary line between North Side & Middle Island	526
" " form a new dist. No. 10 from several dists	529
" " alter line between 15th & 16th dists	186
" " " District in Manor	187
" " divide district in the fireplace	188
" " change site of school house in Moriches	528
" " Joint dist. No. 2 altered to include part of Islip	528
Collectors Books, &c. to be cast up	26
Committee to take charge of J. Tooker's property	36
" to View the Flax pond at Crane Neck	42
" to view the bay, in Setauket, where Selah Strong has petitioned, for Dam & Mill	47
Convention, 1801, delegates elected	45
" 1821, Election to determine	231
" 1821, delegates elected to	233
" 1822, Estimate of votes given	235
Congress, Representative elected, 1799	24

"	"	1800, p. 33	1802, p. 54	1804, p. 76
"	"	'06, 103	'08, 122	'10, 140
"	"	'12, 160		Dec. '12, 167
"	"	'14, 183	'16, 201	'18, 209
"	"	'21, 230	'22, 244	'24, 264
"	"	'26, 282	'28, 291	'30, 306

Conscience Bay at St Georges Manor	262
Coroner, candidates, votes for, 1828	293
" " " 1831	316
County Poor House, vote taken on the question of, 1831	311
" " " " " whether to erect, 1839	362
Crambary Marsh, the pond called	58
Cranes Neck and flax pond	192

D. Book, Introduction. 81
Dam, Benjamin Strong to build, Setauket Harbor................ 70
  " permission across little Patchogue Stream................. 327

TABLE OF CONTENTS.   ix

	PAGE
Daytons swamp, distance from Beaver Dam	372
Dear or other Game, No foreigner to hunt	8
Deer, No furener Shall Chase within this Town With Howns	17
Dispute, Negro Man, Tite, B'haven & Smithtown	17, 21
" Brookhaven & Smithtown, boundary at S. Brook	387
" Southern boundary of lanes at Bellport	435
" Smalling & Smith, division fence, decided	439
Distance from Winthrop's Patent to Yaphank line	372
" " Yap'k line, south end, to Beaver D. Swamp	372
" " Beaver Dam Swamp to Dayton's Swamp	372
" " Dayton's Swamp to little Division	372
Divisions, great & little, survey in, by B. Woodhull	368
" " " Transcript of a survey, 1839	371
Dock, liberty to build, Swan Neck creek	63
" " " Benj'n Petty	99
" " " Nethaniel Woodruff	110
" Trustees join John Wilsey in Building	115
" Application and grant, Zecheriah Sandford	130
" John Wilsey, Drown Meadow Bay	132
" Liberty, Geo. Hallock, S. B. Harbor, deep hole	133–34
" " Elkanah Smith, Blue Point	142
" " Geo. Hallock, to extend	169
" " Zophar Tooker, to set up frame	213
" " Smith Mott, into the South Bay	213
" " John Willse, in Drown Meadow	218
" " Epenetus Mills, Blue Point	240
" Israel Davis, to keep in good repair, drown meadow	266
" Brewster Hawkins, Robbins's Point, Setauket	272
" Geo. Hallock, right & privilege forever	277–8
" Coll. Wm. Howell, Thomas & John Bell	296
" Cha's D. Hallock, complaint about wharfage	304
" Jonas Smith, west meadow creek, S. B	312
" at Stony Brook, wharfage raised	314
" Stoney Brook, 4 rods square, free from incumbrance	315
" Charles Osborn, in South Bay, 1833	321
" Smith & Darling, Drown Meadow	332
" Cha's D. Hallock, lease of land to extend	342
" Wm. L. Jones, Drown Meadow Bay	365
" James R. Davis, formerly to John Wilsie	376
" Sylvester Smith & M. Darling, Drown meadow	377
" Jonas Smith, with rates for wharfage	406–7
" Cha's S. Newey, or railway, South Bay	413
" Willet Griffing, South side, Patchogue	422

X   TABLE OF CONTENTS.

	PAGE
Dock, W. C. Smith & Walter Howell, Patchogue	423
" Cha's Homan, of Islip, into Bay	427
" Austin Roe, South Bay, on his own land	434
" Mary Smith, application to extend	434
" Ahira Hawkins & Wm. Darling at Port Jeff	440–450
" Bedell & Darling, petition presented by, 1851	443
" " " privilege of building, P. J. Bay	448
" I. L. Jones, complaint, obstructions about	457
" Jonas Smith's, Committee to view	462
" Wm. L. Jones, head of Drown Meadow Bay	464
" information, constructing in Islip, without grant	509–511
" Lewis Hulse, application for renewal	537
Docks at Port Jeff. all obstructions to be removed	490
Drift, inhabitants not to be hindered from taking	75
" on Road at the Bay, to belong to Warden Toby	80
Drown Meadow (now called Port Jefferson), 1850	436

E, Book, beginning... 475

East Bay, grass on Islands, J. Robinson to dispose of	501
" " new made Islands in, leased for 5 yrs. 1856	546
Eels, application to catch, in great west Bay	499
" right to catch, to be put up at auction	500
" several applications to take for foreign market	510
" in great South Bay, applications for priv. and Right	510
" Lease to Individuals or companies in West Bay	510
" Notices, forbidding in Great West Bay, without License	518
Eeling privileges in W. Bay, to advertise & sell to highest Bidder	522
Eels, no person shall catch with Seine or nets in the waters on the North side of town	550

Fiddleton, sale of grass on the Islands of	457
Fish not to be carried out of the Town	8
" " " " " penalty	32
" permission to Elias Hedges to catch, But, &c	55
" penalty for catching in the South Bay	66
" " & forfeit, for catching & carrying out	59
" " catching for the purpose of sending to market	97
" Liberty to Geo. Brown & others, to catch for market	67
" penalty for catching and taking out	123

TABLE OF CONTENTS.

	PAGE
Fish Act concerning, reinacted....................................	79
" penalty for attempting to sell to a foreign market, or to any "foreignor"..	149
" law prohibiting taking any kind, in full force & Virtue.......	185
" " " " " " "	174
" " " " " " "	194
" penalty for taking in the Bays, Rivers or Creeks........	206
" Inhabitants to catch for their own Consumption.....	148
" forfeit for taking, except on Tuesday and Friday............	327
Fishing in South Bay, E. Chichester allowed to catch and carry to market..	42
" let to Josiah Smith and H. Howell........................	113
" & Fowling, Act to regulate.................................	141
" " " " in South Bay...................	163
" & clambing in flax pond, reserved..........................	219
" in West Bay, leased to Alexander Smith.....................	472
" " " " "	530
Fisheries, boundary fixed bet. B'haven & Islip.....................	340
Fish House, liberty to set on Moger's shore.......................	398
Flax pond, committee to view, to let into the sound................	42
" " division of, by Commissioners........................	193
" " all the Right in, sold by the Trustees.................	219
Fowl, wild, ordinance against carrying out of South Bay..........	56
" permission to Wm. Alibeen, to fowl for a tenth.............	56
" wild, not to be killed after May 7, 1803.....................	67
" " Act concerning, revived & reinacted.....	78
" " Law prohibiting killing in full force & Virtue.........	174
" " " " " " "	185
" " " " " " "	194
" " forfeit for killing in the Bays, Rivers or Creeks, without first obtaining leave................................	206
Fowling in South Bay hired to Wm. Alibeen.....................	19
" " " to the Highest Bidder, Willet Rayner & Co..	31
" " " for market, to Willet Rayner...............	42
" " " hired to Hampton Howell.....	113
" toleration on, $50 in full, from Willet Rayner............	31
Fox, bounty of 50 cents for Each fox caught, 1806.................	103
Foxes, " vote for the destruction of, 1833.....................	327
Flax pond, application to lay down oysters in, 1855................	537
" " right of fishing and clambing, reserved for inhab'ts....	219
Gate, One Good Easy Swinging, Owner to hang................	61
" an Easy Swinging, Tho's S. Strong, to Hang.............	100

TABLE OF CONTENTS.

	PAGE
Gates, Good handy Swinging, Owners to Erect...................	9
" two good easy swing, at Millers place......................	195
" two or more good easy swinging, on Granny Road..........	269
Governor & Lieut. Gov., Election of 1801........................	43

"	"	1804, p.	76	1807, p. 112	1810, p.	139
"	"	'11,	147	'13, 176	'16,	200
"	"	'17,	204	'20, 224	'22,	243
"	"	'24,	264	'26, 281	'28,	291-2
"	"				'30,	306

	PAGE
Grass on the Islands in the west Bay, vote to sell.................	456
" " out shore Ridge, lease to H. F. Osborn................. ..	459
" " Pelican Island " " Capt. Cha's Rider...............	531
" " Islands in West Bay, D. Hedges to sell................	500
" " " in East " J. Robinson to dispose of	501
Grove place & gipsey Square.....................................	517
Gunning for market, to Willet Rayner, for four persons	42
" " Excepting Such Persons as Has Hired the Previlege of ".	107
" not to debar inhabitant, except on their own Bars.........	113
" privileges in west Bay, W. C. Booth to attend to..........	469
" " West Bay, lease to John Homan............	472
" " South Bay, lease to John B. Dan, from Fiddleton to Wm. Smith line...............	519

Halsie's Manor, grant of land in, Phebe Howell to Zephaniah Bowers....................................... 11
" " Oliver Smith to Benj'n Downs... 12
" " Wm. Floyd, bond, lot in, to B. Downs.......... 13
Hannah Hanabel bound, her Daughter Hannah.................... 30
Highway, (see Road).
"Hoggs," not to run on Commons without yokes, &c.............29-73
Hogs, not to run, &c. penalty.... 33
" Town meeting, votes against running on highways..... 54
" "No Hogs Except Sucking Piggs Shall Run or go On Commons"... 64
" Act concerning, reinacted &c............................... 78
" on Commons, to be Yoked and Ringed...... 128
" Vote, Act, concerning, to be revised......................... 159
Hog, Suffered to run on Commons, penalty for.................... 280
" " No Hog or Shoat Sucking Piggs Onely Excepted shall Run ". 107
Horsefish, not to be taken out of the town........................ 58
" no person shall Smuther or Bury them &c.............. 68
" Act concerning, reinacted........ 78
" not to be carried out, under any Pretense............... 106

TABLE OF CONTENTS. xiii

	PAGE
Horsefish, Law respecting, confirmed	114
" Act concerning, Revised and to Continue	124
" Act passed June 1806, Revised & confirmed on penalty of Twenty Dollars	131
Hot water Pond	58
" " Street, through Halsie's Manor	58
Hope Flat Beach Co., for planting Oysters	478

Indenture, Trustees to Geo. Davis, land in Stony Brook......47–48
            & Geo. Davis's allowance to Joseph Davis .. 48
"   " to Rich'd Floyd & others, half of Flax pond..49–50
" to John Taylor, E. &. P. Morin acknowledge......... 79
" " Cha's D. Hallock, lease in Stony Brook............ 341
" " Lewis Hulse, lease of shore for Railways.......... 346
" " " use & improvement of common land.. 374
" " Silvester Randal, land for blacksmith shop......... 375
" " James R. Davis, Dock formerly to John Wilsie...... 376
" " Rob't Hawkins, west side of Beaver Dam River.... 386
" " Jonas Smith, sand flat at Stony Brook............ 406
" " Willet Griffing, dock, South side, Patchogue....... 422
" " Wm. C. Smith & Walter Howell, dock, " 423
" " C. L. & J. M. Bayles, railway, renewal of lease..... 424
" " Charles Homan of Islip, privilege, building dock.... 427
" " Mary Smith, to enlarge dock at Port Jeff.......... 436
" " Jer. Darling & Ed'd Bedell, priv. of a dock......... 448
" " A. Hawkins & W. Darling, " " 450
" Consequence of refusal of Austin Roe, to execute..... 452
" to J. R. Mather & T. B. Hawkins, Stone wall, P. J. Bay 462
" " Wm. L. Jones, grant for Railway, continued....... 464
" " " Liberty to construct, 1836............ 464
" " Edm'd T. Darling, land for Boat Builders Shop ... 470
" " V. & M. Dickerson, for Ship Yard................. 473
" " Harvey West, Beach or Shore, head of P. J. Bay... 493
" " Edm'd Darling, " " " ... 494
" " C. L. Bayles, Railway at Port Jefferson & work Shop at Port Jefferson.......................... 547
" " Elizabeth Darling, right to construct a Pier........ 548
Inspectors of Common School, vote, allowing fifty Cents a day..... 362
" " Com. Schools, vote, " one Dollar a Day..... 381

Justice of Peace, vote to elect by the people..................... 283
    " Canvass of votes for, 1827...................... 287

TABLE OF CONTENTS.

	PAGE
Justice of Peace, Supervisor & Justices ballot for term	288
" Election of 1828	292
" votes for, inspectors certify, 1829	300

Laurel Hill, negro burial ground laid out at	496
" Trustees, to defend the sale of timber on	510
" piece of land in Setauket, quit claimed	261
Lubber Street or Dickersons Settlement	178
" Grove place	517

Meeting, (See Town and Trustees).
Mill, permission to erect, to Benj'n Strong & Bro's	70
" at Wading River, grant examined	137
" Liberty to build, to Daniel Homan	232
Monument erected at Wading River, between Brookhaven & Riverhead	385

Neat Cattle, horse or sheep not to run on the west meadow Beach.	251
Negro Burying Ground, Laurel Hill, Setauket	496
" " Committee appointed to view	500
" " alleged trespass upon	501
" " timber standing on, to be sold	508
" " application to exchange land for what timber may grow on	521

Oald mans path	97
Old Field Beach, 150 feet for ship yard	456
" " grant extended 5 years	469
" " for ship yard	473
Oosence, branch or creek of Connecticut River	117
Ottor Swamp, Beaver Dam River	117
Overseers of highways, List of, for 1833	325
Oysters, Voted, No Oys. or fish " Be Ketched By foreigners "	8
" " " " Clambs, by persons not inhabitants	8
" " to carry out, shall first obtain liberty	8
" & Clambs, law concerning, confirmed	20
" or shells, not to be sent out of the town	21
" Privilege to Dan'l Smith, to Lay Down	25
" or shells, not to be sent out within certain dates	35
" " penalty for removing, in South Bay	45
" privilege to lay down, in Drown M. Harbor, John Woolsey.	47
" or shells, not to be taken out of the town	58

TABLE OF CONTENTS. XV

	PAGE
Oysters, Great Destruction of, Act to prevent	106
" or shells, law passed to prevent, repealed	109
" Law passed in June 1806 confirmed	114
" Act to preserve young, growing in S. Bay	118
" permission to take in case of sickness	119
" in Case of sickness, Tobey & Baker to give permits	119
" Act revised, no permits to be given	123
" Inhabitants not to be prevented, provided &c	126
" Act to preserve for town & heirs of Wm. Smith	130
" if found on board of any vessel, excepting	131
" permission to take, restrictions	132
" Agent to regulate quantity & receive Acc't	132
" all foreigners excluded from Catching	133
" Agent, Epenetus Mills appointed	133
" penalty for taking without a permit	143
" or Shells, Act of May, 1810, prohibiting, repealed	143
" in the South Bay, Catching prohibited	149
" & shells, between May & Oct. penalty for catching	291
" laying down & taking up, entire priv., Wm. Tooker	294
" penalty for taking between May & Oct., 1829	298
" shells of, from Oyster Beds, penalty for taking away	298
" privilege of laying down, to Wm. Smith	298
" penalty for selling to or for any foreign market	382
" no person shall Dredge or drag for, 1841	405
" Act for the preservation of, 1847	408–9
" " against dredging repealed, 1848	413
" " of 1847, public notice enforcing	434
" " " amended, forfeit for catching	439
" no person to dredge or drag for after Feb., 1851	440
" allotment for planting in west Bay	442
" lots for planting in Great west Bay, leased	456–9
" lots for planting, Beach flats near Quanch	459
" persons to sell, required to obtain license	491
Oystering, Mr. Booth to hire out, in west Bay	440
" in Suffolk Co., to remonstrate against action of the Legislature	445
" license to all applicants who pay in advance	500
" privilege of, rent for, 1851	453
" & fishing, to regulate the Bye Laws, as to penalties	459
" privileges for market, refusal to pay for, subject to prosecution	469
" privileges, agents to, appointed for Great West Bay	470
" " Daines & Newins appointed agents, G. W. B.	472

TABLE OF CONTENTS.

	PAGE
Oystering privileges, N. M. Terrill to superintend, in G. S. B. 1853.	492
" " Mr. Case to take charge of, 1853	501
" " N. M. Terrill, to oversee in the West Bay	502
" " of the West Bay, decided to sell to the highest Bidder	522
" " of the South Bay, decided to sell at public auction	551
Oyster planting, annual rents to be paid Foremen, or forfeit	478
Oysters or shells, no authority to grant liberty to dredge for	531
" dredging for, petition to Supervisors to amend the law	535

Palace Brook (so-called) Patchogue............................ 454
Partnership, (See West & South Bay).
    " Cha's L. & James M. Bayles, agree to dissolve........ 547
Pelican Island, grass growing on, to be leased.................... 531
Peperidge tree, monument erected where it stood in Wading River. 385
Pigs, sucking excepted, on the Commons..................... 64, 107
Pomp & Sarah Arch bind their sons, Wm. & Sonney.............. 30
Poor, Support of, Am't raised, 1802............................. 55

"	"	1803, p. 68	1806, p. 109	1807, p. 116
"	"	'08, 124	'10, 143	'11, 153
"	"	'23,	'24,	'25, 270
"	"	'26, 276	'27, 276	'30, 305
"	"	'31, 317	'34, 333	'48, 418
"	"	'49, 426	'50, 435	'51, 460
"	"	'52, 488	'53, 502	'54, 519

" House, vote to provide, Town Meeting, 1817................. 204
" " County, vote taken on the question of, 1831............ 311
" " " " whether to erect, 1839.................. 362
Punks hole, " An Easterly Course unto "......................... 10

Quanch, Beach flats, oyster lots granted near................... 459

Railway, permission to build at Drown Meadow................ 328
   " Road or way, to Smith and Darling " 333
   " ways, to Lewis Hulse, Drown Meadow Bay................ 347
   " way, renewal of lease to C. L. & J. M. Bayles............ 425
   " " Lewis Hulse's annuity reduced....................... 481
Ram Sheep not to run on the Commons......................... 73
" vote not to run between Aug. & Nov.......................... 159
Rams, Act to prevent running at large........................... 162

TABLE OF CONTENTS. xvii

	PAGE
Rams, Act to prevent running, &c. Revised	174
" " " " in full force & Virtue	194
Ram found running, forfeit for securing	280
" " " without being sufficiently hoppled, penalty of two Dollars	280
Rams or Swine, vote to prevent, running in commons	274
Road, through the Land, By name, the Hundred Acres	9
" the above made Void, 1801	9
" across the land of Isaac Satterly	9
" from the corner to the mill Dam	9
" " Wading River Road to St. George's Manor	10
" " Jeremiah Randals to John Bayles lot	14
" " the Granny Road to fulling mill	15
" " B. Smith's house to Winthrops Patent	17
" " John M. Longs Sawmill to Little Branch	18
" all and Every, in Brookfield, confirmed	20
" altered, Millers Place, Hay Path	22
" " from Ezra Tuthill's, Smith's Neck Road	22
" " Mooneponds	29
" from Sheeppasture Road, Setauket	38
" West of Simeon Hawkinses, Null & Void	38
" joining Yaphank Line to be shut up	40
" from Elijah Davises to Dan'l Bayle's shut up	43
" Exchange of, across Old Mill Dam, Setauket	57
" in Halsies Manor, Hotwater Street	58
" to Wading River Great Lots	60
" " Scidmores Landing	61
" Alter, from Charles's Pond to the Mooneponds	62
" Regulations to repair in East Setauket	69
" John Wilsies House, (at Drownmeadow)	74
" In Tookers Neck, at Bluepoint	79
" at Comsewague, also a part shut up	97
" Alteration from Christopher Swezeys Mills	108
" from Chrystle Brook Hollow to Benjamins R	115
" Stopped up & laid out, Beaver Dam River	117
" " &c. between Wm. Hawkins & John Munsil	125
" Western part of Setauket	136
" Old Mans, to Wading River, continued	136
" from Stoney Brook to Setauket town	146
" " Daniel Homan's Mill to South Country Road	146
" " Rocky pond to Setauket	146
" Private, laid out for N. Overton	153
" at the North End of the Long Lots	154

TABLE OF CONTENTS.

	PAGE
Road, in the fireplace to Bartoe's Landing Place	155
" Shut up between Nassakeag Road &c.	156
" established between N. Tuthill & J. Woodhull	157
" " to Landing place of N. Tuthill	157
" altered in Millers place	159
" at Patchogue, through land of Dan'l Smith &c.	166
" from " to Coram	166
" " Middle Island to Dan'l Swezeys Landing	166
" in the fireplace, from Gerard's R. Southward, stopped	168
" laid out from S. W. corner of Lot five	168
" altered, East side of Beaver Dam Swamp	168
" old pine Neck, Coram Road to horse Block	171
" in Lubber Street, beginning at temps House	187
" from Rocky point R. to M. S. Woodhull's Landing	195
" at Moriches, southwesterly, swift stream	217
" in the village of Westfield	219
" in Stony Brook, staked out	220
" through the land of John Elderkin	225
" Jury of inquest to appraise damage of	227
" from Westfield to Coram	235
" leading to John Mott's Mills, Patchogue	241
" from Patchogue creek, west, closed	248
" " Old Mans to Drown meadow, widened	254
" two pole, opened, bet. Stores of Parsons & Hulse	255
Roads, two certain, in Middle Island, closed	255
Road, from C. Swezey's to Rob't Hawkins's Mills, altered	256
" at the East line of the late Joshua Smith	260
" in the renewal of the grant to Geo. Hallock, S. B	280
" that leads down the fireplace neck altered	288
" from the highway between Setauket & Drown M. inspected, defined & opened	299
" districts numbered & set off, 1830	308–9
" from paper Mill in Moriches to Maple Hollow	320
" " Bell's Dock, northerly	323
" " Bellville Dock, consent to lay out	324
" land for, in Patchogue, release of Sillick Wicks	325
" in Setauket staked out	330
" " to dock of Jonas Smith	334
" from S. Glover's to R. Hawkins's Mills, alteration	339
" commencing near the Meeting House in Old Mans	346
" private, on application of Isaac Overton	352
" from Setauket to Tho's S. Strong's altered	355
" through lands of Jos. Avery & others, to the Bay at Blue Point	356

TABLE OF CONTENTS.   xix

	PAGE

Road, South Post R. Survey of, through Moriches................ 373
    "   Westerly from the Beaver Dam, ancient Section established.. 390
    "   from the South Country R. Northwardly (Yaphank Av.)..... 396
    "   " Dan'l Homan's Mill dam to Gerard's R. stopped......... 397
Roads, at Manor Station, release of............................ 417
Road   "   through Sundry lands........................... 418
    "   to run Westerly to Patchogue Millpond.................. 426
    "   Release of the foregoing, North Street, Patchogue.......... 426
    "   South Country, west of little Patchogue stream, altered..... 432
    "   South Street, alteration of, Patchogue................... 434
    "   above, Hawkins & Chadeayne, release for damages.......... 434
    "   from Carman's Mills to Fireplace neck altered.............. 438
    "   Slippery Lane, survey of, 1850........................... 444
    "   from Bellport to Tookers turnout, L. I. R. R...............454–5
    "   " Head of the neck on Bellport Dock Road.............. 456
    "   South Country, adjoining Parish Ground, Moriches.......... 458
    "   in Moriches, suit for taking earth from................... 458
    "   from Seatuck Mills to Hot water Street.................... 460
    "   " land of Josiah Smith to S. Country Road, East Moriches 461
    "   " the Bay Shore, east side of little Patchogue creek...... 466
    "   near Congregational Church in Patchogue................. 474
    "   " Moriches Church to Wading River Road.............. 479
    "   from Fireplace neck to Coram........................... 482
    "   between D. Robinson & W. Avery to the Bay Shore......... 482
    "   from Bellport Station, L. I. R. R. nearly north............. 483
    "   release all claim to damages, W. E. Conkling & others...... 484
    "   "   "   " D. Robinson & Wm. Avery..... 484
    "   "   "   " Wm. H. Newins & others....... 485
    "   from South Country R. to the South Bay.................. 486
    "   " above road, along shore to Swan creek................ 486
    "   " South Country R. near Wm. Avery's to S. Bay......... 487
    "   " Rocky Pt. R. to M. S. Woodhull's landing Millers Place 489
    "   " Medford Station to old Coram Road................... 492
    "   " Horse Block R. to Waverly Station & southward.....503–4
    "   on fireplace Neck, from highway to South Bay, near west
          line of J. L. Ireland.................................505–6–7
    "   to Rose's landing discontinued.......................... 507
    "   Southerly through Port Jeff. altered from two to three rods. 509
    "   Application for a new road in Moriches.................... 539
    "   South Bay to South Country Road in Moriches nearly opposite
          Methodist Church.... 542
    "   from Centre of Moriches to S. Bay, Quit claim.............. 544
    "   " Patchogue to Mott's Mills, Canaan.. 549
Robbins's point in Setauket harbour, dock........................ 272

XX   TABLE OF CONTENTS.

                                                                    PAGE
Saints Orchard, westermost point of............................ 47
Sand, petition to fence, to preserve meadows................... 74
  "   not to be taken without tolerating....................... 159
  "   Act to prevent taking.................................... 173
  "   taking without leave, guilty of trespass................. 212
Seaweed, No person entitled to, By Heaping..................... 7
Senate, (see Assembly).
Shore, about Setauket Harbor, obstructions to be removed....... 457
School Districts, Town divided into, 1813...................... 178
  "   "   renumbered by the Comm'rs, 1842................ 525
  "   "   30, 31, & 32 altered by Supts................... 529
  "   district, Second, set apart, separate D.................. 205
  "   "   First, divided................................. 252
  "   "   Part No. 1, Wading River....................... 254
  "   "   partly in B'haven & partly in R'head........... 261
  "   "   Trustees No. 18 versus Trustees No. 19......... 522
  "   "   decision of V. M. Rice, in above............... 525
  "   House, Liberty to build in Stony Brook................... 39
  "   "   petition & liberty to build in Fireplace........ 52
  "   "   Hill, committee to view, for Academy............ 538
Sheepshead, toleration for selling............................. 148
Sheriff, candidates, votes for, 1828........................... 293
Shells, Act to prevent Catching, 1810.......................... 141
  "   "   "   "   repealed....................... 143
Shell fish, forfeit for taking in the Waters or harbors on the North
    side of the Island... 217
Slaves, Manumission of, under Act of 1788.
Slave, Mrs. Ruth Woodhull, applies for, Ben.................... 7
  "   Thomas Helme   "   " Jack.................... 14
  "   Elisha Hammond   "   " Ziporah................. 23
  "   Dr. David Woodhull   "   " Silos................... 36
  "   Noah Hallock   "   " Pompe & Candis.......... 39
  "   Tho's S. Strong   "   " Keder & Susan........... 71
  "   Abraham Woodhull   "   " Juleaner................ 98
  "   John Homan   "   " Phelis.................. 99
  "   Wm. Tooker   "   " Primous................. 99
  "   John Howard   "   " Pompe................... 105
  "   Noah Hallock   "   " Tim..................... 114
  "   Wm. Helme   "   " Viner................... 114
  "   Selah Strong   "   " Seylvia................. 124
  "   Joseph Homan   "   " Jude.................... 124
  "   Mariam Brown   "   " Jude.................... 125
  "   Joseph Davis   "   " Elizabeth............... 135

TABLE OF CONTENTS.   xxi

		PAGE
Slave, Jeremiah Havens, applies for, David		135
" Wessell Sell " " Titus		150
" Joseph Jayne " " Limas		156
" Phillips Roe " " Betty		162
" Jonas Hawkins Jr. & Tho's S. Mount, apply for Harry		172
" "personally came and appeared" Killis		177
" Hannah Woodhull, applies for Tamer		180
" Thomas Strong " " Killis		180
" Theophilus Smith " " Sarah		180
" Robert Hawkins " " Margett		186
" Wessell Sell " " Juleanor		186
" Gideon Mills & Rich'd Oakley, apply, for Sampson		187
" Dan'l Davis, applies for Matilda		194
" Tho's S. Strong " Abel		196
" Rich'd Robinson " Clarisa & Jeremiah		196
" Tho's S. Strong " Rose Akerly		197
" Elizabeth Smith " Stephen		197
" Sarah Helme " Nimrod		197
" Henry Smith " Richard		206
" Elizabeth Smith " Candas		210
" Daniel Jones " Rhoda		211–2
" Timothy Miller " Huldah		216
" Zophar Hallock " Philopenea		221
" Mary Davis " Permelia		225
" Wm. Helme " Oliver		226
" Henry Smith " Jemima		227
" Woodhull Smith " Samuel		233
" Tho's S. Strong " Darcas		234
" Henry P. Orsbon " Thomas		236
" Tho's R. Smith " Irenea		237
" Josiah Smith " John Perdue		242
" " " " Dorothy		243
" Tho's S. Strong " Unice		248
" Sam'l L. Thompson, applies for Simon		248
" Abraham Woodhull " " Harry		249
" Wm. Howell " " Peter		254
" Ebenezer Smith " " Joel		256
" John Havens " " Ira		257 & 263
" John Woodhull " " Benjamin Rafe		257
" Mills Brewster " " Peter		269
" Henry P. Osborn " " Reuben		269
" " " " Judas		270
" Wm. Tooker " " Aaron		275

xxii   TABLE OF CONTENTS.

                                                                          PAGE
Slave, Sam'l L. Thompson, applies for Hannah.................... 281
  "   Nathaniel Miller   "   " Jeremiah.................. 307

                 Birth Records, Children of Slaves.

Slave, Born of a, Aner, Reported by Sam'l Smith................. 23
  "   "   "   Rachel & Hector, Reported by Gen'l Wm. Floyd..24–5
  "   "   "   Selah, Reported by Sam'l Carman................ 25
  "   "   "   Peter   "   Jehiel Woodruff............. 27
  "   "   "   Paul   "   Ruth Woodhull............... 36
  "   "   "   Dence   "   M. S. Woodhull.............. 37
  "   "   "   Elisabeth "   Joseph Davis................ 37
  "   "   "   Lew   "   Coll. Nicoll Floyd.......... 37
  "   "   "   Rachel   "   Joseph Brewster............. 37
  "   "   "   Peter   "   Dan'l Robart................ 56
  "   "   "   Bet & Jim "   Oliver Smith................ 61
  "   "   "   Jim   "   Coll. Nicoll Floyd.......... 61
  "   "   "   Tamer   "   Wd. Ruth Woodhull........... 62
  "   "   "   Rosawell   "   Joanna Smith................ 62
  "   "   "   Aaron   "   Wm. Tooker.................. 62
  "   "   "   Apolis   "   James Woodhull.............. 62
  "   "   "   Nel   "   Oliver Smith................ 71
  "   "   "   Primus   "   Wm. Smith................... 81
  "   "   "   Paul ⎫
  "   "   "   Rachel⎬   "   Wm. Smith................... 82
  "   "   "   Lucy ⎭
  "   "   "   Phillip⎫   "   Nicoll Floyd................ 82
  "   "   "   Cyrus ⎭
  "   "   "   Phillip   "   Rich'd Robinson............. 82
  "   "   "   Charles   "   Dan'l Petty................. 82
  "   "   "   Peter   "   Josiah Smith................ 83
  "   "   "   Silas   "   Goldsmith Davis............. 83
  "   "   "   Dick ⎫   "   Sarah Hallock............... 83
  "   "   "   Viner ⎭
  "   "   "   Rachel⎫
  "   "   "   Tamar ⎬   "   Tho's S. Strong............. 83
  "   "   "   Cealia⎪
  "   "   "   Ellen ⎭
  "   "   "   Elijah,⎫
  "   "   "   Sam   ⎬ Reported by Nicoll Floyd........ 84
  "   "   "   Sam   ⎪
  "   "   "   Charity Ann,⎭
  "   "   "   Peggy⎫ Reported by Wm. Smith............... 84
  "   "   "   Mary ⎭
  "   "   "   Herculas⎫ "   John Woodhull............... 85
  "   "   "   Ben   ⎭

TABLE OF CONTENTS.

					PAGE
Slave, Born of a,	Jane,	Reported by	Timothy Miller		85
"	"	Isaac Jayne "	Elizabeth Smith		85
"	"	Lunn "	Wm. Smith		85
"	"	(male child) "	Ebenezer Jones		85
" "	" "	Sarah } Tamer }	"	Nicoll Floyd	86
"	"	Sebra "	Nath'l Tuthill		86
" "	" "	Sam'l Jayne } Charlotte }	Reported by John Smith Gen		86
"	"	Tamer	"	Mary Woodhull	86
"	"	Margett Cicera	"	Rob't Hawkins	87
"	"	Fan	"	Wm. Smith	87
" " " " " " "	" " " " " " "	Dinah Charlott Margarett Franics Pedro Isabellah Arthur	"	Mrs. Mary Robert	87
" " " "	" " " "	Sampson Rose Hannah Fanny	"	Theophilus Smith	88
" "	" "	Ally } Experience }	"	Woodhull Smith	88
"	"	Richard	"	Coll. Nicoll Floyd	89
" "	" "	Huldah Ann } Harriet }	"	Ruth Thompson	89
"	"	David Bowse	"	Elizabeth Smith	89
"	"	Silas	"	Capt. Josiah Smith	89
"	"	Thankful	"	Benj. Woodhull	89
"	"	Oliver	"	Rich'd Robinson	90
" "	" "	Armina } Charles }	"	Sarah Miller	90
"	"	Apollas	"	Joseph Miller	90
"	"	Jeremiah	"	Timothy Miller	90
" "	" "	Tamer } Ben }	"	Nicoll Floyd	90
"	"	Cloe	"	Amos Smith	91
" " "	" " "	Charles Isaac Lil	"	Coll. Nicoll Floyd	91
"	"	Phillis	"	Joseph Jayne	91
"	"	Hannah	"	Stephan Swezey	91
" "	" "	Harry } Mary }	"	Josiah Smith	92
"	"	Mary	"	Sarah Miller	92

TABLE OF CONTENTS.

					PAGE
Slave, born of a,	Sharper	Reported by	Selah Strong		92
"	"	Zacheus	"	John Payne	92
"	"	Mary	"	Gen'l John Smith	92
"	"	Silos } Harry }	"	Rich'd Robinson	92
"	"	Silve } Phebe } Oliver }	"	Judge Selah Strong	93
"	"	David	"	Judge Ab'm Woodhull.	93
"	"	Katura	"	Rob't Hawkins Jr	93
"	"	Margaritt	"	Sam'l Turner	93
"	"	Pomp	"	Coll. Nicoll Floyd	93
"	"	Tite	"	Oliver Smith	93
"	"	Jesse } female child }	"	Capt. Joseph Hedges	94
"	"	Corier	"	Woodhull Smith	94
"	"	Horrace } Paris }	"	Gen'l John Smith	108

Slippery Lane road, centre line of, (Patchogue)...................... 444
South Bay, belonging to Town and Wm. Smith............45, 55, 56, 59
"   "   "   "   " and Heirs of   " 141, 143, 163, 174
"   "   "   "   " and Wm. S. Smith or Wm. Smith..... 206
"   "   that belongs to " & Heirs of Capt. Wm. Smith......... 194
"   "   belonging to   " and Wm. S. Smith......291, 297, 382, 409,
439, 440, 491
"   "   in Company with the Heirs of Wm. Smith............ 141
"   "   "   Town & "   "   "   "   142
"   "   in Co. with   " & "   "   "   "   163
"   "   in Partnership   " & Wm. Smith, 1798............   8
"   "   "   "   "   "   "   " 56–109
"   "   "   "   " & Capt. Wm. Smith..31, 42, 59, 66, 67
"   "   "   "   " & heirs of Major Wm. Smith. ... 105
"   "   "   "   " &c...................107, 113, 126
"   "   "   "   " & Heirs of Wm. Smith...118, 126, 130
148, 185
"   "   "   "   " and Wm. Sidney Smith.......... 492
"   "   Complaint, penalty for staking out..................... 164
Sail Boat, Geo. W. Robinson sells to Oliver Robinson............. 530
Steam boats, wharfage for, June, 1851........................ 457
Stone or Stones, penalty for taking, from public Shores............ 252
Swine, not to run on Commons, ringed & yoked................. 145
"   (Sucking Pigs excepted) not to run on Commons........... 149
"   Act to prevent, revised 1812............................ 162
"   "   "   " 1813............................ 174

TABLE OF CONTENTS.

	PAGE
Swine, Act to prevent, in full force & Virtue.	185
" " " " "	194
Terry, Nelson, sells to W. Carman Terry, goods & chattels.	451
Tockhouse, Robin, Consent to indenture to Tho's S. Strong.	56
Tolerateing master Be a resident of Sd Town.	7
Toleration for Clambs, Two Cents on a Bushel, 1805.	97
" " " three " " " 1806.	131
" " " " " " 1813.	173
" " " not to be carried away, without.	159
" on Fowling, Fifty Dollars, in full from Willet Rayner.	31
" " Oysters, pay to Agent, Six Cents per 100.	133
" " " two Cents on every Bushel.	382
" " " four cents, law passed May, 1841, repealed.	382
" " Bass, three Cents for every.	148
" " Sheepshead, six Cents for every.	148
" " any fish, selling or carrying out without paying, forfeit.	149
" " Sand, from shores or harbours, one Cent pr Bushel.	173
" men, S. L. Newins & N. Daines, agents, west Bay.	452
Tolerators, Hawkins, Baker & Mills appointed.	149

Town Meeting, 1798, p. 6   1799, p. 15.

"	"	1800,	27	1801,	40	1802, p. 53		
"	"	'03,	63	'04,	72	'05,	94	1806, p. 101
"	"	'07,	110	'08,	119	'09,	126	'10, 139
"	"	'11,	143	'12,	157	'13,	172	'14, 181
"	"	'15,	189	'16,	197	'17,	202	'18, 207
"	"	'19,	213	'20,	221	'21,	227	'22, 237
"	"	'23,	249	'24,	257	'25,	266	'26, 273
"	"	'27,	284	'28,	288	'29,	294	'30, 302
"	"	'31,	309	'32,	317	'33,	322	'34, 330
"	"	'35,	335	'36,	349	'37,	353	'38, 359
"	"	'39,	362	'40,	368	'41,	378	'42, 382
"	"	'43,	390	'44,	393	'45,	398	'46, 402
"	"	'47,	409	'48,	414	'49,	419	'50, 428
"	"	'51,	445	'52,	475	'53,	496	'54, 512
"	"	'55,	532					

"	"	Special Comm'rs of Schools, Counstable, &c., 1799.	20
"	"	" Constable & a number of Fence Viewers, 1801.	46
"	"	" to determine by Ballot, Licence or no, 1846.	404
"	"	" " elect Supervisor in room of, 1847.	410
"	"	" " determin by Ballot, licence or no. to Sell Strong & Spirituous liquors, 1847.	412

xxvi   TABLE OF CONTENTS.

                                                                    PAGE
Town Meeting, Special, to fill vacancy in the office of Trustee, 1849.. 419
    "   "   Called Expressly for that Purpose, "Counstable,"
                       1802. 60
    "   "   vote taken, propriety of dividing the town, 1830.. 303
    "   "   "   "   proposed division of the " 1831.. 311
    "   "   "   by Ballot for & against division of " 1841.. 381
    "   "   vote next town M. be held at house of Rich'd W..
                       Smith, 1841................................ 380
    "   "   vote the next Annual meeting at House of Lester
                       H. Davis, 1848............ 414
    "   Superintendent sets off South portion of District 26 into a
              separate district.................................. 453

Trustees " 1798, pages 7, 8, 14.
    "   "   '99,   "   17, 19, 21, 23.
    "   "   1800,   "   25, 26, 30, 34, 35, 36.
    "   "   '01,   "   38, 41, 42, 44, 46.
    "   "   '02,   "   52, 53, 55.
    "   "   '03,   "   62, 66, 67, 68, 69.
    "   "   '04,   "   71, 78, 79.
    "   "   '05,   "   97, 98, 99.
    "   "   '06,   "   105, 106, 108, 109.
    "   "   '07,   "   113, 115, 116.
    "   "   '08,   "   117, 123, 124, 126.
    "   "   '09,   "   129, 130, 132, 133.
    "   "   '10,   "   142, 143.
    "   "   '11,   "   148, 152.
    "   "   '12,   "   161, 164, 165.
    "   "   '13,   "   169, 170   '14, pp. 185, 386.
    "   "   '15,   "   188, 194   '16, " 196.
    "   "   '17,   "   197   '18, p. 206.
    "   "   '19,   "   206, 212, 213, 216, 218, 219.
    "   "   '20,   "   221, 226   '21, p. 226.
    "   "   '22,   "   242   '23, p. 248.
    "   "   '24,   "   256   '25, pp. 257, 268, 269.
    "   "   '26,   "   275, 276, 280   '27 p. 276.
    "   "   '28,   "   291   '29, pp. 296, 298.
    "   "   '30,   "   305   '31, "   307, 311, 314, 317.
    "   "   '32,   no record.
    "   "   '33,   "   322, 327, 329   '34, pp. 333, 546.
    "   "   '35,   "   333, 341   '36, p. 362   '37, p. 365.
    "   "   '38,   "   377   ('39, p. 377)   '40, pp. 373, 376.
    "   "   '41,   "   382, 463   '42 and '43, no record.

TABLE OF CONTENTS. xvii

PAGE

Trustees Meeting, '44, pages 400, 405   '45 pp. 401, 398   '46, p. 401.
"   "   '47,   "   409, 413   '48, " 413, 418   '49, pp. 422, 424, 425.
"   "   '50,   "   427, 431, 433, 434, 436, 437, 438, 441.
"   "   '51,   "   439, 442, 443, 444, 448, 452, 456, 458, 461, 462, 468.
"   "   '52,   "   469, 471, 478, 480, 487, 488, 489, 552.
"   "   '53,   "   490, 491, 499, 500, 501, 502.
"   "   '54,   "   508, 509, 510, 518, 519, 521.
"   "   '55,   "   521, 522, 530, 531, 534, 537, 538, 545.
"   "   '56 Jan. p. 546, Feb. p. 546, March, p. 550.
"   Sell a house & land in Setauket........................... 116
"   death of president, Selah Strong appointed.............. 135
"   sell Jacob Hawkins land in Setauket..................... 156
"   grant to Smith Mott to set up a frame................... 162
"   " liberty to set a dwelling house.................... 164
"   sell to B. Brown land E. side Beaver dam River......... 171
"   should provide a Poor House, 1817...................... 204
"   sell to John Rose land in the fireplace................ 210
"   sold to "   " & Dr. Nath'l Miller, land, &c......... 211
"   " Isaac Brewster & others, Right in Flax pond...... 219
"   grant to Dan'l Homan to build a mill.................... 232
"   " Tho's S. Strong, Esq., dam and bridge, Setauket.. 262
"   Committee of, locate a highway in Stony Brook.......... 280
"   order Cha's D. Hallock to remove a certain log.......... 362
"   grant to Cha's Phillips to set a fish House............. 398
"   reduce annuity, Lewis Hulse, Railways, &c..........401, 481
"   grant Cha's D. Hallock rates for sundry articles........ 481
"   vote Overseers of Poor keep acc'ts separate............. 431
"   " Dr. Brown as Alms House Physician............... 433
"   adjust dispute about lanes at Bellport.................. 435
"   case of the Colored Boy at Rich'd Corwins............. 437–8
"   to Hawkins & Mather to build a stone wall.............. 439
"   decided, Mrs. Horton have money to convey her to N. Y.. 441
"   allotment for oystering in west Bay..................... 443
"   decided not to pay bill of Rich'd Corwin..............443–5
"   in relation to lunatic son of David Smalling............ 452
"   application, E. T. Darling, Boat Builder's Shop........452–7
"   resolve, Dr. Brown, Alms House physician, 1851......... 452
"   vote to sell grass on Islands, 1851..................... 456
"   " lease Oyster lots for 5 years..................... 456
"   contract with V. & M. Dickerson, shipyard............... 456
"   proceed to sell grass on Islands of Fiddleton........... 457

TABLE OF CONTENTS.

		PAGE
Trustees	to consult Counsel respecting Islands, &c.	457
"	grant Oyster lots near Quanch, Brown & Woodruff.	459
"	similar grants in Great west Bay.	459
"	indemnify parties, suit, taking earth from highway.	459
"	lease grass on out shore Ridge.	459
"	" V. & M. Dickerson 150 ft. Old field Beach.	459
"	Resolved, suit for obstructions in Setauket Harb.	459
"	" D. Smalling, Lunatic, conveyed to Alms House.	461
"	" B. Brewster take Wm. F. Ruland from the house.	468
"	propriety of Binding Ann Duick's Child to J. Biggs.	468
"	Messrs. Vinson & M. Dickerson, grant extended.	469
"	lease Fishing privilege of West Bay for 3 years.	472
"	decided to quitclaim land to Henry Hawkins.	472
"	decided that Frances Howell be indentured.	472
"	lease of Old field Beach for ship yard.	473
"	resolved to Lease Mrs. Bowen adjoining old field strand.	478
"	" Mr. Wickham's bill, defending road suit, allowed.	478
"	Boundary bet. Town & Islip, Supervisor, a true survey.	481
"	request Hawkins & Hallock to remove obstructions.	481
"	resolve, suit against B. Hawkins, causing obstructions.	488–9
"	Mrs. E. Darling liberty to build a Pier.	488
"	lease land on Port Jefferson Beach.	490
"	Notice be posted, licence to catch & sell oysters.	491
"	lease to E. T. Darling 50 ft. shore, P. J. Bay.	491
"	Mr. Swezey to procure printed licences for oyster'g.	492
"	lease Harvey West, shore, head of P. J. Bay.	493
"	Clerk of Board to receive same compensation as Trus.	499
"	decided public notices to lease Shores or Beaches.	499
"	" that John Pinkard be kept at the alms House.	501
"	appoint Joel Robinson, grass on Islands in E. Bay.	501
"	decided to raise Rent of Lewis Hulse's Dock, &c.	502
"	resolve to sell timber on Negro Burying ground.	508
"	authorise sale of timber on " " "	510
"	lease to Capt. H. Tyler, renewed, shore, at Setauket Harb.	510
"	" Cha's L. Bayles liberty to Set a shop, 1854.	519
"	resolve to petition Supervisors to amend law for dredging.	535
"	quit claim to Sam'l L. Thompson narrow scrap of land.	539
"	" " Wm. M. Jones a piece of meadow.	538
"	voted to lease to E. T. Moore & others 50 or 60 acres in Great South Bay.	538

TABLE OF CONTENTS.   xxix

	PAGE

Trustees lease new made Islands in E. Bay to J. M. Fanning....... 546
    "   meeting, Jan. 1856, "Nothing of much importance was transacted.. 546

West Bay, in partnership, Town & Wm. Sidney Smith.......... 443
    "   "   Great, "   "   "   "   " 499
    "   "   right & privilege of Oystering to Austin Roe........ 443
    "   "   for planting Oysters leased for 5 years............. 456
    "   "   grass on Islands in, Wm. C. Booth to sell.......... 456
    "   "   "   "   D. Hedges   " 500
    "   "   Oystering privileges, agents to be appointed........ 470
    "   "   Eeling forbidden without licence.................... 518
    "   "   10 lots leased for planting oysters.................. 521
    "   "   Oystering & Eeling to the highest Bidder........... 522
    "   "   fishing privilege leased to Alex. Smith of Huntington, 1855....................................... 530
Watring Place, for use of inhabitants, reserved.................... 211
Wharfage, rates for, (see in the grants for Docks).
    "   raised, Cha's D. Hallocks Dock at Stoney brook......... 314
    "   addition to, allowed Capt. C. D. Hallock............ 457
Woodhull, Mitty, condition & wants to be inquired into......... 459

  Note. The careful reader may, perhaps, find many treasures in this volume not indicated in the foregoing Table, but probably the list will be found sufficiently comprehensive and minute for all practical purposes.   W. J. W.

YAPHANK, Aug., 1888.

INTRODUCTION.

BOOK A.—PART II.

This book consists of two parts. The first part to page 76 contains a copy of the records found in two older books in the clerk's office, copied in accordance with a resolution recorded on the first page of said Book A, as follows:

"Whereas there is two old Books of Record very much out of repair. The Trustees at a meeting on the 4 day of february 1773, passed a Vote that the said old Books Shall be Transcribed and entered in this Book by Daniel Smith and his Son Elijah Smith which said Transcription is done in the pages following."

The transcription ends about the year 1686.

On page 209, the regular records of the town are resumed in their order, beginning in April 1790.

The word PAGE, and the number annexed refer to the page of the original book in the town clerk's office.

PAGE 307.

At a Meeting of the Freeholders and Inhabitants of the Town of Brookhaven held agreeable to a Law of the State for Regulating Town meetings the following Town Oficers ware Chosen this 3d Day of April 1798 (Being the first Tuesday)

Daniel Roe presdt

Joseph Brewster Junr.
Meritt S. Woodhull
Richard Robinson
Capt John Havens
Austin Roe
Caleb M. Hulse } Trustees

Isaac Hulse Clerk & Treasurer

Genl. John Smith Supervisor

Selah Strong
Merritt S. Woodhull
Caleb M. Hulse
Genl John Smith
Joseph Hedges
Capt Wm. Smith
Daniel Saxton } Assessors

Joshua Smith Collector

Capt James Smith
Stephan Swezey
Jonathan Worth } Commissioners of Highways

Joseph Brewster Jun
Caleb M. Hulse
John Bayles
Merit S. Woodhull
Austin Roe } Commissioners of Schools.

Jesse Hulse
Isaac Millar
Joshua Smith

PAGE 308.

Higbe Rayner
Obediah Reve
Samuel Bishop
Simeon Smith } Constables

OVERSEERS OF ROADS.
Abraham Woodhull
William Swezey
Nethanl Tooker

FENCE VIEWERS
Timothy Millar and
Samuel Phillips
Isaac Satterly

Caleb Helme
Wessel Sell
David Carter
James Swezey
Henry Dayton
Jeffery Randal
Obediah Reve
John Luvet
Caleb Perie
Isaac Smith Hills
Daniel Terry
Briant Norton
Jonas Hawkins
John Hallock
Zephaniah Conkling

Jonathan Dickerson
Henry Rayner
Saml Roberson
Goldsmith Davis
Nethanl Overton
Micael Ruland
Wm. Newins
Mordica Homan
Richard Hulse
Jeremiah Wheelar
William Hawkins

PAGE 309.

Brookhaven 5 March 1798

We the Undersigned in Conformity to the Act of the Legislature of the State of New york intitled an Act Concerning Slaves passed 22 feb-y 1788—do hereby Certify that on Application of Genl. Smith in behalf of Mrs Ruth Woodhull have Examined a Certain Negro man Slave Named Ben and are of Opinion that Said Negroman is of Sufficiant ability to provide for himself and that the Said Negro man is Under the Age of fifty Years

NICOLL FLOYD
RICHARD ROBINSON   } Trustees
STEPHAN OVERTON
JOSEPH BREWSTER JUR

CALEB M. HULSE   } Justices
MERITT S. WOODHULL

PAGE 310.

It is Voted By the Inhabitants of sd Town April 3d 1798—that No person is Intitled to Seaweed By Heaping it up on public Beaches also voted that a Tolarateing master Be A resedent of Sd Town

Voted that No Cattle Run at Large West Meadow Beach

under the Pennalty of Two Shillings for Every Head for Every Offence—

Also Voted that No Oysters Or fish Be Ketched By foreigners

Also Voted that No forigners Hunt Dear or Other Game in said Town—

PAGE 311.

At a meeting of the Trustees of the free holders and Commonality of the Town of Brookhaven Held this 7th day of May 1798

Present at Sd Meeting

      Daniel Roe Presdt.

      Austin Roe
      Caleb M. Hulse
      Joseph Brewster Junr } Trustees
      Meritt S. Woodhull
      & John Havens,

At Said Meeting it was Voted and Agreed that No fish Should Be Carried Out of the Town, under Any Protence whatever—

Also it Was further Voted and Agreed that No Oysters or Clambs Shall be Catched in the South Bay in Partnership with Wm Smith and the Town By Any Person Or Persons who are Not Inhabitants of said Town

Also it is further Voted and Agreed that If Any Oysters or Clambs are Carried Out of said Town—the Person or Persons that Carries Sd Oysters Out of Said Town shall first Obtain Liberty of said Trustees or their Agent and Pay the sum of five Shillings for Every Tons Burden of the Craft or Vessel that Carries them Out of said Town or the sum of Eight Pence for Every Hundred Oysters—and the Sum of Two pence for Every Hundred Clambs so Carried to Market.

PAGE 312.

Also it is further Voted and agreed that Every Person or Persons that Catches fish Oysters Or Clambs Contrary to the

True Intent and Meaning of this Law Shall forfit to said Town the Sum of Ten Pounds to Be Sued for and Recovered as any Other Debt Before Any Justice of the Peice in Said Town together with Costs of Suit

DANIEL ROE Presdt L S

We the Commissioners Being Called by Nathaniel Tooker and Nathaniel Akerly and Others to Open a Road Threw the Land known By the Name of the Hundred Acres (Shut up By Simeon Hawkins and Benjamin Hawkins) We Order the Owners of said Land to Take away the fence and Erect Good handy Swinging Gates as Many as Appears to them Requisite to Enclose their Land and Any Person to Pass or Repass—in Testimony Whereof and for the True performing of Everything herein Contained We have hereunto Set Our hands and Seals this Twenty third Day of April 1798—and Sente it to Be Recorded

JAMES SMITH L S) Commissioners
STEPHAN SWEZY L S (of Highways

March 10th 1801 the above Road maid Void*

PAGE 313.

Brookhaven May the 8 1798—

Whereas we the Commissioners of the Town of Brookhaven being Called By Isaac Satterly have Seen fit to Lay Out and Order a Road Opened from the End of the Road a Cross the Land of Isaac Satterly then Comeing into the Road that Now is Occupyed and also we Commissioners of Said Town do Order Daniel Satterly to move his fence further Out of the Road, to the Bounds that we Commissioners have staked Out—and we further Do Order Isaac Satterly to Make and Maintain a Road Twenty feet wide from the Corner of the Road to the mill Dam that is Now in Building By sd Isaac Satterly and we further Do Order the said Isaac Satterly and Daniel Satterly to Move their fence to the

[*NOTE.—See page 356.—Committee.]

Bounds that We the said Commissioners have Staked Out—
By the first Day of August Next Ensueing
 Given Under Our hands and Seals and Ordered On the Town Record.

JAMES SMITH L S } Commissioners
STEPHAN SWEZEY L S } of Highways

N. B. the first stakes the North one By a Cherry Tree in Isaac Satterlys fence marked thus X Second 22 feet from a Large willow in Daniel Satterlies Garden the third 7 feet from a Damson Tree in the Corner of the X in the corner of the Gerden

PAGE 314.

We the Commissioners Being Called by Wm. Smith and Others to Lay Out, a Road* Beginning on the Wadeing River Road Between Wm. Phillips and Henry Dayton's Land On the North side of the Line Between sd Phillips and Daytons Land So Runing to St. Georges Manner and from thence An Easterly Course unto Punks hole in Testimony Whereof and for the True Proforming of Every thing herein Contained
 We have hereunto Set Our Hands and Seals this 8th Day of May 1798—

JAMES SMITH L S } Commissioners
STEPHAN SWEZEY L S } of Highways.

PAGE 315.

To all people to whome these presents Shall Come Greeting know ye that I Phebe Howell of Bridghampton in the County of Suffolk and State of New york, for a Valuable Consideration Received to the full Satisfaction of Zephaniah Bowers of Kilingsworth in the County of Middlesex and State of Connecticut do Give Grant Sell and Make Over to the Said Zephaniah Bowers his Heirs and assigns a Certain

---
[*NOTE.—Called and known as the New Road, leading from Middle Island to Manorville.—Com.]

Tract of Land Lieing in Southampton on Long Island State of New york at a place Called Halsies Manner in the North Division formerly belonging to my Hond. father John Howell Being the One Half of the Lot Number Seven in said Manner Containg By Estimation Two Hundred Acres Be the Same More or Less bounded North by the River West By Land Belonging to Mathew Smith's widow—South By Hot water Street—East By the Lot Number Six—it Being the Tract of the Land I have in that Place; To Have and To Hold to him the said Zephaniah Bower his heirs and Assigns forever the Above Discribed premisses with all the previdledges and Appurtenances to the Same Belonging to their proper use Benefit and Behoof—and that I the Said phebe Howell have Good Right to Sell the same in Manner & form as above Written—and that the Same is free of all Incumbrance what Ever, and furthermore The Said Phebe Howell do By these presents Bind My Self My Heirs Executors & Administrators, to Warrant Secure and Defend the above Granted Premises to him the Said Zephaniah Bowers his heirs and Assigns against all Claims and Demands whatsoever—In Witness I have hereunto Set my hand and Seal this 22nd Day of June AD 1789—

PHEBE HOWELL L S

Signed Sealed and Dilivered In presents of
MARY CLARK
MIRIAM CLARK.

PAGE 316.

Middlesex County ss Kilingsworth September the 6th 1790—

Parsonally Appeared Phebe Howell Signer & Sealer of the foregoing Instrument and acknowledged the Same to be her free act and Deed before me,

HEZH LANE Justice of Peace.

This Indenture Made this Eighteenth Day of January In the Year of Our Lord One Thousand Seven Hundred and

Ninety Eight; Between Oliver Smith of Moriches of the first Part, & Benjamin Downs of River Head Town of the Second Part Witnesseth that the Said party of the first part for and In Consideration of the Sum of Two Hundred & Eighty five Pounds five Shillings Lawfull Money of the State of New York To Him in Hand paid by the Said Party of the Second part, the Receipt Whareof is hereby Acknowledged Hath Given Granted Bargained Sold Aliened Remised Released and Confirmed unto the Said party of the Seccond part, his Heirs and Assignes forever the One Equal undivided Half of Lot Num 10 in the North Division of Halcys Mannar in the Township of Brookhaven County of Suffolk & State of New york Bounding as follows: on the North by the Peaconick River East By Lot Num, 11 Laid out to Mathew Smith South By the Highway west By Lot Num. 9 Laid out to James petty Containing Eight Hundred and Seventy three Acres, together with all & singular the Heriditaments and Appurtenances there unto Belonging Or in any wise Apertaining and the Revertion & Revertions Remainder and Remainders

PAGE 317.

Rents Issues and profits thereof and all the Estate Right Title Interest Claim and Demand Whatsoever of the Said party of the first part. Either in Law Or Equity of in and to the above Granted and Bargained premises with the Said Hereditaments & Appurtenances TO HAVE AND TO HOLD the said Half of the Said Lot of Land with the Appurtenances to the Only Proper use and Behoof of the Said Party of the Seccond part His Heirs and Assigns for Ever—

And the said party of the first part for Him Self His Heirs Executors & Administrators Doth Covenant Bargain Promise & Agree to and with the Said Party of the Second part His Heirs and assigns to Warrant and for Ever Defend the Above Bargained premises and Every part and parcel thereof Now Being in the Quiet and Peassible possession of the said party of the first part his Heirs and Executors Administrators & Assigns & a gainst Every Other Person Or persons Claiming or to Claim the Said Premises Or Any part Or parcel thereof By Him Or under Him Or them, Or any of them

In Witness Whereof the Said party of the first part Hath Hereunto Set his hand and seal the Day and year first above written.

OLIVER SMITH L S

Sealed & Dilivered in presents of
JOSIAH SMITH
SALLY SMITH
a True Coppy pr Luis G Stanberry

PAGE 318.

Know all men By the Presents that I William Floyd of Brookhaven in the County of Suffolk and State of New york am Held and firmly Bound unto Benjamin Downs of River Head Town in the County & State afforesaid in the Sum of Two Hundred and fifty pounds Curent Money of Said State for which payment well and Truely to Be made I do Bind my Self my Heirs Executors and Administrators Sealed with my Seal and dated this Eigtheenth Day of January in the year of Our Lord One Thousand Seven Hundred and Ninety Eight—1798—

The Condition of this Obligation is Such that If the above Bound William Floyd his Heirs Executors administrators or Assigns Shall and will Give or Cause to Be Given or Rendered unto the Said Benjamin Downs his Heirs Executors administrators Or Assigns a Good and Sufficiant Warented Deed Whenever Nethaniel Smith Son of Hugh Smith Shall Arrive at Lawfull Age for the One Equal undivided Half of Lot No. 10 in the North Division of Halcies Manner, the Whole Lot Bounded on the North By peaconick River On the East by Lot N- 11 Laid Out to Mathew

Smith South by the Highway and West By Lot N.- 9 Laid
Out to James petty. Containing Eight Hundred and Seventy
three Acres More Or Less then this Obligation to Be Void
Other Wise to Remain in full force and Virtue
sealed and Dilivered
in presents of
NANCY STRONG }   WM FLOYD L S
NICOLL FLOYD

A true Coppy by me Luis G. Stanbrough

PAGE 319 BLANK.

PAGE 320.

These may Certify all Whome it may Concern that
Thomas Helme Esqr of the Town of Brookhaven has made
Application to the Trustees of the Freeholders and Commonality of Said Town to Manumate and set free a Certain
Negro Slave By the Name of Jack—a Greeable to an Act of
the Legislature. for that purpose passed the 22 Day of
february 1798—and the Trustees aforesaid haveing Examined Said Negro and finding him to be under the Age of
fifty years of Age and of Sufficiant Ability to provide for
himself—have Given this Setificate Agreeable to Said Law—

Given under Our hands this first Day of October 1798—

                DANL ROE Presdt
                JOSEPH BREWSTER
                AUSTIN ROE   } Trustes
                CALEB M HULSE
                CALEB M HULSE   } Justice
                MERITT S WOODHULL

PAGE 321.

Brookhaven January 24th, 1799—

We the Commissioners of highways have Consulted those
Who this Road most Concerns & we do think it most
Proper that the Road from Jeremiah Randals Should Run
a Westerly Course to the North-west Corner of John Bay-

les Lot then Runing along sd Bayles Cordwood Road. about Eighty Rods—then a more westerly Course to Drown meadow Road & we do Take of the Road that Was Laid Out to the west of Stephan Swezys Gate. the aforesaid Road to Be three Rods wide
to Be Recorded   JONATHAN WORTH } Commissioners
                           STEPHAN SWEZY   } of Highways

Brookhaven february the 15 1799

We the Commissioners Being Called to Lay out a three Rod Road* from the Granny Road Begining at the Northwest corner of Ebenezar Homans South Lot Easterly with the fence a Cross the Oald Path then Southerly a Cross sd homans Land to Daniel Terrys Land then In the Oald path to the End of the Hedge fence, then Runing North East to a white Oak Sapling in the fence Between Sd Terry and Christophar Swezey Land, then Runing a Crost Said Swezys Land to the fulling mill, then with the Oald path to the Road that Goes from Robert Homans to John Bayles
                       STEPHAN SWEZEY } Commissioners
                       JAMES SMITH   } of Highways

PAGE 322 BLANK.

PAGE 323.

Town Meeting 1799— { At A Meeting of the freeholders and Inhabitants of the Town of Brookhaven held this 2 Day of April in the Year of 1799 Being Anual Town meeting—Agreeable to a law of the State of New York

Daniel Roe Presdt

Joseph Brewster Jun
Meritt S. Woodhull
Richard Robinson } Trustees
John Havens
Austin Roe
Caleb M. Hulse

[*NOTE.—This road was closed in 1823.—See records p. 199, Book D.—Com.]

Isaac Hulse Clerk & Treasurer
Meritt S. Woodhull Supervisor

Wm Jayne Junr ⎫
Meritt S. Woodhull ⎪
John Robinson ⎪
Genl John Smith ⎬ Assessor
Austin Roe ⎪
John Akerly ⎪
Isaac Hulse ⎭

Joshua Smith Collector

Majr Jonas Hawkins ⎫
John Bayles ⎬ Commisson of highway
Daniel Saxton ⎭

Jesse Hulse ⎫
Isaac Millar ⎬
Higby Rayner ⎭

PAGE 324.

Wardin Toby ⎫
Jacob Newton ⎬ Cunstables
Joseph Hulse ⎭

OVERSEERS OF HIGHWAYS.

Capt James Smith   Elijah Ackerly
Daniel Jones   Capt James Davis
Benjamin Eaton   James Woodhull
Henry Rayner   Azel Robinson
Thomas Aldridge   Theofelas Smith
Richard Hulse   Rogers Avery
Benajah Risley   John Woodhull
Wm Tooker,   Henry Smith
Justus Overton   John Overton
John Bayles   Gillard Mills
Wm Hawkins

PAGE 325.

FENCE VIEWERS

Israel Bennet   Benjamin Hawkins
James Davis   Timothy Millar
James Woodhul   Nethane Tuthill
Henry Rayner   Higby Rayner

Obediah Reves
Jesse Rose
Wm Newins
Geo. Hallock
John Overton

Oliver Smith
Joseph Terry
Nathan Mulfor,d
Geo. Mills
Joshua Smith

Voted that No furener Shall Chase Deer within this Town With Howns

Voted that No hogs Shall Run on the Commons with out Rings

PAGE 326.

At a meeting of the Trustees of the freeholders and Commonality of the Town of Brookhaven Held in Said Town this 2d of April 1799

Present at Said Meeting

DANIE ROE—Presdt

AUSTIN ROE
MERITT S. WOODHULL
RICHARD ROBINSON
JOSEPH BREWSTER
JOHN HAVENS
CALEB M. HULSE
} Trustees

At Said Meeting the Said Trustees and Samuel Smith of Smithtown Administrator to the Estate of John Havens Late of Brookhaven Decst Did Jointly and Seaverly Agree to Leave all Their Desputes Concerning Maintaining a Negro Man By the Name of Tite to Refferance to Be Decided By John Cooper Josiah Fauster & Capt. Josiah Howell Esqrs of the Town of Southampton—and that the Cost of Said Refferance should follow the suit

Brookhaven September. 1798—

We the Commissioners of Roads Being Called By Benjamin Smith to Open a Road that Leads from his House to Winthrops Pattent Shut up By John Woodhull—Which we the Commissioners Do Order to Be Opened as a Publick Road

N B the Return of the above Road was Made to the Reccord after sd Commissioners were out of office—Townd meeting Day April the 2, 1799—Sd Road made void or a part altered——343

JAMES SMITH } Commisioners
STEPHAN SWEZEY } of Highways

PAGE 327.

March—1799—

We the Commissioners Being Called upon By anumber of Inhabitance for Laying Out a publick Highway—and By Advise and Consent of the Owners of the Land we have Laid Out a Publick Road three Rods Wide from John M Longs Saw mill Dam Southwesterly to the Little Branch then Southerly as the Line Runs haveing Theofelus Smiths & Higby Rayners Land & Samuel Rayners Land On One Side and Enos Swezys And Samuel Rayners Land on the Other Side to Samuel Rayners Barn and So to the Middle Road

STEPHAN SWEZEY } Commissioners
JONATHAN WORTH } of Highways.

PAGE 328.

We the Inspectors of the Election in and for the Town of Brookhaven have Proceeded to Close the Poll of Said Election as the Law Directs—and further agreeable to an Amendment of Said Law have proceeded to Open the Ballots and do hereby Certify the Names of Candidates and Number of Votes Taken for Senate and Assemblymen to Be as followeth Viz

FOR SENATE

Piere Vancortland Junr Sixty five Votes
Ezekiel Robins Sixty Six Votes
John B. Coles fifty three Votes

Richard Hatfield fifty three Votes
FOR ASSEMBLY
Nicoll Floyd Seventy Seven Votes
Silos Wood One Hundred & Twenty Six Votes
Jerard Landon Sixty Eight Votes
John Howard fifty one Votes
Jonathan Rogers fifty Six Votes
Doct John Smith Seventy Two Votes
— James Reve fifty Eight Votes
as Witness Our hands

Done this 3d Day of may 1799 | MERITT S WOODHULL
WM JAYNE JUNR
AUSTIN ROE } Inspectors.

I do hereby Certify the above to Be a True Coppy of the Returns made to the Reccord By the above Said Inspectors

ISAAC HULSE Town Clk

N B John Overton Debt Seriff and Isaac Hulse served as Clerks of sd Election—

PAGE 329.

At a Meeting of the Trustees of the freeholders and Commonality of the Town of Brook haven held this 6th of May 1799—

Present at sd, Meeting

DANIEL ROE Presdt
RICHARD ROBINSON
AUSTIN ROE
CALEB M. HULSE
JOSEPH BREWSTER } Trustees
MERITT S. WOODHULL
JOHN HAVENS

At sd Meeting the Fowling in the South Bay in Partnership With Capt Wm Smith and Sd Town Was Hired to Wm Alibeen for One Year from the above Date Reserveing to the Inhabitants of sd Town the Previledge of fowling in

Said south Bay, and the sd Alibeen Agreed to pay to the sd Trustees for the sd Previledge the Sum of forty Two Dollars and fifty Cents—

Also at the above said meet it was voted and Agreed By sd Trustees that the Law Concering Oysters & Clambs Pased the 7th Day of may 1798 and Entered in Page 311 is hereby Confirmed By sd Trustees until a further Vote of sd Trustees—and Entered By me By Order of sd Trustees & Joseph Homan to tolerate for the same

Isaac Hulse Town Clk

PAGE 330.

To all Whome it may Concern

We the Commissioners of Highways for the Town of Brookhaven haveing Been Called to Brookfield By a Number of the Inhabitants of that Place To Regulate Highways in said Brookfield and We Do hereby Lay Out and Confirm all and Every Highway or Road in sd Place as they Was Laid Down on the map of said Pattent By the Commissioners Appointed By the Court for Makeing Partition of sd Pattent—as they was Laid Out in the Year of 1793 and as May Appear By the Map and Return of the Survey of Brookfield Refferance thereto Being Had Done By us in May in the Year of One Thousand Seven Hundred & Ninety Nine

John Bayles } Commissioners
Jonas Hawkins } of Highways

PAGE 331.

At a Meeting of the freeholders and Inhabitants of the Town of Brookhaven the 3d of June 1799 Being a Special Town Meeting for the Purpose of Voting in Commissioners of Schools One Counstable &c Notified for that Purpose

JOSEPH BREWSTER
MERRITT S. WOODHULL } Commissioners of Schools
JOHN BAYLES

SAMUEL BISHOP—Constable

JAMES WOODHULL
NETHANIEL TUTTEL } fence Viewers

At a Meeting of the Trustees of the freeholders and Commonalitoy of the Town of Brookhaven this 3, of June 1799

Present at sd Meeting

DANL ROE Presdt
CALEB M. HULSE
MERITT S. WOODHULL
JOSEPH BREWSTER } Trustees
JOHN HAVENS
AUSTIN ROE

At sd Meeting sd Trustees Voted and agreed that No Oysters or Shells Shall be Taken up in the South Bay for to Be Sent Out of the Town Or to Be Laid Down in the Water from and after the fifteenth of June Instant until the first of September Next Ensueing

PAGE 332.

under the Penalty of Twenty Dollars for Every offence to Be Sued for and Recovered Before Any Justice in sd Town With Costs of suit Danl Roe Pesdt

at sd Meeting on the 3 of June Capt Joseph Brewster By a Geement of the Trustees Was to Go to Saml Smith of Smith Town and Draw notes to Leave the Dispute Between sd Smith and sd Town to Reffrores

PAGE 333.

We the Commissioners of Brookhaven Being Called By the People of Millars Place and the Eastern Part of Coram, to alter a Certain Road or highway that Turns out of the Town Road in Millars Place on the East Side of Timothy and Joseph Millars house that they Now Live in & Runing

Northerly & Westerly until it Comes to the foot of the Beach—known By the Name of the Hay Path which alteration Takes Place By Moving the fence at the Begining Two Rods East and Runing a Straight Course Northerly to a Certain Bar-Poast Standing in the Line fence Between the Lands of the Heirs of NethanielMillar Decst and Nethaniel Davis thence Leading to the Oald Road that Goes to Millars Landing Two Rods Wide until it Comes within fifteen Rods of the Broken Groundwhere On Cordwood is Lain. tis Ment it should Be four Rods wide West of Said Road fifteen Rods in Length and from thence three Rods wide to the Sound—and do Give the forementioned Road in Exchange Reserving the Previledge to Justice Helme Timothy and Joseph Millar and their Heirs and Assigns forever of Carting up Hay Subjecting to Shuting Gates—also it is Our Meaning that the New Road Should Be Subject to the same Which We Return to Be Recorded this 18th Day of June 1799

      JONAS HAWKINS } Commissioners
      JOHN BAYLES   } of Highways

PAGE 334.

We the Commissioners Being Called to Alter a Road Laid Out that Leads from Ezra Tuthills to the Oald Smiths Neck Road we Order said Road to Run from Said Tuthills as it Now Runs until it Comes to the Countery Road then Turning Westerly a Long the Countery Road until it Comes to the Line Between Wardin Tobys Land and the Land of John Rider from Thence Turning Between the Land of sd Toby and Rider until it Comes to the Said Smiths Neck Road Which we Return To be Recorded three Rods wide
 Brookhaven December the 2, 1799—

      DANIEL SAXTON } Commissioners
      JONAS HAWKINS } of Highways

We the Commissioners Order a Road to Be Opened thirty feet wide Begining at Reve Howells so Runing southerly as the Lane Now Leads until it Comes to the Bars Turning into Nethaniel Homans Lot from thence Going threw the Lot Nearly where the Road Now Runs until it Comes to the Granny Road from thence Runing Westerly until it Comes to the West Line of John Howells Land from thence Southerly On the Line Between John Howells an Reve Howells Land until it Comes to the Top of the hill North of Isaac Howells House then Takeing the Best of the Ground for a Road East of Isaac Howells House to the Coram Road

Brookhaven December the 2, 1799

JOHN BAYLES } Commissioners
DANIEL SAXTON } of Highway

PAGE 335.

Agreeable to a Law of this state for the Gradual Abolition of Slavery Passed the 29 of march 1799 Samuel Smith of the Town of Brookhaven Makes Return to the Reccord of sd Town that he had a feemale Child Born of a Slave of his On the first Day of September 1799 Childs Name is Aner—Entered the 24 of December 1799

Pr me ISAAC HULSE Town Clk

These may Certify all Whom it may Concern that Elisha Hammond of the Town of Brookhaven has made Application To the Trustees of the freeholders and Commonality of the Town (of Brookhaven aforesaid) to manumate and set free a Certain Negro female Slave By the Name of Ziporah Agreeable to an act of the Legislator of the State of New york in Such Cases made the 22 of february 1788—the Trustees Aforesaid Haveing Examined the Said Negro and finding her to Be under fifty years of Age and of Sufficcant Ability to Provide for herself have Given this Setificate Agreeable To sd Law Given under Our hands in Brookhaven this second Day of December 1799—

> Daniel Roe Presdt
> Austin Roe
> John Havens   } Trustees
> Richar Robinson
> Joseph Brewster
> Caleb M. Hulse   } Justices
> Meritt S. Woodhull

PAGE 336.

We the Inspectors of the Election for the Town of Brookhaven haveing Proceeded as the Law of this State Directs for Regulateing Elections and Closed the Poll for the Representitive in Congress of the United States—and Counted the Votes and find them to Be as follows that is for (General) John Smith One hundred and Twenty Nine Votes—

for Silos Wood forty Eight Votes—

as Witness Our Hands in Brookhaven this 30th Day of December 1799—

> Meritt S. Woodhull
> John Robinson   } Inspectors
> Austin Roe

N B Wm Jayne Esqr } Servd as Clerks of sd
and Isaac Hulse   Election

January the 6th 1800

I Do hereby Certify that the above is a True Coppy of the Returns from the Inspectors of the election to Brookhaven Reccord

Pr Isaac Hulse Town Clk.

PAGE 337.

Agreeable to a Law of the State of New York for the Gradual Abolition of Slavery Passed the 29th of march 1799—General Wm Floyd of the Town of Brookhaven Made Return to the Reccord of said Town that he had a feemale Child Born of a slave of his on the Third Day of October 1799 Sd Childs name is Rachel.

Entered By me Isaac Hulse Town Clk
January the 28, 1800—
Agreeable to a Law of the State New york for the gradual Abolition of Slavery Passed the 29th of March 1799— Samuel Carman of the Town of Brookhaven made Return to the Record that he had a male Child born of a Slave of his on the furth of August 1800—Childs name Selah
Entered 24 August 1801

Apollos Wetmore Town Clk

Agreeable to a law of this State Genrl Wm Floy made return to the Record of Brookhaven that he had a male child born of a Slave of his on the 23rd Day of November 1801—Childs Name is Hector—Recorded April 5th 1802

A Wetmore T Clerk

Page 338.

At a Meeting of the Trustees of the freeholders and Commonality of the Town of Brookhaven held in said Town this 3d day of January 1800

Present at sd meeting

Daniel Roe Presdt ⎫
Meritt S Woodhull ⎪
John Havens ⎬ Trustees
Austin Roe ⎪
Richard Robinson ⎭

At Said meeting sd Trustees Voted and Agreed that Daniel Smith in Setauket in sd Town should have the Previledge of a Part of Drown meadow Bay herein After Limited to Lay Down Oysters Viz On the West side of said Bay Bounded By the west End of the third Salt Pond so Extending to the North End of the fourth Salt Pond and so to Extend thirty Rods Out Into the Bay from Low Water mark—the sd Previledge above Granted to Be the Property of sd Daniel Smith

Done By the Trustees above sd—

DANL ROE Presdt

PAGE 339.

year 1800 Brookhaven March 5

At a meeting of the Trustees of the freeholders and Commonality of the Town of Brookhaven

Present at Said meeting

Daniel Roe Presdt
Austin Roe   ⎫
Richard Robinson ⎪
John Havens   ⎬ Trustees
Caleb M. Hulse   ⎪
Meritt S. Woodhull ⎭

At Sd meeting Said Trustees Appointed Meritt S. Woodhull Esq. and Mr Richard Robinson Two of the aforesaid Trustees to Cast up the Collectors Books and the Receipts Paid there on and See How much money there is Comeing to the Town from said Collector

At a meeting of the Trustees of the freehelders and Commonality of the Town of Brookhaven held this 31 of march 1800—

Present at sd Meeting

Daniel Roe Presdt   ⎫
Austin Roe   ⎪
Meritt S. Woodhull   ⎪
Caleb M. Hulse   ⎬ Trustees
Richard Robinson   ⎪
John Havens   ⎪
Joseph Brewster Junr   ⎭

at sd Meeting It was voted and agreed that sd Trustees Take the Estate of *

into their Hands as the Law Directs If it Be agreeable to Samuel Smith of Smith Town the Executor to sd Estate

PAGE 340.

---

* NOTE.—Blank in the original record.—Com.

We Daniel Roe & Caleb M. Hulse being Appoind a Committee to View Charles,es pond do Return that Richard Hudson Shall have the Privaledge Set of to him for the term of Ten years and Longer If agreeable to the Succeeding Trustees—the Said Richard Hudson Paying to the Trustees of Brookhaven Annually the Sum of 25 Cents

Agreeable to a Law of the State of New York for the gradual abolition of Slavery Passed the 29th of March 1799—Jehiel Woodruff of the Town of Brookhaven made return to the Record that he had a Male Child Born of A Slave of his Named Tamar on the third day of August 1806 Childs name is Peter—

MORDECAI HOMAN Town Clk

PAGE 341.

At a meeting of the Freeholders and Inhabitans of the Town of Brookhaven held this first Day of April 1800 Agreeable to a Law of the State of New york in Such Cases made—& agreeable to the Pattent of sd Town Incorporateing the Same the following Town Officers Were Chosen

Viz   Meritt S Woodhull Presdt ⎫
      Joseph Brewster Junr   ⎪
      Richard Robinson   ⎪
      John Havens   ⎬ Trustees
      Austin Roe   ⎪
      Caleb M. Hulse   ⎪
      Stephan Swezy   ⎭
         Isaac Hulse Clerk & Treasurer—
         Meritt S. Woodhull supervisor—
         Wm Jayne   ⎫
         Meritt S. Woodhull ⎪
         John Robinson   ⎬ Assessors.
         Austin Roe   ⎪
         Isaac Hulse   ⎭
            Isaac Millar Collector

Richard Floyd }
Isaac Hulse } Commissioners of Highway
Danl Saxton }

Richard Floyd }
Isaac Hulse }
John Havens } Commissioners of Schools
Danl Comstock }

Jesse Hulse }
Isaac Millar }
James Robinson } Counstables
Samuel Bishop }
Samuel Hammond }

PAGE 342.

OVERSEERS OF HIGHWAYS

Isaac Brewster
Benjamin Hawkins
Benjamin Eaton
Joseph Rayner
Jeremiah Havens
Daniel Smith
Wm Tooker
Jonas Davis
Palmer Overton
Stephan Randal

Wm Swezey
Wells Davis
James Woodhull
David Robinson
Oliver Hulse
Wm Newins
Jeremiah Wheelar
Daniel Tooker
John Turner
Zophar Garard

FENCE VIEWERS

Jeremiah Havens
Zackery Sanford
Goldsmith Davis
Nethaniel Overton
John Van Brunt
Wm Swezy
Joseph Wells
Henry Smith
John Mott
Moses Wicks
Nathan Post

Jeremiah Wheelar
John Hallock
James Davis
Timothy Millar
James Woodhull
Nethaneel Tuthll
Barnabas Winds
Israel Bennet
Jacob Hawkins
Zephaniah Conklin

PAGE 343.

April the 1, 1800 in Open Town Meeting the following

Votes were Taken No Hoggs Shall Run On the Commons with Out haveing yokes On that Shall be thought to Be Sufficcend By the fence viewers and Rings in their Noses and Marked with the Owners Proper Ear mark also that no fishery or Guning should be hired Out—
To Danl

Brookhaven April the 5th 1800

We the Commissioners of Highways for said Town Being Called By a number of the Inhabitants of sd Town to Alter a highway in the Neighbourhood of the Mooneponds in sd Town—and after Vieweing the Premises we do hereby Order a Certain Road made Void that was Laid out By Stephan Swezey & James Smith and Entered in Page 326. that Turns Out of the Road Leading from Mary Wickses to Abel Biggses Threw Isaac Ketcham,s & John Woodhulls Land until it meets the Road here After Laid Out viz Begining and Turning Out of the Road at the Northeast Corner of the wd Mary Wickse,s Garden so Runing Southerly On the East side of sd Gardain until It Comes to the South East Corner thereof then Turning Gradually Onto the Line Between Benjamin Smiths

PAGE 344.

and Caleb Newtons Land until it comes to the Portion Road then Turning a Long the Portion Road Easterly until It Comes to a Certain Road Begining on Jacob Smiths Land thence Runing Southeasterly as sd Road now Runs until it Comes to the Oald Road Runing to Islip Patent—It is to be Understood it is to Be three Rods Wide On the East side of sd Mary Wicks,s Garden until It Comes to the South end thereof—then Turning Gradually onto the Line Between Benjamin Smiths and Caleb Newtons Land three Rods wide One half on Each Side sd Line to the Portion Road then Continueing three Rods wide as far as Before Mentioned Leading to Islip Which we Return to Be

Recorded

          RICHARD FLOYD ⎫
          ISAAC HULSE   ⎬ Commissioners of highways
          DANIEL SAXTON ⎭

PAGE 345.

Brookhaven Moriches April the 8th 1800

  Personally Appeared before me Benjamin Edwards one of the Justices of the Peace Pomp a Melatter man & Sary Arch his wife and Acknowledged that they of their Own free and Voluntary Will have Bound their Son named William unto David Day to Serve him untill he Arrives to the age of Twenty One years—

                              BENJAMIN EDWARDS Justice

Brookhaven Moriches April the 8, 1800—

  Personally Appeared before me Benjamin Edwards Justice of the Peace Pomp a Melltterman & Sarah Arch his Wife and Acknowledged that they of their Own free and Voluntary Will have Bound their Son Named Sonney unto Capt--John Havens to Serve him he Arrives to the Age of Twenty One years of age

                              BENJAMIN EDWARDS Justice

Suffolk ⎫
County ⎬ This may Certify that Hannah Hanabel hath bound her Daughter Hannah to William Skidmore for the term of Ten Years from the first day of June next with my approbation

                              BENJAMIN PETTY Justice

Recorded Augus 3rd 1801

PAGE 346.

  At a meeting of the Trustees of the freeholders and Commonality of the Town of Brookhaven held in sd Town this fifth day of May 1800

Present at sd Meeting

                              Meritt S. Woodhull Presdt

Austin Roe }
John Havens }
Caleb M. Hulse } Trustees
Joseph Brewster }
Stephan Swezy }

At sd Meeting sd Trustees Voted & Agreed that the fowling in the South Bay in Partnership with sd Town and Capt Wm Smith Shall be hired for One year from this Date at Vendue to the Highest Bidder Provideing Always that no more than four Persons Shall Occupy the Previledge of sd folling at Any One Time—And always the Previledge of fowling To the Inhabitants of sd Town the Above sd Previledge is hired to Willet Rayner and Co. for fifty Dollars and they Are te Occupy two Certain Bars that they may Chuse in any Place in the Bay to the Exclusiance of Any of the Inhabitants of sd Town By four Persons Onely

Recivd Brookhaven 4th May 1801 from Willet Rayner Fifty Dollars in full for the toleration on Fowling in the South Bay in Pertnership with Capt Wm Smith

PAGE 347.

At a Meeting of the Trustees of the freeholders and Commonality of the Town of Brookhaven held in sd. Town this fifth Day of May 1800

Present at sd meeting

Meritt S. Woodhull Presdt
Austin Roe
Joseph Brewster
John Havens
Caleb M Hulse
Stephan Swezy

At sd Meeting the sd Trustees Takeing into Consideration the Great Destruction of fish in the South Bay in Partnership With sd Trustees and Capt Wm Smith By the fish Being Carried Out of sd Town to Market—

sd Trustees at Said meeting Voted and agreed and hereby Enacted that No fish Should be Caried Out of sd Town By Any Person or Persons What soever under the Penalty of Twenty five Dollars On Every Person that Catches fish with an Intention to Carry or send them Out of the Town or Carries them Out of the Town—to Be Sued for and Recovered before any Justice of the Peace in Said Town Together with full Costs of Suit for the Bennefit of the Town

MERITT S. WOODHULL Presdt L S

PAGE 348.

At a meeting of the Trustees of the freeholders and Commonality of the Town of Brookhaven Held in Sd Town this 5th Day of may 1800—

Present at sd Meeting

Meritt S. Woodhull Presdt
John Havens ⎫
Stephan Swezy ⎪
Austin Roe ⎬ Trustees
Caleb M Hulse ⎪
Joseph Brewster Junr ⎭

At Sd Meeting sd Trustees Considering the Great Damage that Hogs do in Runinging on the Commons in Sd Town With Out Rings or yokes Do in Compliance With the Vote of the freeholders & Inhabitants of Sd Town at their Anual Town Meeting held the first Day of April Last for the Preventing sd Damage Being Done in future—It is Voted and agreed And hereby Enacted By sd Trustees that If Any Hog Or Shoat Excepting Sucking Piggs onely, shall Be found on any of the Commons in sd Town Or on any Persons Inclosed Land—Excepting the Inclosed Lands of the Owner of sd Hogs—with Out Being yoked with Good and Sufficient yokes and Ringed in the Nose With Sufficiant Rings and Markd With the Owners Proper Ear marks, then the Owner or Owners or Possessor of Such hog or hogs so found On the Commons or On any Other Persons Inclosed Land Except the Owner,s—Then the Person Or persons that Owns Such Hog or hogs shall forfit the Sum of Seventy five Cents for Each and Every Hog so Transgressing this Law to Be Sued for And Recovered, By any free Person in sd Town as any Other Debt together with Costs of suit Before Any Justice of the Peice in sd Town

MERITT S. WOODHULL Presdt

PAGE 349.

Election Returns 1800

We the Inspectors of the Election of the Town of Brookhaven Haveing held an Election Agreeable to a Law of this state for a Representative in Congress and Canvesed the Votes and find them to Be as follows Viz

Genl John Smith Seventy nine } May 2—1800
Silos Wood One Hundred and Six }

We the Inspectors of Election for the Town of Brookhaveing Held An Election for Senators for the southern District of the state of new york and Canvessed the Votes and find them to be as follows Viz

Selah Strong One Hundred & one
Samuel Jones Ninety Seven
Samuel Height Ninety five
Benjamin Hunting Fifty five
Ebenezar Purdy Forty Nine
William Dening fifty

We the Inspectors of the Election for the Town of Brookhaven Haveing held an Election for Members of Assembly for the County of Suffolk agreeable To Law, ond Convesed the Votes and find them to Be as follows Viz—

Nicoll Floyd one Hundred & Sixty five
John Howord One Hundred & Seven
John L. Gardner One Hundred & Seven
Josiah Reves One Hundred and Thirty one

Mills Phillips thirty Eight
Abraham Millar thirty Two
Jerard Landon thirty One
Israel Carll—One (John Smith One)

Given under Our Hands In Brookhaven this 2d Day of May 1800—

MERITT S. WOODHULL
AUSTIN ROE
WM JAYNE
JOHN ROBINSON

} Inspectors of the above sd Election

PAGE 350.

At a Meeting of the Trustees of the freeholders and Commonality of the Town of Brookhaven held this Second day of June 1800—

Present at sd Meeting

Meritt S. Woodhull Presdt
John Havens
Stephan Swezey
Austin Roe
Richard Robinson
Joseph Brewster
Caleb M. Hulse
} Trustees

At sd Meeting sd Trustees Voted and Agreed and hereby Enacted that no Clambs or Other Shell fish shall Be Carried Out of the south Bay East of Woodhulls Point or Catched for the Purpose of Carrieing them Out of sd Town—under the Penalty of Twenty five Dollars on Every Person for Every Offence to Be Sued for and Recovered By the Trustees as any Other Debt With full Costs of suit Before any Justice in the Town—Except the Person or Persons that Catches sd Clambs Or Shell fish for the Purpose of Carrieing them Out of the Town shall fish Obtain a permit from the Trustees Thofles Smith or their Agent and Pay the sum of three Cents Pr Bushel for Every Bushel of Clambs Or other Shell fish they shall Catch for the Purpose of Carrying them Out of the Town

MERTT S. WOODHULL Presdt

PAGE 351.

At a Meeting of the Trustees of the freeholders and Commonality of the Town of Brookhaven held this Second Day of June 1800

Present at sd Meeting

Meritt S Woodhull Presdt
Richard Robinson ⎫
Caleb M. Hulse   ⎪
Stephan Swezey   ⎬ Trustees
Joseph Brewster   ⎪
John Havens   ⎪
Austin Roe   ⎭

At sd Meeting sd Trustees Voted and agreed that No Oysters or Shells Shall Be Taken up in the South Bay—to Be sent Out of the Town Or Be Laid Down in the Water from and after the fifth Day of June Instant until the Twentieth Day of August next Ensueing—under the Penality of Twenty Dollars On Every Person for Every offence to Be Sued for and Recovered Before any Justice in the Town With full Costs of suit

MERITT S WOODHULL Presdt

PAGE 352.

At a Meeting of the Trustees of the freeholders and Commonality of the Town of Brookhaven held at the House of John Bayles in sd Town this 4 Day of August 1800

Present at sd Meeting

Meritt S Woodhull Presdt
John Havens   ⎫
Caleb M. Hulse   ⎪
Richard Robinson ⎬ Trustees
Austin Roe   ⎪
Joseph Brewster   ⎪
Stephan Swezey   ⎭

at sd Meeting Doctor David Woodhull Made Aplication to Manumate and set free a Certain male Slave By the name of Silos agreeable to a Law of the State of New york in Such Cases made and provided pased the 22 of february 1788 the Trustees aforesaid haveing Examined said Negro and finding him to Be of Sufficiant Ability to Provide for himself and under fifty years of Age—We have Given this Setificate agreeable to sd Law for the Purpose to Manumate and set free said Negroman

Given under Our hands this 4th of August 1800

CALEB M: HULSE

PAGE 353.

Agreeable to a Law of the State of New york for the Gradual Abolition of Slavery Passed the 29th of March 1799—the Wido Ruth Woodhull of the Town of Brookhaven had a Male Child Born of a Slave of hers on the 18th Day of October in the year of 1800—Childs, name is Paul

Entered November 3 -- 1800

Pr ISAAC HULSE

At a Meeting of the Trustees of the Freeholders & Commonality of theTown of Brook Haven held in sd Town this 3d of Novr. 1800

Present at sd Meeting

Meritt S. Woodhull Presdt

Richard Robinson ⎫
Stephan Swezey　 ⎪
Austin Roe　　　 ⎬ Trustees
Caleb M. Hulse　 ⎪
John Havens　　　⎪
Joseph Brewster ⎭

At sd meeting sd Trustees Voteded and Agreed that Meritt S. Woodhull and Joseph Brewster Esqrs Be a Committy to Take the Charge of Joseph Tookers, Property and Sell as much wood as they Shall think Best for the Support of sd Tooker and family and to Dispose of sd Tooker as they Shall think Best for him—

PAGE 354.

Agreeable to a Law of the State of New york for the Gradual Abolision of Slavery Passed the 29 of March 1799—

Meritt S. Woodhull Esqr of the Town of Brookhaven Made Return to the Record of sd Town that he had a feemale Child Born of a Slave of His On the 7th Day of July 1800—sd Childs Name is Dence—

Entered By me this 12 Day of December 1800

ISAAC HULSE Town Clk

Agreeable To a Law of the State of New York for the Gradual Abolission of Slavery Passed the 29th Day of March 1799—Joseph Davis of the Oaldmans in the Town of Brookhaven Made Return to the Record of Sd Town that he had a female Child Born of a Slave of his on the first Day of July 1800 Sd Childs name is Elisabeth

Entered By me this 12 Day of December 1800—

ISAAC HULSE Town Clk

PAGE 355.

Agreeable to a Law of the State of New york for the Gradual Abolition of Slavery Pased the 29th of March 1799 Coll. Nicoll Floyd of Town of Brookhaven had a male Negro Child Born of a Slave of His on the Twenty Eight of November 1800—Sd Boys Name is Lew—

Entered the 3 Day of January 1800—

Pr ISAAC HULSE Town Clk

Agreeable to a Law of the State of New york for the Gradual Abolition of Slavery Passed the 29th Day of March 1799—Joseph Brewster Esqr of the Town of Brookhaven had a female Child Born of a Slave of his on the third day of November in the year 1800 sd Childs Name is Rachel

Pr Isaac Hulse Town Clk

Page 356.

We the Commissioners of highways of Brookhaven Being Pettitioned to By Sixty Eight of the freeholders and Inhabitants of Setauket in Said Town to Lay Out a Road from Setauket Southerly Agreeable to sd Petition We have Laid Out sd Road from the Sheeppasture Road By Saml Hawkins Southerly threw a Peice of Land that is Called the Hundred Acres Runing Between Simeon Hawkins House & Barn So to Continue Southerly as the the Oald Tract Now goes to the Countery Road or Post Road at a Place Called the Marked Trees—Also Agreeable to sd Petition we have Laid sd Road four Rods Wide—

Also agreeable to sd Petition we have made Null & Void a Road Runing Round West of Simeon Hawkinses from Niccolls Road to Where it Comes into the above sd Road Southward of Simeon Hawkins House which was Laid Out By James Smith & Stephan Swezy and Entered in Page 312 Which we Return to Be Recorded Done By us March 10. 1801

     Isaac Hulse   Commissioners
     Richd Floyd   of
     Daniel Saxton   Highways

Page 357.

At a Meeting of the Trustees of the freeholders and Commonality of the Town of Brookhaven held in sd Town this 6 of April 1801—

Present at sd Meeting

   Meritt S. Woodhull Prst
   Caleb M Hulse
   Austin Roe
   John Havens   } Trustees
   Richard Robinson
   Joseph Brewster Junr
   Stephan Swezy

At sd Meeting the following Genteemen of Stony Brook Namely George Hallock Caleb Davis & George Mills Petitioned sd Trustees for Leberty to Build a School House Northward & westward of Isaac Davises Blacksmiths Shop in Stony Brook—the said Trustees hereby Grants Liberty to set sd School House in said Place Where they shall think Most Convenient so as not to Incumber the Highway—
Entered By Order of the Trustees
By me ISAAC HUDSE Town Clk

PAGE 358.

At a Meeting of the Trustees of the freeholdors & Commonality of the Town of Brookhaven held in sd Town this 6 of April 1801—
Present at sd Meeting

Meritt S. Woodhull Presdt
Caleb M Hulse ⎫
Austin Roe ⎪
John Havens ⎬ Trustees
Richard Robinson ⎪
Joseph Brewster ⎪
Stephan Swezey ⎭

at Sd Meeting Noah Hallock Made Application to Manumate and Set free a Male Slave By the Name of Pompe and a feemale Slave By the Name of Candis Agreeable to a Law of the state of New york Pased the 22 Day of february 1788—The Trustees aforesaid haveing Examined sd Slaves Namely Pompe and Candis—and do find them to Be under fifty years of Age and of Sufficiant Ability to maintain themselves do hereby Agreeable to sd Law Manumate and set free sd Pompe and Candis

Given under sd Trustees Hands—
MERITT S WOODHULL Prest
Recorded By me
ISAAC HULSE Town Clk

Page 360.

At a Meeting of the Trustees of the freeholders & Commonality of the Town of Brookhaven held in sd Town this 7 of April 1801—

Present

    Meritt S. Woodhull
    Richard Robinson
    Caleb M. Hulse,
    Austin Roe   } Trustees.
    Joseph Brewster Junr
    John Havens
    Stephan Swezey.

At sd Meeting it was agreed By sd Trustees that Isaac Homan Should Shut up the Road Joining yaphank Line Reserved By the Town a Crost Connecticut River and In Lue there of Leave one Open the Same Wedth Between fifty & one Hundred Rods to the Westward Where there are Two Pine Trees Marked With the Letter D

[NOTE.—Page 359 is occupied with the same record as page 357.—Com.]

Page 361.

At a Meeting of the Freeholders and Inhabitants of the Town of Brookhaven held this 7 Day of April 1801—Being first Tuesday Being Town Meeting Day By the Law of this State the following Officers Were Chosen Viz

    Meritt S Woodhull Presdt
    Joseph Brewster Junr
    Richard Robinson
    Nicoll Floyd   } Trustees
    Joseph Hedges
    Caleb M. Hulse
    Stephan Swezey

Apollos Wetmore Clerk & Treasurer,
Meritt S. Woodhull Supervisor—

    William Jayne
    Caleb M Hulse } Assessors.
    John Rose

Isaac Millar—Collector

Elijah Akerly } Middle { Commissioners
John Woodhull } Island { of
John Rose—   Highways

Jesse Hulse   }
Isaac Millar |
James Robinson |
Samuel Bishop   } Counstables
Joseph Hulse |
Ebenezer Hulse |

PAGE 362.

OVERSEERS OF HIGHWAYS

Jonathan Mills   Oliver Hulse
Isaac Brewster   Zophar Hawkins
George Munroe   Annanias Smith
Capt. James Davis   Jonas Payn
Timothy Millar   Simeon Smith
James Woodhull   Briant Norton
Joseph Rayner   Stephan Overton
Azer Robinson   George Hallock
Thomas Stanbrow   Davis Overton
Josiah Smith   John Bailey
William Hawkins   Gilliard Mills
                        Jeffery Randal

FENCE VIEWERS.

Israel Bennet   Thomas Stanbrow
Nethaniel Tooker Junr   John Mott
James Swezey   Moses Wicks
Stephan Overton   John Homan
Timothy Millar   Joseph Terry
Timothy Norton   Joseph Wells
Benjamin Woodhull   Henry Smith
Nethaniel Tuthill   Timothy Rose
Davis Overton   Oliver Hulse
John Robinson

PAGE 363.

At a Meeting of the Trustees of the Free holders and commonalty of the Town of Brookhaven held in sd Town

of Brookhaven this 4th day of May 1801
Present at sd meeting—

Merrit S Woodhull President
Caleb M Hulse—
Joseph Brewster—
Stephen Swezey—
Joseph Hedges—
} Trustees

At sd Meeting it was agreed that Merrit S Woodhull—Caleb M Hulse, & Joseph Brewster should be appointed a committe to View the Flax pond at Crane Neck & see if it would answer to let it out into the sound agreeable to the request of Vincent Jones & Richard Floyd

At sd meeting the said Trustees agreed to sell the privaledge of Fowling in the South Bay in partnership with said Town and Capt Wm Smith to Willet Rayner and it is hereby agreed to in the manner following viz—that the said Willet Rayner shall for the Consideration of forty Dollars have the previlege of Gunning for market for four persons on the bars lying in the Bay belonging to William Smith & this Town for the term of one year from this date—

PAGE 364.

At a Meeting of the Trustees of the free-Holders and commonalty of the Town of Brookhaven held in sd Town this 1st day of June 1801—
Present at sd Meeting

Merrit S. Woodhull
Caleb M Hulse—
Joseph Brewster—
Stephen Swezey
Joseph Hedges
Nicoll Floyd
} Trustees

At said Meeting it was agreed that the priviledge of Fishing in the South Bay should be hired out untill the first day of November next, accordingly it was hired out to Elijah Chichester for One Hundred Dollars for said term of time—And furthermore there is no other person or persons allow'd to fish or catch any fish in said Bay to carry out of the Town to any market—

Brookhaven April 21st 1801—

Whereas we the Commissioners being duly called by Elija Davis and a number of others and requested us to stop up a certain Highway or road that appears to them to be useless leading from Elijah Davises to Daniel Bayle's in the old mans and we the said Commissioners having Reviewed the sd Road do allow it to be shut up

JOHN ROSE
JOHN WOODHULL } Commissioners
ELIJAH AKERLY

PAGE 365.

Election Returns with a Statement of Vote

County of Suffolk ss

Stement of Votes taken at the Anniversary Election for Governor Lieut Governor and Senators which commenced on the last Tuesday of Aprill one thousand Eight Hundred and one

For Govornor

George Clinton One Hundred & thirty five } Votes
Stephen Van Rensellaer one Hund & twenty thre

Lieut Govornor

Jeremiah Van Rensellaer—One Hundred & thirty } Votes
  four
James Watson—One Hundred & twenty seven

Senators

Ezra LHommedieu—one Hundred & twenty six } Votes
Selah Strong—one Hundred & twenty seven

We certify the above to be a true statement and estimate of the votes taken in the Town of Brookhaven at the aforesaid Election closed April the thirtieth day eighteen hundred and one

MERRITT S. WOODHULL
WILLIAM JAYNE— } Inspct
JOHN ROSE—

C M Hulse } Clks
A Wetmore }

Attest a true Coppy Apollos Wetmore } Town Clerk

Page 366.

County of Suffolk } ss

Statement of Votes take at the anniversary Election for Members of Assembly which commenced on the last Tuesday of April one thousand eight hundred & one—

Isaac Hulse Two Hundred & twenty two
Israel Carll Two Hundred & thirty five
Abraham Miller Eighty five—
Jared Langdon Eighty Six
Tredwell Skudder Seventeen
John Howard One
Abraham Woodhull One
Edward King One
} Votes

We Certify the above to be a true Statement and Estimate of the Votes taken in the Town of Brookhaven at the aforesaid Election closed April 30th 1801—

Merritt S Woodhull
William Jayne—
John Rose—
} Inspectors

A true Coppy Attest Apollos Wetmore Town Ck

Page 367.

At a Meeting of the Trustees of the freeholders and Commonality of the Town of Brookhaven held this 16th day of June 1801—

Present—

Merritt S Woodhull } President
Caleb M Hulse—
Richard Robinson
Joseph Brewster— } Trustees
Nicoll Floyd—
Joseph Hedges—
Stephen Swezey—

Be it enected by the trustees aforesaid that if any person or persons shall take and carry out of the South bay (belonging to the Town of Brookhaven and William Smith) or lay down in the Water any Oysters or Shells after the 20th of June Inst and before the first day of September next he or they so offending shall forfeit and pay the sum of twenty Dollars for every such offence to be sued for and recoverd before any Justice of the Peace with costs of suit

Meritt S Woodhull } President L S

True Coppy Attest Apollos Wetmore Town Clk

Page 368.

County of Suffolk } ss

Statement of Votes taken at the Election for Delegates to meet in Convention agreeable to a Law of the State of New York passed the sixth day of April one Thousand eight hundred and one 1801——

Samuel L Hommedieu	forty five	Benjn Tyler—	one
Ezra L Hommedieu	Forty eight	Justice Roe—	two
Wm Floyd—	Fifty one	Stephen Edwards—	one
Joshua Smith Jun—	Forty nine	Isaac Brewster	one
Selah Strong—	Nine	Saml Thompson	one
James Reeve—	Six	Isaac Satterly	one
John Woodhull—	four	Nathl Woodhull	one
John Howard—	four	Jacob V Brunt	one
B B Blydenburg	four	Joseph Jayne	one
Richard Udle—	four	Danl Smith	one
Isaac Hulse—	four	George M Punderson	one
Thomas Smith—	One	Richard Dewick	one
Henry Smith—	One	Benjn Jones—	one
Benjn Floyd—	One	Benjn Tyler Jur	one
Daniel Jones—	One	Simeon Hawkins	one
James Smith—	Two	Wikam Mills—	one
Moses Blachley—	one	John Floyd—	one
Jedediah Williamson	two	Thomas Floyd	one
Mills Phillops—	One	George Hallock	one
Nicol Floyd—	one	Alx Hawkins—	one
Benjn Edwards	one	Abm Woodhull—	one
John Havens—	one	Elijah Akerly—	one
Jacob Hawkins	two	Charles Dollas—	one

Selah Smith—	one	Stephen Jayne—	one
Thomas Mount—	two	Wm Jayne—	one
Jonas Hawkins	one	Wm Tooker—	one
Richard Floyd	three	Thos Strong—	one
Isaac Hawkins	one	Morris Jayne—	one
Phillops Ree	one	Robrt Jayne—	one
Jonathan Mills	one	John Denton—	on
Jonath' Dickerson	one	Vinsent Jones—	one
Joseph Brewster	two		

PAGE 369.

Return of the Electors in Brookhaven Is as follows Electors possessing freeholds of 100£ 462 of, 20£ 31 and Renters 81—The above Census taken in august 1801 By Caleb M Hulse, Wm Jayne and John Rose—

PAGE 370.

At a Meeting of the Freeholders and Inhabitance of the Town of Brookhaven on the 2nd day of November 1801 It being a special Town Meeting for the purpose of choosing a Constable & a number of Fence Viewers The following persons were chosen by a unan a mous Vote Viz

Richard Hudson—Constable

Joseph Terry
John Homan
Abm Cherry
Laban Worth
} Fence Viewers

At a Meeting of the Trustees of the Freeholders and Commonality of the town of Brookhaven held this 7th Day of December 1801—

Present

Meritt S Woodhull President
Caleb M Hulse
Richard Robinson
Joseph Brewster Jun
Nicoll Floyd
Joseph Hedges
Stephen Swezey
} Trustees

It was Voted and agree that Meritt S Woodhull Caleb M Hulse & Joseph Brewster be a Committee to view the bay in Setaukett where Selah Strongs has pititioned for the priviledge of erecting a Dam & Mill and see upon what condition he shall the privildge—

PAGE 371.

Decemb. 7th 1801

At said Meeting it was also agreed by said Trustees that John Woolsey should have the privilege of a certain piece of Land under water lying in Drown Meadow Harbor Bounded as follows Viz—beginning at the wester most corner of the Dweling House of sd Woolsey from thence west twenty Rods to the bay or Harbor from thence on a direct line to the westermost point of Saints Orchard, To HAVE and To HOLD the said Land under Water to him the said John Woolsey and to his Heirs and Assigns for ever for the sole purpose of planting or laying down oysters, reserving to the Town the right of improving the sd premises for any other purpose—

MERITT S WOODHULL President

Recorded December 8th 1801

APOLLOS WETMORE Town Clerk

NOTE.—Saints Orchard is upon the east side of Port Jefferson harbor.—Com.

THIS INDENTURE made the seventh day of December in the year of our Lord one Thousand Eight Hundred and one Between The Trustees of the Freeholders and commonality of the Township of Brookhaven in the County of Suffolk & State of New York of the one part and George Davis of the Township, County & State aforesaid of the other part Witnesseth that the said Trustees of the Freeholders and Commonality of the Township of Brookhaven for and in considiration of the Value of Ten Pounds currant money of New York, as exchange of Lands. to them in hand paid by

George Davis at or before the ensealing and delivery of these presents, the Receipt whereof is hereby Acknowledged Hath granted bargain Sold aliend, conveyed and confirmed & by these Presents

PAGE 372.

doth grant, bargain, sell, alien convey & confirm unto the said George Davis and to his Heirs & Assigns for ever, All of a certain Tract and parcel of Land situate at a place called Stoney Brook in the Township of Brookhaven aforesaid & bounded as follows viz—Westerly by the road that leads to the Landing, easterly by the road running through said Stoney Brook ending opposite Joseph Wells' House Northwardly by the Land that said George Davis bought of George Hallock—together with all and singular the privileges, profits, commodities Hereditaments & Appurtenances thereunto belonging or in any wise appurtaining To Have & To Hold the said Tract or parcel of Land and all and singular the premisis hereby granted & sold unto the said George Davis his Heirs & Assigns for ever, to the only use and behoof of the said George Davis his Heirs & Assigns for ever—

Signed Sealed & deliverd In presenc of
APOLLOS WETMORE

MERRITT S WOODHULL
NICOLL FLOYD
JOSEPH BREWSTOR JUNR
RICHARD ROBINSON
JOSEPH HEDGES
STEPHEN SWEZEY
CALEB M HULSE

Town Seal

Recorded 8th Dec 1801 By
A WETMORE
Town Clk.

To the Trustees of the freeholders & commonality of the Township of Brookhaven—These lines may certify that I do and will allow unto Joseph Davis the Land his House stands on with six feet therefrom dureing his natural life, meaning the Land that is Deeded to me from s,d Town but it is my meaning that at his death said house should be remooved.

Witness my hand & Seal this seventh day of December 1801—

 Jonas Hawkins }   George Davis l s
 George Burton {
 Recorded p A W 8th Dec 1801

Page 373.

This Indenture made between Meritt S Woodhull Caleb M. Hulse, Richard Robinson, Joseph Brewster Stephen Swezey Joseph Hedges & Nicoll Floyd—Trustees of the freeholders and commonality of the town of Brookhaven, in the county of Suffolk & State of New York, of the one part, and Richard Floyd Vincent Jones, and Jonathan Mills of the same place of the other part Witnesseth that the said Trustees for and in consideration of the sum of Fifteen Dollars, do give, grant, bargain sell and convey unto the said Richard Floyd Vincent Jones & Jonathan Mills the one equal undivided half part of a certain Pond or Marsh, situate lying & being in s,d Town of Brookhaven known by the name of the Flax Pond in the Old Field containing agreeable to a Map of the same fild in the Clarks office of s,d Town fifty nine Acres one quarter and twenty one Rods be the same more or less, it is bounded as follows, Viz. Beginning nine chains and sixty four Links north twenty-five and a half Degrees east from the North East corner of sd Vincent Jone's barn then running agreeable to sd Map and field Book south forty four Degrees east two Chains Twelve Links, east one Chain forty one Links North forty one degrees east one chain eighty nine Links, south seventy nine Degrees east three Chains seventy five Links south fifty eight Degrees east three chains fifty five Links, North fifty Degrees east three Chains ninety four Links, North five Degrees West one Chain ninety two Links north seventy Degrees east three Chains North sixty three deg East three Chains thirty six Links North seventy four deg east two Chains ninety four Links South eighty one Deg East three Chains sixteen Links, North seventy six Deg East three Chains eighteen Links to Henery Smith's bound or Line then North fifty four degrees East two Chains Sixty sevn Links North forty Deg West two Ch nine Links North forty seven deg east One Chain North Sixty nine Deg East one Chain

PAGE 374.

North fifteen Degrees east one Chain north thirty Degrees East two Chains thirty four Links North Five deg West one chain forty three Links North Twenty five Deg west one chain sixty nine Links to Richard Floyds bounds then North forty five Deg West One Chain North six Deg west one Chain North twenty three Deg East one Chain sixteen Links north five deg West three chains forty eight Links North fifty five dg West three Chains nineteen Links South thirty two deg west one chain forty five Links South Sixty five deg west two chains four Links West five Chains fourteen Links to the Inlet of sd Pond then South eighty deg West one chain seventy five Links South seventy Deg West one chain forty two Links South thirteen deg east one chain seventy one Links South sixty five deg west two chains fifteen Links South seventy five deg West one Chain seventy links South sixty five deg West one Chain seventy seven Links South eighty deg West three chains seven links South eighty three deg West four chains sixty links South twenty two deg West three Chains twenty two links South sixty five deg West one chain fifty three Links North seventy two degrees West one chain South fifty eight deg West two chains South twelve deg East one Chain thirty one Links South Sixty four deg West four chains thirty six links South One Chain South sixty two deg West three chains sixty Links South seventeen deg east two chains fifty five links south forty five deg east four chains four links South eighty deg east four chains south thirty eight deg east one chain ninety Links to the place of beginning, To have & To Hold the above granted and described premises unto the said Richard Floyd Vincent Jones & Jonathan Mills together with all the previledges & Appurtenances thereunto belonging or in any

PAGE 375.

Wise Appurtaining unto sd Richard Floy, Vincent Jones and Jonathan Mills and their Heirs and Assigns forever. Excepting and reserving at the same time and before the signing and delivery hereof the sole and exclusive right of Fishing Clambing & Oystering for ever unto said Trustees and their successors & the Inhabitance of said Town of Brookhaven for ever and the said Trustees Viz. Meritt S Woodhull Caleb M Hulse Richard Robinson Joseph Brewster Stephen Swezey Joseph Hedges & Nicoll Floyd do hereby covenant and agree to and with the s,d Richard Floyd Vincent Jones & Jonathan Mills and their heirs and assigns for ever that at and before the signing sealing & delivery of these presents the s,d Trustees had full power & lawfull authority to grant and sell the before described Premises in manner and form before mentioned by Virtue of the power and Authority vested in them by the Letters Pattent of sd Town of Brookhaven and the several Laws of the state of New York in such cases made—

In Testimony whereof the said Trustees have hereunto set their hands and caused the common seal of sd Town to be fix'd this seventh day of December in the year of our Lord one thousand eight hundred and one 1801

Signed sealed & delivered In the presence of us—
JOHN WOOLSE

MERITT S WOODHULL
JOSEPH BREWSTER Junr
CALEB M HULSE
STEPHEN SWEZEY

{ Town Seal }

APOLLOS WETMORE RICHARD ROBINSON
                 JOSEPH HEDGES—

Recorded Jany 1st 1802
A WETMORE T Clk

PAGE 376.

At a meeting of the Trustees of the Freeholders & commonality of the Town of Brookhaven held this forth Day of January 1802
Present

Meritt S Woodhull President
Joseph Brewster Jur ⎫
Caleb M Hulse—   ⎪
Richard Robinson   ⎬ Trustees
Stephen Swezey—   ⎪
Joseph Hedges—   ⎭

At sd Meeting there was a petition from the Inhabitance of Fireplace handed in by John Rose and signed by sd John Rose James Greenfed Nothaniel Woodruff Phinehas Rose Nathan Post Timothy Rose Jonathan Howel &c Praying or petitioning sd Trustees for the priviledge of building a School house on the Highway between the House of the late Skudder Ketcham decd. and the lot of land owned by John Turner, so as not to interfere with the Road but to leave it four Rods wide on the east side of the School House, taking two Rods wide & four Rods long for sd privilege beginning Ten feet North of the School House—sd Trustees do hereby grand the liberty to the Petitioners to set a School House in sd Place so as not to incumber the Road—

Entered by order of the Trustees

A WETMORE Town Clk

Jany 18' 1802

PAGE 377.

At a Meeting of the Freeholders and Inhabitance of the

Town of Brookhaven held this Sixth day of April in the year 1802 It being the first Tuesday in sd Month and held as Town Meeting day agreeable to a Law of this State— The following persons were Chosen to hold their Respective officees Viz

Nicoll Floyd President

Richard Floyd
James Woodhull
John Rose
Palmer Overton
Thomas Strong
William Tooker } Trustees

Isaac Hulse Clek & Treasurer & Supervisor

Abraham Woodhull
John Rose
William Smith Capt } Assessors

Isaac Miller } Collector

Isaac Hulse
William Tooker
Isaac Satterly } Commissioners of Highways

Jesse Hulse—
James Robinson—
Samuel Bishop—
Richard Hudson—
Oliver Hulse—
Daniel Davis 2d } Constables

PAGE 378.

OVERSEERS OF HIGHWAYS

Jacob Hawkins	James Smith Senr
William Swezey	James Davis Junr
Nathaniel Davis	Nathaniel Ruggles
Joseph Rayner	David Robinson
Jonathan Worth	William Hawkins
Josiah Smith	David Homan
Isaac Munsil	William Risley
Micah Ruland	John Hammond
William Hawkins	John Overton Senr
Isaac Howell	Daniel Homan.

Henry Dayton   Jeffery Randle
Woodhull Smith

Fence Viewers

Isaac Davis Stoney Brook
Henry Smith   John Homan Senr
Nathaniel Tooker Jr David Davis Senr
Israel Bennet   Davis Overton
Moses Weekes   Isaac Howell
Samuel Bishop   Jeffry Randle
Abraham Cherry   Jonathan Worth
Laban Worth   Jacob Newton
Phinehas Rose   James Smith monpnd
William Rose

At sd Town Meeting it was also voted & agreed that no Hogs should go in the public Highways & Strees unless, they are Yok,d Ringed & mark with the owners proper Ear Mark—&c

Page 379.

At an Election Held in the Town of Brookhaven on the 27th—28th and 29 Days of April in the year of 1802—and After Examining the Votes it is found that Genl John Smith for Representitive To Congress had One Hundred and Two Votes—

and Samuel Jones for Member of the Senate of the Southern District of the state of New york Had Seventy Two Votes—

John Schenk for Member of senate for sd Southern District of sd State had fifty Seven Votes—

for Members of Assembly for the County of Suffolk the following Persons had the following Number of Votes— Viz

      Israel Carll Ninety One
      Josiah Reve Eighty Six
      David Hedges forty five
      Jonathan Dayton forty Seven
      John Smith Two
      Isaac Hobes One

John Overton Two
John Rose One
Given under our hands this 29th Day of April 1802

ABRAHAM WOODHULL }
JOHN ROSE— } Inspectors
WM. SMITH } of Election
ISAAC HULSE }

JOHN OVERTON JNR. }
ZACHARIAH HAWKINS } Clerks

PAGE 380.

At a Meeting of the Trustees of the freeholders and Commonality of the Town of Brookhaven held in sd. Town this 3 Day May 1802—
Present at sd. Meeting

Nicoll Floyd Presdt.
Richard Floyd }
Palmer Overton }
Thomas S Strong } Trustees
John Rose }
Wm. Tooker }
James Woodhull }

At said Meeting it Was Voted & a Greed By sd Trustees that the sd Town of Brookhaven Shall Raise By Tax on the freeholders & Inhabitants for the support of the Poor of sd Town and other Contingent Charges of sd Town the Sum of One Thousand Dollars at sd. Meeting Permission is hereby Given to Elias Hedges To Take or Catch Fish in the Bay Belonging to the Town of Brookhaven and William Smith But not To Carry any fish Out of the sd Town He paying therefor forty Dollars for One year from this Day May 3d. 1802—

NICCOL FLOYD Presdt
Attest ISAAC HULSE T,Clk

PAGE 381.

May 3 } at the Before Recited Meeting of the
1802 } Trustees Entered on pag 380 it Was Ordained as followeth Viz Be it Ordained By the sd Trustees

of the freeholders and Commonality of the Town of Brookhaven that is If any Person or Persons Shall Take or Carry away any Wild Fowl out of the South Bay belonging To the sd. Town and Wm Smith after the Date hereof Without Leave first Obtained of the sd. Trustees— he or they Shall forfit and Pay the Sum of Twenty five dollars for every offence to Be sued for and Recovered with Costs of Suit By the Trustees or their Order Together with Costs of Suit

By Vote and Order of sd Trustees
May 3 1802   NICCOLL FLOYD Presdt.
Attest ISAAC HULSE T Clk

At the Before Recited Meeting sd Trustees Gave Permission To William Alibeen To fowl in the south Bay in Partnership with sd Town and Wm. Smith he Paying the Trustees for the Town and Wm. Smith One Tenth of the Money the fowls Sells for—

Attest ISAAC HULSE T Clk   NICCOLL FLOYD Presdt,

Agreeable to a Law of the state of New york for the Gradual Abolition of Slavery Past the 29th March 1799— Entered that Daniel Robart of the Town of Brookhaven had a Male Child Born of a Slave of his on the 24 of May year of 1801—sd Childs Name is Peter

Entered this 11 Day of May 1802
By me ISAAC HULSE Town Clk

PAGE 382.

I Meritt S Woodhull Esquire one of the Justices of the Peice for the County of Suffolk do hereby Declare my Concent to the Puting fourth an Indian Boy Named Robin Tockhouse as will appear by an Indenture Given By John Tockhouse and Cretia his Squaw) an Apprentice To Thomas S. Strong According to the Intent and Meaning of the sd.

Indenture
Brookhaven february 20" 1802—
August the 20" 1801
We the Commissioners of Highways of Brookhaven Being Called By Isaac Satterly to Take a View of a Certain Road in Setauket Runing a Crost the Stream Below the Oald Mill Dam—we the said Commissioners have Attended And Viewed the Said Road and finding it Inconvenient for the Publick—We therefore Do Agree with sd. Satterly to Exchange the former Road—for the One Acrost the Oald Mill Dam & the sd. satterly Obligateing Himself to keep up the flew at his Own Expence and sd Isaac Satterly is To Have the Oald Road for the One a Crost the Dam In Exchange—

Returned to Be Recorded.   JOHN WOODHULL } Commissioners
                            JOHN ROSE   } of Highways

PAGE 383.

At a Meeting of the Trustees of the freeholders and Commonality of the Town of Brookhaven held in sd. Town this 7 June 1802

Present at sd. Meeting

Nicol Floyd Presdt
Thomas S Strong ⎫
Wm. Tooker   ⎪
Palmer Overton   ⎬ Trustees
James Woodhull   ⎪
John Rose   ⎪
Richard Floyd   ⎭

Resolved By sd. Trustees at sd Meeting that in the Case of Barney O Goram that the Overseers of the Poor of the City of New york and that Thomas S Strong Esqr Be Appointed By the Trustees To Take the Care of Him

Resolved that Phebe Smith Daughter of John Smith be bound to David Cole untill she arrives at the age of eighteen years the Trustees paying him twenty two Dollars 50-100—

We the Commissioners of Highways for the Town of Brookhaven do Lay Out a Road threw Halsies Manner Between the North and South Devisions of Lots as the same is Laid Out and Reserved on the Card of sd Manner By the Name of Hotwater Street as follows Viz Begining at Brookfield East Line so Runing North 88 degrees East 190 Chain then North 50 Degrees East 109 Chains four Rods Wide with sd. Reserve to Southampton Line, also the pond Called Crambary Marsh we order throwed Out as the same is Laid Out on sd. Card four Rods wide all Round sd pond also a Small pond Designated on sd Card By the Name of Hot water Pond we order thrown Out the wedth of sd pond from Hot water Street four Rods wide upon the North East and South west sides of sd pond we do hereby Return the same To be Recorded Novr 18 1800

                        RICHARD FLOYD ⎫ Commissioners
                        ISAAC HULSE   ⎭ of Highways

PAGE 384.

At the Before Recited Meeting of the Trustees Present as aforesd. this 7 June 1802—

It was Voted and Agreed and hereby Enacted By sd. Trustees that No Oysters Shells Clambs or Horse fish Shall Be Taken or Carried Out of the Town—By Any Person or Persons Whatsoever from the Present Date until the Twentieth Day of September Next Ensueing under the Penalty of Twenty five Dollars on Each Person for Every Offence to Be Sued for & Recovered By sd. Trustees Before Any Justice in sd. Town Together With Costs of suit

                                NICCOLL FLOYD Presdt.

PAGE 385.

At a meeting of the Trustees of the Freeholders and Commonality of the Town of Brookhaven Held in sd. Town this Third Day of May 1802

Present at Sd Meeting

Nicoll Floyd Presdt.
Thomas S. Strong ⎫
Richard Floyd
Palmer Overton
John Rose ⎬ Trustees
Wm Tooker
James Woodhull ⎭

at sd Meeting it Was Voted and Agreed and hereby Enacted By sd. Trustees That No Fish Should Be Katched In the South Bay in Partnership with Capt. Wm. Smith and sd. Trustees or Caried Out of the sd Town of Brookhaven By any Person Or Persons Whatsoever under the Penalty of Twenty five Dollars on Every Person for Every offence to Be Sued for and Recovered With full Costs of Suit Signed By Order of the Trustees

Attest   Niccoll Floyd Presdt
Isaac Hulse Town Clk

PAGE 386.

At a Meeting of the Trustees of the freeholders and Commonality of the Town of Brookhaven held at Corum on the third Day of May One Thousand Eight Hundred and Two—

Present   Nicoll Floyd President
Thomas S Strong ⎫
Richard Floyd
Palmer Overton
John Rose ⎬ Trustees
Wm. Tooker
James Woodhull ⎭

Be it Ordained By the athority of the Trustees aforesaid that If Any Person or Persons Shall Catch any fish in the South Bay Belonging To the Town of Brookhaven and William Smith or Carry Any Out of the Town Being Taken in the Bay Aforesaid—he or they So offending shall forfit and Pay for Every Such Offence Twenty five Dollars, to be Sued for and Recovered in the Name of the Trustees Aforesaid

L S   NICOLL FLOYD President

June the 10 1802

At a Town Meeting Held at Isaac Brewsters in the Town of Brookhaven Daniel Robbins was Elected and Chosen Counstable at a Town-Meeting Called Expressly for that Purpose it Being Previously Notifyed a Greeable to a Law of this State In Such Cases made

PAGE 387.

We the Commissioners of Highways for the Town of Brookhaven Being Called By a Large Number of Inhabitants freeholders of sd. Town to Lay Out a Publick Highway in sd. Town from the North Country Road to Scidmores Landing We the sd Commissioners do hereby Lay Out a Publick Open Highway from sd. North Country Road in the Same Track Where the Road Now Goes to Scidmores Landing—as far Northward from sd. Country Road—as the Division of Lots Runs Called Wading river Great Lots—a Greeable to a Reserve for Roads in sd. Division—we Lay sd. Road three Rods wide from the west Hedge Easterly to the North End of sd. Lots as the Reccords of Brookhaven of sd Lots May Appear—

and we Return the Same Road To Be Recorded—Done By us August the 4 1802

         ISAAC HULSE   } Commissioners
         ISAAC SATTERLY } of Highways
         WM. TOOKER   }

PAGE 388.

We the Commissioners of Highways for the Town of Brookhaven Being Called by a Large Number of freeholders Inhabitants of sd Town to Lay out a Publick highway from the North End of the Great Lots where we Laid Out a road to on the 4 Day of this Instant—We Meeting with Two Justices of the peice of the County of Suffolk and

Twelve freeholders Inhabitants of Smith Town Save One which was of RiverHead Both Towns in Sd. County who Did Apprise Sd Road at Ninety Dollars and we Return the Same Road To be Recorded in the following Manner. Viz Begining Where the Before Mentioned Road stoped at the North End of the Long Lots in the Same Tract where the Road Now goes to Scidmores Landing Runing three Rods Wide from the East Hedge By sd Road Westerly until It Comes to the Cherry trees By the House where John Scidmore Now Lives—So keeping the Same Tract from the Cherry Trees four Rods Wide Viz Two Rods Wide on Each Side of the Tract that goes Down the Gully to Run to the Sound to Lowe water mark and We Do Allow the Owner of sd Land threw which sd. Road Runs to hang One Good Easy Swinging Gate on sd Road Wid Enough for a Waggon & Cart way at any Place where they Shall Chouse from sd Cherry trees By sd House To the North End of sd Long Lots Supposed to be Where a Gate post now stands about 80 Rods from the Shore we Order sd. Road To be Recorded August 9th 1802

ISAAC HULSE
ISAAC SATTERLY } Commissioners of Highways
WM. TOOKER

PAGE 389.

I Oliver smith of Brookhaven Suffolk County do Certify that a female Child Named Bet was Born in my House of a Slave on the 23d Day of December in the year of 1800

The aforesaid Oliver Smith of the Town and County aforesaid do hereby Certify that That A male Child Born of a Slave of mine in my House on the 23d Day of September 1802 Childs Name is Jim

Born the 4th Day of July 1802 of a Slave in the family of Coll Nicoll Floyd a Male Child Named Jim—

Born the 13th Day of february 1802 a female Child Named

Tamer of a Slave of the Wd. Ruth Woodhull—

Born of a Slave of Joanna Smith Corum feemale Child on the 28 of July 1802 sd Child Name is Rosawell—

Born of a Slave of William Tooker Mooneponds in sd Town a Male Child on the first of March 1802 Sd Childs Name is Aaron

Meritt S. Woodhull Esquire Had A Negro Boy Born of a Slave of His On the first Day of December 1801 Sd Boys Name is Ben—

PAGE 390.

James Woodhull of the Town of Brookhaven Suffolk County Does hereby Certify that a Male Childs Named Apolis was Born of a Slave of his in family on the fifth Day of February 1803

PAGE 391.

We the Commissioners of Highways do hereby Alter the Road that Goes from Charles's Pond to the Mooneponds as far as it Runs a Crost the 29 Lot in sd Division of Land and do Lay Out the same Where the Road Now Goes a Crost sd Lot and Leave the Other part of sd Road as it Was formerly Laid Out three Rods Wide

January 3 1803—

      ISAAC HULSE } Commissioners
      WM. TOOKER } of Highways

PAGE 392.

At a Meeting of the Trustee of the Freeholders And Commonality of the Town of Brookhaven Held this 7th of March 1803

Present at sd Meeting

    Nicoll Floyd prs,dt
    James Woodhull
    John Rose
    Palmer Overton
    Tho. S. Strong

Wm. Tooker

At Sd Meeting Annanias Smith Made Application to sd Trustees for Leberty to Build a Dock from the Shore of his Own Land on Swan Creek Neck Where He now Lives Out into the South Bay where his Dock Now is and Said Trustees Agreeable to His Request Granted Said Annanias Smith Liberty to Build Sd. Dock

PAGE 393.

At a Publick Town meeting of the Freeholders and freemen of the Town of Brookhaven held in Said Town this 5th Day of April 1803 Agreeable To the Town patent & the Law of the State of New-york in Such Cases made (it Being the first Tuesday of April) The following Town Officers Ware Chosen By Majority of Votes Viz—

Selah Strong Presdt
Meritt S. Woodhull
William Tooker
Palmer Overton   } Trustees
John Rose
Benjamin Petty
Isaac Overton

Isaac Hulse Clerk & Treasurer
Meritt S. Woodhull Supervisor
Isaac Millar Collector

Joseph Brewster
John Rose   } Assessors
Wm. Smith Capt
Mritt S. Woodhull

Isaac Satterly   } Commissioners
John Woodhull   of Highways
Stephan Swezey

Amos Smith
Samuel Bishop—
Richard Hudson   } Constables
Nehemiah Hulse
James Robinson
George Norton Junr

Page 394.

Overseers of Highways

Jedediah Williamson
Israel Bennet
Alvaham Woodhull
Daniel Jones
Wells Davis
Peter Skidmore
Jonathan Worth
Jeffry Randal
Timothy Millar
Phillip Hallock
Luis Gurden
James Stan Brow

Robert Hawkins Junr
Jehiel Woodruff
John Overton Crum
Daniel Tooker
Joshua Terry
Samuel Muncel
William Newins
Austin Roe
Isaac Overton
Oliver Hulse
James Post
Ebenezar Hart

Fence Viewers

Joseph Hawkins
Henry Smith
Elenerser Smith
Wm Dickerson
Joseph Brewster
James Smith
James Davis
Daniel Davis
Meritt S Woodhull
Nethaniel Davis
Jonathan Worth
Jefery Randal
Barney Wines

James Robinson
Henry Dayton
David Davis J
Caleb M Hulse
Danl Roe
James Smith V
Jeremiah Wheelar
Humphry Avery
Warden Toby
James Greenfield
Nathl WoodRuff
Ebenezar Hart
Josiah Smith

Page 395.

Also at the foregoing Town meeting it Was Voted By a Majority of Votes that No Hogs Except Sucking Piggs Shall Run or go On the Commons in the Town of Brookhaven Except they Be Ringed in the Nose With Sufficiant Rings and yoaked With Good and Sufficiant yoaks under the Penalty of 75 Cents for Every Hog for Every Offence If a Despute Shall Arise Concerning the Sufficiany of Either Rings Or yoaks to Be Determined By the Two Nearest fence Viewers——

County of Suffolk } ss a Statement of Votes Taken at the Anniversary Election for a Senator which Comminced on the Last Tuesday of April one Thousand Eight Hundred and Three

Egbert Benson Eighty three } Votes
John Broom Eighty four

We Certify the Above to Be a True Statement and Estimate of the Votes Taken in the Town of Brookhaven at the aforesaid Election Closed April the Twenty Eighth One Thousand Eight Hundred & three

MERITT S. WOODHULL }
JOSEPH BREWSTER JUR } Inspectors
JOHN ROSE

PAGE 396.

County of Suffolk } ss Statement of Votes Taken at the Annaversary Election for Members of Assembly which Commenced on the Last Tuesday of April One Thousand Eight Hundred and Three

Israel Carll—one Hundred & nine
David Hedges—one Hundred & Two
William Smith—Forty Six—
Sylvester Dering thirty four—
Benjamin Floyd Eleven—
Isaac Hulse Ten
John Overton three } Votes
Daniel Roe Two
John Rose Two
John Mott one
Joseph Brewster one
Apolis Wetmore one
Thomas Aldridge one
Thomas Strong one

We Certify the Above to Be a True Statement and Estimate of the Votes Taken in the Town of Brookhaven at the aforesaid Election Closed the Twenty Eight Day of April one Thousand Eigh Hundred & Three

MERITT S WOODHULL⎫
JOSEPH BREWSTER ⎬ Inspectors
JOHN ROSE ⎭

PAGE 397.

At a Meeting of the Trustees of the Freeholders and Commonality of the Town of Brookhaven Held in sd Town this 2 Day of May 1803

Present at sd. Meeting

Selah Strong President ⎫
Meritt S. Woodhull
Palmer Overton
John Rose ⎬ Trustees
William Tooker
Benjamin Petty
Isaac Overton ⎭

At sd A meeting it Was Voted and Agreed and hereby Enacted By the a thority a foresaid that If any Person or Persons Shall Catch fish in the South Bay in Pertnership with sd Town and Capt. Wm Smith—Or In the Bay in Partnership with Genl. John Smith and sd Town for the Purpose of Conveying them Out of sd Town to Market Or Carry them Out of the sd Town to Market Being Taken in Either of the Bays aforesaid—Every Person, Or Persons So Offending Shall forfit and pay for Every Such Offence Twenty five Dollars to Be Sued for and Recovered in the Name of the Trustees aforesaid Together with Costs—Except Such Persons as may or Shall have Obtained Leave of sd Trustees for the Purpose of Catching fish and Carrying them Out of sd Town. and Be it further Inacted By the Athority aforesaid that all Laws of the Town Conserning fish which have been Passed Before the Date hereof Shall be and hereby Are Repealed—

PAGE 398.

At a Meeting of the Trustees of the Freeholders and Commonality of the Town of Brookhaven Held in sd Town

this 2 Day of may 1803
Present at sd Meeting

Selah Strong Presdt
Meritt S. Woodhull ⎫
Palmer Overton ⎪
Wm Tooker ⎪
John Rose ⎬ Trustees
Benjamin Petty ⎪
Isaac Overton ⎭

At Sd. Meeting sd Trustees for the Consideration of One Hundred Dollars To them In hand Paid By George Brown John Turner and Isaac Wells—have hereby Granted Liberty to sd Geo. Brown John Turner Or any Other Person Or Persons to be Authourised By them to Catch fish in the South Bay in Pertnership With sd Town and Capt William Smith for the Term of One year from the Date Here of and Send them To Market Where and how they Please

Signed in Behalf of the Trustees Town Seal hereunto fixed

SELAH STRONG Prsdt L S

Attest ISAAC HULSE Clk

PAGE 399.

At a Meeting of the Trustees of the Freeholders And Commonality of the Town of Brookhaven Held in Said Town this 2d Day of may 1803—

Present at sd. Meeting

Selah Strong Presdt ⎫
Meritt S Woodhull ⎪
Palmer Overton ⎪
John Rose ⎬ Trustees
Wm. Tooker ⎪
Benjn Petty ⎪
Isaac Overton ⎭

At sd. Meeting sd Trustees Hereby Resolved that No Person Or Persons Shall After the 7th Day of this Instant kill any Wild fowl In the South Bay in Partnership With sd Town and Capt. Wm. Smith or in the Bay in Partnership With sd Town & Genl. John Smith or On any of the Islands in Either of sd Bays or On any of the Beaches Adjoining thereto for the Purpose of Carrying them Out of sd Town or shall Carry them Out of sd town Shall forfit and Pay Twenty five Dollars for Every Offence to Be Sued for and Recovered in the Name of the Trustees with Costs Allways Excepting Such Persons as hath or Shall Obtain Leve of sd Trustees By Order of sd Trustees

ISAAC HULSE Town Clk

PAGE 400.

At a Meeting of the Trustees of the Freeholders and Commonality of the Town of Brookhaven Held in Said Town this 6 Day of June 1803

Present at Sd. Meeting

Selah Strong Presdt
Meritt S Woodhull
Palmer Overton
John Rose } Trustees
Wm. Tooker
Benjn Petty
Isaac Overton

At Sd. Meeting the Trustees Voted and Agreed and here Enacted that No Person Or Persons Shall Catch Horse fish in the South Bay for the Purpose of Plowing them in Or Burying them or after Being Catched Shall Smuther or Bury them or Plow them in to make Menure or Send them Out of the Town Every Person that Shall Be Guilty of Either of the Aforesaid Offences Shall forfit and Pay for Either of the aforesaid offences Shall forfit and Pay for Every Offence the Sum of Ten Dollars To be Sued for and Recovered in the Name of the Trustees

Also at sd. Meeting sd Trustees Voted and agreed that there Shall be Six Hundred Dollars Rased in sd Town By a Rate on the Inhabitants for the Support of the Poor and for Other Contingent Charge of sd Town for the Present year.

PAGE 401 BLANK.

PAGE 402.

Be it Remembered On the Eighteenth Day of June 1803 We the Commissioners of Brookhaven being Called upon By a number of the Inhabitants aforeSaid To Alter and Lay Out the Regulations How to mend and Repair the Highways of The East part of Setauket that Is to say that the Inhabitants Shall mend and Repair all the Said Roads in their District Begining at the East End of the Oald mill Dam Going Eastward to the Drownmeadow Runs on that Road and Also the Southermost Road To the Top of Drownmeadow Hills also the Country Road Leading from Town that is To say one Half of the way to Corum

Given under Our Hands and Seals the Day and year first above Mentioned We do Order the Same To be Recorded on the Town Reccords

ISAAC SATTERLY L S   Commissioners
STEPHAN SWEZY L S   of Highways

PAGE 403.

At a Meeting of the Trustees of the Freeholders and Commonality of the Town of Brookhaven Held at the House of Goldsmith Davis the 5 Day of Septr. 1803.

Present

Selah Strong Presdt.
Meritt S. Woodhull
Palmer Overton
John Rose   } Trustees
Wm. Tooker
Isaac Overton

Whereas Thomas S Strong Benjamin Strong and Joseph Strong have Application to this Board, for the privilege of Erecting a Dam and Mill a Cross the Channel Between the

Point of Land belonging To Selah Strong Esquire and the Shore Oposite to the Land Belonging to Coll. Benjamin Floyd Within Setauket Harbour—

It Was thereupon Voted and Agreed that the Said Thomas S Strong Benjn Strong & Joseph Strong their Heirs and Assigns should Be Permitted to Build & Erect a Dam And Mill a Crost the Said Channel upon the following Conditions—first that the Said Thomas S. Strong Benjn Strong & Joseph Strong shall Pay to sd Trustees the Sum of Seventy five Dollars for the said Previledge—in full Consideration for their Right and Title for the Same Vested in the sd Town or their Successors—

Secondly—the Said Thomas S. Strong Benjn Strong & Joseph Strong for them Selves their heirs and Assigns Doth Covenant and Agree that So Soon as the said Dam and Mill are Erected and Compleated Ready to Grind

PAGE 404.

That they Will Reserve One Run of stones to Grind for the Inhabitants of the Said Town as Long as the Mill is kept up and in Order to make flower and meal—and that they Will when the Quantity of Grain Will admit make Good & Wholesome flower and Meal Reserving for the use of sd Mill as Toal One Tenth Part of the Grain So Manufactured—Thirdly the Said Thomas S Strong Benjn Strong and Joseph Strong for them Selves their Heirs & Assigns doth further Covenant and Agree, to Have the said Dam and Mill Erected and Compleated within Eight years from the Date of this Grant or to forfit the Previledge—of the Same —and also Not to Deprive the Inhabitants of the Said Town of Brookhaven from the same priviledge They are Now Entitled To of fishing and fowling in the said pond & Bay—

And the Said Trustees for themselves and their Successors do further Grant to the Sd Thomas S Strong Benjn Strong & Joseph Strong their Heirs and Assigns all their right and Title to that Certain Point or Peice of land near the Place Where the Dam is to Be Built and on which Pompes House formerly Stood—to Be used in makeing the Said Dam—Provided the same is Dug so low—as to Be Overflowed at High water by Common Tides

In Testimony Whereof the Trustees have affixed to these Presents the Common Seal of the Said Town and Signed the same By their President this fifth Day of Septr 1803—

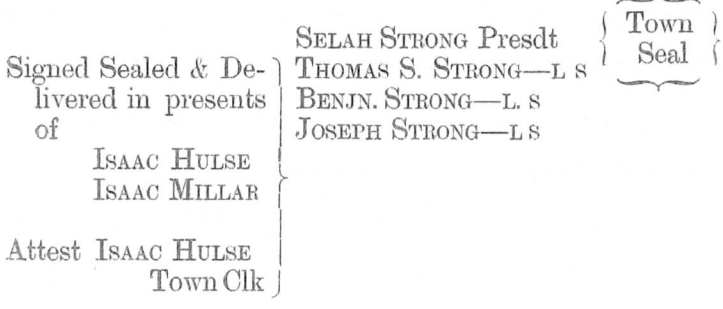

Signed Sealed & Delivered in presents of
    Isaac Hulse
    Isaac Millar

Selah Strong Presdt
Thomas S. Strong—l s
Benjn. Strong—l. s
Joseph Strong—l s

{ Town Seal }

Attest Isaac Hulse
    Town Clk

Page 405

Born Of a Slave in the family of Oliver Smith a female Child By the Name of Nel Born On the 12 of May 1803

At a Meeting of The Trustees of the Freeholders and Commonality of the Town of Brookhaven Held in sd Town the 5 Day of March 1804

Present at sd. Meeting
    Selah Strong Presdt.
    Meritt S Woodhull
    Isaac Overton
    John Rose
    Wm Tooker   } Trustees
    Benjn. Petty
    Palmore Overton

This may Certify that we the Undersigned Overseers of the Poor in the Town of Brookhaven have Examined into the age of Keder a Black man and Susan a Black Woman Late the Property of Thomas S Strong, and finding that the Said Negroes are under the Age of fifty years and Appear to Be Helthy Persons and able to Get their Liveing——

BrookHaven march 5th 1804 the Trustees & Overseers of the Poor—

{ L S } SELAH STRONG Presdt

PAGE 406 BLANK.
PAGE 407.

At a Town Meeting of the freeholders and freemen of the Town of Brookhaven held this 3 Day of April 1804 Agreeable to A Law of the State of N. york in Such Cases made the following officers was Chosen

Selah Strong Presdt ⎫
Meritt S Woodhull   ⎪
William Tooker—   ⎬ Trustees
Samuel Davis—   ⎪
John Rose   ⎪
James Post—   ⎭
David Davis Junr.

Isaac Hulse Clerk & Treasurer
Meritt S Woodhull Supervisor
Isaac Miller Collector

Joseph Brewster Junr   ⎫
Meritt S. Woodhull   ⎪
John Rose   ⎬ Assessors
Henry Rayner Brookfield ⎪
William Tooker   ⎭

John Woodhull M ponds ⎫ Commissioners
James Smith Capt—   ⎬ of Highways
Josiah Smith—   ⎭

Amos Smith   ⎫
Samuel Bishop   ⎪
Richard Hudson   ⎬ Constables
James Robinson   ⎪
Samuel Homan   ⎪
Isaac Millar   ⎭

Overseers of Highways

Isaac Smith Corum	Isaac Hulse
Abraham Woodhull Judge	Jonas Hawkins
John Taylor	Tho S Strong
Daniel Davis 2d oaldmans	Nethaniel Tooker
William Skidmore	Jonathan Worth
Briant Norton	

Page 408.

Phillop Hallock	Azel Robinson
James Stanbrow	Geo Brown
Henry Dayton	Theoflis Smith
John Leek	Richard hulse
Nethanl Woodruff	Benjamin Laws
Caleb M, Hulse	Joshua Terry
John Davis	Joseph Robinson
David Smith	Sam. Smith

Fence Viewers

Stephen Edwards	John Rider
Isrel Bennet	Wardin Toby
John Mott	Isaac Akerly
Nathan Mulford	Jeremiah Wheelar
Richard Hulse	Benjamin Garrard
Nathaniel Hawkins	Isaac Hammond
James Stanbrow	Caleb M. Hulse
Justus Overton	Daniel Roe
Wm Penny	Jonathan Worth
Peter Havens	Jeffery Randal
Isaac Smith	Capt James Davis
Daniel Overton	Danl Davis
Henry Smith	

Page 409.

also Voted that No Ram Sheep Shall Run on the Commons in sd Town from the Last of July Next for three months—

No Hogg to Run on the Commons With Out Being Ringed in the Nose & Yoaked.

Page 410.

Be It Remembered on the 18 Day of June 1803 We the Commissioners of Brookhaven Being Called Upon By a Number of the Inhabitants for to Lay Out a Regular Road John Wilsies House (at Drownmeadow) Begining at a Corner Chesnut post Marked X Standing in the Corner of Wilsies fence from thence Runing Southwstrly Course Three Rods from the Post then to Run Parrallel With mr Wilsies fence To Lowwatermark—makeing the Road three Rods Wide

Given Under Our Hands & Seals the Day and Date above Mentioned

Commissioners } Isaac Satterly (l s)
of Highways } Stephan Swezy (l s)

Page 411.

Whereas a Number of the Inhabitants of the Town of Brookhaven have by their petition Represented to the Trustees of the freeholders and Commonality of the Town aforesaid, that by feeding off the Grass that Groes on the West meadow beach it Causes the Sand to Blow On the Meadows ajoining to Said Beach and Cover up the Same therefore they Pray for Leave and Liberty to fence So much of the Same as Will Be of use to preserve their Meadows—

at a Meeting of the sd. Trustees the 3 Day of April 1804 held at the House of Goldsmith Davis in sd Town
Present at sd Meeting

    Selah Strong Presdt.
    Isaac Overton
    Meritt S Woodhull
    Wm. Tooker
    Palmer Overton
    John Rose
    Benjn. Petty

It Was Voted and agreed at sd. Meeting that the Owners of sd. meadow Should have Leave and Liberty to fence the Beach on the Higest Part of the Same, so as to Leave the Space of One Rod Wide on the Sound Shore above Highwater mark for all Persons to pass with Teams and Cariages for the Purpose of Collecting the Drift that Comes on the same, and also to make as many Bars or Gates as Shall Be Sufficient for the Inhabitents to Go within the fence to put Down the Said Drift or Spread their Thatch or for any Other Purpose Whatsoever—and also not to Prevent any Person or persons Parsons passing on any Highway Already Laid Out, or that may hereafter be Laid Out: and also Whenever Ten Substantial Freeholders being Inhabitants Shall Request the

PAGE 412.

fence Taken down and the Beach Lay in Common as at Present it Shall be Complied with and the Owners of said Meadow Shall Remove their fence—and it is also further Agreed that this Liberty Granted Shall not Operate So far as to Give the Owners of the said meadow notwithstanding any Right Or Title to the Said Beach nor Shall this Liberty Granted to them of fenceing the same Operate so as to Impower the Owners of sd Medow to hender any (Personsons) Inhabitants of sd Town from Takeing any Kind of Hay or Mulch, or any other thing Whatsoever that Shall Either Be Drifted By the Tide Carted or any of them Within the same and as hereto to pass and Repass freely without Molistation or henderance with Teams Carts Waggons Horses or any Other Way or manner as they Shall think proper or Do within the same by Drawing Bars or Opening Gates from Time To Time and at all Times forever hereafter—the Inhabitants of the Town that Pass Carefull To Shut up Bars and Gates after them

PAGE 413.

Haveing held and Closed the Poll of the Election in the

Town of Brookhaven the Twenty seventh Day of April One Thousand Eight hundred and four and Canvessed the Votes agreeable to the Act Entitled an Act for Regulateing Elections Passed the Twenty fourth Day of March One Thousand Eight Hundred and One do find the votes to be as followeth Viz

For Gouvornor Morgan Luis One Hundred & fifty one votes

and Aaron Burr One hundred and four Votes. For Leut Governor John Broom One Hundred and forty Nine Votes ——and Oliver Phelps One Hundred and four Votes—

For Senators—
William Denning Two Hundred and Twenty Eight Votes
Ebenezar Purdy One Hundred and Thirty five Votes
Thomas Thomas One Hundred and Thirty five Votes
Cornelious C. Rosevelt One Hundred and Two Votes
John Smith One Hundred Votes—
William Edgar Five Votes
William Smith three Votes

MERITT S. WOODHULL
JOHN ROSE
JOSEPH BREWSTER } Inspectors
HENRY RAYNER
WILLIAM TOOKER

Haveing held and Cosed the poll of Election for the Town of Brookhaven the Twenty Seventh Day of April One Thousand Eight Hundred and four and Canvesed the Votes agreeable to an Act passed the Twenty fourth Day of March One Thousand Eight Hundred and One for the Purpose of Regulateing Elections do find the Votes to Be as followeth Viz for Congress to fill the Vacancy of Genl. John Smith. Elifalet Wicks had One Hundred and Six Votes

Joshua Smith Sixty Three Votes
Samuel Riker had three Votes

Meritt S. Woodhull
John Rose
Joseph Brewster } Inspectors
Henry Rayner
Wm. Tooker

Page 414.

Haveing held and Closed the Poll of the Election in the Town of Brookhaven the Twenty sixth Day of April One Thousand Eight hundred and four and Canvesed the Votes a Greeable to the Act Entitled an Act for Regulateing Elections Passed the Twenty fourth Day of March, One Thousand Eight Hundred and One" do find the Votes to Be as followeth Viz

For Representitive To Congres

Eliphalet Wicks One Hundred & Seventeen Votes
Joshua Smith Ninety five Votes
Samuel Riker four Votes

Meritt S. Woodhull
John Rose
Joseph Brewster } Inspectors
Henry Rayner
William Tooker

Brookhaven april the Twenty seventh Day of April Eighteen Hundred and four held and Closed the Pole of Election and Canvesed the Votes. agreeable To a Law Passed the Twenty fourth Day of March Eighteen Hundred and one for the Purpose of Regulateing to find the Votes to Be as followeth Viz for Member of Assembly for the County of Suffolk

  Jared Landon had Ninety one Votes
  Jonathan Dayton had Eighty Nine Votes
  Israel Carll had Ninety Votes
  Silvester Deering had four Votes
  David Warner had One Vote
  John Rose had One Vote

John Mott had One Vote
William Tooker had One Vote
Calico Hawkins had Nine Votes

MERITT S. WOODHULL }
JOHN ROSE
JOSEPH BREWSTER } Inspectors
HENRY RAYNER
WILLIAM TOOKER

PAGE 415.

At a Meeting of the Trustees of the Freeholders and Commonality of the Town of Brookhaven held in sd Town this 7 of May 1804

Present at sd Meeting

Selah Strong Presdt }
John Rose
Meritt S. Woodhull
Wm Tooker } Trustees
Saml Davis
David Davis
James Post

At sd Meeting sd Trustees Voted and a Greed that the Act Concerning Hoggs Runing on the Commons Passed By the Trustees of the freeholders and Commonality of the Town of Brookhaven On the 5 Day of May 1800 Is hereby Reinacted & Revived and Declared By sd Trustees to Be a Law of this Town sd Act was Entered in page 348—

Also at sd Meeting sd Trustees Voted and a Greed that the Act Concerning Wild fowl Passed the 2d of May 1803 and Entered in page 399— is hereby Revived and Reinacted By sd Trustees and is Declared to Be a Law of this Town

also at sd Meeting sd Trustees Voted and Agreed that the Act Concerning Horse fish which was Passed on the 6th Day of June 1803 and Entered in page 400 is hereby Rein Acted and Revived and Declared to Be a Law of this Town

also at sd Meeting sd Trustees Voted and agreed that the

Act Concerning Catching fish Passed the 2d Day of May 1803 and Entered in Page 397 is hereby Revived and Reinacted and is a Law of this Town—

PAGE 416.

At a Meeting of the Trustees of the Freeholders and Commonality of the Town of Brookhaven held in sd Town this 7 of May 1804—
Present at sd Meeting

Selah Strong Presdt
Meritt S. Woodhull
John Rose
Wm Tooker } Trustees
Saml Davis
David Davis
James Post

PAGE 417.

Brookhaven October third 1803—

Be it Remembered that on this Day Personally Appeared Before me Joseph Brewster one of the peoples Justices in and for the County of Suffolk Edmon Morin & Phebe Morin his Wife Who Acknowledged their Indenture Given to John Taylor to Be of their Own free act and Deed Taken Before me the Day and year above Written

JOSEPH BREWSTER Justice

Whereas there was a Highway Laid Out In Tookers Neck at Bluepoint In the year of 1790 By Daniel Roe Wm Phillips and Austin Roe 20 feet Wide from the Bay Entered in Page 223 they Not saying where sd Road Goes from the Bay—and We the Commissioners of Highways Haveing Viewed the premises and sd Road we do hereby Order that the West side of sd Road shall go from the Bay In Range of the East End of Worden Tobys Two Houses Viz Bringing the East End of sd Tobis Two Houses in Range so Going 20 feet Eastward By the Bay so Keeping sd Wedth until it Comes within 20 feet of sd Tobys House By the Bay then Turning Gradualy East ward so as to Clear the south East Corner of sd House 3 foots Keeping the Wedth of 20 feet from thence following the Road as it Was Laid Out To the Country Road

as Witness Our Hands Brookhaven February 1806

JOHN WILEY ⎱ Commissioner
ISAAC HULSE ⎰ of Highways

N B, it was agreed By sd Commissioners that the Drift that Comes Onto the Road at the Bay Shall Belong to Warden Toby

RECORDS OF BROOKHAVEN.

BOOK D.

INTRODUCTION.

A number of the pages in the beginning of Book D, up to the page numbered 3 are occupied with the register of the births of children of slave parents belonging to various residents of the town at the time they were entered.

They are copied in the order in which they occur in the original records.

Twelve pages in the beginning are not numbered; they have been marked for reference with the letters A, B, C, &c.

Two pages are each numbered 1.

Two pages are each numbered 12.

This form | SEAL | at the end of a record indicates an actual seal on the page of the record, while the letters L S which appear in the records, represent only a nominal seal.

COMMITTEE.

PAGE A.

William Smith of the Manor of St. George made return that he had a Male child Born of a Slave of his on the 11th day of April 1832 childs name is Primus enterd this 27th March 1833—

William Smith of the Manor of St. George made return

that he has a male Child Born of a Servant of his on the 4th day of November 1834 Childs Name is Paul enterd this 12th January 1836

Page B.

William Smith Made return that he had a female child Born of a Slave of his on the 11th day of October 1820 Child name is Rachel enterd this 10th day of March agreeable to the Law of this State for the Abolition of slavery

Attest MORDECAI HOMAN town Clerk

Nicoll Floyd made return that he had a male child born of a slave of his on the first day of April 1822 Childs name is Phillip born of hannah enterd this 8th November 1823—for the Abolition of Slavery

Attst MORDECAI HOMAN town Clerk

Richard Robinson made return that he had a male child Born of a slave of his on the 15th of March 1813 Childs name is Phillip—

Enterd this 3d July 1824

M. HOMAN town Clerk

Daniel Petty made return that he had a male child born of a slave of his on the 17th June 1817 child name is Charles enterd this 27th July 1825.

William Smith made return that he had a female Child born of a Slave of his on the 29" May 1822 chils name Lucey

Enterd this 6th August 1825—

M. HOMAN town Clerk

Nicol Floyd made return that he had a Male child born of a slave of his named Hannad Childs Name is Cyrus Enterd this 16th May Child Born on the 12th September 1825

MORDECAI HOMAN town Clerk

Page C.

Josiah Smith made return that he had Male child Born

of a slave of his named Dorothy on the 25th September 1819 Childs names is Peter enterd this 4th day of April 1820 According to the Act for the Abolition of Slavery

Attest MORDECAI HOMAN Town Clerk

Goldsmith Davis made return that he had Male child Born of a Slave of his on the 4th day of february 1821. Childs Name is Silas Enterd this 3rd April 1821 According to the Act for the Abolition of Slavery

Attest— M. HOMAN Town Clerk

Sarah Hallock made return that she had a Male Child Named Dick. Born of a slave of hers in April 16 1808 enterd this 7th April 1821. According to the Act for the Abolition of Slavery

Attest MORDECAI HOMAN Town Clerk

Also Sarah Hallock made Return that she had a female Child Named Viner Born of a Slave of hers on the tenth day of January 1818 Enterd this 7th day of April 1821 According to the Act for the Abolition of Slavery

Attest MORDECAI HOMAN Town Clerk

Suffolk County ss. Thomas S. Strong of the Town of Brookhaven in the County of suffolk being duly sworn deposeth and saith that he owns and posesses four female Children who are slaves whose names and ages are as follows Viz.

Rachel Born 22nd day of August 1805—
Tamar Born 25th day of September 1807
Cealia Born 15th day of January 1810 and
Ellen or Nell Born 23rd day of October 1815
that the said slave are all the Children of Unice who was a slave of the deponents at the time of their Respective Births

Sworn the 4th day of December 1821 before me   THOMAS S. STRONG

    RICHARD UDLE Justice

Enterd according to the law of this state for the abolition

of Slavery

Attest Mordecai Homan Town Clerk

Page D.

Nicoll Floyd made Return that he had a Child Born of a Slave of his on the 15th april 1818—sd Childs name is Elijah Born of Rose

Also Nicol Floyd made return that he had a Child Born of a Slave of his. Childs Name is Sam Born of Hannah on the 21st January 1818

Enterd this 5th day of June 1818

Attest Mordecai Homan Town Clerk

William Smith of the Manor of St. George made return that he had a female Child Born of a Slave on his on the first day of September 1817 Childs name is Peggy

Enterd this 20th day of Octr 1818—

Attest Mordecai Homan Town Clerk

Nicoll Floyd made return that he had a Male child Born of a Slave of his on the 28th day of January 1818 Named Sam.

Enterd this 8th day of December 1818 According to Law

Sworn before James fanning Esq.

attest Mordecai Homan Town Clerk

William Smith of the Manor of St. George Made Return that he had a female Child Born of a Slave of his on the tenth day of April 1818 Childs name is Mary

Enterd this 19th April 1819. According to Law for the Abolition of Slavery—

Attest Mordecai Homan Town Clerk

Nicoll Floyd made return that he hand a female Child Born of a Slave of his on the twenty first day of June 1819. Childs name is Charity Ann.

Sworn before Thomas S. Strong Judge

Entered this 2d Nov. 1819 According to Law

MORDECAI HOMAN town Clerk
PAGE E.

John Woodhull Made return of a Slave of his Named Herculas that was Born on the 19th day of September 1798 Enterd this 13th February 1816

MORDECAI HOMAN Clerk

John Woodhull Made return that he had a Male Slave Named Ben. that was Born on the 22nd November 1801— Enterd this 13th day of february 1816

MORDECAI HOMAN Town Clerk

Timothy Miller Made return that he had a female Child Born of a Slave of his on the 8th day of June 1815 Child Name is Jane

Enterd this 20th March 1816 Agreeable to the Law of this State for the Abolition of Slavery.

MORDECAI HOMAN Town Clerk

Elizabeth Smith Widow of Gen. John Smith Made return that she had a Male Child Born of a Slave of her's on the 16th day of March 1816 Childs Name is Isaac Jayne

Enterd this 6th day of November agreeable to the Law of this State for the Abolition of Slavery

MORDECAI HOMAN Town Clerk

William Smith Made return that he had a Male Child Born of a Slave of his on the 24th Day of March in the Year 1816 Childs name is Lunn

Enterd this 25th day of March 1817

MORDECAI HOMAN Town Clerk

Ebenezer Jones Made return that he had a male Child Born of a Slave of his on the 20th June 1808 said Wenech being the property of Daniel Jones

Enterd 4th february 1818

MORDECAI HOMAN Town Clerk

PAGE F.

Nicoll Floyd made return that he had a female Child

Born of a slave of his Named Hannah on the first day of March 1814 Childs Name is Sarah

Enterd According to Law for the Abolition of Slavery— this 9th day of March 1815

MORDECAI HOMAN Town Clerk

Also Nicoll Floyd made return that he had a female Child Born of a Slave of his on the 29th day of November 1814. Named Rose Childs Name is Tamer—

Enterd this 9th Day of March 1815 According to Law for the Abolition of Slavery—

MORDECAI HOMAN Town Clerk

Nathaniel Tuthill made Return that he had a Male Child Born of a Slave of his on the 2nd day of November 1803 Childs Names is Sebra

Enterd for the Abolition of Slavery

pr. MORDECAI HOMAN Town Clerk

John Smith Gen. Made Return that he had a Male Child Born of a Slave of his on the 9th day of Sept. 1814 Named Samuel Jayne

Enterd this 12th day of Octr 1815

MORDECAI HOMAN Town Clerk

Also John Smith Gen. Made return that he had a female Child Born of a Slave of his on the 4th day of April 1815 Named Charlotte

Enterd this 12th day of Octr 1815—

MORDECAI HOMAN Town Clerk

Mary Woodhull made return that she had a female Child Born of a Slave of hers on the 8th day of September 1815 —Childs Name is Tamer

Enterd this 13th febuary 1816 for the Abolition of Slavery.

MORDECAI HOMAN Town Clerk

PAGE G.

Robert Hawkins Made return that he had a female Child

Born of a Slave of his on the fifth day of September 1811 Named Margett Cicera enterd this fourth day of May According to Law for the Abolition of Slavery

MORDECAI HOMAN Town Clerk

William Smith made return that he had a female Child Born of a Slave of his on the Ninth day of November 1813—Childs name is Fan. enterd this 10th day of November 1814 for the Abolition of Slavery

MORDECAI HOMAN Town Clerk

Mrs Mary Robert made return that she had a female Child Born of a Slave of hers on the 20th July 1803 Child Nam is Dinah—

Also Mrs Mary Robert made return that She had a female Child Born of a Slave of hers on the 20th day of Octr 1806—Childs Name is Charlott.

Also Mrs Mary Robert made return that she had a female Child Born of a Slave of hers on the 30th April 1808. Chils name is Margarett

Also Mrs Mary Robert Made Return that she had a female Child born of a Slave of hers on the 12th October 1808—Chils Name is franics—

Also Mrs Mary Robert made Return that she had a male Child Born of a Slave of hers on the 3rd day of May 1813 Childs Names is Pedro.

Also Mrs Mary Robert made Return that she had a female Child Born of a Slave of hers on the 7th day of Jan 1814—Childs Name is Isabellah

Also Mrs Mary Robert made Return that she had a Male Child Born of a Slave of hers on the 12th day of October 1814—Childs Name is Arthur—

Enter According to Law for the Abolition of Slavery

PAGE H.

Theophilus Smith made return that he had a male Child Born of a Slave of his on the fifteenth day of November

One Thousand Eight hundred and Eight Named Sampson

Also a female Child Born of a Slave of his on the twelvth day of November one thousand Eight hundred and Ten Childs name is Rose

Also a female Child Born of a Slave of his on the twentieth day of October on Thousand Eight hundred and twelve Childs name is Hannah—

Also a female Child Born of a Slave of his on the fourth day of April one thousand Eight Hundred and Thirteen Childs name is Fanny—and also at the same time the sd Theophilus Smith did Elict to Abandon the s,d Child Named Fanny

entered this first day of March one thousand Eight Hundred and fourteen agreeable to the Statute of the State of New York for the Abolition of Slavery

Enterd this first day of }
March 1814— } MORDECAI HOMAN Town Clerk

Woodhul Smith made return that he had a Male Child Born of a Slave of his on the first day of March 1808 Named Ally enterd this fourth day of May 1814 agreeable to the Statute of this State for the abolition of Slavery—

MORDECAI HOMAN Town Clerk

Also Woodhull Smith Made return that he had a female Child Born of a Slave of his on the first Day of December 1811 Named Experience

Enterd this fourth day of May 1814 agreeable to the Statute of this state for the Abolition of Slavery

MORDECAI HOMAN Town Clerk

PAGE I.

Coll. Nicoll floyd made return that he had a Male Child Born of a Slave of his on the third day of October in the Year of our Lord one thousand Eight hundred and twelve

enterd this 28th day of February 1813 agreeable to the Statute of this State for the Abolition of Slavery Child

Name is Richard

MORDECAI HOMAN town Clerk

Brookhaven 5th April 1813

Ruth Thompson made return that she had a female Child born of a Slave of hers on the 14th June 1811—Childs name is Huldah Ann enterd this 6th day of April 1813 agreeable to the Statute of this State for the Abolition of Slavery

MORDECAI HOMAN Town Clk

Ruth Thompson made return that she had a female Child Born of a Slave of hers on the third day of January 1813—Childs Name is Harriet

Enterd this sixth day of April 1813 agreeable to the Statute of the State of New York for Abolition of Slavery—

MORDECAI HOMAN Town Clk

Elizabeth Smith made return that she had a Male Child Born of a Slave of hers on the 1st day of April 1812 Childs Name is David Bowse Entered this fifteenth day of february 1814 agreeable to Statute of the State of New York for the Abolition of Slavery

MORDECAI HOMAN Town Clerk

PAGE J.

Capt. Josiah Smith made return that he had a Male Child Born of a Slave of his on the tenth Day of February 1811 Child Name is Silas

Enterd this 22nd May 1811—agreeable to a Statute of the State of New York—

Benjamin Woodhull made return that he had a female Child Born of a Slave of his on the tenth day of April 1811 —Childs Name is Thankful

Enterd agreeable to the Statute of the State of New York this 13th September 1811—

by me MORDECAI HOMAN Town Clerk

Richard Robinson made Return that he had a Male Child

Born of a Slave of his on the 21st day of March in the Year one Thousand and Eight hundred and Eleven Child's Name is Oliver—Enterd this 22nd June 1812 Agreeable to the Statute of the State of New York for the Abolition of Slavery by me

MORDECAI HOMAN Town Clerk

Sarah Miller made return that she had a female Child Born of a slave of hers—on the 14th day of february 1812 Childs Name is Armina

Enterd this 12th February 1813 agreeable to the Statute of the State of New York for the Abolition of Slavery

MORDECAI HOMAN Town Clk

PAGE K.

Joseph Hedges made return that he had a male Child Born of a Slave of his on the Twenty Second day of September 1809—Child,s Name is Apollas enterd this Seventh day of Dec. 1809 agreeable to the Statute of New York for the Abolition of Slavery—

Timothy Miller made Return that he had a male Child Born of a Slave of his on the first of December 1809 Childs name is Jeremiah Enterd this Seventeenth day of May 1810 agreeable to the Statute of the State of New York for the Abolition of Slavery

Nicoll Floyd made return that he had a Women Child Born of a Slave of his on the 15th June 1810 Childs name is Tamer

Also a Male Child Born of a Slave of his on the 5th March 1809 Boys name is Ben. Enterd this 4th September 1810 Agreeable to an Act of the Assembly for the Abolition of Slavery.

MORDECAI HOMAN Town Clrk

Sarah Miller made return that she had a male Child Born of a Slave of hers on the fourteenth Day of October 1809 Childs Name is Charles Enterd this 4th Day of March 1811

agreeable to an Act of Legislature of New York——
MORDECAI HOMAN Town Clerk

PAGE L.

Amos Smith made return that he had a female Child Born of a Slave of his on the 12th Day of March 1803 Childs name is Cloe
    enterd the 6 April 1808 agreeable to a law of this State for the Abolition of Slavery——
    Agreeable to a Law of the State of New York for the gradual abolition of Slavery Coll. Nicoll Floyd made return that he had a male Child born of a Slave of his on the 24th November 1804 Boys Names is Charles——
    Also one other Male Child Born of a slave of his on the 22nd June 1806—Boys name is Isaac
    Also one female Child Born on the 9th November 1807 Girls Name is Lil—
    Enterd this 8th Day February 1809—
by me MORDECAI HOMAN Town Clerk

Joseph Jayne made return that he had a female Child Born of a Slave of his on the 30th day of April in the year 1805 Childs Name is Phillis
    enterd agreeable to an act of the Legislature
    Enterd this 4th April 1809—
by me MORDECAI HOMAN Town Clerk

Nicol Floyd made Return that he had a male Child Born of a Slave of his on the fifth day of March 1809—Bys Name is Ben.
    Enterd this 16 May 1809—agreeable to an Act of the Legislature of New York
by me MORDECAI HOMAN Town Clerk

PAGE 1.

A Negro Girl Born of A Slave of Stephan Swezey on the third day of October 1802 Girls name is Hannah

Entered Agreeable to A Law of this state for the Gradual Abolition of Slavery—

Josiah Smith Made return that he had a Male Child Named Harry Born of A slave of his on the twenty Sixth day of July 1802 enterd agreeable to a Law of this State for the gradual abolition of Slavery

Also Josiah Smith made return at the same time of A Female Child Named Mary Born of A Slave of his on the 12th of August 1806

Enterd agreeable to A Law of this State for the Gradual Abolition of Slavery this 6th Day of May 1807

By me MORDECAI HOMAN Clk

A Negro girl Born of A Slave of Sarah Miller on the 15th Day of Sept last Viz 1806 Girl,s Name is Mary enterd agreeable to a Law of this State for the Gradual Abolition of Slavery

Selah Strong Made Return that he had a male Child Born of a Slave of his on the Second day of february 1807— Childs Name is Sharper

Recorded this 1st March according to the Stature Law—

John Payne made return that he had a male Child named Zacheus Born of a Slave of his on the 13th day of August 1807 Childs Mothers name is Fan.

Recorded this 23rd March 1808 agreeable to Law for the abolition of Slavery—

MORDECAI HOMAN Clk

PAGE 1. (SECOND).

A Negro Girl, born of a Slave of Genl. John Smith on the 4 of April 1803 Gerls name is mary Entered a Greeable to a Law of this State for the Gradual Abolition of Slavery——

A negro Male Child Born of a Slave of Richard Robinson on the 8th Day of October 1802 sd Boys Name is Silos

One Other Male Child Born of a Slave of sd Richard

Robinson on the 4th Day of June 1804 Sd Boys Name is Harry

Entered According to a Law of this state of New york for the Gradual Abolition of Slavery

A Negro female Child Born of a Slave of Judge Selah Strong November the 20 1799—Sd Girls Name is Silve—

One Other female Child Born of a Slave of sd Judge Selah Strong March the 24th 1802 Sd Girls Name is Phebe—

One Other Male Child Born of a Slave of sd Judge Selah Strong on the 6th of March 1804 Sd Boys Name is Oliver—

Entered Agreeable to a Law of the State of New york in Such Cases Made—

these may Certify, that Judge Abraham Woodhull of sd Town had a Male Child Born of a Slave of his on the seventeenth Day of January Last past sd Boys Name David

sd Judge Woodhull does further Certify that he shall Not abandon sd Child But shall Keep him as his Property until he Shall Arive to the age of 28 years

Entered this 8th Day of August 1805

PAGE 2.

A Negro Girl Named Katura Born of a Slave of Robert Hawkins Junier on the Seventeenth Day of September 1804

Entered Agreeable to a Law of this State

Samuel Turner Turner Had a female Child Born of a slave of his on the 8th Day of february in the year of 1803 sd Girls Name is Margaritt

These May Certify that Coll Niccoll Floyd Had a Negro Boy Named Pomp born of a Slave of His on the 17 Day of August 1805—

Recorded on the 29th of Decr 1805 agreeable to Law

Mr Oliver Smith makes Return that he had a Child Born of a Slave of his on the 14 Day of february 1805 sd Child is a Male Child his name is Tite

Capt Joseph Hedges makes Return that he had a Male Child Born of a Slave of His on the third Day of October 1803—Childs Name Is Jesse—at the Same Time sd Joseph Hedges makes Return that he Had a feemale Child Born of a slave of His in his family on the 5th Day of November 1805—

Woodhull Smith makes Return that he had a female Child Born of a Slave of His on the fifteenth Day of October 1804 Childs name is Corier—

This may Certify that there was this day in my presents and By my Concent, an Indian Boy Named James & aged four Years Ten months and 26 Days oald Bound By an Indenture to James Foster of Southampton until he Arives to the Age of Twenty One Years—by Sary Arch the 26 day of March 1806—

JOHN ROSE Justice

PAGE 3.

at a Meeting of the Freeholders and Inhabitants of the Town of Brookhaven held this 2 Day of April 1805 it Being the first Tuesday and Town Meeting Day Agreeable to a Law of the State of New york in such Cases made and Provded the following Town officers ware Chosen Viz

       Selah Strong Presd

       Meritt S Woodhull ⎫
       William Tooker |
       Joseph B Roe   } Trustees
       John Rose |
       John Robinson |
       David Davis   ⎭

          Isaac Hulse Clk & Tresury
           John Rose Supervisor

     Meritt S Woodhull   ⎫
     Joseph Brewster Jur |
     Wm Tooker   } Assessors.
     Henry Rayner |
     John Rose   ⎭

John Wilsey \
Niccol Floyd } Commissioners of Highways
Isaac Hulse /

Amos Smith Collector

CONSTABLES

Amos Smith
Saml. Bishop
Richard Hudson
Ebenezar Pain

James Robinson
George Norton
Saml Homan

OVERSEERS OF ROADS

Majar Jonas Hawkin
Simeon Hawkins
Joseph Brewster
Daniel Jones
Capt James Davis

Phillip Hallock
Thomas Strong
Merritt S Woodhull
Wm. Skidmore

PAGE 4.

Johathan Worth
Justus Overton
Luis Gurdon
Nethanl Smith
Michh Ruland
Jacob Newton
Benjamin Garard
Briant Davis
Josiah Tuthill

John Leek
Richd Hulse
Nehanl Woodruf
John Mott Esqr
Johathan T Baker
John Akerly
Elisha Hammond
John Overton Sherif
Wm Randal
Briant Norton

FENCE VIEWERS & DAMAGE PRISERS

Jonathan Worth—
Peter Skidmore—
George Hallock—
Elenezar Smith—
Micah Ruland—
John Mott—
Laban Worth—
James Post
Iccebud Carter
Nethaniel Muncel
Mordecai Homan.

Saml Bishop
Terry Baker
Woodhull Smith
Nathl Akerly
Wm Newins
Nathan Mulford
Enos Cherry
Jonathan Robinson.
John Robinson
John Turner
Zophar Tooker

PAGE 5.

Haveing Held and Closed the Poll of the Election in the Town of Brookhaven this Second day of May in the year of one Thousand Eight Hundred and five, and Canvesed the Votes agreeable To the act, Intitled an Act for Regulateing Elections passed the Twenty fourth Day of March one one Thousand Eight Hundred and one, and Do find the Votes to be as follows, Viz for Senators

  Dewit Clinton fifty Eight Votes
  Ezra LeHumiedieu fifty Two Votes
  John Floyd Nineteen Votes

MERITT S. WOODHULL
JOHN ROSE
WILLIAM TOOKER
HENRY RAYNOR
   } Inspectors

Haveing Held and Closed the Poll of the Election in the Town of Brookhaven this Seccond Day of May one Thousand Eight Hundred and five and Canvesed the same Votes agreeable to the Act Entitled an act for Regulateing Elections passed the Twenty fourth Day of March One Thousand Eight Hundred and one and Do find the Votes to Be as follows

for Assembly Jarrard Landon had Thirty Nine Votes
  David Hedges had Sixty one Votes
  David Warner had twenty nine Votes
  Israel Carll had Sixty One Votes

MERITT S. WOODHULL
JOHN ROSE
WILLIAM TOOKER
HENRY RAYNER
   } Inspectors

PAGE 6.

At a Meeting of the Trustees of the Freeholders and Commonality of the Town of Brookhaven Held in sd. Town this 7th of May 1805

Present at sd. Meeting

Selah Strong Presdt ⎫
Meritt S. Woodhull ⎪
David Davis ⎬ Trustees
William Tooker ⎪
John Rose ⎪
John Robinson ⎭

at sd. Meeting sd. Trustees Voted and a Greed and hereby Enacted that No fish Shall Be Catched In the South Bay in sd. Town for the Purpose of Sending or Carrieing them out of said Town or Be Carried Out of the Town To Market By any Person Or persons, Except such persons as Are Authorised and permited to Catch sd fish and Carry them to Market on penalty of Twenty five Dollars fine, To Be paid By Every Person for Every offence—also It was Voted and a Greed and hereby Enacted By sd. Trustees that No Clambs shall Be Carried Out of sd Town By any Person or persons Without first Obtaining Leave and Paying Two Cents on a Bushel as Toleration on penalty of Paying Twenty five Dollars fine On Every Person or Persons for Every Offence

L S   SELAH STRONG Presdt.

PAGE 7.

We the Commissioners of Highways for the Town of Brookhaven Being Called To View a Road or Highway near Setauket at a place Called Comsewague Leading from the Oald mans Path By the Corner of Phillips Roes Lot to Daniel Jone's Bars we do Allow the Owners of the Land to Keep one Gate on said Road at the Oald mans Path. and from thence we do hereby Allow the Road as it Runs from Daniel Jonese,s Bars Southerly Between Daniel Jones Land and Benjamin Jones In part and William Jaynes and Daniel Jones,s In part until it Comes to the Long Lots we do Allow to Be Shut up Given under our Hands this 4th of June 1805—

ISAAC HULSE } Commissioners
JOHN WILLSE } of Highways

At a Meeting of the Trustees of the freeholders and Commonality of the Town of Brookhaven Held at the House of Goldsmith Davis this 4th Day of June 1805
Present at sd Meeting

Selah Strong Presdt.
Meritt S. Woodhull
John Rose
Joseph B Roe } Trustees
David Davis
Wm Tooker
John Robinson

Upon Aplication of Abraham Woodhull Esquire of sd Town To sd Trustees To Manumate a Negro Woman slave Named Juleaner—and the said Negro woman Slave Named Elianer appearing To sd Trustees To Be Healthy and of sufficiant Ability to support Her Self, & To Be under fifty years of Age, it was voted and Agreed that the said Negro woman Slave Eliner should Be Manumated and set free According to Law

PAGE 8.

At a Meeting of the Trustees of the Freeholders and Commonality of the Town of Brookhaven Held in sd. Town this 5th Day of November 1805—
Present at sd. Meeting

Selah Strong Presdt
Meritt S. Woodhull } Trustees
David Davis } &
Wm. Tooker } overseers
John Rose } of the
John Robinson } poor—
Joseph B Roe }

at sd. Meeting Aplication was made To sd Trustees By Samuel Homan in Behalf of John Homan senr to Manumate and set free A Certain Negro woman Now a Slave To sd

John Homan Named Phelis—and Agreeable To a Law of the state of New york Passed the 8th day of April 1801 sd Trustees & overseers of the Poor Haveing Examined sd. slave and finding Her To Be under fifty Years of Age and of Sufficient Ability To Maintain Herself Do Hereby Manumate and set Her free

Attest ISAAC HULSE Town Clk----

at sd Meeting Application was Made To sd. Trustees By William Tooker To Manumate and set free a Certain Negro man a Slave To sd Wm Tooker Named Primous—and agreeable To a Law of the state of New York Passed the 8th Day of April 1801 sd Trustees & overseers of the Poor Haveing Examined sd Slave and finding Him To Be under fifty years of Age and of sufficient Ability to Maintain Himself Do Hereby Manumate and set him free

Attest ISAAC HULSE Town Clk----

PAGE 9.

at a Meeting of the Trustees of the Freeholders and Commonality of the Town of Brookhaven Held in sd. Town this 5th Day of November 1805

Present at sd Meeting

Selah Strong Presdt. ⎫
Meritt S Woodhull ⎪
David Davis ⎪
John Rose ⎬ Trustees
John Robinson ⎪
William Tooker ⎪
Joseph B Roe— ⎭

at sd Meeting Application Was Made To sd Trustees By Benjamin Petty Esqr fr Liberty to Dock out Into the south Bay from the Bottom of the Neck where he Now Lives at Moriches in sd Town—and after hereing sd Aplication or petition sd. Trustees Granted Liberty to sd. Benjamin Petty Esqr To Dock out into the Bay from the Bottom of his sd Neck of Land—

We the Subscribers are Willing that Thomas S Strong Shou,d Be permited to Hang and Erect an Easy Swinging Gate a Cross the Road that Leads from Ebenezar Pains To the said Thomas S. Strongs, To be Hung at the North End of the Watering place To the Northward of sd pain, and also the said Thomas S. Strong to Be permited Hang an Easy Swinging Gate a Crost the Road that Leads from John Wilceys to sd Thomas S. Strongs to Be Placed East of the Road that Turns to the Left as you Go west to William Swezys—Provided that the sd Thomas S. Strong Keeps the Gates in Good Repair at his own Expence, and further we do not think that the sd

PAGE 10.

Gates will be any Inconvenance to the publulick as the said Roads are Used But Very Little By the Publick Brookhaven February the 19th 1806

EBENZAR PAYN	JOSEPH MILLAR
NETHANIEL DAVIS	TIMOTHY MILLAR
JAMES DAVIS	ELISHA PETTY
PHILIPS BROWN	PHILIPS ROE
DANIEL DAVIS	JNO. TAYLOR
SPICER DAVIS	BERIAH PETTY
DANIEL BAILES	WILLIAM SWEZEY
BENJN. CLARK	THOS BELL
DAVID ROBINS	ISAAC SATTERLY
ELISHA DAVIS	RICHARD DAVIS
JOSEPH DAVIS	HENRY TOOKER
WELLS DAVIS	DANIEL DAVIS
SAML. HOPKINS	JESSE DAVIS
THOMAS BAYLES	ISRAEL DAVIS
WILLIAM GARRARD	JOSEPH GARARD
ELISHA BAYLES	GEO NORTON SENR
JOHN DAVIS	

Agreeable To the petition of Thomas S. Strong Esq Accompanyed with the foregoing Names Requesting the Commissioners of the Town of Brookhaven to allow him sd. Thomas S Strong Esq To Hang Good Easy Swinging

BROOKHAVEN TOWN RECORDS.   101

Gates at the places mentioned in sd petition—We the Commissioners of Highways for sd Town Haveing Examined sd premises and petition and Do Allow sd Gates to Be Hung at the following places Viz one at the North End of the watering place By Ebenezar Payns One other a Cross the Road that Leads from John Wilceys To Thomas S. Strongs to be Placed East of the Road that Turns to the Left as you Go West To William Swezeys—sd Thomas S. Strong to Keep sd Gates In Good Repair at his Own Expence Done By us this 17th Day of March 1806—

      ISAAC HULSE } Commissioners
      JOHN WILCEY } of Highways
Attest ISAAC HULSE Town Clk

PAGE 11.

At a Meeting of the freeholders and Inhabitants of the Town of Brookhaven, Held this first Day of April 1806— Being first Tuesday and Town Meeting Day Agreeable To a Law of the State of New york in such Cases Made and Provided—

The following Town Officers Were Chosen By a Majority of Votes—

Viz Selah Strong Presdt ⎫
   Meritt S Woodhull ⎪
   Wm. Tooker   ⎪
   Caleb M. Hulse   ⎬ Trustees
   John Rose   ⎪
   Josiah Smith Moriches ⎪
   Isaac Homan   ⎭

  Isaac Hulse Clerk & Treasurer—
    John Rose Supervisor
    Amos Smith Collector

  Meritt S. Woodhull ⎫
  Joseph Brewster Esqr ⎪
  Wm. Tooker   ⎬ Assessors
  Josiah Smith   ⎪
  John Rose   ⎭

John Wilcey
Wm Smith Moriches, } Commissioners of Highways
Joseph B Roe

Constables

Amos Smith
Richard Swezey
James Robinson
Saml. Homan

Saml. Bishop
Wm Howell
David Overton Junr
Henry Dayton

Page 12.

Stephan Edwards—
Jonas Hawkins—
Nethanl Davis oald mans—
Phillip Hallock—
Jonathan Worth—
Gilbert Homan—
Jacob Corwin B. Smith—
Isaac Rayner—
Barnabas Wines—
Ebenezar Hart—
Stephan Reves—
Micah Ruladd—
Danl Tooker –
John Roseman—
Humphry Avery—

Simeon Hawkins
John Taylor
Nethanl Davis, Merchant
Wm. Skidmore
Wm. Randal
Stephan Swezy
Isaac Homan
Asel Robinson
John Barker
Briant Davis
Stephan Robinson
John Mott
Wm Tooker
John Overton sheriff
Danl Roe. Esqr

Elisha Hammond—the above Named is Overseers of Highways for this year—

Fence Viewers

Israel Hawkins
Nethaniel Akerly
Jonathan Worth
Capt David Davis
Danl Davis
Robert Elison
John Mott
Micah Ruland
John Bishop
Zacharier Sanford
Capt. John Robinson
Saml. Bishop

Jonas Davis
Ebenezar Bayles
Peter Skidmore
Danl Swezy
Wells Davis
Richard Corwin
Joseph Hedges
Wm. Newins
Laban Worth
Saml. Terry
James Stanbrow

Voted that there Shall Be a bounty of 50 Cents for Each fox that Shall be Ketched

voted that thare shall Be No Clambs Catched in the Town By fourigners.

PAGE 12. (SECOND).

Suffolk County ss

Statement of Votes taken at the Annavarsary Election for senators Which Commenced on the Last Tuesday of April one Thousand Eight Hundred and six

Senators

Benjamin Coe one Hundred & fifteen } Votes
Jonathan Ward one Hundred & fifteen }

Samuel Jones forty Seven } Votes
James Moris Forty Six }

We Certify the above to Be a True statement and Estimate of the Votes Taken in the Town of Brookhaven at the aforesaid Election May first one Thousand Eight Hundred and six

MERITT S. WOODHULL }
ISAAC HULSE } Inspectors
WILLIAM TOOKER }
JOHN ROSE }

Suffolk County ss

Statement or Votes taken at the Anniversary Election for Congressmen Which Commenced on the Last Tuesday of April one Thousand Eight Hundred and six

Congressmen

Samuel Riker one Hundred & Thirty Two Votes

Eliphalet Wicks One Vote—

We certify the above to be a True Statement & Estimate of the votes taken in the Town of Brookhaven at the aforesaid Election May first 1806—

MERITT S. WOODHULL }
WILLIAM TOOKER } Inspectors
JOHN ROSE }
ISAAC HULSE }

PAGE 13.

Suffolk County ss

Statement of Votes Taken at the Annaversary Election for Members of Assembly Which Commenced on the Last Tuesday of April one Thousand Eight Hundred & six viz

David Hedges one Hundred and Thirty Two ⎫
Israel Carll one Hundred and Thirty Two ⎬ Votes
David Warner one Hundred and Thirty Two ⎭

James Reve one ⎫
B B Blindingburgh one ⎬ Vote
Richard Udall one ⎭

We Certify the above to be a True statement and Estimate of the Votes Taken in the Town of Brookhaven at the afore sd Election may first 1806—

MERITT S. WOODHULL ⎫
JOHN ROSE ⎬ Inspectors
WILLIAM TOOKER ⎬
ISAAC HULSE ⎭

December the fourteenth Day Eighteen Hundred and five this Day Keeder Bur and Margarett Bur his Wife Bound their son Shadrick Bur Now of the Age of Eight Years seven months and thirteen Days to Gabraell Mills

before me— MERITT S WOODHULL Justice

December the fourteenth Day Eighteen Hundred and five This Day Keeder Bur and Margarett Bur his Wife—Bound their son James Bur Now of the Age of six years Eleven months and Two Days To Gabrell Mills before me

MERITT S. WOODHULL Justice

PAGE 14.

At a Meeting of the Trustees of the freeholders and Commonality of the Town of Brookhaven Held in said Town this third Day of June 1806

Present at said Meeting

Selah Strong Presdt.
Meritt S. Woodhull.

Caleb M. Hulse
Wm. Tooker
John Rose
Josiah Smith
Isaac Homan
} Trustees

At sd. Meeting John Howard Esquire made Application to sd Trustees to manumate and set free a Certain Male Slave By the name of Pompe the property of the Estate of David Howell Late of Brookhaven Deceast. said Trustees Haveing satisfactory Evidence that sd Pompe is under fifty years of Age, and of Sufficiant ability to provide for and Maintain Himself We do hereby Manumate and set sd Negro man Pompe a Greeable To a Law of the State of New york Passed the 8 Day of April 1801

Attest Isaac Hulse Town Clk.

Page 15.

At a Meeting the Trustees of the freeholders and Commonality of the Town of Brookhaven Held in said Town this third Day of June 1806—

Presant at said Meeting

Selah Strong Presdt.
Meritt S. Woodhull
Caleb M. Hulse
Wm. Tooker
John Rose
Josiah Smith
Isaac Homan
} Trustees

at said Meeting it was Represented to said Trustees that there Hath Been Great Destruction Made to the young Oysters By Reason of the Inhabitants Catching and Takeing up Young Oysters and Shells With Them in the South Bay in Partnership With said Town & the Heirs of Major Wm. Smith—Now therefore for the Preventing of such Destruction, to said young Oysters Being Done hereafter said Trustees Hath Voted and Agreed and hereby Enacted By the athority a fore said that If any Person or Persons shall

Catch or Take up any Oysters or Shells from the Beds on Which they Lay with in said Bay Every Person Or Persons Shall forfit and Pay Twenty Dollars for Every offence To be sued for and Recovered In the Name of the Trustees for the Use of the Town—
Attest Isaac Hulse Town Clk
                            Selah Strong Presdt l s

Page 16.

At a meeting of the Trustees of the Freeholders and Commonality of the Town of Brookhaven Held in Said Town this third Day of June 1806—Present at said meeting—

> Selah Strong Presdt.
> Merritt S. Woodhull
> Caleb M. Hulse
> John Rose   } Trustees
> Wm. Tooker
> Josiah Smith
> Isaac Homan

at said meeting sd Trustees Voted and Agreed and Hereby Enacted By the a thority a foresaid that If any Person Or persons Shall Catch any Clambs or Horsefish in any of the Bays or Harborus Within the Limits of the said Town for the Purpose of Carrying them Out of the Town, Or Carry them Out of the said Town To Market Being Catched or Taken in Either of the Bays or Harbours Within the Limits or Bounds of sd Town Every Person or Persons shall forfit and Pay Twenty Dollars for Every Such offence, to Be Sued for and Recovered In the Name of the Trustees for the use of sd Town allways Excepting such Persons as Shall Obtain Leave of sd Trustees or their Agent To Carry Clambs Out of said Town, and Pay to said Trustees or their Agent three Cents for Each and Every Bushel of Clambs Intended To be Carried Out of said Town, But Not to Carry Horsefish Out of sd. Town under any Pretence

Selah Strong Presdt　⎫
Caleb M Hulse　　　⎪
Meritt S. Woodhull　⎪
Wm. Tooker　　　　⎬ Trustees.
John Rose　　　　　⎪
Isaac Homan　　　　⎪
Josiah Smith　　　　⎭

Whereas said Trustees Passed a Law on the third day of June Last for the preventing any Oysters Or Shells Being Catched in the South Bay in Partnership with the Town and Wm. Smith—and at the above said Meeting a Greeable to the Request and partition of a Number of the Inhabitants of sd Town sd Trustees at their above said meeting Have Passed a Law Repealing so much of the first Mentioned Law—as to Grant Liberty to the Inhabitants of sd Town To Take shells and Oysters in that part of sd Bay that Lieth East ward of a south Line from a Creek on the East side of Pine Neck Called Muddy Creek Extending sd Line to the south Beach—

SELAH STRONG Presdt

PAGE 20.

At a Meeting of the Trustees of the Freeholders and Commonality of the Town of Brookhaven Held in said Town this 2 Day of September 1806

Present at sd Meeting

Selah Strong Presdt　⎫
Meritt S. Woodhull　⎪
Caleb M. Hulse　　　⎬ Trustes
John Rose　　　　　⎪
Wm. Tooker　　　　⎪
Isaac Homan　　　　⎭

at s,d Meeting the said Trustees Voted and Agreed that there Should Be One Thousand Dollars Raised in said Town By a Rate on the Inhabitants of said Town for the Support of the Poor and the Town Expences

Attest—　　　　　　　　ISAAC HULSE Town Clk

At a meeting of the Trustees of the freeholders and

Commonality of the Town of Brook haven Held in sd Town this 6 Day of January in the year of 1807
   Present at said Meeting

        Selah Strong Presdt
        Meritt S. Woodhull
        Caleb M. Hulse   Trustees
        John Rose
        Wm Tooker
        Isaac Homan

at said Meeting said Trustees Voted and a Greed that Nethaniel Woodruff should Have Liberty to Build a wharf or Dock Out into the south Bay against his Own Land which he Now Possesses

PAGE 21.

so as to Extend Out in to said Bay Six Rods and the said Trustees doth hereby Confirm unto said Nethaniel Woodruff the Right To Build said Wharf and to Occupy the same as his Own Property

   Attest ISAAC HULSE Town Clk

   This may Certify that there is this day Bound by Ephraim and Phillis Black People by an Indenture to Cephas Foster Isaac their Son aged three years old the fifth day of January Instant to serve until he is twenty one Years old done in the presence and by the consent of me this 19 Day of January 1807

                      JOHN ROSE Justice

PAGE 22.

   At a Meeting of the freeholders and Inhabitants of the Town of Brook Haven Held in said Town this 7th Day of April 1807 it Being Town Meeting Day Agreeable to a Law of this state the following Town Officers was Unanimously Chosen Viz

        Selah Strong Presdt
        Meritt S. Woodhull
        William Tooker
        Daniel Roe   Trustees

John Rose Esqr
William Smith
Capt. David Davis
Mordecai Homan Town Clerk & Treasurer
John Rose Esqr Supervisor
Amos Smith Collector

William Jayne
Meritt S. Woodhull
William Tooker } Assessors
John Rose Esqr
Josiah Smith

John Rose Esqr
Meritt S Woodhull } Commissioners of Highways
William Jayne

PAGE 23.

CONSTABLES

Amos Smith	William Howell
Elisha Davis	Saml. Bishop
James Robinson	Saml. Davis Junior
Saml Homan	Israel Smith

OVERSEER OF HIGHWAYS.

Zecheriah Hawkins	Richard Hulse
Joseph Miller	William Howell
Phillip Hallock	Barnabas Smith
Peter Skidmore	Humphrey Avery
Jonathan Worth	Isaac Mills
Capt. James Davis	Jehiel Woodruff
Ichabod Carter	David Davis
Azael Robinson	Saml Hammond
Henry Rayner	Isaac Smith
Ebenezer Hartt	John Hulse
Willm. Smith	William Tooker
Michal Ruland	Jesse Overton
Jonas Hawkins	Capt Benjamin Jones
Morris Jayne	Benjamin Smith
Capt David Davis	

FENCE VEIWERS & DAMAGE PRIZERS

Nathl. Akerly	Philip Hallock
Ebenezer Bayless	Hendrick Hallock

John Van brunt   Jonathan Worth
Jesse Roe   James Woodhull
Jesse Davis   Justus Overton
Capt James Davis   Barnabas Wines

PAGE 24.

Nathan Post   James Post
Stephen Robinson   William Smith
Joseph Hedges   Titus Goold
Barnabas Smith   Jeremiah Whelor
Ketcham Terry   Daniel Tooker
William Newins   Bryant Norton
Jehiel Woodruff   John Bishop
Benjamin Hutchinson   Robert Hawkins Junr
Saml. Bishop   Humphrey Avery

Suffolk County ss.

Statement of Votes taken at the Annaversary Election for Governor Lieut. Governor & Senator which Commenced on the Last Tuesday of April one thousand Eight Hundred and Seven

Governor

Daniel D. Tompkins one Hundred and Ninty four ⎫ Votes
Morgan Lewis one Hundred and Six   ⎭

Lieut Governor

John Broom one Hundred and Ninety Seven ⎫
Thomas Storn one Hundred and two   ⎬ Votes
Thomas Lewis one—   ⎭

Senators

Dewitt Clinton one Hundred and Eighty Nine ⎫ Votes
Samuel Jones one Hundred and three   ⎭

We Certify the above to be a true Statement and estimate of the Votes taken in the town of Brookhaven at the afores,d Election May the first one thousand Eight Hundred and Seven

    MERIT S. WOODHULL JOHN ROSE   ⎫ Inspectors
    WILLIAM JAYN   WILLIAM TOOKER ⎭

PAGE 25.

Suffolk County ss.

Statement of Votes taken at the Annaversary Election

for Members of Assembly which commenced on the last Tuesday of April one thousand Eight Hundrd and Seven

Assembly.—

Jonathan Dayton One Hundred and Sixty four. ⎫
Israel Carle One Hundred and Sixty five   ⎪
Daniel T. Terry Ninety three—   ⎬ Votes
Thomas S. Lester Seventy one—   ⎪
David Warner one—   ⎪
David Hedges one—   ⎭

We Certify the above to be a true Statement and Estimate of the Votes taken in the town of Brookhaven at the aforesaid Election May the first one thousand Eight Hundred and Seven——

MERIT S. WOODHULL ⎫
JOHN ROSE   ⎬ Inspectors
WILLIAM JAYNE   ⎪
WILLIAM TOOKER   ⎭

PAGE 26.

At a meeting of the Freeholders and Commonalty of the Town of Brookhaven held this 5th Day of May 1807 Present at s,d Meeting

Selah Strong Presdt ⎫
Merit S. Woodhull   ⎪
Daniel Roe   ⎬ Trustees
David Davis   ⎪
Wm Tooker   ⎪
John Rose   ⎭

* At sd Meeting the Priviledge of Fowling in the South Bay Belonging between the Town and the Heirs of Major Wm Smith Deceas,d was hired out to Hampton Howell for fifty Dollars for one Year from this date With the Priviledge of Vending them wheresoever they Can find a Market but not to debar the Inhabitants of s,d Town from Gunning except on their own Bars

*Also the Priviledge of fishing in s,d Bay in Partnership with s,d Town and s,d Wm. Smith Was let out upon Shares to Capt. Josiah Smith and Hampton Howell who is to pay unto the Trustees one tenth part of all the fish they Catch in s,d Limits—but not to hinder the Inhabitants of s,d Town from fishing

Also at s,d Meeting it was agreed By s,d Trustees that the Law respecting Oysters and Clambs and Horsefish Passed the third day of June 1806 is hereby confirmed or revised by s,d Trustees until a further Vote of s,d Trustees—

Enterd by me By order of s,d Trustees—

Mordecai Homan Town Clerk

Page 27.

Brookhaven 2nd June 1807

this May Certify that on the Second day of June on thousand Eight Hundred and Seven Noah Hallock of S,d Town Made application to the Trustees to Set free A Negro Male Slave of his by the Name of Tim and s,d Trustees having Satisfactory evidence the s,d Tim is under the age of fifty Years and of Sufficient ability to provide for and Maintain himself we the s,d Trustees do hereby Manumate and Set free s,d Negro Man Tim agreeable to a Law of the State of New York Passed the 8th Day of April 1801—

Attest Mordecai Homan Town Clk

this May Certify that on the Second day of June one thousand eight Hundred and seven Wm Helme of s,d Town Made application to the Trustees of s,d Town to Manumate and set free A Woman Slave of his by the Name of Viner and s,d Trustees having Satisfactory evidence that s,d Viner is under the age of fifty Years and of Sufficient ability to provide for and Maintain herself we the s,d Trustees do hereby Manumate and set free s,d Negro Woman Viner agreeable to a Law of the State of New York Passed the 8th Day of April 1801—

Attest Mordecai Homan Town Clk

*Note.—The two items above were found crossed and a note on the margin as follows: "Entered in cash book."—Com.

PAGE 28.

Brookhaven 18th June 1807—

We the Commissioners of high Ways of the Town of Brookhaven being Called upon by William Still Samuel Hammond and others to lay out a Road from Chrystle Brook hollow Road to a Road Calld Benjamins Road therefore We the s,d Commissioners having Viewed the premises and Supposing it Nessasary have laid out a Public high Way three Rods wide beginning at the Road Calld Chrystle Brook hollow Road Near the North East Corner of William Stills Lot Running North Westerly to a Road Call,d Benjamins Road—and We the s,d Commissioners do order the same to be enterd on the town Record as Witness our hands

MERITT S. WOODHULL } Commissioners
WILLIAM JAYNE   } of
JOHN ROSE   } highways

Attest MORDECAI HOMAN Town Clerk

PAGE 29.

At A meeting of the Trustees of the Commonalty and freeholders of the Town of Brookhaven held this 7th July 1807 present at sd Meeting

Selah Strong President
Meritt S. Woodhull
Daniel Roe } Trustees
David Davis
John Rose

At S,d Meeting the Trustees agreed to Join John Wilsey in Building a Dock at the head of Drown Meadow Bay on the Towns priviledge Jointly in partnership and appointed Judge Strong Merritt S. Woodhull and Daniel Roe as A Committee to View the premises—

At a Meeting of the Trustees of the freeholders and Commonalty of the Town of Brookhaven held in s,d Town this 1st of Septr 1807

Present at s,d Meeting

Selah Strong President
Merrit S. Woodhul ⎫
Daniel Roe   ⎪
Wm. Tooker   ⎬ Trustees
Wm. Smith   ⎪
John Rose   ⎭

At s,d Meeting s,d Trustees Voted and agreed that there should be one thousand Dollars Raised in said Town by a Tax or Rate on the Inhabitance of s,d Town for the support of the poor and Town Expences—
          Attest MORDECAI HOMAN Town Clerk.

PAGE 30.

Brookhaven 1st Septr 1807—

This may Certify that on the first day of September AD 1807 the Trustees of s,d Town Sold a House and piece of land belonging to s,d Town lying in Setauket on the Road that leads to Morris Jayns from Isaac Satterlys Mill dam s,d premise Was sold to Wm. Hulse for Two Hundred and Forty five Dollars—
          attest MORDECAI HOMAN Town Clerk

Brookhaven 2nd Feb 1808

at a Meeting of the Trustees for the Time being held on s,d day it was desired by s,d Wm Hulse above Written that the Deed given to him for the above s,d premises should be Changed to Stephen Hulse and Jesse Hulse the Trustees therefore at the Request of sd Parties took the Deed given to Wm Hulse back again and gave a Deed for the same premises to sd Stephen and Jesse Hulse
          attest MORDECAI HOMAN Clerk

PAGE 31.

Brookhaven 13 Jan 1808—

We the Commissioners of high Ways being Called by Robert and Charles Ellison and others to stop up the Road Laid out on the West side of the Beaver Dam River having Viewed s,d Road do Judge it to be intirely useless and unnessary to accommodate the Public have Stoped it up from the head of the Beaver Dam River or Swamp on the West side of s,d River to the Lower going Over and have Laid out a Road from the head of the ottor Swamp Northeasterly as it now Runs Crossing the Beaver Dam River at a place Called the uper going Over sd Road to be four Rods Wide the old Road Stopped up and the New one Laid out by us this thirteenth Day of January AD 1808

WILLIAM JAYNE } Commissioners
JOHN ROSE

Attest MORDECAI HOMAN Town Clerk

PAGE 32.

Suffolk }
County } ss   Personally appeared before me Meritt S. Woodhull one of the Justices of the Peace in and for the s,d County Robert Hawkins Sinior and upon his Oath doth Say that a Certain Branch or Creek putting out of Connecticut River on the West Side at a hill of upland and running Northwesterly is Called Oosence and is and has always Been considered the Northwestermost Bounds of Yaphank.

Sworn before me }   His
MERITT S. WOODHULL }   ROBERT X HAWKINS
Justice }   Mark

22nd. February 1808—enterd by me

MORDECAI HOMAN—Town Clerk

OYSTER ACT—At a Meeting of the Trustees of the freeholders and Commonalty of the Town of Brookhaven held at the House of Goldsmith Davis Inn Keeper in s,d Town on Tuesday the first day of March in the Year of our LORD one thousand Eight Hundred and Eight present at s,d Meeting—

Selah Strong President.

Merrit S. Woodhull
Daniel Roe
John Rose
William Tooker   } Trustees
David Davis
William Smith

PAGE 33.

Whereas it hath been represented to the s,d Trustees by a number of the Inhabitance of s,d Town that there is great Quantities of young Oysters growing in South Bay within the limits and Bounds of s,d Town that is in partnership with s,d Town and the Heirs of William Smith Deceas,d and if they could be preserved and not taken or Catched during the continuance of the following Act, or order it would not only be very beneficial to a number of Individuals but to the Inhabitance of s,d Town in general, therefore in order to preserve the s,d Oysters in s,d Bay it was Voted and agreed on at s,d Meeting that no Oysters nor shells of Oysters shall be taken or Catched out of s,d Bay as aforesaid by any Person or Persons after the fourth day March Instant on penalty of forfeiting to the s,d Trustees or their order the sum of Twenty Dollars for each and every offence to be applied to the use of s,d Town to be Sueed for and recovered as any other Debt before any Justice of the Peace of s,d Town. And also at s,d Meeting it was Voted and agreed that if any Oysters or Shells of Oysters shall be found on Board of any Boat or small Craft belonging to any Person or Persons within the Bounds and limits as aforesaid or if any Person or persons shall aid or assist in conveying or shall Carry any oysters or Shell of Oysters out of s,d Town or who shall have any Oysters or shells of Oysters found in his or their possession taken or Catched after the passing of this Act it shall be deemed sufficient proof to convict him or them of the offence aforesaid Provided such owner as aforesaid shall not make it appear that s,d Oysters or shell of Oysters were put on Board of s,d Boat or small Craft or in his or their possession by some evil dispos,d person for the purpose of fraud

Page 34

and also at s,d Meeting it was further Voted and agreed notwithstanding the aforesaid act that where any Person or family shall be Visited with severe sickness or other indisposition and the afflicted peson or family shall be desirous of some Oysters that in Such Case any person or persons applying to the Trustees or their order shall have a permit for such Quantity as may be deemed sufficient for the purpose aforesaid such permit specifying the Quantity to be taken and the s,d Oysters to be left with such person for inspection as the trustees shall appoint, this Act to continue in force until Repealed by the s,d Trustees or their successors.—all former Acts or orders of s,d Trustees Respecting Oysters and shells of Oysters are hereby Repealed—

N. B. it was also Voted and agreed that Warden Tobey at Blue point and William Baker at Patchogue be appointed to give permits agreeable to the aforesaid acts in Case of sickness.

SELAH STRONG President [L S]
Attest, MORDECAI HOMAN Town Clerk

Page 35 blank

Page 36.

At a Meeting of the Freeholders and Inhabitance of the Town of Brookhaven held in s,d Town this fifth day of April in the Year of our Lord one thousand Eight Hundred and Eight it Being Town Meeting Day agreeable to a Law of this State the following Town Officers were unanimously Chosen

Viz—

    Wm Jayne President
    Thomas Strong   ⎫
    Daniel Saxton |
    Benjamin Hallock | Trustees
    Ebeneser Hartt |
    John Rose |
    Barnabas Smith   ⎭
Mordecai Homan Town Clerk and Treasurer
    John Rose Sepirvisor
    Amos Smith Collector

Wm Jayne   ⎫
Merritt S. Woodhull |
John Rose   } Assessors
William Beale |
Josiah Smith   ⎭

John Rose Esq.   ⎫
Merritt S. Woodhull } Commissioner of
John Wilsey   ⎭   high Ways

PAGE 37.

Amos Smith   ⎫
Daniel Brown |
Ebeneser Payn |
Sylvanus Overton |
James Robinson } Constables
Israel Smith |
Nathan Post |
Samuel Homan |
Samuel Bishop   ⎭

Jonas Hawkins—Major   Charles Garrard
Jacob Hawkins   John Bishop
John Vanbrunt.   Wm Swezey
Samuel Davis   Briant Norton
George Norton   Brewster Terry
Nathaniel Davis   Jeremiah Wheeler
Nathaniel Davis Millersplace Jeremiah Sqires
Phillip Hallock   John Bishop Moriches
Daniel Brown   Wm Smith
John Robinson   Joseph Hedges

Capt Worth Jonathan   David Leek
Joseph Raynor   Esqr. Horten
Justus Overton   Micah Ruland
Azel Robinson   Ebeneser Hawkins
Gilbert Homan   Ebeneser Bailey
Thomas Aldrich   Isaac Brewster
Stephen Swezey   David Case
Benjamin Hallock   Josiah Tuthill

PAGE 38.

FENCE VIEWERS

Ebenezer Hawkins   Isaac Hammond
Ebenezer Bailey   John Vanbrunt
John Davis   Josept Jayne
Daniel Davis   Zechriah Sanford
Nathaniel Davis   Benjamin Petty
Merrit S Woodhull   Mordecai Homan
Jonathan Worth   Charles Ellison
John Robinson   Mical Ruland
Jeremiah Wines   Samuel Bishop
Ebenezer Wines   Moses Wick
Henry Dayton   Wm Arthur Jur
John Turner   Barnabas Smith
Robert Hawkins   Josept Hedges
John Bishop   Nathan Mulford
Wm Swezey   Esq Horton

PAGE 39.

Suffolk County ss

Statement of Votes taken at the annaversary Election for Senators which Commenced on the last Tuesday of April one thousand Eight Hundred and Eight——

Senators

Samuel Jones one hundred and fourteen
James Morris one hundred and fourteen
William W. Gilbert one hundred and forty eight } Votes
Benjamin Coe, one hundred and fifty

We Certify the above to be a true statement of the Votes taken in the Town of Brookhaven at the aforesaid Election April 29th 1808—

MERRITT S. WOODHULL
JOHN ROSE
JOSIAH SMITH
WILLIAM JAYNE
} Inspectors

Suffolk County } ss Statement of Votes taken at the Annaversary Election for Representatives in Congress which Commenced the last Tuesday in April one thousand Eight hundred and Eight—

Representatives in Congress

Ebeneser Sage Twenty six
Benjamin B. Blydenburgh one hundred and Twenty two
John W. Seamon one Hundred and fifty
} Votes

We Certify the above to be a true Statement and Estimate of the Votes taken in the Town of Brookhaven at the aforesaid Election—29 April 1808

MERRITT S. WOODHULL
JOHN ROSE
JOSIAH SMITH
WILLIAM JAYNE
} Inspectors

PAGE 40.

Suffolk County ss

Statement of Votes taken at the Annaversary Election for Assembly which commenced the last Tuesday in April one thousand Eight hundred and Eight

Assembly

Thomas S. Lester one hundred and Seventy two
Abraham Rose one hundred and forty
Mills Phillips one Hundred and Eighty
Capt. Nethiel Smith one Hundred and seventeen
Daniel Terry Ten.
David Hedges thirty five
John Woodhull one
} Votes

We Certify the above Statement and Estimate of the Votes taken in the Town of Brookhaven at the aforesaid Election this 29th April 1808

MERRITT S. WOODHULL
JOHN ROSE
JOSUAH SMITH
WILLIAM JAYNE
} Inspectors

PAGE 41.

At a Meeting of the Trustees of the freeholders and commonalty of the Town of Brookhaven held in s,d Town this third day of May one thousand Eight Hundred and Eight Present at S,d Meeting William Jayne President Thomas Strong Daniel Saxton Benjamin Hallock Ebenezer Hartt John Rose Barnabas Smith Trustees

At s,d Meeting it was Voted and agreed on by s,d Trustees and hereby Enacted by the authority of the Same that if any Person or Persons Shall Catch any fish in any of the Bays or harbours belonging to s,d Town or if any Person or Persons shall Carry any fish out of s,d Town every person or persons so offending shall pay to the Trustees aforesaid the sum of Twenty Dollars for each and every Offence to be sued for by s,d Trustees or their order in any Court having Cognizance thereof to be applied to the use of s,d Town——

Also at s,d meeting s,d Trustees Voted and agreed and hereby Enacted by the authority aforesaid that the Act Respecting Oysters and shells of Oysters passed the first day of March 1808 should be Revised until a further order of s,d Trustees except that Certain Clause in s,d Act that was to grant permits in Certain cases which is hereby prohibited Viz. there is no permits to be given in any Case whatever——

PAGE 42.

Also at s,d Meeting s,d Trustees Voted and agreed and hereby Enacted by the authority aforesaid that the Act Concerning Clambs and horsfish passed the third day of June 1806 should be Revised and the foregoing Acts are

hereby Revised and to Continue in force until Repealed or a further order from s,d Trustees or their Successors—
            WILLIAM JAYNE President L S
attest MORDECAI HOMAN Clerk
At a Meeting of the Trustees of the freeholders and Commonalty of the Town of Brook haven held this 6th Day of Sept. 1808   Present at sd Meeting
            Wm. Jayne President
            Daniel Saxton   ⎫
            Thomas S. Strong   ⎪
            Barnabas Smith   ⎬ Trustees
            John Rose   ⎪
            Ebenezer hart   ⎪
            Benjamin Hallock   ⎭
At s,d Meeting s,d Trustees Voted and agreed that there should be Eight hundred dollars Raised in s,d Town for the use of the Poor and other expenses thereof
            MORDECAI HOMAN Town Clerk

PAGE 43.

This May Certify that on the sixth day of September in the Year of our Lord one thousand Eight Hundred and Eight Selah Strong Made application to the Trustees of S,d Town to Manumate and Set free a Woman Slave of his Named Seylvia and s,d Negro Woman appearing to s,d Trustees to be under the age of fifty Years and of Sufficient ability to provide for and Maintain herself We the s,d Trustees do therefore Manumate and Set free s,d Slave according to a Law of the State of New York passed the 8th Day of April 1801—
            Attest MORDECAI HOMAN Clerk
This may Certify that on the Sixth day of April in the Year of our Lord one thousand Eight Hundred and Eight Joseph Homan made application to the Trustees of s,d Town to Manumate and set free a Negro Slave of his Named Jude and s,d Negro Woman appearing to s,d Trus-

tees to be under the age of fifty Years and of Sufficient ability to provide for and maintain herself we the s,d Trustees do therefore Manumate and set free s,d Negro Woman Jude agreeable to a Law of the State of New York passed the 8th. day of April 1801—

Attest MORDECAI HOMAN Clerk

PAGE 44.

Brookhaven the 6th September 1808—

We the Commissioners of highways for the town of Brookhaven being Call'd by John Munsell William Hawkins Junr. and others to stop up a Road begining at the south Country Road to the East of John Munsels House Runing North to the Middle of the Island and to Lay it out in the Line between Wm. Hawkins Junr. John Munsll and Isaac Overton Esqr. we the s,d Commissioners having Viewed the premises do think it necessary and Convenient for the Public and have ordered it Recorded Accordingly given under our hands this day and date above Written

MERRITT S. WOODHULL } Commissioners
JOHN ROSE

Attest MORDECAI HOMAN Clerk

PAGE 45.

This may certify that on the first day of November in the year of our Lord one thousand Eight hundred and eight Mariam Brown made application to the Trustees of the Town of Brookhaven to manumate and set free a Women Slave of hers Named Jude and s,d Trustees being Satisfied that s,d Jude is under the age of fifty Years and of Sufficient ability to support and maintain herself We the s,d Trustees do therefore manumate and set free s,d Jude agreeable to a Law of the State of New york made and provided in such cases

Attest——MORDECAI HOMAN Clerk

At a Meeting of the Trustees of the Freeholders and

Commonalty of the Town of Brookhaven held this first Day of Nov. 1808 Present at s,d Meeting Wm. Jayne President John Rose Ebenezer Hartt Thomas Strong Daniel Saxton Barnabas Smith Trustees at s,d Meeting s,d Trustees Voted and agreed that they would not prosecute any Inhabitant or Persons of the Town of Brookhaven for Catching Oysters in the South Bay that is in partnership with s,d Town and the Heirs of Major William Smith Deceas,d providing s,d person or persons do not carry any of s,d Oysters out of s,d Town or dispose of any of s,d Oysters to any foreigner or person for the purpose of Carrying S,d Oysters out of s,d Town—

PAGE 46.

Also at s,d Meeting it was Voted and agreed and hereby Enacted by the authority of the Same that if any Person or Persons do kill any Brant or other Wild foul in the South Bay that is in partnership with s,d Town and the Heirs of Wm. Smith Deceas,d or that is in partnership with s,d Town and Gen. John Smith or shall carry them out of s,d Town every Person so offending shall forfeit and pay to the Trustees aforesaid or their order the Sum of Twenty Dollars for each and every offence to be sued for and recovered by s,d Trustees or their order before any Court having Cognizance thereof to be applied to the use of s,d Town

Attest MORDECAI HOMAN Clerk

PAGE 47.

At a Meeting of the freeholders and Inhabitance of the Town of Brookhaven held at the House of Goldsmith Davis,s Inn keeper in Coram on Tuesday the fourth day of April 1809—it Being Town Meeting Day agreeable to a Law of the State of New York and the following Town officers were unanumously Chosen—

Viz—   Caleb M. Hulse President

Isaac Davis Stoney Brook }
William Helme
Isaac Overton Esq.
Daniel Tooker
Benjamin Hallock
Barnabas Wines
Mordecai Homan Town Clerk and Treasurer
John Rose Supervisor—
Amos Smith Collector

Jonas Hawkins }
William Helme
Benjamin Hallock } Assessors
Isaac Overton Esq.
John Robinson

John Wilsee }
Jacob Hawkins } Commissioners
James Robinson

PAGE 48.

Amos Smith
Ebenezer Pam
James Robinson
Nathan Post } Constables
Samuel Homan
Israel Smith
Sylvenas Overton

OVERSEERS OF HIGHWAYS

Jonas Hawkins   Jonathan Hallock
Nathaniel Akerly   John Robinson
Wm Jayne   Isaac Homan
Ebenezer Jones   Henry Dayton
Daniel Bailey   George Brown
Nathaniel Davis   Thomas Aldrilch
Timothy Miller   Benjamin Halock
Ichabod Carter PAGE 49. Samuel Hammond
Joseph Raynor   Isaac Smith Hills
David Robinson   Wm. Still
Jeremiah Havens Junr. John Hulse
and Benjamin Smith   William Swezey
James Moore

James Conklin
William Hawkins
Phiehas Robinson
Daniel Smith
Ketcham Terry

David Davis
Briant Norton
Caleb Newton
William Tooker
Isreal Hawkins

FENCE VIEWERS

Jonas Davis
Timothy Davis
Ebenezer Baile
Benjamin Hawkins
Wm Jayne
Isaac Brewster   PAGE 50.
James Davis
Nathaniel Davis
Nathaniel Davis
William Helme
Peter Skidmore
Jonathan Worth
Ebenezer Wines
Jerrus Wines
James Stansbro
Ichabod Carter

Benjamin Smith
Mordecai Homan
Ira Downs
Joseph Hedges
Barnabas Smith
Daniel Smith
Moses Wicks
Samuel Bishop
Epenetus Mills
Mordecai Homan
William Phillips
Nehemiah Overton
Brewster Terry
William Swezey
Isaac Hammond
James Post

PAGE 51.

Voted that all hogs runing on the Commons to be Yoked and Rignd—

PAGE 52.

Suffolk County ss.

Statement of Votes taken at the Anniversary Electon for Senators which Commencd on the last Tuesday of April one thousand Eight hundred and Nine

Senators

Isreal Carll two hundred and thirty three ⎫
Benjamin B. Blydenburgh one hundred and Nineteen ⎬ Votes
Benjamin Blydenburgh two—— ⎪
Brewster B. Blydenburgh one ⎭

We certify the above to be a true Statement and Estimate of the Votes taken in the Town of Brookhaven at the aforesaid Election this Twenty Seventh day of April 1809

JOHN ROSE
ISAAC OVERTON
WILLIAM H. HELME } Inspectors
JONAS HAWKINS
JOHN ROBINSON

Attest MORDECAI HOMAN Town Clerk

PAGE 53.

Suffolk County ss.

Statement of Votes taken at the anniversary Election for Assembly which Commenced on the last Tuesday in April one thousand Eight hundred and Nine—

ASSEMBLY

John Rose two hundred and Seventy
Abraham Rose two hundred and Seventy one
Tredwell Scudder two hundred and Seventy one } Votes
Merritt S. Woodhull one hundred and thirty one
John Woodhull one hundred and thirty
Cornelius Sleight one hundred and twenty Nine

We Certify the above to be a true Statement and Estimate of the Votes taken at the aforesaid Election this 27th April 1809—

JOHN ROSE
ISAAC OVERTON
WILLIAM H HELME } Inspectors
JONAS HAWKINS
JOHN ROBINSON

Attest MORDECAI HOMAN Town Clerk

PAGE 54.

At a Meeting of the Trustees of the freeholders and Commonalty of the Town of Brookhaven held this 6th day of June 1809—Present at s,d Meeting

Caleb M. Hulse President

William Helme }
Isaac Overton }
Isaac Davis } Trustees
Benjamin Halliock }
Barnabas Wines }

At s,d Meeting application was made to sd, Trustees by Zecheriah Sandford to Build a dock out into the South Bay against his own Land and the s,d Trustees after Consulting the Matter Granted the Request accordingly Vis. that Zechariah Sandford should have Liberty to Build a Dock out into the South Bay against his own Land

Attest MORDECAI HOMAN Town Clerk

PAGE 55.

ACTS OF TRUSTEES at a Meeting of the Trustees of the freeholders and Commonalty of the Town of Brookhaven held in s,d Town this first Day of May in the Year of our Lord one thousand Eight hundred and Nine present at s,d Meeting Caleb M. Hulse President Isaac Davis William Helme Isaac Overton Benjamin Halliock Daniel Tooker Barnabas Wines Trustees at s,d Meeting s,d Trustees in order to preserve the Oysters that is in the south Bay for the benefit of the Inhabitance of s,d Town in general and the heirs of Wm. Smith Deceas,d, therefore we the s,d Trustees have Voted and agreed and hereby Enacted by the Authority in us invested that no Oysters nor shells of Oysters shall be taken or Catched in the south Bay that is in partnership with s,d Town and the Heirs of William Smith Deceas,d by any person or persons whoever after the Eighth Day of May Instant on penalty of forfeiting to the s,d Trustees or their Successors the Sum of Twenty Dollars for each and every offence to be Sued for as any other debt by the s,d Trustees or their order and recovered in any Court having Cognizance thereof to be applied to the use of S,d Town &C and it is hereby Enacted by the Authority aforesaid that if any Oysters or shells of Oysters

Page 56.

Shall be found on Board of any Vessell or Small Craft within the Bounds or Limits as aforesaid or if any Person or Persons shall aid or assist in Conveying or shall carry any Oysters or Shells of Oysters out of s,d Town or if any person or Persons whoever shall have any Oysters or shells of Oysters found in his her or their possession it shall be deemed Sufficient proof to convict the offender as aforesaid unless such person or persons shall make it appear to the satisfaction of s,d Trustees that such Oysters or Shells of Oysters were put on Board of such Vessel or Small Craft or in his her or their possession for the purpose of fraud all former Acts orders or Resolves Respecting Oysters or shells of Oysters are hereby Repealed——

Also an Act passed the third day of June in the year of our Lord one thousand Eight hundred and Six which prohibits the taking or Catching any Clambs or Horsfish in any of the Bays or Harbors within the Bonds or Limits of the Town of Brookhaven for the purpose of Conveying them out of s,d Town or shall Carry them out of s,d Town is hereby Revised and confirmed on penalty of Twenty Dollars for each and every Offence excepting such persons as shall obtain leave of the sd Trustees or their order to Carry Clambs out of sd Town on paying a toleration of three Cents on every Bushel to be Carry,d out of s,d Town

CALEB M. HULSE President
Attest MORDECAI HOMAN Town Clerk

Page 57.

Also at the aforesaid Meeting Josiah Smith of Morriches and Epenetus Mills at Bluepoint were appointed tolerating Masters to tolerate people to Catch Clambs for the purpose of Carrying them out of the Town on paying three Cents on every Bushel

Attest, MORDECAI HOMAN Town Clerk

At a Meeting of the Trustees of the freeholders and Commonalty of the Town of Brookhaven held this first day of August one thousand Eight hundred and Nine Caleb M. Hulse President Isaac Davis Daniel Tooker Wm. Helme Benjamin Halliock Isaac Overton Barnabas Wines Trustees at s,d Meeting John Wilsey made application for Liberty to Dock out into Drown Meadow Bay against his own Land and the Trustees having Consulted on the Businesses do by these presents grant Liberty to the s,d John Wilsey to Dock out into Drown Meadow Bay against his own Land the Distance of Six Rods from Common low Water Reserving a Right for the Inhabitance of Brookhaven to pass and Repass on s,d Dock free from any Tax or Toll with any Bundle or Burthen not exceeding one hundred Weight—

Attest, MORDECAI HOMAN Town Clerk

Page 58.

Brookhaven 12th Sept. 1809

At a Meeting of the Trustees of the freeholders and Commonalty of the Town of Brookhaven for the time being held in s,d Town this fifth Day of September one thousand Eight hundred and Nine at s,d Meeting s,d Trustees Voted and agreed and hereby Enacted that any Inhabitant of the Town of Brookhaven and those persons living within the outlines of s,d Town Viz a South Line from Stoney Brook to the South Bay shall after the first Day of October Ensueing have liberty to Catch Oysters in the South Bay for their own Consumption and the Inhabitance of s,d Town providing such Person do not Act Contrary to the Restrictions hereafter mentioned Viz—No Person or Persons are permitted Either foreignor or Inhabitant of s,d Town to Carry any Oysters out of s,d Town unless Such Person shall obtain a permitt of the Agent of s,d Trustees appointed for that purpose for Such Quantity of Oysters as shall be thought proper by s,d Agent and shall give a true

Account thereof unto the s,d Agent and before they depart from s,d Town with their Vessels Crafts or Carriages shall be inspected by s,d Agent and shall pay unto the sd Agent Six Cents on every hundred of Oysters they shall so have as a toleration for the use of the

PAGE 59.

Town of Brookhaven.—any Person Acting contrary to these restrictions shall be considered as transgressors and shall pay unto the sd Trustees or their order the forfieture of Twenty Dollars for each and every offense to be sued for by the s,d Trustees or their order and recovered in any Court having Cognizance thereof and applied to the use of s,d Town. and if any Person or Persons shall put any Oysters on Board of any Vessell Craft or Carriage or dispose of any Oysters to any Person for foreign Market the Owner whereof or Person having not obtaine,d permission as aforesaid such person shall be considered as an offender and subject to the aforesaid penalty, Also the privilege of Catching s,d Oysters is reserved for the Inhabitance of s,d Town and all foreigners are hereby excluded from Catching s,d Oysters on penalty as aforesaid as Witness my hand and the Seal of Brookhaven Day and date above Written.

CALEB M. HULSE President L S

Attest. MORDECAI HOMAN Town Clerk

N. B Epenetus Mills at Blue point is appointed as Agent in sd Business——

PAGE 60.

At a Meeting of the Trustees of the freeholders and Commonalty of the Town of Brookhaven for the time Being held in s,d Town this fifth Day of November in the Year of our LORD one thousand Eight Hundred and Nine—

Whereas George Hallock of s,d Town hath made application to s,d Trustees for Liberty to Build a Dock or Wharff at Stoney Brook Harbor at a place Call,d the deep hole adjoining his own Land and the s,d Trustees after duly Considing the matter do by information and what they

PAGE 61.

know of the matter consider it to be of Material Advantage not only to individuals but to the public in general therefore we the s,d Trustees do hereby Grant Liberty to the s,d George Hallock to Build a Dock or Whrff at s,d place adjoining his own Land under the following Restrictions Viz. the s,d George Hallock is hereby permitted to Build a Dock or Whrff at the aforementioned place one Hundred feet in Length on the shore and fifty feet in Width from Common high Water mark but not to hinder or obstruct people from passing or repassing to and from the West meadow as usual and the s,d George Hallock is hereby allowed the Sum of Seventy five Cents for any Vessel of thirty Tons Burthen or upwards to load or unload at s,d Dock to be paid by the Master or Owener of such Vessel and all light Vessels making fast to s,d Dock and Lying a day or part of a Day shall pay the sum of twelve and half Cents unless such Vessell makes fast to s,d Dock for the purpose of geting under Way only and all empty Vessells shall make way for Vessels to Load or unload and the s,d George Hallock is to keep s,d Dock in good Repair otherwise this Grant to be Void and of no effect and any person shall have the priviledge of making fast to s,d Dock with their small Crafts and pass and repass on sd Dock with any Bundle or Burthen not exceeding five Hundred Weight free from any Tax or Toll—As Witness our hands this day and Date above Written——

CALEB M. HULSE president
Attest by me MORDECAI HOMAN Town Clerk.

PAGE 62.

This doth certify that on the Second day of January one

thousand Eight Hundred and Ten Joseph Davis of the Town of Brookhaven Made application to the Trustees of s,d Town for the time being to Manumate a Negro Woman of his by the name or named Elizabeth and the s,d Trustees Being satisfied that the sd Negro Woman is under the age of forty five years and of Sufficient ability to support herself do therefore at the Request of the s,d Joseph Davis Manumate and set free s,d Elizabeth according to the Statute Law of the State of New York made and provided in such cases——

Attest,d MORDECAI HOMAN Town Clerk

This doth certify that on the Second day of January one thousand Eight hundred and Ten Jeremiah Havens of the Town of Brookhaven made application to the Trustees of s,d Town for the time Being to Manumate a Negre Slave of his named David and s,d Trustees being Satisfied that s,d Negro Man is under the age of forty five Years and of Sufficient abilities to support himself do therefore at the request of the s,d Jeremiah Havens Manumate and set free s,d David agreeable to a Statute Law of the State of New made and provided in such cases—

Attest,d MORDECAI HOMAN Town Clerk

PAGE 63.

Suffolk County ss—

Whereas providence hath removed by Death the president of the Trustees of the freeholders and Commonalty of the Town of Brookhaven and whereas the Statute Law of the State of New York Relative to the duties and priviledge of the Several Towns in this State Bearing date the Twenty seventh of March one thousand Eight Hundred and one wherein s,d Act makes it the duty of three Justices of the Peace in the Same County Residing near to Such Town we whose names are hereunder Written do Nominate and appoint Selah Strong Esq.—To act as president of s,d Trustees until the next Annual Town Meeting given under our hands and Seals this Sixth Day of February in the year of our Lord one thousand Eight Hundred and Ten

        JONAS HAWKINS }
        JOHN NEWTON } Justices
        ISAAC SATTERLY }

Enterd by order of s,d Justices
    Attest,d MORDECAI HOMAN Town Clerk

PAGE 64.

Brookhaven 5th March 1810

Description of a Road Laid out by Jacob Hawkins James Robinson and John Wilsie—We the Commissioners of high Ways for the Town of Brookhaven being petitioned by a Number of freeholders of sd Town have proceeded agreeable to Law to Lay out a Road in the Western part of Setaket Beginning at a large Chesnut tree upon the South Side of the highway leading from the Mill at Setaket to the Landing at Stoney Brook (by the House of Nehemiah Hawkins) thence Running Easterly across the Land of Isreal Bennit the Second Eighteen Rods more or less to the end of Ditch in the Land of Israel Hawkins three Rods Wide as Witness our hands

      JACOB HAWKINS } Commissioners
      JAMES ROBINSON } of highway
      JOHN WILSIE   }

Enterd 7th March 1810 by MORDECAI Town Clerk

We the Commissioners of highway for the Town of Brookhaven on examining the Record we find a highway Laid out from the old Mans to the Wading River we Continue the s,d public highway to the Middle of Mr. Jonathan Worths Mill pond to a Certain Stake we set up by his Consent

as Witness our hands in Brook haven this Tenth Day of March 1810

JOHN WILSIE } Commissioners
JAMES ROBINSON

Enterd this 12th March 1810
    by me MORDECAI HOMAN Town Clerk

PAGE 65.

Brookhaven 10th April 1810.

Whereas Jonathan Worth of the Wading River insd Town made application to the Trustees of s,d Town to appoint a Committee from the Body of Trustees to examen into the Grant that was Given by the Town to Build a Mill at the Wading River and we the s,d Committee having Viewed the s,d premises do give it as our Opinion that he the sd Jonathan Worth has not gone beyond his Limits or Grant as Witness our hands this 13rd Day of April 1810

WILLIAM H. HELME } Committee
BENJAMIN HALLOCK

Enterd this 13d April 1810
    by me MORDECAI HOMAN Town Clerk

NOTE.—Page 66 blank. Com.

PAGE 67.

OVERSEERS OF HIGHWAYS.

Jonas Hawkins	Isreal Bennett
Jedediah Hartt	John Wilsee
Spicer Davis	Nethaniel Davis
Nethaniel Davis Millrs place	Jonathan Hallock
Daniel Swezey	Zopher Mills
Benjamin Raynor	Noadiah Carter
David Robinson	Jeremiah Havens
Ebenezer Hartt	Wm. Smith
Joseph Homan	Wm Hawkins
Phinehas Robinson	Justus Roe
David Leek	Charles Gerard
Jacob Corwin	George Brown
Jeremiah Randal	Benj. Hallock
Samuel Hamond	Brewster Terry
Noah Overton	Wm. Swezey
David Davis	Briant Norton
Wm. Tooker	Caleb Newton

Isreal Hawkins   Daniel Saxton
              FENCE VIEWERS.

Jonas Davis   Timothy Davis
Jacob Hawkins Jr   Nethaniel Tooker
Wm Jayne   Isaac Brewster
Nethaniel Davis   Timothy Miller
James Davis   Nethaniel Davis
Peter Skidmore   Jonathan Worth
James Robinson   Justus Overton
James Post   Benj Smith
Timothy Rose   Robert Ellison
Wm. Beale   Justus Roe
Samuel Bishop   Epenetus Mills
Barnabas Smith   Joseph Hedges
Daniel Saxton   James Smith
Nathan Corwin   Wm. Saxton
David Davis   Henry Dayton
Brewster Terry   Daniel Overton

PAGE 68.

Nicoll Floyd President of trustees
James Davis   ⎫
Justus Overton   ⎪
John Robinson   ⎬ Trustees
Benjamin Hallock   ⎪
Robert Ellison   ⎪
Abraham Woodhull   ⎭

Jonas Hawkins Supervisor
Mordecai Homan Town Clerk & Treasurer
Nathan Post Collector

Josiah Smith
Daniel Tooker
Merritt S. Woodhull
James Smith
William Helme or Isaac Overton

William Helme   ⎫
Jacob Hawkins   ⎬ Commissioners
Isaac Overton E   ⎭

CONSTABLES

Samuel Homan   Nathan Post
Isreal Smith   Ebenezer Payne
John Bishop   Timothy Davis
Richard Robinson   Amos Smith

NOTE.—The records do not state when the above town officers were elected. Com.

PAGE 69.

Suffolk County s s

Statement of Votes taken at the Anniversary Election for Govenor Lieut. Govenor and Senator which Commenced on the last Tuesday of April one thousand Eight hundred and Ten

GOVENOR

Daniel D. Tompkins had two hundred and forty nine } Votes
Jonas Platt had one hundred and thirty one }

LIEUT. GOVENOR

John Broom had two hundred and forty Nine } Votes
Nicholas Fish had one hundred and thirty one }

SENATOR,S

Ebenezer White had two hundred and forty Eight } Votes
Richard hatfield had one hundred and thirty one }

We certify the foregoing to be a true Statement and Estimate of the Votes taken in the Town of Brookhaven at the aforesaid Election 27th April 1810

JONAS HAWKINS }
MERRITT S. WOODHULL } Assessors
JAMES SMITH }
WILLIAM H. HELME }

Attest MORDECAI HOMAN Town Clerk

PAGE 70.

Suffolk County s s

Statement of Votes taken at the Anniversary Election for Representative to Congress which Commenced on the Last Tuesday in April one thousand Eight hundred and

Ten
CONGRESS

Ebenezer Sage had two hundred and Eighty two
David Gardiner had one hundred and Twenty four } Votes

We Certify the above Statement and Estimate of the Votes taken in the Town of Brookhaven at the aforesaid Election April 27th. 1810

JONAS HAWKINS
MERRITT S. WOODHULL
JAMES SMITH
WILLIAM H. HELME } Inspectors

Attest. MORDECAI HOMAN Town Clerk

PAGE 71.

Suffolk County ss

Statement of Votes taken at the Anniversary Election for Assembly which Commenced on the last Tuesday in April one thousand Eight hundred and Ten

ASSEMBLY

Jonathan S. Conklin had two hundred and Eighty three
Thomas S. Lester had two hundred and Eighty four } Votes

Tredwell Scudder had two hundred and Eighty three
Samuel Jayne had one hundred and twelve
Charles Colyer had one hundred and Eighteen } Votes

We Certify the above Statement and Estimate of the Votes taken at the aforesaid Election April 27th. 1810

JONAS HAWKINS
MERRITT S. WOODHULL
JAMES SMITH
WILLIAM H HELME

Attest,—MORDECAI HOMAN Town Clerk

PAGE 72.

An Act to regulate the fishing and fowling in the South Bay passed this Second day of May one thousand Eight hundred and Ten

Be it Ordained by the Trustees of the freeholders and Commonalty of the Town of Brookhaven that if any person or persons shall kill or take any Wild fowl on any of the Barrs or flatts lying in the South Bay in Company with the Heirs of William Smith Deceasd or in Company with Gen. John Smith without leave first obtained of the s,d Trustees or their Agent he or they for every such Offence shall forfeit and pay to the sd Trustees the Sum of twenty five Dollars to be Sued for and recovered in the Name of the Trustees aforesaid—

And be it further ordained by the Authority aforesaid that if any person or persons shall take or Catch any fish of any kind whatsoever in the South Bay belonging to the Town of Brookhaven the Heirs of William Smith Deceas,d and General John Smith without leave first obtain,d of the Trustees or their Agent he or they so offending shall forfeit and pay the sum of Twenty five Dollars to be sued for and recovered in the Name of the Trustees aforesaid. And be it further Ordain,d by the Authority aforesaid that all former Acts relating to Shooting or killing Wild fowl and taking or Catching fish

PAGE 73.

of any kind whatsoever in the Town aforesaid shall and are hereby Repealed.

{ SEAL. }   NICOLL FLOYD President

An Act to prevent the Catching or taking Shells passed this Second day of May 1810

Be it ordained by the Trustees of the freeholders of the Commonalty of the town of Brookhaven that if any person or persons shall Catch or take any shells in the South Bay in Company with the Town of Brookhaven the Heirs of William Smith Decd and General John Smith without leave first Obtained from the sd Trustees or their agent he or they for every Ofence shall forfeit and pay to the sd Trustees the sum of Twenty five Dollars to be Sued for and recovered in the Name of the Trustees aforesaid

{ SEAL }   NICOLL FLOYD President

NOTE. Page 74 Record cancelled. Com.

PAGE 75.

At a Meeting of the Trustees of the Freeholders and Commonalty of the Town of Brook Haven held on the 7th day of August 1810
Present

         Nicoll Floyd president
         Abraham Woodhull ⎫
         James Davis |
         Justus Overton   } Trustees
         John Robinson |
         & Robert Ellison   ⎭

Liberty was Given unto Elkanah Smith to build a Dock opposite the land of the said Elkanah Smith at Blue point to extend six rods into the bay at right angles with the shore the inhabitants of the Town aforesaid not to be deprived of the priviledge of using the dock provided they do not incumber or damage it

By order of the Trustees

         NICOLL FLOYD President
Attest, MORDECAI HOMAN Town Clerk

PAGE 76.

At a Meeting of the Trustees of the freeholders and Commonalty of the Town of Brookhaven held on the 4th day of September 1810
Present

Nicoll Floyd president
Abraham Woodhull ⎫
James Davis ⎪
Benjamin Hallock ⎬ Trustees
Justus Overton ⎪
Robert Ellison ⎭

It was Ordaind that if any person shall take any Oysters in the South Bay belonging to the Town aforesaid and the Heirs of William Smith Deceas,d or carry any out of the Town being taken or Catch,d therein without first obtaining a permit from the Trustees or their Agent and paying Eight pence for every hundred so taken shall for every such offence pay the Sum of Twenty five Dollars to be Sued for and recover,d in the name of the Trustees aforesaid—

And be it further ordaind that so much of that Act pass,d on the Second day of May last as relates to the prohibition of the Cathing of Oysters and Shells in the South Bay is hereby Repealed.

{ SEAL }   NICOLL FLOYD President

PAGE 77.

This doth Certify that on the fourth Day of September 1810 the Trustees of the Freeholders and Commonalty of the Town of Brookhaven for the time being agreed to raise one thousand Dollars by a Tax on the Inhabitance of sd Town to defray the Charges of the Poor and other Expences of sd Town

Attest. MORDECAI HOMAN Town Clerk

PAGE 78.

At a Meeting of the Freeholders and Inhabitance of the Town of Brook haven held in the sd Town on the 2nd. Day of April 1811—at the House of Goldsmith Davis Innkeeper in sd Town it being Town Meeting day the following Town Officers were unnanomously Elected agreeable to a

144   BROOKHAVEN TOWN RECORDS.

Law of the State of New York in such case directing—

OVERSEERS OF HIGHWAYS

Jonas Hawkins	Michael Wiggints
Nethaniel Tooker	Wm. Newins
Gilbert Floyd	Robert Hawkins
George Munroe	Jacob Corwin
Spicer Davis	George Brown
Isreal Davis	Jeremiah Randal
Wm H. Helme	Benj Hallock
Jonathan Hallock	Samuel Hammond
James Moore Senr	Brewster Terry
Zopher Mills	Noah Overton
Freeman Lane	David Davis
Lewis Gorden	William Swezey
John Havens	Wm Tooker
John Leek, Jur	Caleb Newton
Joseph Homan	Daniel Saxton
Elias Parshall	Isreal Hawkins
Isaac Woodruff	Asa Swezey

FENCE VIEWERS

Timothy Davis	Nathan Bartoe
Jonas Davis	Wm Beale
Jacob Hawkins	Justus Roe
Nethaniel Tooker	Samuel Bishop
Wm-Jayne	Epenetus Mills
Isaac Brewster	Austin Roe
Daniel Davis	Phinehes Robinson
Wells Davis	Daniel Saxton
Joseph Miller	John Akerly
Samuel Davis	Nathan Corwin
Peter Skidmore	John Bishop
Jonathan Worth	Davis Overton
Isaac Raynor	Daniel Terry
Joseph Raynor	James Howell
James Post	Wm Swezey
Benjamin Smith	David Davis
Nethaniel Hawkins	Nath. Munsel

PAGE 79.

Also a Vote Was taken by the freeholders that no Swine

should run in the Commons unless it is Sufficiently ringed and Yoked—and if they were found trespassing without being sufficiently ring,d and Yoked that the Owners thereof should pay such a fine as the Trustees of the Town shall inflict

PAGE 80.

Abraham Woodhull President

James Davis } Trustees
Benjamin Hallock
Justus Overton
William Beale
Timothy Rose
Zecheriah Sandford

Mordecai Homan Town Clerk & Treasurer
John Rose Supervisor
Nathan Post Collector

Merritt S. Woodhull } Assessors
James Smith
Josiah Smith
William Beale
Barnabas Wines

Elias Parshall } Commissioners of highways
Isaac Davis
Timothy Miller

Samuel Homan } Constables
Nathan Post,
Isreal Smith
Noah Overton
Elias Norton
Timothy Davis
Amos Smith
Richard Robinson
Isaac Woodruff

PAGE 81.

County of Suffolk }
Brookhaven.

We the Commissioners of highways of said Town being

Call,d by Doctr. Samuel Thompson and others have laid out a Public highway three Rods wide through Isreal Bennitt Junr. Land in said Town—begining at a Chesnut tree Standing on the West Side of said Land by the Road leading from Stoney Brook to Setaket town between the two houses of Israel and Nehemiah Hawkins and runing Easterly Across sd Land until it Comes to Israel Hawkins Line where the Path now goes for which we have agreed that the Town of Brookhaven shall pay unto the sd Isreal Bennitt the Sum of Twenty one Dollars and fifty Cents which we return to be recorded this 11th March 1811.

    JACOB HAWKINS }
    WILLIAM H. HELME Commissioners
    ISAAC OVERTON }
     Attest MORDECAI HOMAN Town Clerk

Enterd 3rd. April 1811

PAGE 82.

We the Commissioners for the Town of Brookhaven being Call,d by Daniel Homan and others have laid out a Road begining at the South end of Daniel Homans Mill Dam and runing Southerly where the Road now is that is calld Hubbards Road. until it Comes to Gerards Road thence southwesterly until it comes to the South east Corner of Barnabas Riders Cleared Lot—South of the Horseblock Road thence a direct Course to the South Country Road at the place where the Road leading to the head of the Beaver dam River parts from the South Country Road the sd Road is to be three Rods Wide Layd out 3rd. August 1810

    JACOB HAWKINS }
    WM. H. HELME Commissioners
    ISAAC OVERTON }

Enterd 3rd. April 1811

We the Commissioners for the Town of Brookhaven being Calld by George Lee and others to alter and Lay out a Road leading or runing from Rocky pond to Setauket we have laid it out from Zophar Hawkins,s House by the fence on the East side of the fence till it Comes to the Country Road four Rods Wide and then where the Said Road comes on the Line Between Ezra Hawkins and George Lee then we have altered it again and laid it out four Rods wide on the Line Between them till it Comes to the End of the Ditch then a Northwest Course til it Comes to the old Road—Laid out 30th August 1810—

JACOB HAWKINS
WILLIAM H. HELME } Commissioners
ISAAC OVERTON

Enterd 3rd. April 1811

Attest. MORDECAI HOMAN Town Clerk

PAGE 83.

Suffolk } ss
County

Statement of Votes taken at the Anniversary Election for Lieut. Govenor and Senator which Commenced on the last Tuesday of April one thousand Eight hundred and Eleven—

LIEUTENANT GOVENOR

Dewitt Clinton had one hundred and Seventy
Marinus Willet had forty two } Votes
Nicholas Fish had Eighty six

SENATORS

Nathan Sandford had two hundred and fourteen } Votes
John Vanderbilt Jun had Eighty two

We certify the foregoing to be a true Statement and Estimate of the Votes taken in the Town of Brookhaven at the aforesaid Election May 2nd. 1811

JOHN ROSE
MERRITT S. WOODHULL } Inspectors
JOSIAH SMITH
BARNABAS WINES

Attest. MORDECAI HOMAN Town Clerk

PAGE 84.

Suffolk County } ss

Statement of Votes taken at the Anniversary Election which Commenced on the last Tuesday of April one thousand Eight hundred and Eleven for Members of Assembly—

ASSEMBLY

Abraham Rose Two hundred and thirty five ⎫
Nathaniel Potter Two hundred and thirty Six ⎟
Usher H. Moore one hundred and Seventy ⎬ Votes
five ⎟
Thomas S. Lester Sixty one— ⎭

We Certify the foregoing to be a true Statement and Estimate of the Votes taken in the Town of Brookhaven at the aforesaid Election this 2nd. of May 1811—

JOHN ROSE ⎫
MERRITT S. WOODHULL ⎬ Inspectors
JOSIAH SMITH ⎟
BARNABAS WINES ⎭

Attest MORDECAI HOMAN Town Clerk

PAGE 85.

At a Meeting of the Trustees of the freeholders and Commonalty of the Town of Brookhaven held this Seventh day of May in the Year of our Lord one thousand Eight Hundred and Eleven at sd Meeting it was Voted and agreed and hereby Ordained by the Authority aforesaid that any Inhabitant of the Town of Brookhaven shall have Liberty to Catch fish in the South Bay that is in partnership with the Town of Brookhaven and the Hiers of William Smith Decesd or General John Smith and make use of them for their own Consumption and for the Consumption of the Inhabitance of s,d Town but not to Sell any Such fish to any foreignor or send or sell them for any foreign Market unless such person shall pay unto the Trustees aforesaid or their Agents a toleration of six Cents for every sheepshead and three Cents for every Bass that they (or any person) shall so attempt or wish to Carry to any foreign Market and any person or Persons who shall be guilty of Selling any fish to any foreignor or whoever shall Carry and fish out of the Town of Brookhaven without first having their fish Inspected by the Agent or Agents appointed by this Board for that purpose and paying the toleration before mentioned every person or persons so offending shall forfeit and pay unto the Trustees or their Order the Sum of Twenty five Dollars to be Sued for and recoverd in the Name of the Trustees aforesaid in any Court having Cognisance thereof and applied to the use of the Town and any person who shall be guilty of sending

PAGE 86.

or Selling any fish as aforesaid shall be debarred from the priviledge of Catching fish and be liable to be fined as was specified in an Act passed the 2nd. May 1810 and be it further Ordained that all and every person are prohibited from Catching any Oysters in the South Bay from this date until a further order of sd Trustees, and William Hawkins William Baker and Epenetus Mills is appointed as Agents and tolerators to inspect and receive the toleration above mentioned

ABRAHAM WOODHULL President { SEAL }

7th May 1811   Attest MORDECAI HOMAN Town Ck.—

An Act to prevent Swine from runing in the Commons unless Sufficiently ringed and Yoked

Be it ordained by the Trustees of the freeholders and Commonalty of the Town of Brookhaven that no Swine shall be permitted to run on any of the Commons belonging to the Town of Brookhaven (Sucking Pigs excepted) unless such Swine is Sufficient Yoked and ringed in the Nose on penalty of twelve and half Cents for every day such swine shall run on the Commons aforesaid to be Sued for and recovered in the Name of the Trustees aforesaid and applied to the use of the Town

                ABRAHAM WOODHULL   { President Seal }
Attest MORDECAI HOMAN Town Clk

PAGE 87.

This doth Certify that Wessell Sell of the Town of Brook haven on the 7th April 1811—made application to the Trustees of the Town of Brook haven to Manumate a Negro Slave of his named Titus and S,d Trustees being Satisfied that sd Negro Slave was under the age of forty five Years and of Sufficient ability to Support and maintain himself—do therefore Manumate and Set free sd Negro Slave according to the Satute of this State in such Cases made and provided

                        ABRAHAM WOODHULL
      Attest MORDECAI HOMAN Town Clerk

PAGE 88.

At a Meeting of the members and Congregation of the first Presbyterian Church in the Town of Brookhaven in Suffolk County held the Twenty fourth day of January in the Year of our LORD one thousand Eight Hundred and Eleven 1811 it was agreed to by all the s,d Members and Congregation whose names are hereunto Subscribed that the Worship of the true GOD is infinately important and is esteemed by his sincere friends and followers the greatest and most precious priviledge they enjoy on Earth. In Ancient Days the Tabernacle the Temple and afterwards the Synagogues were Erected for that purpose.

In them GOD met his people blessed and comforted them and from the Introduction of the Gospel by the Son of God the priviledges and Blessings of his Deciples have been greater and more extensive and wherever they with meekness and unanimity Build a house for his Honour and Worship there they have reason humbly to hope he will Come and Record his Name and graciously establish enlarge and Build them up in the pure Doctrins and faith of the Gospel—

Therefore in the View of these benign and Christian sentiments we the aforesaid Members and Congregation of the first Presbyterian Church in the Town of Brookhaven in Suffolk County and State of New York having taken into

PAGE 89.

Consideration the necessity of a New convenient and comfortable House for the public and honorable Worship of GOD, do unanimously agree to the following Articles which shall be Binding upon ourselves and our Heirs—Viz—

Article first—

We mean to be known by the title of the first Presbyterian Church and Congregation in Brookhaven and be Governed According to the word of God as explained and understood in the Directory of the Presbyterian Church in the United States of AMERICA—

Article 2nd.

The House shall be known by the Name of the first Presbyterian Church in Brookhaven

Article 3rd.

The use and priviledge of the pulpit shall uniformly be under the controul and directions of the Stated Pastor of the Church and Congregation and shall not be occupied occasionally by any other person except by the Consent of the Church session whose decision shall ever be in conformity to the Presbyterian Church in the United States of America—

PAGE 90.

Article 4th.

All persons desirous of uniting with this Church and Congregation in their mode of Worship and being willing to bear their proportion of expence shall be admitted to such priviledges.—

Article 5th.

When the Church is compleated and fit for use it shall be free for the Members and Congregation who have hereunto Subscribed their names to take their Seats where they think proper only with the exception of a Seat reserved for the Ministers family and a due respect to old age and it shall Continue in this Situation till a Majority of the proprietors Judg it necessary to make other Arangments—

At the Same Meeting Abraham Woodhull Thomas Strong Isaac Brewster Isaac Satterly John Mount Nethaniel Akerly and Jacob Hawkins were Chosen Trustees to Erect the sd Meeting House.

Registered by me this 4th June 1811—

MORDECAI HOMAN Town Clerk

PAGE 91.

At a Meeting of the Trustees of the freeholders and commonalty of the Town of Brookhaven held in sd Town this third day of September 1811 Present at sd Meeting —Abraham Woodhull President James Davis Zecheriah Sandford Justus Overton Timothy Rose Benjamin Hallick William Beale Trustees.—Application being made to the Trustees aforesaid that they would Grant unto the Society of the first Presbyterian Church in the Town of Brookhaven a Certain piece of Land Situate in Setaket and the sd Trustees after a due consideration had in the premises, do hereby grant unto the sd Society and to their Successors a Certain Piece of Land belonging to s,d Town lying in Setaket, Begining at the Northwest Corner of Benjamin Floyd,s home lot near the Episcopal Church running a Strait Line Southerly to a Certain Rock nearly level with the Ground and about two Rods or thereabout lying westerly in front of the New first Presbyterian Church in the Town of Brookhaven and from thence a strait Line runing

Southerly to the Southwest Corner of the Burying Ground in Witness whereunto the President of the Trustees has set his hand and afixed the Seal of the Town of Brookhaven in the name of the Trustees aforesaid day and date above Written

in presence of Mordecai Homan Samuel Bishop

ABRAHAM WOODHULL President L S

{ SEAL }   Registerd by me MORDECAI HOMAN
                                        Town Clerk

PAGE 92.

Be it remembered that on the 3rd. day of September 1811—the Trustees of the Town of Brookhaven agreed to raise Eight hundred Dollars as a Tax on the Inhabitance of the Town aforesaid for the Support of the Poor and other expences of sd Town for the ensueing Year

Attest—MORDECAI HOMAN Town Ck.

We the Commissioners of highways for the Town of Brookhaven being Call,d by Nehemiah Overton to Lay out a private Road for his use Across the Land of Isaac Smith Whitehead K. Hulse and Caleb M. Hulse and we the sd Commissioners after having Viewed the premises have laid out a Private Road for the use of the s,d Nehemiah Overton Twenty feet in Width turning Easterly out of the Road that runs from the House of Joshua Smith,s Deceas,d to Isaac Smith, at a Certain place where there is a Cartway and where we have fixed the Bounds Extending Eastward across the Land of s,d Isaac Smith and Whitehead Hulse until it Come to the Road Leading Northward from David Overton thence Northard along the sd Road a few Rods until it Comes to a Road leading Eastward acros Caleb M. Hulse,s Land so Continuing Eastward on s,d Road until it Comes

PAGE 93.

to the Land of the sd Nehemiah Overton sd Road is to be Twenty feet wide Viz ten feet each way from the center of the oald Road and good easy swinging Gate allowed to be kept in Repair by the owners of the Land which we order to be Recorded—as Witness our hands in Brookhaven this 25 September in the Year 1811—

Isaac Davis
Timothy Miller } Commissioners
Parshall Elias   of highways

Enterd by me Mordecai Homan Town Clerk

We the Commissioners of highways for the Town of Brookhaven being Call,d by a number of Inhabitance of s,d Town to lay out a highway at the North End of the Long Lotts and after Viewing the primises do think it proper and Convenient therefore we the sd Commissioners have laid out a Public highway beginning at the Road Runing from Stoney Brook to Titus Gould,s at the North End of the Long Lotts in the first Division Runing Easterly by and with s,d long Lotts until it comes to the Eleventh Lott and to extend to the Northward the width of three Rods which we order to be Recorded this 11th October 1811.

Isaac Davis   } Commissioners
Timothy Miller   of
Elias Parshall   highways

Enterd by me Mordecai Homan Town Clerk

Page 94.

We the Commissioners of highways for the Town of Brookhaven Being duly Call,d by a Sufficient number of freeholders of s,d Town to Lay out a highway in the fireplace down through the Neck of Land belongin to Widow Elizabeth Terry and Stephen Bartoe and after Viewing the premises do Consider it necessary and Convenient for the Public and have therefore Laid out a Public highway with Gates Beginning a little to the Westward of the sd Elizabeth Terry,s House at the South Country Road and to run on the West Side of the sd Mrs Terrys Land and to run Southerly across her Lot adjoining the s,d Country Road Twenty feet in width then continuing Southerly acros the Land of the sd Mrs Terry as the Road now runs as far as the Gate Between her and Stephen Bartoe two Rods wide with the priviledge of six easy swinging Gates and then Continuing Southerly as the Road now Runs across the Land of the s,d Stephen Bartoe until it Comes to his Landing Place or the River where he has a Dock already Built or dam and the s,d Road is to be two Rods in width across the Land of s,d Bartoe from the Gate Between him and the sd Mrs Terry until it Come to the fence below his Barn and then three Rods in Width across the Lott and meadow to the Landing place or River which s,d three Rods is allowed for to accommodate the Public to Lay Wood Coal Lumber &.C. so as not to hinder people from passing and repassing reserving to the sd Stephen Bartoe the Right of two easy swinging Gates on sd Road to be by him kept in repair and a right for him to Straiten

Page 95.

the Road through his woods in such manner as will not discommode or hurt the highway which s,d highway with all its priviledges we order to be Recorded in the Book of Records for the Town of Brookhaven Given under our hand in Brookhaven this 15th day of Octr. 1811—

Isaac Davis } Commissioners
Elias Parshall } of highways

Enterd by me Mordecai Homan Town Clerk

A Jury of View was Call,d to prize sd Road and allowed unto the s,d Mrs Terry the Sum of Seventy five Dollars and to Mr Bartoe Ninety Dollars for their Land and damage—

Suffolk } Brookhaven 10th October 1811—
County }

We the Commissioners of highways being Call,d by Benjamin Jones and Stephen Edwards to Stop up a Road which had been used Occasionally by the Inhabitance of s,d Town and after taking a View of the Same and finding Said Road to lie between the Nassakeag Road and the Road leading from Setaket to Coram and on finding s,d Road to be of little use to the public do order the Same to be shut up at the discretion of the Owners of the Land through which it Runs which we return to be Recorded

     Isaac Davis
     Elias Parshall } Commissioners
     Timothy Miller

  Enterd by me Mordecai Homan Town Clerk

Page 96.

Be it Remembered that on the Second day of December 1811 Joseph Jayne of the Town of Brookhaven Made application to the Trustees of sd Town of Brookhaven to Manumate and set free a Certain Man Slave of his named Limas and sd Trustees being Satisfied that sd Servent is under the age of fifty Years and of Sufficient ability to Support and maintain himself do therefore at the request of the Master and agreeable to the Statute of the State of New York Manumate and Set free sd Servent Accordingly

    Attest, Mordecai Homan Town Clerk

Brook haven 2nd Dec. 1811

This doth certify that on the 7th day of January 1812 in the Year of our Lord the Trustees of Brookhaven Sold unto Jacob Hawkins a piece of Land belonging to sd Town lying in Setaket Bounded West by the Road that goes to old field North so as to take in the House of Samuel Sibbs East by the Bank and South by the Land and Meadow of the sd Jacob Hawkins Containing about two acres—more or less sd Land was Sold for the Sum of Ten Dollars—1812

Attest—Mordecai Homan Town Clerk

Page 97.

We the Commissioners of highways for the Town of Brookhaven being Call,d to View and Establish a Road or highway that runs between the Land of Nathaniel Tuthill and James Woodhull and having Viewed the Same do adjudge and order the Same to be where it now Runs—

And also we the Subscribers have established a Road to the Landing place setting off from the highway between Nathaniel Tuthill and James Woodhull and running through the Land of Nathaniel Tuthill as the Road now Runs to the Landing place of the sd Nathaniel Tuthill and request the same to be Recorded—

Elias Parshall } Commissioners
Timothy Miller } of highways

Brookhaven 14th March 1812 Mordecai Homan Town Clerk

Page 98.

At a general Town Meeting of the freeholders and Inhabitance of the Town of Brookhaven held this 7th. day of April 1812 at the House of Goldsmith Davis Inn keeper in Coram for the purpose of Choosing Town Officers agreeable the Law of this State in such Case directing the following Persons were unanimously elected

William H. Helme President

Joseph B. Roe
Nathan Post
Benjamin Hutchenson
William Beale } Trustees
Isaac Satterly
John Robinson

John Rose Supervisor
Mordecai Homan Town Clerk
Nathan Post Collector

Josiah Smith
Isaac Satterly } Assessors
William Beale

Benjamin Hallock
Merritt S. Woodhull } Commissioners of highways
Nethaniel Akerly
John Rose
Benjamin Hallock

Nathan Post
Samuel Smith
Nathaniel Robinson
Hedges Osborn } Constables
David Carter
Elias Norton
Stephen Still

PAGE 99.

OVERSEERS OF HIGHWAYS.

Jonas Hawkins	Daniel Tooker Deacon
Samuel Satterly	Ebenezer Jones
Spicer Davis	Isreal Davis
Isaac Miller	Phillip Hallock
Hendrickson Hallock	Zopher Mills
Aron Robinson	Lewis Gorden
John Havens	John Leek Jur
Joseph Homan	Elias Parshall
Joseph Robinson	Michael Wiggints
David Leek	Humpry Avery
Isaac Mills	Jacob Corwin Jur
George Brown	Jeremiah Randal
Joshua Swezey Jur.	Samuel Hammond
Brewster Terry	Noah Overton
David Davis	William Swezey
William Tooker	Caleb Newton
Daniel Saxton	Isreal Hawkins
Samuel Lane	

FENCE VIEWERS

Timothy Davis	Jonas Davis
Jacob Hawkins	Nethaniel Tooker
William Jayne	Isaac Brewster
Daniel Davis	Wells Davis
Joseph Miller	Samuel Hopkins
Peter Skidmore	Jonathan Worth

Isaac Raynor	Joseph Raynor
James Post	Benj. Smith
Nethaniel Hawkins	Nathan Bartoe
Phinehas Robinson	Hedges Osbon
Wm. Beale	Justus Roe
Epenetus Mills	Joseph Homan
Daniel Saxton	Gideon Mills
Nathan Corwin	Davis Overton
James Howell	William Swezey
George Munroe	Willard Ruland
William Phillips	Nathaniel Munsel
David Terry	

PAGE 100.

By a Vote of the freeholders and commonalty the Act concerning hogs runing in the commons should be revised—

Also A Vote that no person should take any sand from this town without tolerating wishd that Joseph Hawkins should be inspeter—also that no Clambs should be carryed away without toleration Also that no Ram should run in the Commons between the last day of August until the first day of November

We the Commissioners of highways for the Town of Brookhaven being Call,d by Merritt S Woodhull to view and alter a Road that runs Eastward through the Millers place towards the Landing place of the s,d Merritt S. Woodhull Viz the Road that now Runs Between his Dwelling house and Store house and after having Viewed the same and finding that it will not discommode the public to alter s,d Road do hereby allow and permit the sd Merritt S. Woodhull to stop up the s,d Road and open it from the Corner of James Davis,s Land and so to Continue it along by the side of James Davis Land to the pond of Water which lies in the open way near the House of the sd James Davis which we return to be recorded in the Record of Brookhaven as witness our hands this 30th April 1812

    JOHN ROSE } Commissioners
    BENJAMIN HALLECK

Attest Mordecai Homan Town Clerk

Page 101.

Suffolk } ss
County }

Statement of Votes taken at the Annivarsary Election for Senators which commenced on the last tuesday in April one thousand Eight hundred and twelve—

William Furman had two hundred and thirty three
John Garretson had two hundred and thirty three
Peter W. Radcliff had Ninety Six
Elbert H. Jones had Ninety Six
John Bingham had two
Robert Moore had two
} Votes

We Certify the foregoing to be a true Statement and estimate of the Votes taken in the town of Brookhaven at the aforesaid Election this 30th April 1812

Merritt S. Woodhull
John Rose
Isaac Satterly
Benjamin Hallick
Josiah Smith
} Inspectors

Suffolk } ss
County }

Statement of Votes taken at the Anniversary Election for Congress which commenced on the Last tuesday in April one thousand Eight Hundred and twelve—

Ebenezer Sage had two hundred Seventy five
John Floyd one hundred and eleven
} Votes

We Certify the above to be a true Estimate and Statement of the Votes taken in the Town of Brookhaven at the aforesaid Election this 30th April 1812—

John Rose
Merritt S. Woodhull
Isaac Satterly
Benjamin Hallick
} Inspectors

Page 102.

Suffolk }
County }
Statment of Votes taken at the anniversary Election for Members of Assembly which commenced on the last tuesday of April one thousand Eight hundred and twelve

Caleb Smith had two hundred and seventy
Henry Rhodes had two hundred and Seventy one
Benjamin F. Thompson had two hundred and Sixty
Nathaniel Potter had Eight
John Jermain had one hundred thirteen
William Blydenburgh had one hundred thirteen
John Woodhull had one hundred fourteen
} Votes

We Certify the above to be a true Estimate and Statement of the Votes taken in the Town of Brookhaven at the aforesaid Election this 30th april 1812—

JOHN ROSE
MERRITT S. WOODHULL
ISAAC SATTERLY
BENJAMIN HALLICK
JOSIAH SMITH
} Inspectors

At a Meeting of the Trustees of the freeholders and Commalty of the Town of Brookhaven held in sd Town this fifth day of May 1812   Present at sd Meeting William H. Helme President William Beale Isaac Satterly Nathan Post Joseph B. Roe Benjamin Hutchinson John Robinson Trustees.

At sd Meeting Smith Mott made Application to sd Trustees for liberty to set up a frame in the South Bay about twenty-five Rods from the Shore opposite his own Land for the purpose of laying his Wood on and We the sd

Page 103.

Trustees after due consideration had in the premises do

consider that the sd priviledge will not discommode the public Navigation nor in nowise injure the public, do hereby grant liberty to the sd Smith Mott to set up a frame as aforesaid in the South Bay nearly opposite his own Land a little to the Westward of Connecticut River for the conveniancy of laying his wood on for Vessels to Land from s,d frame is to be forty feet by Sixteen and this Grant is Given for two Years and no longer which is done Accordingly—

WILLIAM H. HELME President—
Attest MORDECAI HOMAN Town Clrk

Also at the aforesaid Meeting the Act to prevent Swine from Running in the commons without being sufficiently Yoked and ringed in the Nose which was passed the 7th May 1811 is hereby revised

WILLIAM H. HELME President
Attest MORDECAI HOMAN Town Clerk.

PAGE 104.

This doth Certify that on the Second day of June 1812 Phillips Roe made application to the Trustees of the freeholders and commalty of the Town of Brookhaven to Manumate a Woman Slave of his named Betty. and the sd Trustees being Satisfied that sd Slave is under the age of fifty Years and of sufficient ability to provide for and maintain herself do therefore Manumate and Set free sd Woman Slave According to the Statute of the State of New York in such case directing——

Attest—MORDECAI HOMAN Town Clk

An Act to prevent Rams from runing at large for a certain time passed this second day of June one thousand Eight Hundred and twelve—Be it Ordained by the Trustees of the freeholders and Commonalty of the Town of

Brookhaven that if any Ram shall be found runing in the Commons or out of its Owners Inclosure Between the last day of August and the first day of November Ensueing the Owner thereof shall for Each and every such offence forfeit and pay the sum of fifty Cents to be sued for and Recover,d by any person who will sue for the Same According to the true intent and meaning of this Act.

WILLIAM H. HELME President

PAGE 105.

An Act to regulate the fishing and fowling in the South Bay passed this Second day of June 1812 Be it Ordained by the Trustees of the freeholders and commonalty of the Town of Brookhaven that if any person or persons shall kill or take any wild fowl on any of the Barrs flats or Waters in the South Bay that is in Co with the Town of Brookhaven the Heirs of William Smith deceas,d or General John Smith without leave first obtaind of the sd Trustees or their Agent he or they for every such Ofence shall forfeit and pay to the sd Trustees or their Order the sum of twenty five Dollars to be Sued for and recovered in the name of the Trustees Aforesaid—

And be it further Ordained by the Authority aforesaid that if any person or persons shall take any fish of any kind whatsoever in the South Bay belonging to the Town of Brookhaven the Heirs of William Smith deceas,d or General John Smith without leave first obtained of the sd Trustees or their Agent he or they for Each and every such offence shall forfeit and pay to the sd Trustees or their order the sum of Twenty five dollars to be sued for and recovered in the Name of the Trustees aforesaid and applied to the use of the Town—in witness whereof we have Caused the Seal of our s,d town to be affixed Isaac Overton and William Hawkins Jun is appointed Agents or Inspectors in the aforesaid premises—

William H. Helme { President. Seal }

Attest Mordecai Homan Town C.k

PAGE 106.

At a Meeting of the Trustees of the freeholders and Commonalty of the Town of Brookhaven held in s,d Town this first day of September 1812—complaint being made to sd Trustees that some persons have Staked out into the South Bay which greatly obstructs the Navigation thereof and prevents the drift from having its Natural course to the great disadvantage of Individuals and the public in general—therefore Be it Ordained by the Authority aforesaid that if any person or persons shall Stake dock or fence out into the South Bay below low Water Mark without leave first obtain,d of s,d Trustees and if any person having made any such Obstruction and shall not within one Week from the passing of this Act remoove and take away the same shall be considered an Offence and shall for each and every such offence forfeit and pay unto the s,d Trustees or their order the Sum of Ten Dollars to be sued for and recove,d by the s,d Trustees or their order in any Court having cognizance thereof and applied the use of sd Town—Provided always that this Act shall not prevent any person from making fence out into the South Bay at such place and places and to such a distance into the Bay as will be absolutely necessary to fence against Cattle and if any dispute shall arise concerning the place that is Necessary and the distance into the Water such dispute shall be decided by the fence Viewers of the Same district in Witness whereunto we have Set our hands and Caused the Seal our s,d Town to be fixed—

Isaac Satterly } Trustees
Nathan Post

Attest MORDECAI HOMAN Town Clerk   { Seal }

PAGE 107.

At a Meeting of the Trustees of the freeholders and Commonalty of the Town of Brookhaven held on the first day of September in the Year one thousand Eight hundred and twelve a petition was presented to the s,d Trustees for James Homan Junr. to have liberty to Set a dwelling House on the Common Land belonging to the town in the fireplace Between the House of Richard Corwins and Robert Ellison, on the West side of the highway and the s,d Trustees after due consideration had do hereby Grant liberty to the s,d James Homan to set a dwelling house on the West side of the highway Between the House of Robert Ellisons and Richard Corwins on the Common Land that belongs to s,d Town and also to have the privilege of one Quarter of an Acre of Ground for the use of a garden which grant is on the following Viz. the s,d James Homan shall not discommode the highway and shall take his House from off s,d Land at any time when ever the s,d Trustees shall see fit on their giving him three Months Notice or the House shall be forfeit and also when such order shall be given the Land is to return back to the Town again and the sd Homan shall have liberty to remove or sell his house to be removed at any time until it is forfeited but shall not Settle any other family there without a further grant from sd Trustees or their successors which is granted accordingly

Attest, MORDECAI HOMAN, Town Clk

PAGE 108.

We the Commissioners of high Ways for the Town of Brookhaven being call,d by Goldsmith Davis and others to lay out a public highway at Patchogue and having Viewed and examined into the premises have laid out a Road begining at the Country Road, Runing Southward til it comes to the head of Jonathan Bakers Meadow the width of the same being thirty feet from thence Runing the same direction to the Bay the Width of Eighteen feet we also allow one Easy swinging Gate on sd Road at the North end by the Country Road sd Road is to Run through the Lands of Daniel Smith Nathan Mulford and Jacob Baker and we do order and allow the Same to be recorded—given under our hands in Brookhaven this 3rd. day of June 1812—

    JOHN ROSE   } Commissioners
    BENJAMIN HALLICK

Attest MORDECAI HOMAN Town Clk.

We the Commissioners of highways being Calld by a Number of the Inhabitance of Patchogue to Lay out a Certain Road runing from sd place to Coram & having Viewed sd Road do think it Necessary for the public in general do therefore Lay out sd Road three Rods Wide begining at the south Country Road a little to the westward of John Mills, House from thence Runing Northward to Coram as the Road now runs—wich we allow and order to be recorded—

    JOHN ROSE   } Commissioners
    BENJAMIN HALLICK

Brookhaven 18th Dec 1812

PAGE 109.

We the Commissioners of highways for the Town of Brookhaven being Call,d by a Number of petioning Inhabitance of the Town of Brookhaven to lay out a highway Runing from the Middle Island to Daniel Swezeys Landing and having Viewed sd Road do think it is really necessary and convinient for the public or people adjoining thereunto in general we the sd Commissioners do Accordlay out sd highway begining at the Middle Country Road a few Rods Eastward of Mr. Jacob Corwins house from thence Runing Northwardly Across the sd Corwins Lott and so Continuing Northwardly to the North Country Road to the place where the Road goes down the hill to sd Swezeys Landing sd Road is three Rods in Width and is to run where the Road is now used and we also allow the sd Jacob Corwin to keep two good easy Swinging Gates on sd Road Viz one Each Side of his home Lott adjoinig the Country Road which s,d Road and the priviledges Respecting the same we do hereby order to be enterd on Brookhaven Record—

JOHN ROSE } Commissioners
BENJAMIN HALLICK }

Brookhaven 18th. December 1812

Attest MORDECAI HOMAN Town Clerk

The allowance of gates was released by J. Rockwell Smith for $30 in 1835 and release is found filed—B. T. H. Clerk.

PAGE 110.

Suffolk }
County }

Statement of Votes taken at the Election held for Representatives in Congress which Commenced on the third Tuesday in December one thousand Eight hundred and twelve—

Ebenezer Sage had three hundred and six }
John Lefferts had three hundred and Seven }
Benjamin B. Blydenburgh had one hundred and Twenty Six } Votes
Peter A. Jay had one hundred and Twenty Seven }

We Certify the Above to be a true Statement and Estimate of the Votes taken in the Town of Brookhaven at the aforesaid Election—

MERRITT S. WOODHULL }
JOSIAH SMITH } Commionrs
ISAAC SATTERLY } or
BENJAMIN HALLICK } Inspectors

Enterd pr MORDECAI HOMAN Town Ck

Suffolk } ss
County }

We the Commissioners of Highways for the town of Brookhaven being Called by a number of the Inhabitance of sd town to Stop a Road in the fireplace leading from Gerards Road Southward to the South Country Road which was laid out by Isaac Overton Esq. and William H. Helme Commissioners on the third day of August 1810 which s,d Road we have Stoped as far Northward as Gerards Road and have laid out another Road begining at the Southwest Corner of the Lott No-five at the South Country Road three Rods Wide Runing upon the West side of sd Lott to

PAGE 112.

the North end of the Cleared Land then turning Northeast til it comes to the old Road then Northerly as the old Road now runs til it comes near the South end of Nehemiah Hands Cleared Land thence Northeasterly til it Crosses the Lot No. four thence Northerly til it strikes the Road then with the Road to gerards Road which s,d Road we return to be enterd of Record as Witness our hands this 2nd. day of February 1813

JOHN ROSE } Commissioners
BENJAMIN HALLICK } of highways

Suffolk } ss
County }

We the Commissioners of highways for the town of Brookhaven being Call,d by the Trustees of s,d Town to lessen a Road on the East side of Beaver dam swamp in the fireplace and after having Viewed the premises do alter and lessen the same from a six Rod Road to four Rods from the going over at Mrs. Ketchams Northward to the head of the Beaver dam swamp which sd Road is Bounded East by the fence as the fence now stands leaving the Common Land on the West side of sd Road which we allow and return to be enterd on the Record of Brookhaven as Witness our hands in Brookhaven this second day of february 1813—

JOHN ROSE } Commissioners
BENJAMIN HALLICK } of highways

PAGE 113.

Be it remembred that at a Meeting of the Trustees of the freeholders and commonalty of the Town of Brookhaven for the time being, held on the fifth day of November in the Year of Our Lord one thousand Eight Hundred and Nine George Hallock of s,d town made application to the sd Trustees for liberty to Build a Dock or Wharff at a place Calld the deep hole in Stoney Brook harbour against his own Land and sd Trustees after due Consideration had in the premises did grant that the sd George Hallock should Build a Dock or Wharff at the aforementioned place one hundred feet in Length on the shore and fifty feet in Width from common high Water Mark—under Certain restrictions and regulations—

And whereas the sd George hallock did on the fifth day of December one thousand Eight hundred and twelve make application to the Trustees of the sd Town of Brookhaven for the time being for liberty to extend his aforesaid dock further to the Northward and to make further regulations concerning the same and the s,d Trustees having appointed a Committee to go and View the s,d premises do therefore According to the report of the sd Committee and after further Consideration had in the premises Grant and allow the s,d George Hallock to extend his said Dock two hundred feet to the Northward and to be equal in width as the former dock Viz fifty feet from Common high Water Mark and the sd George Hallock shall be allowed the sum of one Dollar for any Vessel of thirty Tons or upwards that may load at sd Dock one half to be paid by the Master of the Vessell and the other half by the Farmer or freightier but the sd George Hallock

PAGE 114.

is to Consider the Owner of the sd Vessells accountable to him for the whole sum and all light Vessels making fast to sd Dock and laying a day or part of a day shall pay to the sd George Hallock the sum of twelve and half Cents pr day except such Vessell shall make fast to sd Dock for the purpose of getting under way only, and all light Vessells shall make way or give room for Vessels to load or unload at s,d Dock—And the sd George Hallock for and in Consideration of the aforesaid Grant doth give unto the s,d Town of Brookhaven a Road twenty feet in width leading from s,d Dock to the Road that leads to Isreal Hawkins,s and also that all homebound Cargoes or Articles which are for the use and conveniance of the Inhabitance of sd Town shall be Landed on s,d Dock free from any expence and the sd George Hallock shall not hinder or Obstruct people from passing and repassing to and from the west Meadow nor hinder people from making fast to sd Dock with small Crafts provided they do not hinder or Obstruct Vessels from Loading or unloading all of which is Granted Accordingly whereunto we have Set our hands and Cused the Seal of our sd Town to be fixed this Second day of february 1813—

ISAAC SATTERLY } L. S. Trustees
WILLIAM BEALE }

Attest MORDECAI HOMAN Town Clerk

PAGE 115.

At a Meeting of the Trustees of the freeholders and commonalty of the Town of Brookhaven held on the Second day of March in the Year of our Lord one thousand Eight hundred and thirteen present at s,d Meeting Isaac Satterly Benjamin Hutchenson Joseph B. Roe John Robinson Nathan Post William Beale Trustees—At sd Meeting the aforesaid Trustees Sold a Certain piece of common Land unto Benjamin Brown lying on the East side of Beaver dam River in the fireplace which sd land was sold for fifty Dollars and Bounded as follows Viz Bengining at the Southeast Corner at a certain Stake Set up about three Rods to the Northward of the going over against Mr. Ketcham,s House from thence Runing Southwest to a Certain Maple Bush Marked in the swamp from thence Runing Northward by the Bank or River about twenty Rods to Certain Bounds fixed from thence runing Eastward to the Road and thence Southward by the Road as the Road has lately been fixed and altered to the aforementioned Bound leaving the Road four Rods Wide which s,d piece of Land Contains about one Acre More or less—

      Isaac Satterly } L. S. Trustees
      William Beale }

Attest, Mordecai Homan Town Clerk

Page 116.

Suffolk } ss
County }

We the Commissioners of highways for the Town of Brookhaven in sd County being Called by a Number of Inhabitance of sd Town to lay out a Road Calld the old pine Neck Road Runing from the Coram Road to the horse Block Road and after Viewing the premises have laid out the aforesaid Road three Rods Wide and order the same to be enterd on the Record of sd Town of Brookhaven as Witness our hands this second day of March 1813—

    John Rose } Commissioners
    Benjamin Hallock } of highways
    Nathaniel Akerly }

Attest Mordecai Homan Town Ck

This doth Certify that on the sixth day of April in the Year of our Lord one thousand Eight Hundred and thirteen Jonas Hawkins Junr and Thomas S. Mount made application to the Trustees of the freeholders and Commonalty of the Town of Brookhaven to Manumate a Certain Man Slave of theirs Named Harry and sd Trustees after examining into the premises do find s,d Negro Man to be under the age of fifty Years and of Sufficient ability to provide for and maintain himself do therefore set free sd Negro Man According to the Satute of this State in such case made and providng

Attest MORDECAI HOMAN Town Clk

PAGE 117.

At a general Town Meeting of the freeholders and Comonalty or Inhabitance of the Town of Brookhaven held this 6th. day of April 1813—at the House of Goldsmith Davis Innkeeper in Coram for the purpose of Choosing Town Officers agreeable to the Statute of this State the following Town Officers were Unanamously Chosen and Elected

Josiah Smith President.

Phillip Hallock
Lewis Rich
Nathan Post
John Mills
Briant Norton
William Dickerson
} Trustees

Constables.

Thomas Mount
David Carter
Nethaniel Robinson
Alexander Wicks
John Leek Jur

Timothy Davis
Nathan Post
Nathan Corwin
Isreal Davis

John Rose Supervisor
Mordecai Homan Town Clk and treasr
Nathan Post Collector

Isaac Satterly
John Davis
Barnabus Wines } Assessors.
William Beale
David Davis–Coram.

Jedediah Williamson
Daniel Overton } Commissioners of highways
Timothy Rose

Benjamin F. Thompson
John Rose } Commisioners of Schools.
Mordecai Homan

PAGE 118.

An Act to prevent people from taking sand or Catching Clambs in any of the Harbours or on or from any of the Shores Belonging to the Town of Brookhaven passed this sixth day of April 1813.

Be it Ordained by the Trustees of the freeholders and commonalty of the Town of Brookhaven for the time being that if any person or persons shall take any sand from any of the shores or harbours of the Town of Brookhaven or if any person shall Catch any Clambs in any of the Bays Creekes harbours or Waters within the Bounds of the Town of Brookhaven aforesaid without first having a permitt from sd Trustees or their order and paying a toleration of one Cent pr Bushel for every Bushel of sand and three Cents for every Bushel Clambs so taken shall be deemed an offender and transgressor and shall pay for each and every such Offence the sum of Twenty Dollars to be Sued for and recovered in the Name of the Trustees aforesaid before any Court having Cognizance thereof and applied to the use of the Town aforesaid given under our hands and Seal in Brookhaven this day and date aforesaid.

ISAAC SATTERLY } Trustees { L S }
JOHN ROBINSON

Attest MORDECAI HOMAN Town Clerk

Page 119.

At a meeting of the Trustees of the freeholders and Commonalty of the Town of Brookhaven held in s,d town this fourth day of May one thousand Eight hundred and thirteen present at sd Meeting Josiah Smith president William Dickerson John Hills Briant Norton David Davis Nathan Post and Lewis Rich Trustees at sd meeting sd Trustees agreed and by the Authority in them Invested did Revise the Laws passed on the Second day of June 1812 which prohibits the taking or Catching of any fish of any kind whatever or of killing any Wild fowl of Any kind whatsoever within the Bounds and Limits of the South Bay or parts belonging to sd Town and the Heirs of William Smith deceasd, or Gen. John Smith which s,d Laws are hereby Revised and to be in full force and Virtue until Repealed—

And also the Act to prevent Rams from runing in the Commons from the last day of August until the first day of November be and is hereby Revised

And also the Act to prevent Swine from runing in the Commons without being sufficiently ringed and yoked passed the 7th day of May 1811 be and the same is hereby revised given under our hands and Seal of the Town of Brookhaven.

JOSIAH SMITH President L S
Attest MORDECAI HOMAN Town Clerk

Page 120.

Rev Zecariah Green
Rev Noah Hallock
Nicoll Floyd
William Beale
Rev Ezra King
Joseph B. Rowe
} Inspectors of Schools

Overseerrs of Highways.

Jedediah Williamson
Ebenezer Baily
Samuel Satterly
Frederick Halsey
Spicer Davis
Isreal Davis
Nethaniel Davis
Jonathan Hallock
Peter Skidmore
Zopher Mills
Aron Robinson
Samuel Lane
Lewis Gorden
John Havens
John Leech Jur
Zopher Tooker
Robert Ellison
William Rose
Jacob Bell

Daniel Smith
William Osborn
David Leek
Warden Tobey
Isaac Mills
Jacob Corwin
Jeremiah Randal
George Brown
William Swezey
John Smith
Samuel Hammond
Brewster Terry
George Smith
David Davis
Justus Overton
Jeremiah Wheeler
Israel Hawkins
David Overton
James Smith

Fence Viewers.

Timothy Davis
Joseph Hawkins
Jacob Hawkin
Nethaniel Tooker
William Jayne
Isaac Satterly
Daniel Davis
Wells Davis
Joseph Miller
Samuel Hopkins
Peter Skidmore
Jonathan Worth
Henry Raynor Jur.
Nethaniel Robinson
James Post
Benjamin Smith
Nehemiah Hand
Nathan Bartoe
Phinehas Robinson

Hedges Osborn
William Beale
Justus Rowe
William Osborn
Humphy Avery
James Smith
Daniel Saxton
Nathan Corwin
Davis Overton
Azariah Hawkins
Justus Overton
George Munroe
Willard Ruland
Robert Hawkins
William Phillips
William Randal
John Laws
Caleb Newton
Zopher Hallock

Page 121.

Suffolk County } ss

Statement of Votes taken at the Anneversary Election for Governor Lieutenant Governor and Senator which commenced on the last Tuesday in April one thousand eight hundred and thirteen.

Governor—

Daniel D. Tompkins had three hundred and fifty one } Votes
Stephen Van Rensselear had one hundred and forty six

Lieutenant Governor

John Tayler had three hundred and fifty one } Votes
George Huntington had one hundred and forty six

Senator—

Jonthan Dayton had three hundred and fifty one } Votes
Jeremiah Johnson had one hundred and forty five

We Certify the foregoing to be a true Statement and Estimate of the Votes taken in the Town of Brookhaven at the aforesaid election this 29th day of April 1813

JOHN ROSE } Inspectors
ISAAC SATTERLY
BARNABAS WINES
DAVID DAVIS

Attest MORDECAI HOMAN Town Clerk

Page 122.

Suffolk County | ss

Statement of Votes taken in the Town of Brookhaven at the Annaversary Election for Members of Assembly which commenced on the last tuesday in April one thousand Eight hundred and thirteen.

Thomas S. Lester had three hundred and Eighty eight
Jonathan S. Conklin had Three hundred and eighty eight } Votes
Nathanel Potter had three Hundred and Eighty eight

Richard Udall had one Hundred fifty four
James Hallock had one Hundred fifty four } Votes
Thomas Beebe had one Hundred fifty four
David S. Conklin had one

We certify the foregoing to be a true Statement and Estimate of the votes taken in the Town of Brookhaven at the aforesaid Election.

JOHN ROSE
ISAAC SATTERLY } Inspectors
DAVID DAVIS
BARNABIS WINES

Attest MORDECAI HOMAN Town Clerk

PAGE 123.

Know all men by these presents that we the undersigned overseers of the Poor of the Town of Brookhaven do hereby Certify that on the day of the date hereof before us personally came and appeared Killis lately a slave to Samuel Thompson physician Deceasd who is now Manumitted by the Executors to the Estate of the said Samuel Thompson deceas,d by Virtue of an agreement entered into Between the sd Samuel Thompson the sd Killis and we do further Certify that the sd Killis appears or is under the age of fifty Years and of Sufficient ability to provide for himself in Witness whereof we have hereunto set our hands this Seventh day of September in the Year of our Lord one thousand Eight hundred and thirteen

Josiah Smith
John Mills   Overseers of the Poor
Nathan Post   of the
Phillip Hallock   Town of Brookhaven
William Dickerson
Attest MORDECAI HOMAN Town Clerk

PAGE 124.

The Commissioners of Common Schools for the Town of Brookhaven met at Coram on Tuesday the 3rd. day of November 1813 and Divided the town into School Districts According to Statute of this State in such Case provided—

JOHN ROSE   ) Commissioners
FRANKLIN B. THOMPSON }   of
MORDECAI HOMAN.   ) Common Schools

No. one is to Embrace the Inhabitants or Neighbourhood of Stoney Brook—

No. two is to Embrace the Western part of Setaket including the Inhabitants of Lubber Street and Dickersons Settlement

No. 3rd. is to Embrace the Eastern part of Setaket

No 4 is to Embrace the Neighbourhood of Drown meadow and Adjoining Inhabitants—

No. 5. is to Embrace the Neighbourhood of oldmans and adjoining Inhabitants—

No 6 is to embrace the Village of Millersplace and hopkins Settlement—

No 7 is to Embrace the Inhabitants of Rocky point and people Adjacent—

No 8 is to embrace the Inhabitants of the Western part of Western Middle Island About Rocconcama Pond to Smithtown line.

No. 9 is to Embrace the Inhabitants or Settlement of New Village as far West as James Hawkins and East to Richard Norton and Joseph Roes—

No 10 is to Embrace the Inhabitants of Coram as far

West as James Nortons

No 11 is to Embrace the Inhabitants of the North part of Middletown and Sweazey town—

12 is to embrace the Inhabitant of the lower part of Middle Island as far west as Isaac Howells (Deceasd) North to James Daytons and West to James Barnaby,s—

PAGE 125.

No 13 is to Embrace the Inhabitants of the Manner as far West as George Cobits and prosper kings and East by Southampton including Halseys Manner

No. 14 is to Embrace the Remainder part of the Manner—

No. 15 is to include the Inhabitants of the Eastern part of Moriches as far West as Havens Mills—

No 16 is to Embrace the remainder part of Morriches as far West as the paper Mill—

No. 17 is to Embrace the Inhabitants of Mastick as far West as fireplace—

No 18 is to Embrace the Inhabitants West of fireplace Mills as far West as Jeffrey Brewsters—

No. 19 is to Embrace the Inhabitants West of Jeffrey Brewsters as far West as Austin Roe,s

No. 20 is to Embrace the Inhabitants West of Austin Roes as far West as Patchogue Stream—

No 21 is to Embrace the Inhabitants West of Patchogue Stream as far West as Islip line

No 22 is to Embrace the Inhabitants East of Thomas Aldrich in Middletown extending East to the Wading River Line

No. 23. is to Embrace the Inhabitants of Coram hills as far East as the Widow Howells—

On the 14th. January 1814 John Rose and Mordecai Homan Commisioners were Calld to alter the Districts in the Manner and did Extend the Western District on the

South Road to include the House Barnabas Wines and on the North as far East as to include Nathaniel Brower,s House—

PAGE 126.

This doth Certify that on the first day of March 1814 Hannah Woodhull made application to the Trustees to Manumit a Certain Slave of hers Named Tamer and s,d Trustees being Satisfied that sd Slave is under the age of forty five Years and of Sufficient ability to provide for and maintain herself do therefore manumitt and set free s,d Tamer as the Law of this State directs

JOSIAH SMITH President

Attest MORDECAI HOMAN Town Clk

This doth certify that on the first day of March 1814 Thomas Strong made applications to the Trustees of the Town of Brookhaven to Manumitt a Certain Negro man a Slave of his Named Killis and sd Trustees being Satisfied that said Killis is under the age of forty five years and of sufficient ability to provide for and maintain himself do Manumitt and set free sd Slave and the Law of this State directs— JOSIAH SMITH President

Attest MORDECAI HOMAN Town Clerk

This doth Certify that on the first day of March 1814 Theophilus Smith made application to the Trustees of the Town of Brookhaven to Manumitt and Set free a Certain Woman Slave of hers Named Sarah and sd Trustees being sadisfied that sd Sarah is under the age of forty five Years and of Sufficient ability to provide for and maintain herself do therefore Manumitt sd Slave as the Law of this State directs-- JOSIAH SMITH President

MORDECAI HOMAN Town Clerk

PAGE 127.

At a general Town meeting held in the Town of Brook-

BROOKHAVEN TOWN RECORDS.   181

haven at the house of Goldsmith Davis on the fifth day of April 1814 by the Inhabitants and Commonalty of s,d Town for the purpose of Choosing Town Officers as the Statute of this State directs the following persons were unanimously Elected—

John Rose President of the Trustees

Daniel Davis }
Benjamin Halliock
William Dickerson } Trustees
Briant Norton
John Mills
Barnabas Wines }

John Rose Supervisor
Mordecai Homan Town Clerk & Treasurer
Nathan Post Collector

Isaac Satterly }
Peter Skidmore
Theophilus Smith } Assessors
William Beale
Benjamin Hallock }

Benjamin F. Thompson }
John Rose } Commisioners of Schools
Mordecai Homan }

Jedediah Williamson }
Lewis Rich } Commissioners of highways
John Rose }

John Denton
Benjamin Hawkins Jur }
David Carter
Nathan Post
Tathaniel Robinson } Constables
Nathan Corwin
Elisha Bailes
John Leek Jur
Samuel Bishop }

Page 128.

Rev. Zechiarah Green
Rev. Noah Hallock
Rev. Ezra King
Nicoll Floyd
Wm Beale
Joseph B. Roe
} Inspectors of Schools

Overseers of Highways

Jedediah Williamson
Daniel Smith Jr
John Davis
Samuel Davis
Peter Skidmore
Henry Raynor
John Havens
Mordecai Homan
Isaac Biggs
Daniel Smith
William Arthur Jr
James Dayton
Herrick Aldrich
Samuel Davis Jur
Willard Ruland
Briant Norton
Phinehas Rose
James Smith

Nathaniel Akerly
Ebenezer Jones
Nathaniel Davis
Jonathan Halliock
Aron Robinson
Lewis Gordon
John Leek
Stephen Overton
Jacob Bell
Isaac Willits
Isaac Mills
John Laws
William Swezey
Isaac Overton
Sylvanus Overton
Azariah Hawkins
Jeremiah Wheeler
Isreal Hawkins

Fence Viewers

Woodhull Smith
Benjamin Hawkins
William Jayne
Daniel Davis 2nd
Joseph Miller
Peter Skidmore
Henry Raynor

Richard Smith
Ebenezer Bailey
Isaac Satterly
Wells Davis
Samuel Hopkins
David Worth
Nathaniel Robinson

Benjamin Smith	Jonathan Hawkins
Zophar Tooker	Mordecai Homan
Phinehas Robinson	Hedges Osborn
Nathan Mulford	Ebenezer Akerly
William Arthur Jr	Samuel Bishop
James Smith	Daniel Saxton
Joshua Overton	Nathan Corwin
Azariah Hawkins	Justus Overton
Willard Ruland	George Munroe
Simmons Laws	Robert Hawkins
William Randal	John Laws
Jeremiah Wheeler	Titus Gould

PAGE 129.

Suffolk } ss
County }

Statement of Votes taken at the Anaversary Election for Senators which Commenced on the last tuesday in April one thousand Eight hundred and fourteen—Viz

Darius Crosby had two hundred and Eighty six } Votes
Abraham Odell had one hundred and Seventeen }

We Certify the above to be a true Statement and Estimate of the Votes taken in the Town of Brookhaven at the aforesaid Election this twenty eighth day of April one thousand Eight hundred and fourteen

Isaac Satterly }
John Rose } Inspectors
Benjamin Hallock }
Peter Skidmore }

Suffolk } ss
County }

Statement of Vote taken at the Anaversary Election for Congress which commenced on the last Tuesday in April one thousand Eight hundred and fourteen Viz—

Henery Crocheron had three hundred and thirty one
George Townsend had three hundred and thirty one
William Townsend had one hundred and twenty six
Cornelius Bedell had one hundred and twenty six
} Votes

We Certify the above to be a true Statement and Estimate of the Votes taken in the Town of Brookhaven at the aforesaid Election this twenty eighth day of April one thousand Eight hundred and fourteen—

Isaac Satterly
John Rose
Benjamin Hallock
Peter Skidmore
} Inspectors

Attest Mordecai Homan Town Clerk

PAGE 130.

Suffolk }
County } ss

Statement of Votes taken at the Anaversary Election for Members of Assembly which Commenced on the last tuesday in April one thousand Eight hundred and fourteen Viz—

John P. Osborn had three hundred and twenty Nine
John Wells had three hundred and twenty Six
Tredwell Scudder had three hundred and twenty Nine
Thomas S. Lester had three——
} Votes

Abraham Vanwyck had one hundred and twenty Nine
James Reeve had one hundred and twenty Nine
Silas Howell had one hundred and twenty Nine
} Votes

We certify the foregoing to be a true Statement of Votes taken in the Town of Brookhaven at the aforesaid Election this twenty eighth day of April one thousand Eight hundred and fourteen.

Isaac Satterly
John Rose
Benjamin Hallock
Peter Skidmore
} Inspectors

Attest Mordecai Homan Town Clerk

PAGE 131.*

At a Meeting of the Trustees of the freeholders and Commonalty of the Town of Brookhaven held in sd town on the fourth day of May 1814 the Law prohibiting the taking or killing Wild fowl : or of taking or Catching fish of any kind whatever passed on the Second day of May 1812 as Respects the South Bay in partnership with the Town of Brook Haven the Heirs of William Smith deceas,d or General John Smith be and they are hereby revised and declared to be in full force and Virtue Given under our hands in Brookhaven this fourth day of May 1814 whereunto we have Caused the Seal of the Town of Brookhaven to be affixed.

JOHN ROSE President. L S

Attest MORDECAI HOMAN Town Clerk

*Note.—The two following pages are each numbered 131 in the Records.—COM.

Also at the aforesaid Meeting the Act passed on the 7th. day of May 1811 which prevents Swine from Runing in the Commons without being ringed and Yoked be and is hereby Revised and declared to be in full force and Virtue Given under our hands and Seal in Brookhaven this 4th day of May 1814   JOHN ROSE President   L S

Attest MORDECAI HOMAN

PAGE 131.

This doth Certify that on the fourth day of May 1814 Robert Hawkins of the Town of Brookhaven made Application to the Trustees or Overseers of the Poor of s,d Town

to Manumitt a Certain Slave of his Named Margett and the s,d Trustees being Satisfied after due Consideration had in the premises that the said Slave Named Margett is under the age of forty five years and of sufficient ability to provide for and Maintain herself do therefore Consent that the s,d Slave shall be Manumitted as the Law in this state directs given under our hands in Brookhaven this day above Written. JOHN ROSE President
Attest MORDECAI HOMAN Town Clerk

We the Commissioners of Common schools for the Town of Brookhaven being Called upon by the mutual Consent of the Inhabitants of the fifteenth and sixteenth school districts to alter the Line or division Between s,d Districts in order to give Each District its Just proportion of Inhabitants do therefore extend the fifteenth District as far West as the Lane that leads down to the house of Isaac Bishops given under our hands in Brookhaven this 10th July 1814

JOHN ROSE } Commissioners
MORDECAI HOMAN } of Common schools

PAGE 131.

This doth Certify that on the 6th day of Sept. 1814 Wessell Sell of the Town of Brookhaven made application to the Trustees thereof to manumitt a certain female Slave of his by the name of Juleanor and sd Trustees being Satisfied that said slave is under the age of forty five Years and of sufficient ability to Support and maintain herself do consent that she should be manumitted as the Law of this state in such case directs—given under our hands in Brookhaven this day aforesaid—

JOHN ROSE President
Attest MORDECAI HOMAN Town Clerk

This doth Certify that on the 7th day of february 1815 Gideon Mills and Richard Oakly of the Town of Brookhaven Made application to the Trustees of s,d Town to Manumitt a Certain Negro Man of theirs Named Sampson formerly the property of John Ackerly Deceas,d and sd Trustees being satisfied that s,d Sampson was under forty five years and of Sufficient ability to provide for and Maintain himself did consent that s,d Negro Man should be manumitted According to the Statute Law of this State given under our hands in Brookhaven this day aforesaid.

JOHN ROSE President

Attest MORDECAI HOMAN Town Clerk

PAGE 132.

We the Commissioners of highways for the Town of Brookhaven being Called upon by Elijah Bailes and others to open a highway in Lubber Street and sd Commissioners after Viewing the premises do order and agree that the Road shall be opened Begining at a place Call,d temps House Runing Westwardly to a Certain Stake at Elijah Bayles Stacking place or spreading place four Rods Wide which we order to be recorded given under our hands in Brookhaven this 7th February 1815—

JOHN ROSE   } Commissioners
JEDEDIAH WILLIAMSON } of highways

Attest MORDECAI HOMAN Town Clerk

This doth Certify that about the 8th. day of December 1814 Mordecai Homan and John Rose were Calld upon as Commissioners of Common Schools to alter the school district in the Manor and did agreeable to the request of the Inabitants form a District on the North Road so as to include all the Inhabitants on said Road from the place or House of Caleb Smith deceas,d to the Eastern part of the Neighbourhood—which Will be No. 24

as Witness our hands MORDECAI HOMAN } Commissioners of
                              JOHN ROSE   } Common Schools

PAGE 133.

At a Meeting of the Trustees of the freeholders and Commonalty of the Town of Brookhaven for the time being held in s,d Town on the Third day of January one thousand Eight hundred and fifteen at s,d meeting Sundry Merchants and others of s,d Town made Application to the Trustees aforesaid praying them to establish a Bank Consisting of Small Bill for the Accommodation of Change and s,d Trustees after due Consideration had in the premises did Vote and agree that there should be a quantity of Bills struck for the Accommodation of Change during the present scarcity of Specie Change. to be sub to the orders and regulation of s,d Trustees and their Successors in Office and Accordingly the sd Trustees did apply to Mr. Alden Spooner Printer and had twelve hundred Nine Dollars and Ninety two Cents. $1200 92-100. Struck which was deposited with Mordecai Homan Town Clerk and Treasurer to be by him Signed and put in Circulation if Call,d for

Be it Rembred that on the 12th. day of May 1815 the Inhabitants of the 18th. District made application to us Commissioners of Common Schools to have their District Divided which we do Accordingly and have set off that part of the fireplace Begining at the point of the Middle Island and the Mill Roads so Extending Across the Neck in a Southeasterly direction so as to include the House of Stephen Bartoe in the 26 District which will be that part towards the Mills and the Remainder to be in the 18th. District.

MORDECAI HOMAN } Commissioners
WILLIAM BEALE } of Schools

PAGE 134.

Suffolk }
County }

Be it remembered that on the first day of May 1817 the Inhabitants of the Neighborhood of Ball,d hills made application to us commissioners of common schools for the Town of Brookhaven to be set off in a District by themselves and we the sd Commissioners after due consideration had in the premises do hereby set them off the West Bound to extend to the east line of Daniel saxtons land so extending Northward so as to include Christopher Tookers and Eastwardly so as to include the house and premises of John Hulse Jur which will be District No. 27. Given under our hands at Brookhaven this day aforesaid

Also Deacon Wheeler and Capt. Wheeler to be united with the Ninth District

MORDECAI HOMAN
WILLIAM BEALE
} Commisioners of Common Schools

On the Ninth day of May 1815 Mordecai Homan and William Beale Two of the Commissioners of Common Schools for the Town of Brook haven were Calld by a number of the Inhabitants living on the extremities of the Ninth and Tenth School District of the Town of Brook haven Stateing to sd Commissioners that their Districts were too large and praying to have a District formd from the two Districts and sd Commissioners after due Consideration had in the premises did set off a district to Include the Inhabitants in that part of the Vilage Calld Westfield which shall include the House now Ocupied by Lemuel Smith Westerly and to extend East so as to include George Smiths on the North side of the Country Road and David Fordham on the South side—which Will be District No. 25—

MORDECAI HOMAN
WILLIAM BEALE
} Commisioners of Common Schools

PAGE 135.

At a General Town Meeting of the freeholders and Commonalty of the Town of Brook haven held at the House of Goldsmith Davis in Coram on the fourth day of April 1815 the following Town Officers were Unanimously Chosen—Viz.

Isaac Satterly President

John Havens ⎫
Daniel Smith ⎪
Benjamin Hallick ⎬ Trustees
Briant Norton ⎪
Robert Hawkins ⎪
Merritt S. Woodhull ⎭

John Rose Supervisor
Mordecai Homan Town Clk and Treasurer
Nathan Post Collector

Hampton Howell ⎫
Ichabod Carter ⎪
Benjamin Hallick ⎬ Assessors
Woodhull Smith ⎪
Merritt S. Woodhull ⎭

Isaac Overton ⎫
Lewis Rich ⎬ Commissioners of highways
Timothy Davis ⎭

William Beale ⎫
Mordecai Homan ⎬ Commissioners of
John R. Satterly ⎭ Common Schools

Nathan Post ⎫
Samuel Bishop ⎪
Nathan Corwin ⎪
John L. Merritt ⎪
William Homan ⎬ Constables
Azel Robinson ⎪
John Leek Jur ⎪
Benjamin Hawkins ⎪
Robert Stivers ⎭

PAGE 136.

Rev. Zecheriah Green ⎫
Rev. Noah Hallock ⎪
Rev. Ezra King ⎬ Inspectors of
Coll Nicoll Floyd ⎪ Common Schools
William Beale ⎪
Joseph B. Roe ⎭

OVERSEERS OF HIGHWAYS

Jonas Hawkins   James Woodhull
Daniel Smith   Elisha Bayles

Spicer Davis
Phillip Hallock
Aaron Robinson
Lewis Gourden
Isaac Petty
Timothy Rose
Joseph Wood
William Arthur
James Dayton
William Swezey Jur
Isaac Overton
Sylvanus Overton
Azra Hawkins

Samuel Davis
Zophar Mills Jur
Joseph Raynor
Jeremiah Culver
Mordecai Homan
Josiah Woodhull
John Mills
Simmons Davis
John Laws
Samuel Darr's
Willard Ruland
Briant Norton
Titus Gould

Isaac N. Gould.

FENCE VIEWERS

Woodhull Smith
Benjamin Hawkins
William Jayne
Elisha Davis
Joseph Miller
Peter Skidmore
Henry Raynor
Benjamin Smith
Zophar Tooker
Phinehas Robinson
Nathan Mulford
William Arthur
James Smith
Joshua Overton
Azariah Hawkins
Willard Ruland
David Davi's
William Randal

Richard Smith
Ebenezer Bailis
James Hulse
John Davis
Samuel Hopkins
David Worth
Nathaniel Robinson
Jonathan Hawkins
Mordecai Homan
Hedges Osborn
Ebenezer Ackerly
Samuel Bishop
Daniel Saxton
Nathan Corwin
Samuel Hammond
George Munroe
Thomas Homan
John Laws

PAGE 137.

Statement of Votes taken at the Anavarsary Election for Senators in the Town of Brookhaven which Commenced on the Last tuesday of April one thousand Eight hundred and fifteen Viz

Jacob Barker had two hundred and forty five } Votes
Leffert Lefferts had Eighty Eight—

We Certy the foregoing to be a true Statement and Estimate of the Votes taken in the Town of Brook haven at the aforesaid Election

John Rose
Ichabod Carter
Merritt S. Woodhull
Hampton Howell
} Inspectors

Statement of Votes taken at the Anavarsary Election for Members of Assembly which Commenced on the last Tuesday in April one thousand Eight hundred and fifteen

Abraham Rose had three hundred and forty eight
Josiah Smith had one hundred and Eighty one
Benjamin F. Thompson had one hundred and Eighty two
John Saxton had Ninety Six—
Isreal Carll had one—
Phinehas Carll had two hundred and fifty six
} Votes

We Certify the foregoing to be a true Statement and Estimate of the Votes taken in the Town of Brookhaven at the aforesaid Election—

John Rose
Merritt S. Woodhull
Ichabod Carter
Hampton Howell
} Inspectors

PAGE 138.

Be it remembered that whereas there is Certain property known the name of the flax pond lying at a place Call,d Cranes Neck in the Town of Brookhaven that is Equally owned by the Town of Brookhaven of the one part and Vincent Jones William Wickham Mills, and Stephen Hulse deceas,d of the other part and the aforesaid parties being desirous to make a Division in the aforesaid premises did Choose us the Undersigned Viz. Timothy Miller William

Dickenson and Mordecai Homan as Commissioners to make a Division thereof and the s,d parties together with Ebenezer Smith did enter into Bonds of one hundred Dollars each to abide and agree to the Division and Bounds that shall be made and fixed by us the aforesaid Commissioners And we the s,d Commissioners after having Viewed and Made a Survey thereof with the Assistance of Mr. Daniel Saxton Surveyor do find it very difficult to Ascertain where the original Bounds were the aforesaid parties did agree that we the s,d Commissioners should make a Division and Set the Bounds According to our Judgment and we the sd Commissioners afer due Consideration and examenation had in the premises do make and establish the Bounds as follows Viz. the Bounds is a Stake Set on the Bank on the South Side of the pond which is due West from a Certain Ceder Tree standing in the fence between the land of the sd Vincent Jones and the flax pond Lane which sd stake Stands five Chains and five Links due West from s,d Ceder tree which Division appears to us Commissioners to be equal

Page 139.

and from sd Stake to run a due North Line to the Northermost side of the s,d pond and Marsh and the s,d parties after haveing heard the Division and seen the Bounds that were fixd did proceed to make Choice as to the share that should belong to them, and the aforesaid Vincent Jones Wm. Wickham Mills and Thomas S. Strong Executor to the Estate of Stephen Hulse Deceas,d did Choose the Westermost half and Coll Isaac Satterly President of the Trustees for the Town of Brookhaven did Choose the Eastermost half, or part in behalf of the Town and the aforesaid parties did agree to pass Quit claims to each other Accordingly given under our hands in Brookhaven this 12th day of April 1815

Timothy Miller ⎫ Commisioners
William Dickenson ⎬ appointed by
Mordecai Homan ⎭ the parties

This doth Certify that on the Seventh day of November 1815, Daniel Davis Made application to the Trustees of the Town of Brookhaven to Manumitt a Certain female Slave of his Named Matilda and s,d Trustees being Satisfied that slave was under forty five years and of sufficient ability to provide for and Maintain herself did Consent that sd Davis should Manumitt sd slave as the Law in such Case directs—

Isaac Satterly President

Attest Mordecai Homan Town Clerk

Page 140.

At a meeting of the Trustees of the freeholders and Commonalty of the Town of Brookhaven held in s,d Town on the 2nd day of May 1815. the Law passed on the 2nd day of June 1812. which prohibits the taking or killing wild fowl or of taking or Catching fish of any kind whatever in the South Bay that belongs to the Town of Brookhaven the Heirs of Capt. William Smith deceas,d or General John Smith be and they are hereby declared to be in full force and Virtue—

Isaac Satterly president

Attest Mordecai Homan Town Clerk

Also the Act passed on the 7th day of May 1811. which prevents Swine from Runing on the Commons without being Ringed and Yoked be and the same is hereby declared to be in full force and Virtue

Isaac Satterly President

Attest Mordecai Homan Town Clerk

Also the Act passed on the 2nd day of June 1812 which prevents Rams from runing on the commons Between the Last day of August and the first day of November be and the same is declared to be in full force and Virtue given under our hands and Seals in Brookhaven this day aforesaid

       Isaac Satterly President
Attest Mordecai Homan Town Clerk

{ SEAL }

Page 141.

Be it Remembred that on the 15th day of June 1815 We the Commissioners of highways for the Town of Brookhaven was Call,d by a number of the Inhabitants of sd Town to lay out a highway at Millers place from the Rocky point Road to Merritt S. Woodhull, Landing and We the s,d Commissioners after Viewing the same did lay out a highway for the public three Rods wide through the land of Lyba Brown Samuel Davis and Merritt S. Woodhull to low Water mark Begining at the Rocky point Road four feet to the West of the West Waggon Rut and extending East so as to make the above mentioned three Rods until it comes to the Land of the s,d Samuel Davis and then through the Land of the s,d Samuel Davis and the Land of the s,d Merritt S. Woodhull the same Width as it was Staked out by the s,d Commissioners. and the s,d Samuel Davis is to have liberty to keep two good easy swing Gates on s,d Road where they now are at his own expense and likewise to have liberty to erect one more gate Easy swinging Gate at some other Convenient place on s,d Road so as not to discommode the traveling any more than the other two Gates does. Likewise the sd Merritt S. Woodhull is to have liberty to Erect one good Easy swinging Gate Across the Road leading from his House to the landing aforesaid at any Convenient place to the Eastward of the the s,d Samuel Davis House which s,d Road we order to be Recorded—

Lewis Ritch } Commissioners
Isaac Overton } of highways

M. Homan Town Ck

Page 142.

This doth Certify that on the 6th day of Febuary 1816 Thomas S. Strong Esq. made application to the Trustees of the freeholders and Commonalty of the Town of Brookhaven to Manmitt a Certain Slave of his Named Abel and s,d Trustees being Satisfied that s,d Slave was under forty five Years and of Sufficient Ability to provide for and maintain himself do Consent that the sd Abel should be Manumitted According to the Statute of this State in such case made and provided

         Isaac Satterly President
Attest Mordecai Homan Town Clerk

This doth Certify that on the 6th day of February 1816 Richard Robinson Made application to Manumitt a Certain Slave of his Named Clarisa and s,d Trustees being Satisfied that sd Slave was under forty five Years and of Sufficient ability to provide for and maintain herself do Consent that the s,d Clarisa should be Manumittd According to the Satute of this state in such Case made and provided

         Isaac Satterly President
Attest Mordecai Homan Town Clerk

Page 143.

This doth Certify that on the fourth day of March 1816 Richard Robinson made application to the Overseers of the poor of the Town of Brookhaven to Manumitt a Certain slave of his Named Jeremiah, and s,d Trustees being Satisfied that sd Slave was under forty five years and of sufficient ability to provide for and Maintain himself do Consent that he should be Manumitted According to the Law of the state in such Case made and provided

Attest Mordecai Homan Town Clerk

This doth Certify that on the sixth day of November 1816 Thomas S. Strong Executor to the Estate of Samuel Thompsen Deceas,d Made application to the Overseers of the poor of the Town of Brookhaven to Manumitt a Certain Slave belonging to said Estate Named Rose Akerly and s,d Overseers being satisfied that said Rose was under forty five years and of Sufficient ability to provide for and Maintain herself do consent that she should be Manumitted According to the Law of this state in such case made and provided

Attest MORDECAI HOMAN Town Ck

PAGE 144.

This doth Certify that on the 2d Day of June 1817 Elizabeth Smith Exeexutrix to the Estate of John Smith Deceasd made Application to the Overseer of the Poor of the Town of Brookhaven to manumitt a certain Slave Belonging to said Estate and said Overseers being Satisfied that said Slave whose name is Stephen is under forty five years and of Sufficient Ability to Maintain himself do consent to his manumition as the law in such Case is made and provided—

Attest MORDECAI HOMAN Tow Clk

This doth Certify that on the 2nd Day of September 1817. Sarah Helme made application to manumitt a certain Slave of hers named Nimrod and the Trustees of the freeholders and commonalty of the Town of Brookhaven being Overseers of the Poor being Satisfied that said Slave is under forty five years and of Sufficient ability to provide for and maintain himself do consent that said Nimrod should be manumitted as the law directs

Attest MORDECAI HOMAN Town Clk

PAGE 145.

At a meeting of the freeholders and Commonalty of the Town of Brook haven held at the house of Goldsmith Davis in Coram on the 2nd. day of April 1816 being the Annual

Town Meeting Day the following persons were Unanomously Elected as Town Officers—

Viz. Thomas S. Strong President

Isaac Brewster ⎫
Benjamin Hallick ⎪
William Tooker ⎬ Trustees
Ichabod Carter ⎪
Issac Hammond ⎪
William Phillips ⎭

Mordecai Homan Town Clerk & Treasurer
John Rose Supervisor
Hendrickson Hallock Collector

Benjamin Hallick ⎫
Hampton Howell ⎪
Josiah Smith ⎬ Assessors
Isaac Brewster ⎪
Timothy Miller ⎭

Isaac Satterly— ⎫
Nicoll Floyd— ⎬ Commissioners of Highways
Benjamin Hutchenson ⎭

John R. Satterly ⎫ Commissioners of
Mordecai Homan ⎬ Common Schools
William Beale ⎭

Henry Dayton ⎫
Nathan Post ⎪
John Penny ⎪
Freeman Lane Jur ⎬ Constables
Samuel Bishop ⎪
Jonathan Still ⎪
Thomas Mount ⎪
Elias Norton ⎭

PAGE 146.

Rev. Zecheriah Green ⎫
Rev. Noah Hallock ⎪ Inspectors
Rev. Ezra King ⎬ of
Nicoll Floyd ⎪ Schools
William Beale ⎪
Joseph B. Roe ⎭

Overseers of Highways

Jonas Hawkins
James Woodhull
Daniel Smith Jur
Zechariah Hawkins
Spicer Davis
Israel Davis
Samuel Davis
Phillip Hallock
Benjamin Robinson
Ebenezer Wines
Joseph Raynor
Christopher Robinson
Bartlett Sandford
Joseph Hawkins Senior
Mordecai Homan
Timothy Rose

Josiah Woodhull
Stephen Roe
John L. Merritt
Sylvester Foster
Daniel Homan
James Dayton
John Laws
William Swezey
Samuel Davis Jur
Isaac Overton
Noah Overton
Willard Ruland
Briant Norton
Azariah Hawkins
Titus Gould
James Smith

William Swezey Patchogue

Fence Viewers

Woodhull Smith
Richard Smith
Benjamin Hawkins
Ebenezer Akerly
William Jayne Esq
James Hulse
Elisha Davis
Daniel Davis
Joseph Miller
Samuel Hopkins
Peter Skidmore
David Worth
Henry Raynor
Nathaniel Robinson
John Penny

Barnabas Smith
Justus Roe
Ebenezer Akerly
Samuel Bishop
John Rider
James Smith
Daniel Saxton
Joshua Overton
Nathan Corwin
Azariah Hawkins
Samuel Hammond
George Munroe
Willard Ruland
William Phillips
Jeffrey Randal

Silas Reeves
Zophar Tooker
Mordecai Homan
Hedges Osborn

William Randal
John Laws
Davis Overton
Brewster Terry

PAGE 147.

Suffolk County } ss

Statement of Votes taken at the Annaversary Election for Governor Lieutenant Governor and Senators which commenced on the Last Tuesday in April 1816—Viz.

Governor

Daniel D. Tompkins had two hundred and Seventy three } Votes
Rufus King had Seventy three

Lieutenant Governor

John Taylor had two hundred and Seventy three } Votes
George Tibbits had Seventy Nine—

Senators

John D. Ditmis had two hundred and Seventy three
Walter Bowne had two hundred and Seventy three } Votes
Elisha W. King had Seventy Eight—
John Johnston had Seventy Eight—

We certify the above to be a true Statement and Estimate of the Votes taken in the Town of Brookhaven at the aforesaid Election this second day of May one thousand Eight hundred and Sixteen

John Rose
Isaac Brewster
Timothy Miller } Inspectors
Hampton Howell
Benjamin Hallick

Attest MORDECAI HOMAN Town Clerk

PAGE 148.

Suffolk County } ss

Statement of Votes taken at the Annaversary Election for Assembly which commenced on the last tuesday in april 1816 Viz.—

Israel Carll had theee hundred and sixteen ⎫
Abraham Parsons had three hundred and Sixteen ⎪
Thomas S. Lester had three hundred and sixteen ⎬ Votes
James Halliock had sixty Nine—69— ⎪
Stephen Mitchael had sixty Eight, 68— ⎪
John H. Jones had sixty Nine 69— ⎭

We Certify the foregoing Statement to be a true Estimate of the Votes taken in the Town of Brookhaven at the aforesaid Election this second day of May one thousand Eight hundred and Sixteen

John Rose ⎫
Isaac Brewster ⎪
Timothy Millr ⎬ Assessors
Hampton Howell ⎪
Benjamin Hallick ⎭

Attest MORDECAI HOMAN Town Clerk—

Suffolk County } ss

Statement of Votes taken at the Annaversary Election for Congress which commenced on the last tuesday in april one thousand Eight hundred and sixteen Viz.

George Townsend had three hundred and twenty five ⎫
Tredwell Scudder had three hnndred and twenty five ⎬ Votes
Samuel Jones Jun had Ninety one— ⎪
Nethaniel Smith had Ninety three— ⎭

We Certify the foregoing to be a true Statement and Estimate of the Votes taken in the Town of Brookhaven at the aforesaid Election this 2nd. day of May 1816

202   BROOKHAVEN TOWN RECORDS.

John Rose
Isaac Brewster
Timothy Miller } Inspectors
Hampton Howell
Benjamin Hallick

Attest MORDECAI HOMAN Town Clerk

PAGE 149.

At a Meeting of the freeholders and Commonalty of the Town of Brookhaven held in said Town on the first day of April in the Year of our LORD one thousand Eight hundred and Seventeen the following Town Officers were unanomously and duly Elected

Nicoll Floyd President

Thomas S. Strong
Isaac Satterly
Justus Overton } Trustees
Daniel Overton
Isaac Overton
William Beale

John Rose Supervisor
Mordecai Homan Town Clerk and Treasurer
Nathan Post Collector

William Tooker
Benjamin Hallock
Isaac Brewster } Inspectors
Timothy Miller
Joseph Raynor

John Rose } Commissioners
William Phillips } of
Isaac Brewster } highways

William Beale } Commissioners of
Mordecai Homan } Common Schools
John R. Satterly

Samuel Bishop ⎫
Silvanus Overton ⎪
Samuel Homan ⎬ Constables
Evi Smith ⎪
James Woodhull ⎪
Thomas S. Mount ⎭

PAGE 150.

Reverend Zecheriah Green ⎫
Rev. Noah Hallock ⎪
Rev. Ezra King ⎬ Inspectors of Schools
Nicoll Floyd ⎪
William Beale ⎪
Joseph B. Roe ⎭

OVERSEERS OF HIGHWAYS

Joseph Hawkins
James Woodhull
Daniel Smith
Zecheriah Hawkins
Spicer Davis
Israel Davis
Samuel Brown
Phillip Hallock
Benjamin Robinson
Zophar Mills
Ebenezer Wines
Isaac Raynor Senior
Christopher Robinson
Henry P. Orsborn
James Fanning
Mordecai Homan South
Doct. Nathaniel Miller

Isaac Overton
Austin Roe
Justus Roe
Isaac Willetts
Isaac Mills
Isaac Haff
John Laws
Joshua Swezey
Samuell Davis
Isaac Overton 2nd
Willard Ruland
Briant Norton
Azariah Hawkins
Edmind Wheeler
James Smith
Caleb Newton
William Swezey

FENCE VIEWERS

Timothy Davis
Joseph Hawkins
Benjamin Hawkins
Ebenezer Bailey
William Jayne

Hedges Orsbon
Barnabas Smith
Justus Roe
Ebenezer Akerly
Samuel Bishop

James Hulse	Isaac Willetts
Elisha Davis	James Smith
Daniel Davis	Daniel Saxton
Joseph Miller	Joshua Overton
Samuel Hopkins	Nathan Corwin
Peter Skidmore	Azariah Hawkins
David Worth	Samuel Hammond
Henry Raynor	David Overton
Nathaniel Robinson	Willard Ruland
John Penny	Robert Hawkins
Silas Reeves	Isaac Mills
Nathan Bartoe	William Randal
Samuel Hawkins	John Laws
Briant Davis	Daniel Overton

PAGE 151.

At the aforesaid Town Meeting a Vote was taken that the Trustees of said Town should provide a poor House for the Accommodation of the poor and to unite with the Towns of Smith Town and Islip for that purpose which was Carried Unanomously in the Affirmative and Nicoll Floyd Thomos S. Strong and William Tooker were appointed as a Committee to meet a Committee for the Towns of Smith Town and Islip for said purpose—

Attest MORDECAI HOMAN, Town Clerk

Suffolk } ss
County }

Statement of Votes taken in the Town of Brookhaven at the Annaversary Election for Governor and Lieut. Governor and Senators which commenced on the last tuesday in April one thousand Eight hundred and Seventeen

Dewitt Clinton had ninety five } Votes for
Peter B. Porter hand Seventeen } Governor

John Taylor had one hundred and Seventeen Votes for Lieutenant Governor—

Senators

Stephen Barnum had one hundred and ten }
Jonathan Dayton had one hundred and seven } Votes
Stephen B. Porter had three—for Senators }

We Certify the foregoing to be a true Statement and Estimate of the Votes taken in the Town of Brookhaven at the aforesaid Election this first day of May 1817

John Rose }
Isaac Bewster }
William Tooker } Inspectors
Joseph Raynor }

PAGE 152.

Suffolk } ss
County }

Statement of Votes taken at the Annaversary Election for members of Assembly in the town of Brookhaven which commenced on the last tuesday in April one thousand eight hundred and seventeen—Viz

John P. Orsborn had one hundred and sixteen }
Nathaniel Miller had one hundred and seventeen } Votes
Charles H. Havens had one hundred and twelve }
Jeffrey Randal had four— }

We certify the foregoing to be a true Statement and Estimate of the Votes taken in the town of Brook haven at the aforesaid Election dated this first day of May 1817.—

John Rose }
Isaac Brewster }
William Tooker } Inspectors
Joseph Raynor }

Brookhaven 2nd June 1817

This is to certify that all that part of the Second School District of the Town of Brookhaven lying South of Benjamin F. Thompsons Esq. and a Certain Road known by the Name of Baileys Hallow is hereby set apart into a Seperate District and are entitled to all the priviledges of the Law to be denominated the 28th School District of the Town of Brookhaven given under our hands in Brook haven this 4th. february 1818—

Mordecai Homan } Commissioners of
John R. Satterly } Common Schools

PAGE 153.

Be it Ordained by the Trustees of the Freeholders and commonalty of the Town of Brookhaven that if any person shall catch or take any fish of any kind whatsoever in any of the Bays Rivers or Creeks belonging to the Town of Brookhaven and William S. Smith or William Smith or shall kill or take any Wild Fowl therein—without first obtaining leave from the Trustees of said Town or their Agent he shall for every such Offence forfeit and pay to said Trustees or their order the sum of Twelve Dollars and fifty Cents. to be sued for and recoverd in the Name of the Trustees aforesaid Dated this 7th day of April 1818 at Brookhaven and sealed with our Seal

Josiah Smith Presdt { Seal }

W Sidney Smith { Seal }

Attest MORDECAI HOMAN town Clerk

Be it remembered that on the 2nd day of february in the Year one thousand Eight hundred and Nineteen Henry Smith made application to the Overseers of the poor for the Town of Brookhaven to Manumitt a Certain Male slave of his namd Richard and s,d Overseers being satisfied that said Richard is under forty five years and of Sufficient ability to provide for and maintain himself do consent that he should be manumitted as the Law of this State directs given under of hands.

Josiah Smith President

MORDECAI HOMAN Town Clerk

PAGE 154.

At a Meeting of the Freeholders and commonalty of the Town of Brookhaven held in said Town of the first Tuesday in April one thousand Eight hundred and Eighteen being Town Meeting day the following Town officers were duly and unanomously elected. Vis—

Josiah Smith President

Isaac Overton
Justus Overton
Daniel Overton } Trustees
Isaac Satterley
Timothy Miller
Joseph Raynor

John Rose Supervisor
Mordecai Homan Town Clerk & Treasurer
Nathan Post Collector

Theophilus Smith
William Beale
Benjamin Hallock } Assessors
Isaac Brewster
Thomas S. Strong

John Rose
William Phillips } Commissioners of highways
Isaac Brewster

Mordecai Homan
William Beale } Commissioners of Common Schools
John R Satterly

Constables

Timothy Davis   Nathan Corwin
James Woodhull   Samuel Bishop
Smith Mott   Israel Davis
Noadiah Carter   Jeremiah Gourden
Daniel Havens   Samuel Homan
Silvanus Overton

PAGE 155.

Rev. Zeceriah Green
Rev. Ezra King
Rev. Noah Hallock } Inspectors of common Schools
Nicoll Floyd
Joseph B. Roe
William Beale

Overseers of Highways

Joseph Hawkins	Selah Hawkins
Jacob Hawkins	Isaac Overton
James Woodhull	George Smith
Daniel Smith Jur	Justus Roe
Zecheriah Hawkins	Nathaniel Smith
Spicer Davis	Simmons Laws
Elisha Davis	Gershom Osbon
Samuel Brown	John Hutchinson
Peter Skidmore	James Dayton
James Woodhull Junr.	Joshua Mott
James Stansbro	James Howell
Isaac Reynor	Samuel Hammond
Christopher Robinson	George Hawkins
Henry P. Osbon	Caleb Newton
James Fanning	Briant Norton
Mordecai Homan	Epenetus Mills

Jeremiah Gourden

Fence Viewers

Jedediah Williamson	Hedges Osbon
William Rudyard	Barnabas Smith
Benjamin Hawkins	Justus Roe
Ebenezer Bailes	William Beale
William Jayne	Samuel Bishop
James Hulse	Epenetus Mills
Andrew Still	James Smith
Alfred Edwars	Daniel Saxton
Elisha Davis	Joshua Overton
John Davis	Nathan Corwin
Joseph Miller	Azariah Hawkins
Samuel Hopkins	Samuel Hammond
Miller J. Woodhull	David Overton Jur
Benjamin Robinson	Willard Ruland
Barnabas Wines	Robert Hawkins

Isaac Mills   John Laws.
William Randal   Daniel Overton
            Briant Davis

PAGE 156.

Suffolk }
County }

Statement of Votes taken at the Annaversary Election for Senators in the Town of Brookhaven which commenced on the last tuesday in April one thousand Eight hundred and Eighteen.

Darias Crosby had Seventy one } Votes
Jacob Dela Montagnie had Seventy two }

We certify the foregoing to be a true Statement and estimate of the Votes taken in the Town of Brookhaven at the aforesaid Election Dated this 30th. April 1818—

John Rose }
Isaac Brewster }
Benjamin Hallock } Inspectors
Theophilus Smith }

Suffolk }
County }

Statement of Votes taken at the Annaversary Election for Congress which commenced in the Town of Brookhaven on the last tuesday in April one thousand Eight hundred and Eighteen—Viz

Ebenezer Sage had Eighty four }
James Guyon Jun. had Eighty three } Votes
Silas Wood had Seventy Nine }
John Garretson had Seventy Nine }

We certify the foregoing to be a true Statement and Estimate of the Votes taken in the town of Brookhaven at the aforesaid Election dated this 30th. April 1818

John Rose }
Isaac Brewster }
Benjamin Hallock } Inspectors
Theophilus Smith }

Page 157.

Suffolk } County }

Statement of Votes taken in the Town of Brookhaven for Members of Assembly which commenced on the last tuesday in April one thousand Eight hundred and Eighteen Viz.

John P. Osborn had one hundred and fifty one
Daniel Youngs had one hundred and fifty one
Isaac conklin had one hundred and forty one
Ebenezer W. Case had one
} Votes

We certify the foregoing to be a true Statement and estimate of the Votes taken in the Town of Brookhaven at the aforesaid Election dated this 30th. April 1818

John Rose
Isaac Brewster
Benjamin Hallock
Theophilus Smith
} Inspectors

This doth certify that on the 2nd. day of August 1818 Mrs Elizabeth Smith Widow of John Smith Deceasd made application to the Trustees of the Town of Brookhaven to Manumitt a certain Woman Slave Belonging to the Estate of said Smith and said Trustees being satisfied that said Woman Slave whose name is Candas is under forty five Years and of sufficient ability to provide for and Maintain herself do consent that said Candas should be manumitted as the law directs and an entry made on the Town Record   JOSIAH SMITH President

Attest
MORDECAI HOMAN Town Clerk

Page 158.

Be it Remembered that on the 2nd. day of August 1818 the Trustees of the freeholders and commonalty of the Town of Brookhaven sold unto to John Rose Esq. a piece of common Land belonging to said Town lying in the fireplace on the east side of Beaver dam River and bounded East by the highway South by the land of Doctr. Nath. Miller West by said River and North to a certain Bound to be set so as to range with the south part of Richard Corwins Milk house—Also one other piece of Land lying four Rods to the Northward of the last mentioned Bound which said four Rods is reserved, extending from the highway to the River for a Watring place for the use of the Inhabitance of said Town which is not to be obstructed the last mentioned piece is Bounded south by the said four Rods West by the Land of Richard Gerard North within two Rods of the going Over Nearly oposite the house of Alexander Hawkins and East by the highway including all the Land belonging to said Town within the Bounds aforesaid the aforesaid Lands was sold for the sum of fifty Eight Dollars at public sale—as may appear by the title given for the same

Sold for the sum of $60.

JOSIAH SMITH President L. S.

Attest MORDECAI HOMAN Town Clerk.

Also on the fourth day of June 1819 the said Trustees sold to John Rose and Doctr. Nathaniel Miller all the Remainder of the common land belonging to s,d town lying to the Northward of the going over against Elizabeth Ellisons house on the Beaver dam River reserving a highway four Rods Wide at said going over

THOMAS S. STRONG President L. S.

Attest M. HOMAN Clerk—
for the sum of forty Dollars

PAGE 159.

Be it remembered that on the 3rd. day of November 1818 Daniel Jones made application to the Trustees of Brookhaven to Manumitt and set free a Certain female

Slave of his named Rhoda and said Trustees being Satisfied that said slave is under forty five Years and of Sufficient Ability to provide for and maintain herself do consent that she should be Manumitted as the Law of this state in such case directs— JOSIAH SMITH President.
Attest
MORDECAI HOMAN Town Clerk

Be it Ordained by the Trustees of the freeholders and commonalty of the Town of Brook haven that if any person or persons shall take any sand from any of the strands or shores belonging to the commons of Brook haven without first obtaining leave from said Trustees or their angent and paying a toleration at the Rate of one Cent for every Bushel so to be taken shall be deemed guilty of Trespass and shall for every such offence forfeit and pay to the said Trustees or their Agent the sum of twelve dollars and fifty Cents to be sued for and recoverd in the Name of the Trustees aforesaid before any Court having Cognizance thereof and applied to the use of said Town and further we do hereby appoint Joseph Hawkins our Lawful Agent, hereby Ratifying and confirming whatever our said Agent may lawfully do in the premises Given under our hand and Seal of Brookhaven this 2nd. day of february 1819

JOSIAH SMITH President

Attest MORDECAI HOMAN Clerk | Seal

PAGE 160.

At a Meeting of the Trustees of the freeholders and commonalty of the Town of Brookhaven for the time being held in said Town on the 2nd. day of february 1819. Zophar Tooker made application to said Trustees for liberty to set a Dock or frame in the south Bay for the purpose of laying Wood on and said Trustees after due consideration had in the premises did Grant liberty to the said Zophar Tooker to set up a frame or Dock in the south Bay a little to the Westward of long point at a place that shall be convenient for Vessels to load at which said Grant is to extend for the space of one Year from this date aforesaid given under our hands in Brookhaven

JOSIAH SMITH President

Attest MORDECAI HOMAN Clk

At a Meeting of the Trustees of the freeholders and commonalty of the Town of Brook haven held on the second day of March 1819. Smith Mott of said Town made application to said Trustees for liberty to Build a Dock in the south Bay against his own Land & said Trustees after due consideration had in the premises did grant liberty to the said Smith Mott to Build a Dock out into the South Bay against and adjoining to his own Land and to extend out into the said Bay to Eighteen Inches Water at common low Water Given under our hands in Brookhaven this second day of March 1819   JOSIAH SMITH President

Attest MORDECAI HOMAN Town Clerk

PAGE 161.

At a Meeting of the freeholders and commonalty of the Town of Brookhaven held in said town on the 6th. day of April 1819—being Town Meeting day the following persons were unanamously Elected as town Officers—Viz.

Thomas S. Strong President of Trustees

Samuel Satterly
Nathaniel Smith
Nicoll Floyd
Daniel Overton } Trustees
Justus Overton
Phillip Hallock

John Rose Supervisor
Mordecai Homan Town Clerk & Treasurer
Nathan Post Collector

Barnabas Wines }
Timothy Miller }
Isaac Satterly } Assessors
William Beale }
Benjamin Hallock }

Nathan Post } Commissioners
Lewis Ritch } of highways
Isaac Brewster }

Mordecai Homan } Commissioners of
Archabald Jayne } Common Schools
Nathaniel Miller }

Timothy Davis }
James Davis Jur }
Stephen Still }
Noadiah Carter }
William C. Overton } Constables
Micah Smith }
Samuel Dayton }
Samuel Homan }
Joseph Bennitt }

Page 162.

John R. Satterly }
Russell Green }
Rev. Ezra King } Inspectors of
Nicoll Floyd } Common Schools
William Beale }
Joseph B. Roe }

Overseers of highways

Joseph Hawkins   Mordecai Homan
Jacob Hawkins   Nathaniel Miller
Isaac Satterly   William Tooker
Daniel Smith   Joseph Hedges

Zecheriah Hawkins
Spicer Davis
Henry C. Mathers
Samuel Brown
Peter Skidmore
Miller I. Woodhull
Wells Davis
James Stansbro
Jacob Carter
David Peterson
Silas Reeves
John S. Havens

Justus Roe
William Arthur
Simmons Laws
Jeffrey Randal
Silvanus Overton
John Hutchenson
Nathan Corwin
Brewster Terry
Daniel Terry
Samuel Hammond
Zophar Hallock
Austin Roe Jur.

Jeremiah Gourden

FENCE VIEWERS

Jedediah Williamson
William Rudyard
James Woodhull
Isaac Jayne
Samuel Satterly
James Hulse
Andrew Still
Alfred Edwards
Wells Davis
John Davis
Joseph Miller
Samuel Hopkins
James Woodhull Jur
Benjamin Robinson
Barnabas Wines
James Stansbro
Samuel Terry
Elisha Raynor
Nathan R Bartoe
Samuel Hawkins

Hedges Osborn
Barnabas Smith
William Beale
Justus Roe
John Rider
Epenetus Mills
James Smith
Daniel Saxton
Joshua Overton
Nathan Corwin
Azariah Hawkins
Samuel Hammond
David Overton Ju
Willard Ruland
Robert Hawkins
Isaac Mills
William Randal
John Laws
Daniel Overton
Briant Davis

216 BROOKHAVEN TOWN RECORDS.

PAGE 163.

Suffolk } ss
County }

Statement of Votes taken at the Annaversary Election for Senators which commenced on the Last tuesday in April one thousand Eight hundred and Nineteen

Pierre Van Cortlandt had one hundred and thirty three
James Tallmadge Jur. had one hundred and thirty five—
Peter R. Livingston had Eighty Nine } Votes
John Townsend had Ninety one
Phillip I Schyler had two
James Morris had two

We certify the foregoing to be a true Statement and Estimate of the Votes taken in the Town of Brookhaven at the aforesaid Election this 29th. April 1819—

Isaac Satterly
Barnabas Wines
Benjamin Hallock } Inspectors
John Rose
Timothy Miller

At a Meeting of the Trustees of the freeholders and commonalty of the town of Brookhaven held on the 2nd. day of April 1819--Timothy Miller made application to manumitt a certain slave of his named Huldah and said Trustees being Satisfied that said slave was under forty five Years and of Sufficient Ability to provide for and maintain herself do give their consent that she should be Manumitted as the Law of this State in such case directs

JOSIAH SMITH President—

Attest
MORDECAI HOMAN Town Clerk—

PAGE 164.

Suffolk } ss
County }

Statement of Votes taken at the Annaversary Election

for Members of Assembly which commenced on the last tuesday in April one thousand Eight hundred and Nineteen—

Israel Carll had one hundred and Seventy Eight
John Rose had one hundred and Ninety one
Ebenezer W. Case had one hundred and Ninety Six
Charles H. Havens had Seventy Eight } Votes
Abraham Parsons had Eighty five
Samuel Dickinson had fifty
Lewis Ritch had one
Ebenezer Case had one—

We certify the foregoing to be a true Statement and Estimate of the Votes taken in the town of Brookhaven at the aforesaid Election this 29th. April 1819—

Be it Ordained by the trustees of the freeholders and commonalty of the town of Brookhaven that if any person or persons shall take or catch any shell fish in any of the Waters or harbours on the North side of the Island belonging to the town Brookhaven he or they so offending shall for every such Offence shall forfeit and pay the sum of twelve dollars and fifty cents Dated this 7th. day of September 1819—

THOS. S. STRONG president

MORDECAI HOMAN | Seal

PAGE 165.

We the commissioners of the town of Brookhaven in the County of Suffolk being call,d upon by a sufficient number of the Inhabitants of said town to lay out a highway at Moriches and after having viewed the premises have laid out a public highway four Rods wide begining at a certain Stake set a little to the eastward of the Mill dam at swift stream and from thence extending Southwesterly across the land of Mr. Silas Woodruff and the land of James Faning to a certain stake set about Eighty seven links to the Eastward of a certain pine stump near the River and from thence extending into the River about thirteen Links and from thence Runing Northeasterly to the highway across the Dam aforesaid four Rods wide. Which we return to be Recorded

                       Nathan Post } Commissioners
                       Lewis Ritch } of highways

the aforesaid road was appraised by a Jury call,d for that purpose by the assistance of John Rose and Barnabas Wines Justices of the peace for said County which said Jury did alow unto Mr. Woodruff the sum of two Dollars and to James Faning the sum of thirty five Dollars for damages of said Road done in Brookhaven this third-day of July 1819—

                  John Rose } Justices
                  Barnabas Wines }

Enterd this 3rd. day of July 1819.
MORDECAI HOMAN Town Clerk

PAGE 166.

At a Meeting of the Trustees of the freeholders and commonalty of the Town of Brookhaven held on the seventh day of September 1819 present at said Meeting Thomas S. Strong President Nicoll Floyd Nathaniel smith Daniel Overton Justus Overton Samuel Satterly Trustees—At said Meeting said Trustees Granted to John Willse the priviledg of Building a Dock or Wharf in Drown Meadow Bay against the Land of John Willse Deceasd for the sum of one Dollar and to have it for the space of twenty one Years to him and to his heirs and Assigns. under the following regulations and restrictions Viz the said John Willse shall be allowed and paid for putting on Board of any Vessel or craft from off of said Dock six Cents for every six feet Cord of Wood and for every Vessel laying along side of said Dock when not loading twelve and half cents pr day for taking in or out Cattle fifteen Cents pr head for Calves or lambs two Cents pr head for every hogshead fifteen Cents for every Barrell of Liquor or pork six Cents for every Barrell of flour four Cents for every thousand of long shingle twenty five Cents and four Cents for every Bundle of short shingle for every thousand feet of plank twenty five Cents for every thousand feet of Boards Eighteen and three quarter Cents. and for every ten Gallon keg three Cents for five Gallon do. two cents Reserving a Right of Landing on said Dock any Article belonging to the corporation of Brookhaven free from duty. and at the expiration of the said 21. Years the aforesaid Grant shall return to said town and the Dock appraised by indiferent men or further arrangments made Between said Trustees or their Successors and the said John Willse his Heirs or Assigns concering the premises.

THOMAS S. STRONG President (L S)

Attest
MORDECAI HOMAN Town Clerk

PAGE 167.

Be it rembered that on the 7th day of December 1819 the Trustees of the freeholders and commonalty of Brookhaven for the sum of three hundred and fifty Dollars sold to Isaac Brewster Stephen Edwards and Ebenezer Smith all the Right in the flax pond belonging to said town. excepting and reserving the right of fishing and clambing in said pond for the Inhabitants of said town. to be under the controul of said Trustees or their Successors—

THOMAS S. STRONG President—

Attest. MORDECAI HOMAN. Town Clerk

We the Commissioners of highways for the Town of Brookhaven being call,d to open a Road in the Village of Westfield begining at the house of Isaac Hammonds and thence to Justus Overtons begining at the said Hammonds

on the South side East to a Road leading South at a Locus tree from thence East to a black Oak tree before Wm Overtons house thence East to a Stake thence East to Joseph Rulands House Intended for one of his sons twenty one feet North from the House from thence to a White oak tree by the hedge fence within four feet of the same from thence as the fence now stands to a certain Locus tree from thence to a black Oak Saplin marked with two notches thence East within two feet of an Apple tree East of Albert Overtons House from thence to a Locus tree before Joseph Rulands house from thence by and with the Roe of Locus trees and from thence to a Black Oak tree Marked from thence East to a stake twenty three feet soth of a large White oak tree standing in the Road from thence east to a black Oak tree west of Justus Overtons Barn from thence East to a Stake in the Ditch at the North east Corner of Joseph Rulands Land the above mentioned Road to be opened four Rods Wide extending North from the above mentioned line which we return to be recorded this 7th. June 1819
as Witness our hands

      Lewis Ritch ⎫ Commissioners
      Nathan Post ⎭ of highways

 Enterd 1st february 1820
 Attest MORDECAI HOMAN Town Clerk

PAGE 168.

We the commissioners of highways for the Town of Brookhaven being call,d to Stake out a Road in the Village of Stoney Brook begining at the Road leading from Setaket to Stoney Brook from the abovesaid Road Westerly to George Hallock Dock begining at a Red Ceder post on the south side twenty feet North thence Westerly to the south-west corner of George Hallock Junr. Garden fence twenty feet North to a Stake thence West to a Red Ceder tree on the North side twenty feet south thence West to a Red ceder stake from thence to a large Red Ceder tree twenty feet south thence Westerly to a Red Ceder on the south side twenty feet North to a stake thence Westerly to Stakes on the North and south side of the above mentioned Road being the Width of twenty feet from the begining to said Hallocks Dock which we return to be Recorded this 8th. day of June 1819—as Witness our hands—

Lewis Ritch ⎱ Commissioners
Nathan Post ⎰ of highways

Enterd this 1st. feb. 1820

Attest MORDECAI HOMAN Town Clerk—

This doth certify that on the fourth day of April in the Year 1820. Zophar Hallock made application to the Trustees of the freeholders and commonalty of the town of Brookhaven to Manumitt and set free a female slave of his named Philopenea and said Trustees being satisfied that said slave is under forty five years of age did consent to said Manumition According to the Statute of this state in such case made and provided. said slave being of sufficient ability to provide for and maintain herself

Attest MORDECAI HOMAN Town Clerk

PAGE 169.

At a Meeting of the freeholders and Inhabitants held in said Town on the fourth day of April 1820 being town Meeting day the following persons were unanimously Elected Viz—

Thomas S. Strong President

Davis Norton ⎫
William Phillips ⎪
Major Nathaniel Smith ⎬ Trustees
Samuel Satterly ⎪
Timothy Miller ⎪
Barnabas Wines ⎭

John Rose Supervisor
Mordecai Homan Town Clerk and treasurer
Nathan Post collector

Nathan Post
Theophilus Smith
Benjamin Hallock } Assessors
Phillip Hallock
Woodhull Smith

Isaac Brewster
Lewis Ritch } commisioners of highways
Isaac Overton

Mordecai Homan
Archabald Jayne } commisioners of common schools
Nathaniel Miller

William C. Overton
Micah Smith
Silvanus Edwards
Joseph Bennitt } Constables
Noadiah Carter
James Robinson

Russell Green
Rev. Ezra King } Inspectors of Schools
William Beale

PAGE 170.

OVERSEERS OF HIGHWAYS

Joseph Hawkins
Jacob Hawkins senior
Thomas Bailey
James Woodhull
Samuel Satterly
James Hulse
Zecheriah Hawkins
Daniel Davis
Isaac Davis
Samuel Davis

Mordecai Homan
Benjamin Guildersleve
William Tooker
Justus Roe
Joseph Avery
William Phillips
Briant Davis
Sylvanus Overton
Joshua Mott
Brewster Terry,

Henry C. Mathers
Zophar Mills
James Robinson
Jacob Carter
Lewis Gourden. Jur.
Samuel Terry
William Penny

Samuel Hammond
Daniel Terry
Zophar Hallock
Austin Roe Jur
Jeremiah Gourden
Daniel Hulse
John Randal

Nicoll Floyd

FENCE VIEWERS

Jedediah Williamson
William Rudyard
James Woodhull
Isaac Jayne
Samuel Satterly
James Hulse
Ebenezer Jones
Alfred Edwards
Elisha Davis
Isaac Davis
Samuel Hopkins
Joseph Miller
James Woodhull Jr
Benjamin Robinson
Isaac Raynor Jur
Joseph Raynor Jur
Samuel Terry,
Elisha Raynor
Nathan R Bartoe
Samuel Hawkins

Joseph Hedges
Barnabas Smith
William Beale
Justus Roe
John Rider
Epenetus Mills
James Smith
Daniel Saxton
Joshua Overton
Joshua Mott
Azariah Hawkins
Samuel Hammond
David Overton Jur
Willard Ruland
Robert Hawkins
Isaac Mills
William Randal
John Laws
Daniel Overton
Briant Davis

PAGE 171.

Suffolk }
County }

Statement of Votes taken at the Annaversary Election in the town of Brookhaven for Governor lieutenant Governor and Senators which commenced on the last tuesday in April one thousand Eight hundred and twenty Viz—

Vote for Governor

Daniel D. Tompkins had two hundred and Eleven
De Witt Clinton had one hundred and forty three

Vote for Lieut. Governor

Benjamin Mooers had two hundred and ten
John Taylor had one hundred and forty four.

Votes for Senators

Walter Bown had two hundred and Eleven
John Lefferts had two hundred and Eleven
Samuel Jones had one hundred and forty one
John C. Vanderveer had one hundred and forty three
Benjamin Hutchenson had one—
W Sidney Smith had one Vote for Lieutenant Governor

We certy the foregoing to be a true Statement and Estimate of the Votes taken in the town of Brookhaven at the aforesaid Election dated this 27th. April 1820

John Rose Benjamin Hallock Woodhull Smith Nathan Post Phillip Hallock Inspectors

Suffolk }
County }

Statement of Votes taken at the Annaversary Election in the town of Brookhaven for Members of Assembly which commenced on the last tuesday in April in the year 1820 Viz.

Votes for Assembly

Isaac Conklin had two hundred and forty four
John P. Orsbon had two hundred and forty three
John M. Williamson had two hundred and forty three
Abraham Rose had one hundred and six
John R Satterly had one hundred and Eight
Jonathan Gardner had one hundred and five

Mordecai Homan had two
Nathan Post had two
Nathaniel Miller had two
Benjamin F Thompson had one

We certify the foregoing to be a true Statement and Estimate of the Vote taken in the town of Brookhaven in said County at the aforesaid Election dated this 27th. May 1820

                    John Rose
                    Benjamin Hallock
                    Woodhull Smith
                    Nathan Post
                    Phillip Hallock
Attest MORDECAI HOMAN town Clerk

PAGE 172.

This doth certify that on the fifth day of September 1820 Mary Davis made application to the Overseers of the poor for the town of Brookhaven to Manumitt a Male slave of hers Named Permelia and said Overseers being satisfied that said slave is under forty five Years of Age and of Sufficient ability to provide for and Maintain herself did consent that she should be Manumitted as the law of this state in such case directs

Attest. MORDECAI HOMAN Town Clerk

Suffolk County ss

We the Commissioners of highways of the town of Brookhaven in the County of Suffolk do hereby certify that a public highway was laid out by us on the twenty eighth day of September 1820 through the lands of Warden Tobey and Henry H. Howell (now the land of John Elderkin) Begining at a certain Chesnut post standing in the fence of Warden Tobey near the Road leading from Isaac Jaynes to Westmeadows by which a Stake is fixed and runing thence northward to the poplar tree standing nearest the House of Henry H. Howell and so on to the south corner of Isaac Satterlys House and then three Rods East nearly to the Mill pond thence south parallel with the aforesaid line till it strikes the same fence which it begins at being three Rods wide throughout given under our hands and seals in Brookhaven this 28th. October 1820

     Lewis Ritch L S   } Commissioners
     Isaac Brewster L S } of highways
     Isaac Overton   }

Enterd this 31. Octr. 1820
by me. Mordecai Homan Town Clerk

Page 173.

Be it Remembred that on the Seventh day of Nov. 1820 William Helme made application to the Trustees of the freeholders and commonalty of Brookhaven to Manumitt a certain Slave of his named Oliver and said Trustees being Satisfied that said slave is under forty five years and of sufficient Ability to provide for and maintain himself do hereby consent that he should be Manumitted as the Statute of this State directs Thomas S. Strong Presdt
 Attest Mordecai Homan. Town Clerk

Be it Remembred that on the 6th. day of March 1821 Henry Smith made Application to the Trustees of the freeholders and commonalty of the town of Brookhaven to Manumitt a certain Slave of his named Jemima and said Trustees being Satisfied that said Slave is under forty five years and of Sufficient ability to provide for and maintain herself do hereby consent that she the said Jemima should be Manumitted as the Law of this State directs
             Thomas S Stong
 Attest Mordecai Homan Town Clerk

Be it remembred that on the 3rd. day of April 1821 Benjamin Jones made Application to the Trustees of the freeholders and commonalty of the town of Brookhaven to

Manumitt a Certain slave of his Named Mingo and said Trustees being satisfied that said Slave is under forty five Years and of Sufficient Ability to provide for and Maintain himself do hereby consent that the said Mingo should be Manumitted as the Law of this state directs—

Attest THOMAS S. STRONG president
MORDECAI HOMAN Town Clerk

Be it remembred that on the 28th. of October 1820 a Jury of Inquest was call,d to appraise the damage of a Road laid out through the land of Warden Tobey and John Elderkin and allowed to Warden Tobey fifty Dollars and to John Elderkin twenty Dollars. said Road was laid out by Lewis Ritch and Isaac Overton on said day and Returns thereof Made

Attest MORDECAI HOMAN Town Clerk

PAGE 174.

At a Meeting of the freeholders and Inhabitants of the town of Brookhaven held on the third day of April 1821 being town Meeting day the following persons were unanimously Elected as town Officers for the ensuing Year Viz.

Nicoll Floyd President of Trustees

Merritt Learned }
John Brewster
Timothy Miller } Trustees
Robert Hawkins
Samuel Davis
Henry P. Orsbon }

John Rose Supervisor

Mordecai Homan Clerk and Treasurer

Nathan Post Collector

Barnabas Wines }
Timothy Miller
Daniel Davis } Assessors.
Nathan Post
Woodhull Smith }

BROOKHAVEN TOWN RECORDS.

Josiah Smith
Benjamin Hutchenson } Commissoners of highways
Isaac Satterly

Mordecai Homan
Nathaniel Miller } Commissioners of Common Schools
Archabald Jayne

William C. Overton
Noadiah D. Carter
Sylvanus Edwards
Micah Smith } Constables
Joseph Bennitt
Daniel I. Havens
Isaac Davis

At said Meeting it was Voted that no Rams should run in the Commons from the first day of Sept. to the first day of Nov.

PAGE 175.

INSPECTORS OF COMMON SCHOOLS

Russell Green   Rev. Ezra King
           William Beale

OVERSEERS OF HIGHWAYS

Joseph Hawkins   Mordecai Homan South
Jacob Hawkins   Benjamin Guildersleve
Thomas Bailey   William Howell
Joseph Bennitt   Daniel G. Gillette
Samuel Satterly   Joseph Avery
James Hulse   Simmons Laws
Zecheriah Hawkins   Samuel N. Hurtin
John Davis   John Hutchenson
David Robbins   Albert Davis
Charles Woodhull   Joshua Mott
Josiah Lupton   Brewster Terry
Daniel Swezey.   Samuel Hammond
Benjamin Robinson   James Howell
James Robinson   Zophar Hallock

Noadiah D. Carter
Lewis Gourden Jur
Bartlett Sandford
Mott Raynor
Nicoll Floyd

Davis Norton
Jeremiah Gourden
Daniel Davis
John Randal
William Swezey

FENCE VIEWERS

Jedediah Williamson
William Rudyard
Morris Jayne
Isaac Jayne
Samuel Satterly
James Hulse
Ebenezer Jones
Alfred Edwards
Elisha Davis
Isaac Davis
Samuel Hopkins
Joseph Miller
Charles Robinson
Moses Swezey.
Isaac Raynor
Joseph Raynor
Joseph Hawkins senior
Elisha Raynor
Nathan R. Bartoe
Samuel Hawkins

Joseph Hedges
Barnabas Smith
Wm. Beale
Justus Roe
John Rider
Epenetus Mills
James Smith
Daniel Saxton
Joshua Mott
Noah Overton
Azariah Hawkins
Sammuel Hammond
David Overton Jur
Willard Ruland
Robert Hawkins
Isaac Mills
Benjamin Hutchenson
Ezra Guildersleve
John Laws.
William Randal

PAGE 176.

No 1. For Senators

Suffolk County } To Wit.
Town of Brookhaven }

A true canvas and estimate of the Votes taken at the annual general Election held on the last tuesday in April 1821 and on the two succeeding days inclusive in the town of Brookhaven in the County of suffolk for the purpose of Electing two Senators for the southers District of the State of New York—to Wit

Peter Stephens had one hundred and sixty one
Abraham Rose had one hundred and sixty three
Abel Huntington had one hundred and thirteen
Abraham Gurnee had one hundred and twelve } Votes

Given under our hands in the said town of Brookhaven this 26 day of April 1821

Timothy Miller
Daniel Davis
Woodhull Smith } Inspectors
John Rose
Barnabas Wines

No. 2. For Members of Congress

Suffolk County—
Town of Brookhaven } To Wit.

A true Canvas and estimate of the Votes taken at the Annual General Election held on the last tuesday in April and on the two succeeding days inclusive in the town of Brookhaven in the County of suffolk for the purpose of Electing two Members of Congress to Represent the first District of the state of New York in the house of Representatives of the united States—To Wit.

Cadwallader D. Colden had two hundred and twenty
Silas Wood had two hundred and thirty Eight
Joshua Smith had one hundred and forty three
Peter sharp had one hundred and twenty seven } Votes

Given under our hands at the said town of Brookhaven in the County of Suffolk this 26,th day of April 1821

Timothy Miller Barnabas Wines
Daniel Davis   John Rose   } Inspectors
Woodhull Smith

PAGE 177.

No 3. For Members of Assembly—

Suffolk County } To Wit
Town of Brook haven }

A true Canvass and Estimate of the Votes taken at the Annual General Election held on the last tuesday in April and on the two succeeding days inclusive in the town of Brook haven in the County of suffolk for the purpose of Electing three Members of Assembly to Represent the said County in the house of Assembly of the state of New York. To. Wit

Mordecai Homan had two hundred and sixteen }
William Platt Buffett had two hundred and twelve }
Oliver Post had two hundred and Eleven }
John M. Williamson had one hundred and twenty five } Votes
Hugh Halsey had one hundred and twenty seven }
Tredwell Scudder had one hundred and twenty four }

Given under our hands at the said town of Brook haven this 26. April 1821

Timothy Miller Daniel Davis } Inspe-
Woodhull Smith John Rose Barnabas Wines } ctors

No. 4. For and against Convention

Suffolk County }
Town of Brook haven }

A true Canvass and Estimate of the Votes taken at the Annual General Election pursuant to the Act entitled an Act reccommending a convention of the people of this passed 13 March 1821. held on the last tuesday in April and on the two succeeding days inclusive in the town of Brook haven in the County of suffolk for the purpose of determining whether a Convention shall be Called pursuant to said Act.

To Wit.

Convention Sixty six—
No Convention two hundred and twenty } Votes

Given under our hands at the said town of Brook haven this 26th. April 1821

Timothy Miller Daniel Davis—
Woodhull Smith John Rose Barnabas Wines } Inspectors

PAGE 178.

Be it Remembred that on the fourth day of May in the Year of our Lord one thousand Eight hundred and twenty Daniel Homan made application to the Trustees of the town of Brookhaven for liberty to Build a Mill or Mills on the River calld Connecticut River Below where his Mills now standeth and said Trustees after due consideration had in the premises did for and in consideration of the sum of five Dollars to them in hand paid Grant unto Daniel Homan and to his Heirs liberty to Dam across the said River at any place between where his Mills now Standeth and Yamphank line and to Erect thereon a Grist Mill Saw Mill and such other Machinery as he or they shall think proper to Erect and to have the priviledge of the town Right to the Stream of Water above Yamphank line for the aforesaid use and the said Homan his Heirs and Assigns shall be allowed the one Eleventh part for Grinding all sorts of Grain and the said Homan his Heirs and Assigns shall keep Sufficient Bolting Cloths for Bolting and provided also the said Mills or a considerable part thereof shall be erected within the term of six Years from this date by the said Homan or his Heirs or otherwise the aforesaid Grant shall return to said town again but in case the said Mills or a considerable part thereof shall be Erected within the term aforesaid by the said Homan or his Heirs then the aforesaid Grant shall extend to his or their Assigns provided also that he or they shall keep the same in good re-

pair and also keep an Approved Miller which is Granted Accordingly
  in presence of
  Mordecai Homan

|L S

Thomas S. Strong President

PAGE 179.

Delegates for Convention

Suffolk County } To Wit
Town of Brook haven }

A true canvas and estimate of the Votes taken on the third tuesday in June 1821 and on the two succeeding days inclusive in the town of Brook haven in the County of Suffolk for the purpose of Elicting Delegates for said County to meet in convention agreeable to the Law of this State passed 13th. March 1821. Viz.

Nicoll Floyd had one hundred and Ninety
Joshua Smith had two hundred and forty three
Ebenezer Sage had two hundred and thirty six
Usher H. Moore had fifty five—
Judge Woodhull had one—
Ebenezer Smith had one—

Given under our hands at the said town of Brook haven in the said County of Suffolk this 21st. day of June 1821.

John Rose—
Daniel Davis—
Timothy Miller— } Inspectors
Barnabas Wines
Woodhull Smith

At a Meeting of the Trustees of the freeholders and commonalty of the town of Brookhaven held on the fourth day of Dec. 1821 Woodhull Smith made application to said trustees to Manumitt a certain Slave of his named Samuel and said Trustees being satisfied that said Slave was under forty five Years and of sufficient ability to provide for and maintain himself do hereby consent to the Manumision of said Samuel as the law of this State directs

 Attest   Nicoll Floyd President
Mordecai Homan Clerk

Page 180.

Be it remembered that on the fourth day of December 1821 Thomas S. Strong made application to the Trustees of the freeholders and commonalty of the town of Brook haven to Manumitt a certain slave of his named Darcas and said Trustees being satisfied that said slave is under forty five years and of sufficient ability to provide for and maintain herself do hereby consent to the Manumition of said Darcas agreeable to the Law of this state in such case made and provided—   Nicoll Floyd President

 Attest Mordecai Homan Town Clerk

Suffolk County ss:

We Thomas S. Strong Joshua Smith and Divine Hewlett three of the Judges of the court of common pleas of the County of suffolk having been call,d to decide an appeal brought by Warden tobey against the proceedings of the commissioners of highways of the town of Brook haven in the said County laying out a public highway in the said town through lands of Henry H. Howell (now of John Elderkin) and of the said Warden Tobey and having heard the proofs and Allegations of the said Warden Tobey and the said commissioners do adjudge that the said highway has been correctly laid out and was required for the convenience of the public and do in all things confirm the said proceedings of the said commissioners in witness whereof we have hereunto set our respective hands and seals this 17th. day of November 1820

 Enterd this
 16th. Dec. 1820   Thomas S. Strong—L S
           Joshua Smith—L S
           Divine Hewlett—L S
Mordecai Homan town Clerk

PAGE 181.

Suffolk County }
town of Brook haven }

A true canvas and estimate of the Votes given in the town of Brook haven and County of Suffolk on the third tuesday in January 1822 and the two days succeeding inclusive under certain resolutions of the late convention of this state submitting to the decission of the people the amended constitution of this state adopted by the said convention. Viz ; one hundred an sixteen Votes were given for the said amended constitution by that number of Ballotts being Written or printed with the word Yes Ninety five Votes were given against the said Amended constitution by that number of Votes being Written or printed with the word No—given under our hands at Brook haven this 17th. January 1822

Woodhull Smith }
Nathan Post }
Daniel Davis } Inspectors
John Rose }

Attest MORDECAI HOMAN Clerk—

We the Commissioners of the town of Brookhaven being calld to open the Road leading from the Village of Westfields to coram and finding the same to be in many places too narrow and much obstructed by fences and other obstructions we hereby order the same to be cleared of all the obstructions above named by the different owners of the Lands adjoining the same on or before the first day of may next. within or on that portion of Road leading from the house of Isaac Hammonds to the house of Justus Overtons the same to commence at a stake by the side of the cross Road between the Lands of Isaac Hammond and William Overton, and running Easterly within two feet of the Northwest corner of sd Wm. Overtons House to a stake then Easterly to a stake standing within twenty feet of the front of Israel Rulands House from thence Easterly to a White Oak tree by the hedge fence within four feet of the Ditch from thence Easterly to a stake standing in the line fence of Albert Overton at or near his Northeast corner from thence the same to continue on Easterly to a Red Oak sapling marked with two Notches on the same from thence Easterly to a stake standing two Rods south of a large white Oak tree at the Northwest corner of Joseph Rulands lott and on the east side of the woodland of Austin Roe from thence Easterly Across said

PAGE 182.

Rulands lott to a Stake Standing in the Ditch on the south side of the Road opposite Justus Overtons Barn the above Road to be opened four Rods in width extending North from the above mentioned Bounds which we return to be recorded this 27th day of October 1821. as Witness our hands

Josiah Smith—
Benjamin Hutchenson } Commissioners
Isaac Satterly— of highways

Enterd this 5th. day of February. 1822 MORDECAI HOMAN Clerk

Be it remembred that on the fifth day of March 1822 Henry P. Orsbon made application to the Trustees of the freeholders and commonalty of the town of Brookhaven to Manumitt a certain slave of his named Thomas and said Trustees being satisfied that said slave is under forty five years and of sufficient ability to provide for and maintain himself do hereby consent to the Manumition of said Thomas agreeable to the Law of this State in such case made and provided. NICOLL FLOYD President

Attest MORDECAI HOMAN Town Clerk

Be it remembred that on the fifth day of March 1822 Thomas R. Smith made application to the Trustees of the

freeholders and commonalty of the town of Brook haven to Manumitt a certain slave of his named Irenea and said Trustees being satisfied that said slave is under forty five years and of sufficient ability to provide for and maintain himself do hereby consent to the Manumition of said Irenea agreeable to the Law of this State in such case made and provided   NICOLL FLOYD. President
Attest MORDECAI HOMAN Town Clerk

PAGE 183.

At a Meeting of the freeholders and commonalty of the town of Brook haven on the first tuesday in April 1822 being town Meeting day the following persons were Elected as town Officers. Viz

Thomas S. Strong President

Nathaniel Smith } Trustees and
Jesse Woodhull } Overseers of the poor

Barnabas Wines ⎫
Briant Davis ⎪
Samuel Davis ⎬ Trustees
Phillip Hallock ⎭

John Rose Supervisor

Mordecai Homan Town Clerk

Nathan Post Collector

Henry P. Orsbon ⎫
Nathan Post ⎪
Justus Overton ⎬ Assessors
Woodhull Smith ⎪
Timothy Miller ⎭

Isaac Satterly ⎫
Samuel Davis ⎬ Commissioners of
Nathaniel Miller ⎭ highways

BROOKHAVEN TOWN RECORDS.

Mordecai Homan   ⎫ Commissioner
Archabald Jayne   ⎬   of
Nathaniel Miller   ⎭ common schools

William C. Overton
Noadiah Carter
Sylvanus Edwards
Micah Smith
Jesse Hulse
Robert Stivers
Israel Davis
James Robinson
John Buckingham

PAGE 184.

Russell Green   ⎫
Ezra King   ⎬ Inspectors of common schools
William Beale   ⎭

OVERSEERS OF HIGHWAYS

Timothy Davis Aceptd
Jacob Hawkins Accepted
Samuel Satterley Acepted
Thomas Bailey
Daniel Smith Acceptd
Isaac Satterly Accepted
Zecheriah Hawkins Acepted
Daniel Davis
Isaac Davis Accepted
William Hopkins
Henry C. Mathers Accepted
Benjamin Robinson Acceptd
James Robinson Accepted
Jacob Carter Accepted
Solomon Bishop Acepted
James Fanning Accepted
Mordecai Homan Acepted
Nathaniel Miller Accepted
William Tooker Accepted

James Woodhull Accepted
Joseph Avery
Jeffrey Randal Accepted
Benjamin Hutchenson Accepted
Albert Davis Accepted
Noah Overton
Elisha Overton Accepted
Samuel Hammond Accepted
Daniel Saxton
Zophar Hallock Accepted
Briant Norton Accepted
Jeremiah Gourden Accepted
Daniel Hulse Accepted
William Randal Accepted
Nicol Floyd Acepted
Appollos Mills Accepted

FENCE VIEWERS

Jedediah Williamson
William Rudyard
Jesse Woodhull
Isaac Jayne
Ebenezer Jones
Zecheriah Hawkins
Samuel Hopkins
Joseph Miller
James Woodhull Jr
Benjamin Robinson
Isaac Raynor Ju
Joseph Raynor Jur
Samuel Hawkins
Nathan R. Bartoe
John Rider
Epenetus Mills
Justus Roe

William Beale
James Smith
Daniel Saxton
Joshua Overton
Daniel Bishop.
Azariah Hawkins
Samuel Hammond
Davis Overton
Willard Ruland
Robert Hawkins
Isaac Mills
William Randal
John Laws
Daniel Overton
Briant Davis
Isaac Davis
Elisha Davis

Page 185.

To all to whome the presents shall come we the Trustees of the freeholders and commonalty of the town of Brookhaven send Greeting, Whereas we have heretofore granted to Warden Tobey the priviledg of erecting and constructing a Dock or Wharfe at a place called Blue point on certain conditions and whereas the said Warden Tobey after having constructed such Dock or wharfe has assigned his right therein to Epenetus Mills of the said town of Brookhaven and whereas the said Epenetus Mills has offered to relinquish the grant made to the said Warden Tobey and assigned to him on the condition that he shall receive a new Grant and whereas we believe that it will be for the convenience and adventage of the freeholders and inhabitants of the said town to make such Grant; Now therefore Know ye that we the said Trustees in consideration of the premises and of one Dollar to us in hand paid by the said Epenetus Mills the receipt whereof is hereby acknowledged, have sold Granted and conveyed and by these presents do sell grant and convey to the said Epenetus Mills his Executors Administrators and Assigns all our right and title to the said Dock or wharfe and the land on which it has been constructed comprehended within the limits or Boundaries mentioned in the original grant to the said Warden Tobey it being understood that the said Dock shall be and continue fourteen feet wide and one hundred and sixty Seven feet long or thereabouts, provided nevertheless and these presents are upon the express condition that the said Epenetus Mills shall not charge any greater rates of wharfage to any freeholder or Inhabitant of the said town than the following to wit, for every four feet cord of Wood lying on the said wharfe over four hours and not exceeding one callended Month the sum of six Cents for every common Waggon load of hay drawn by a common team and lying over four hours and not exceeding twenty four hours the sum of Nine cents for every sail Boat lying at the said Dock over four hours and not exceeding twenty four hours four Cents and every sail Boat paying by the year if not sunk by the Dock one Dollar and twenty five cents the year if lying sunk by the Dock four Cents for every twenty four hours, and all other articles in the same proportion the said trustees however

PAGE 186.

reserving to themselves the right to fix the rate of wharfage for all articles not herein particularly designated, and also to put thereon the goods belonging to the town on such terms as they may thing proper and it is further understood and do hereby grant that if any person shall obstruct the said Dock by setting up stakes Anchoring Boats near thereto or otherwise he or they shall be liable to pay the same wharfage as if the vessel was lying by or other obstruction placed on the said wharfe and all damages occasioned by such obstruction: to have and to hold the said dock or wharfe with the privileges above mentioned, but subject to the conditions above stated to the said Epenetus Mills his Executors Administrators and Assigns to and for his and their own benefit for the period or term of twenty Years from the date of these presents in Witness whereof we have caused these presents to be signed by our president and countersigned by our Clerk and affixed our seal thereto the fifth day of June in the Year one thousand eight hundred and twenty one   NICOLL FLOYD President L. S.

Attest MORDECAI HOMAN town Clerk

We the commisioners of highways for the town of Brookhaven being call,d to open a certain Road at patchogue which was formerly open from the south country Road begining near the house of Justus Roe in patchogue and leading to John Motts Mills but is now shut up by Stephen

Jayne of the said patchogue and others we hereby order the said Stephen Jayne and others to open the said Road where they have shut the same to the width of three Rods the same to commence at and between the Barn of Oliver Russel and the Dwelling house of Justus Roe and running Northerly across the Lands of Stephen Jayne as the Road formerly Ran to the Gate which lets the Road into Ebenezer Akerleys land thence Northwesterly through a small Grove of Oaks till it comes to a ditch to another Gate and from thence Northerly as it is now marked across the Land of said Akerley to the Land of James Smith thence Across his land as it is marked to the Lands of Ebenezer Jones thence Across said Jones Land to the Lands of Stephen Jayne and

PAGE 187.

then across said Jaynes Lands to the house of John Mott senior and thence to continue on the said Road in the place where it now Runs til the same shall hit the Coram Road at sandy Mile Hollow which we return to be recorded this 20th. day of March 1822

      Isaac Satterly } Commissionrs of
      Josiah Smith } highways

Enterd this 3rd. April 1822
MORDECAI HOMAN town Clerk

Be it remembred that on the 4th. day of June 1822 Josiah Smith Made application to the Trustees of the freeholders and commonalty of the town of Brook haven to Manumitt a certain Slave named John Perdue belonging to the Estate of Oliver Smith Deceas,d and said Trustees being Satisfied that s,d Slave is under forty five Years and of Sufficient ability to provide for and Maintain himself do hereby consent to the Manumition of said Slave according to Law of this State in such case provided

      THOMAS S. STRONG President
Attest. MORDECAI HOMAN town Clerk

Be it remembred that on the 4th. day of June 1822 Josiah Smith made application to the Trustees of the freeholders and commonalty of the town of Brook haven to Manumitt a certain slave of his named Dorothy and said Trustees being satisfied that said Slave was under forty five years and of sufficient ability to provide for and maintain herself do hereby consent to the Manumition of said slave According to the Law of this State in such Case provided—

THOMAS S. STRONG President

Attest
MORDECAI HOMAN town Clerk

PAGE 188.

A true Canvass and estimate of the Votes taken at an Election held in the town of Brook haven in the County of Suffolk on the fourth day of November one thousand eight hundred and twenty two and on the two succeeding days inclusive for a Governor Lieutenent Governor and four Senators viz—one hundred and eight votes were given for Joseph C. Yates for the Office of Governor—Seventy one votes were given for Erastus Root for the Office of Lieutenent Governor—

Twenty seven votes were given for Henry Huntington for the Office of Lieutenant Governor—

for the Office of Senator

Sixty eight votes were given for Walter Bown
Sixty eight votes were given for Jasper Ward
Sixty nine votes were given for John Lefferts
Sixty nine votes were given for John A King
twenty five votes were given for abel Huntington
one vote were given for John Rose
one vote were given for Nathan Post
one vote were given for Mordecai Homan

given under our hands at Brook haven this sixth day of November 1822.

> Nathan Post
> John Rose
> Woodhull Smith
> Justus Overton
> Timothy Miller
> } Assessors—

A true Canvas and Estimate of the votes taken at an Election held in the town of Brook haven in the County of Suffolk on the fourth day of November one thousand eight hundred and twenty two and on the two succeeding days inclusive for a Representative to Congress. Viz.

for the Office of Congress

Seventy seven votes were given for John P. Osborn

One hundred and twenty three votes were given for Silas Wood

given under our hands at Brook haven this sixth day of November 1822

> Nathan Post
> John Rose
> Woodhull Smith
> Justus Overton
> Timothy Miller
> } Assessors

Page 189.

A true Canvas and estimate of the votes taken at an Election held in the town of Brook haven in the County of Suffolk on the fourth day of November one thousand eight hundred and twenty two and on the two Succeeding days inclusive for two Members of Assembly one Sherriff one Clerk and four Coroners for the County of Suffolk. Viz :

for the Office of Assembly

Sixty seven votes were given for Samuel Strong

sixty seven votes were given for Joshua Fleet

Sixty three votes were given for Abraham H. Gardiner for the Office of Sherriff—

One vote were given for John G. Gardiner for the Office of Sheriff—

for the Office of Clerk

Sixty three votes were given for Charles H. Havens
One vote were given for Charles A. Floyd—

for the Office of Coroners

Sixty five votes were given for Selah Carll—
Sixty four votes were given for Samuel F. Norton
Sixty four votes were given for Levi Hildreth—
Thirty four votes were given for John S. Conklin
Thirty four votes were given for George L. Conklin

Given under our hands at Brook haven this sixth day of November 1822—

Nathan Post
John Rose
Woodhull Smith } Assessors
Justus Overton
Timothy Miller

Mordecai Homan } Clerks
Henry P. Osborn

Be it remembred that on the eighth day of June 1822 the Inhabitants of the 16th school District made application to the commission of common Schools for the town of Brook haven to divide their district and after due consideration do find the said district too large and have set off all that part of said district lying to the westward of the East line of John Penny so extending westward on the Country Road as far as the house formerly occupied by Ben. a Coulerd man not including the houses down the neck on the west side of the River which said district will be No. twenty nine 29.

Nathaniel A. Miller } Commissionrs
Mordecai Homan of Schools

PAGE 190.

To whome it may concern

We the commissioners of highways of the town of Brook haven in the County of Suffolk having taken a view of the public roads landings and watering places in and about the village of Setauket as directed by the Act entitled an Act to regulate highways in the Counties of suffolk Queens and Kings passed the 2nd. April 1813—and having heard and considered the allegations of the respective parties interested do hereby certify—adjudge and determine the following encroachments upon the highways herein hereafter mentioned and have opened the same to such width as to us seems necessary for the public convenience and as the same were originally laid out and recorded.—

1st We adjudge and determine that the highway and watring place in setauket near the head of the Mill pond and on both sides of the Mill stream are encroached upon by the fences of John Jayne and Warden Toby and have opened and regulated the said highway and watering place by certain stakes and Boundaries fixed by us agreeable to the record of the said highways and watering places as originally laid out and regulated by the commissioners of highways of said town on the 8th. february 1757 as by refference to said Record will more fully and at large appear—

2nd. We adjudge that the highway leading from the house of Samuel Satterly to the harbor is encroached upon in divers places by the fences adjoing the lands of the said Samuel Satterly of Stephen Edwards William Jayne John Cleves Isaac Brewster and Benjamin Jones and have opened the same to certain marked Boundaries fixed by us to designate the said encroachments—

3rd. We do adjudge and certify that the road runing upon the east side of the house occupied by Edward King has become unnecessary for public use or convenience and allow the same to be closed by the person or persons

PAGE 191.

Owning the land coverd by the said road or highway—

4th. we adjudge and determine the division of the road districts of which Samuel Satterly and Daniul Smith Jur. are overseers to be at opposite the North end of the said Edward King house so as the Bridge west of said Kings house shall be in the District of which the said Samuel Satterly is Overseer—

5the. We adjudge and determine that the highway leading from the said Bridge to the head of the lane is encroached upon by the fences of Mills Brewster and have opened the same to the width of four Rods throughout

6th. We adjudge and determine that the highway leading from the public green to coram by the house of John Dewick is encroached upon by the fences of John Brewster Mills Brewster and the said John Dewick and have opened the same accordingly to certain Bounds fixed by us

7th. We adjudge and determine the highway leading from the Mill in setauket to Nassekig is encroached upon by the fences of Benjamin Hawkins and we have opened the same so as the fences of the said Benjamin Hawkins be in a direct line from the southeast corner of the Garden of Obediah D. Wells to the Northeast corner of the homestead of the late Richard Dewick (deceasd) all of which we certify and authorise the town Clerk of Brook haven at any time hereafter to file this document of Record in his office given under our hands and seals this 22nd. May 1822

L S— Nathl. Miller
L S— Isaac Satterly } Commisionr of highways
L S— Samuel Davis

PAGE 192.

We the Commissioners of highways for the Town of Brook haven do hereby certify and determine that we have stopped and closed the Road from patchogue Creek west of the same as heretofore passed betwixt Ebenezer Akerleys and smith Hammonds in exchange for the Road four Rods wide as the same now runs on the north side of the house of Capt. Daniel G. Gillett.

                        Nathl. Miller } Commissioner
                        Samuel Davis } of highways.
                        Isaac Satterly }

Brook haven
4th feb. 1823

    Be it remembred that on the first day of April 1823 Thomas S. Strong made application to the Trustees of the freeholders and commonalty of the town of Brook haven being Overseers of the poor to Manumitt a Certain slave of his named Unice and said Trustees being Satisfied that said slave is under forty five years and of Sufficient Ability to provide for and maintain herself do consent to her Manumission according to the Act in such case made and provided

Attest
  Mordecai Homan
      town Clerk—

Jesse Woodhull
Briant Davis
Samuel Davis } Trusees
Phillip Hallock
Barnabas Wines

    Be it remembrid that on the first day of April 1823 Samuel L. Thompson made application to the Trustees of the freeholders and Commonalty of the town of Brook haven being Overseers of the poor to Manumitt a certain slave of his named Simon and said Trustees being satisfied that said slave is under forty five years and of sufficient ability to provide for and maintain himself do consent that he the Samuel L Thompson should manumitt said slave According to the Act in such case made and provided

                        Thomas S. Strong President
Attest
Mordecai Homan town Clerk

PAGE 193.

Be it remembred that it satisfactorily appears to us the Trustees of the freeholders and commonalty of the town of Brook haven that Harry a coulerd man this day Manumitted by Abraham Woodhull of the said town of Brook haven to whome he has heretofore been a Slave is under the age of forty five years and of Sufficient ability to provide for and maintain himself do hereby consent to his Manumission as Law of this State in such case directs Dated this 1st April 1823

THOMAS S. STRONG President

Attest MORDECAI HOMAN
Town Clerk

At a Meeting of the freeholders and inhabitants of the town of Brook haven on the first tuesday in April being town meeting day the following persons were Elected as town Officers—Viz

Josiah Smith President

Nathl. Smith
Isaac Brewster
William S. Robert
Daniel Overton
Elisha Overton
Samuel Davis Millers place
} Trustees

John Rose Supervisor

Mordecai Homan town Clerk

Nathan Post Collector

Timothy Miller
Barnabas Wines
Daniel Davis
Nathan Post
Woodhull Smith
} Assessors

Timothy Davis
Samuel Davis
Isaac Overton
} Commissioners of highways

Act. Mordecai Homan }
Act. Nathl. Miller   } Commissioners
Archabald Jayne   }   of Schools

Constables

Sylvanus Edwards   James Robinson
George D. Lee   Noadiah D. Carter
Israel Davis   Rumsey Rose
Jesse Hulse   Robert Stivers
Henry Blydenburgh   John B. Overton
John Buckingham   Selah Oakley
           Seth Worth.

PAGE 194.

Russell Green } Act.
Ezra King   }   Inspectors of Schools
William Beale } Act.

OVERSEERS OF HIGHWAYS

Timothy Davis—Act   William Tooker
Jacob Hawkins—Act.   Nathaniel Smith—Act
Thomas Bailes—Act   John Rider
Isaac Satterly   Appollos Mills Act
Samuel Satterly   James Dayton
Samuel Jayne   Benjamin Hutchenson
Israel Davis—Act   William Swezey Act.
Nathaniel Davis   William Randal
John Davis—Act   Joshua Overton Act
Russell Green—Ac,t   Willard Ruland Act
Henry C. Mathers   Davis Norton—Act
James Woodhull Jur   Elijah Terry Act
Jacob Carter   Zophah Hallock Act
James Robinson Act   Benjamin Hallock Act
Silas Reeve Actpt.   Caleb Newton Jur.
James Fanning Act.   Moses Wicks

Sineus C. Miller Act   David Peterson
Nathl. Miller Act   Samuel Hammond Act
            Noadiah Carter Act

Fence Viewers

Jedediah Williamson	William Beale
William Rudyard	James Smith
Jesse Woodhull	Daniel Saxton
Isaac Jayne	George D. Lee
Ebenezer Jones	Daniel Bishop
Zecheriah Hawkins	Austin Roe
Samuel Hopkins	Davis Norton
Joseph Miller	Azariah Hawkins
Charles Robinson	Samuel Hammond
Moses Swezey	Davis Overton
Isaac Raynor Jr	Willard Ruland
Joseph Raynor Jur	Robert Hawkins
Elisha Raynor	Isaac Mills
Samuel Terry	William Randal
Nathan Post	John Laws
Timothy Rose	Daniel Overton
Jonathan Burwell	Briant Davis
Joseph Avery	Isaac Davis
Justus Rowe	Elisha Davis

Page 195.

Be it Ordained by the Trustees of the freeholders and commonalty of the town of Brook haven that if any person or persons shall suffer or permitt any Neat Cattle horse or sheep to run on the west meadow Beach at any time after the tenth day of June Instant shall forfiet and pay unto the said Trustees the sum of fifty Cents pr head for each and every such offence to be sued for and recovered in the name of the said Trustees or any person who will prosecute for the same and applied to the use of the town provided however that nothing in this Act shall prevent people from Carting on said Beach as usual but not to suffer their teams to run at large on said Beach Given under our hands and seal of Office this 3rd. day of June 1823 at Brook haven

  MORDECAI HOMAN   Nath'l Smith
   town Clerk   Wm. S Robert | Seal

 Be it Ordained by the Trustees of the freeholders and commonalty of the town of Brook haven that if any person or persons shall take any Stone or Stones from any of the public Shores or landings belonging to the town of Brook haven without leave be first obtained from the Board of Trustees of said town shall for each and every such offence forfiet and pay to the said trustees or their order the sum of twelve Dollars and fifty Cents to be sued for and recoved in the name of said trustees by them or their order and applied to the use of said town

in witness whereof we affix our names. and seal of Office this 2d. Sept 1823

         Nathl. Smith } Trustees
         Isaac Brewster } | Seal

MORDECAI HOMAN town Clerk

PAGE 196.

 Be it remembred that we the undersigned Commissioners of common Schools for the town of Brook haven being call,d by the inhabitants of the first school District to Divide said District and after having viewed the same have by the mutual consent of said District set off a District begining at and including the houses of Richard Garrett and the Widow of Beriah Petty and to embrace all the North and east part of said first District which said last District will be Number thirty of School Districts in said town given under our hands at Brookhaven this 28th. Octr.

1823—and said District extends Northerly so as to include lubber street—

Nath,l Miller } Commissors
Mordecai Homan } of common Schools

Suffolk County } ss
town of Brook haven }

A true Canvas and estimate of the Votes taken at an Election in the town of Brook haven in the County of Suffolk on the third day of November in the year one thousand eight hundred and twenty three and on the two succeeding days inclusive for the Office of one Senator given under our hands at said town of Brookhaven this fifth day of Nov. 1823

Seventy four votes were given for Abel Huntington for the Office of Senator—

one hundred and Sixty three votes were given for David Gardiner for the Office of Senator—

John Rose
Woodhull Smith
Timothy Miller } Inspectors
Barnabas Wines
Daniel Davis

PAGE 197.

Suffolk County } ss
town of Brookhaven }

A true canvas and estimate of the votes taken at an Election held in the town of Brook haven in the County of Suffolk on the third day of November in the year one thousand Eight hundred and twenty three and on the two succeeding days inclusive for the Office of two Members of Assembly given under our hands at Brook haven this fifth day of Nov. 1823—

fifty six votes were given for Charles H. Havens for the Office of Member of Assembly—

one hundred and seventy four votes were given for Josiah Smith for the Office of Member of Assembly—

two hundred and thirty three votes were given for Hugh Halsey for the Office of Member of Assembly

John Rose
Woodhull Smith
Timothy Miller } Asessors
Barnabas Wines
Daniel Davis

Be it remembred that on the 3d. day of febuary 1824 William Howell made application to us the Trustees of the town of Brook haven to Manumitt a certain slave of his named Peter and it satisfactorily appears to us that said slave is under forty five years and of Sufficient ability to provide for and maintain himself do hereby consent to his Manumition according to the Law of this state in such Case made and provided

Nathl Smith } Trustees
Daniel Overton

Attest MORDECAI HOMAN town Clerk

Part of District No. 1 is to embrace the Inhabitants in Brook Haven Bounded east by Wading River Creek and west by the west line of James Woodhulls Land

Brook Haven   Mordecai Homan } Commissioners
4 Dec. 1823—   Nathl. A. Miller   of Schools

PAGE 198.

We the commissioners of highways for the town of Brook haven being Call,d by a number of the Inhabitants of Drown meadow to widen the road leading from the old mans, Across Drown meadow &.C. and have opened the Road that leads from the old mans to Drown meadow begining near Drown meadow at the shop owned by Benjamin Brown the southwest line begining three feet in front of said shop and runing a strait line to the old part of Lewis

Hulses Store and Celler fifty six feet wide to where the two pole road crosses the same, Also opened the two pole Road between the Store of Solon Parsons, and that of Lewis Hulse,s runing eighteen Inches from the House of Solon Parsons on the west side to the lot of Land belonging to Ebenezer Jones on the east side two pole wide and so to continue on south through Drown meadow two pole wide

7th August 1823 — Isaac Overton, Timothy Davis, Samuel Davis } Commissonrs of highways

We Samuel Davis Isaac Overton and Timothy Davis Commissioners of highways for the town of Brook haven being calld by a number of the Inhabitants of said town to stop up two certain Roads in the Middle of the Island and after having Viewed said Roads do find they are very bad to be repaired and of little or no use to the public in general do accordingly stop up the Road begining at the Road calld the Granny Road near the South East corner of Briant Davises Lott and from thence runing Southerly to the Road that leads from Coram to Christopher Swezeys Mills and also the Road commencing at the same place on the Granny Road and from thence Runing Easterly across the old fulling Mill dam to the Road that runs Northerly from Christopher Swezeys House to the house of Samuel N. Hurtin given under our hands at Brook haven this 2nd. day of August 1823

Enterd 2nd. March 1824 — Isaac Overton, Samuel Davis, Timothy Davis } Commissioners

Page 199.

We Samuel Davis Isaac Overton and Timothy Davis commissioners of highways for the town of Brook haven being call,d by a number of the Inhabitants of said town to alter a Road leading from Christopher Swezeys to Robert Hawkins,s Mill and after having viewed said Road do consider it necessary and beneficial for the public conveniency to alter said Road and have acordingly altered the same by turning out of the old Road about twenty Rods to the Northward of Samuel Randals Barn and from thence runing a Southeasterly course across the land of Samuel Randal and the Land Josiah Corwin until it hits the said Road again as the same is Staked out a little to the southward of Josiah Corwins land crossing the Land of Paul Terry and have given unto the said Samuel Randal ten Dollars in money and his fence against Josiah Corwins land to remain where it now is and the old Road against his other land to the Northward of s,d Corwins land is given in exchange for the new together with the said ten Dollars for the Damage he may sustain and also have given unto the said Josiah Corwin the old Road against his land up to said Randals fence and the fence of Paul Terry extending as far Eastward as the line between said Corwin and said Paul Terry said Road is to be three Rods wide and opened by the first day of October ensueing which we return to be enterd of Record in Brook haven this 2nd. day of September 1823

	Samuel Davis	Commissionrs
Enterd this 2nd. March	Isaac Overton	of
1824	Timothy Davis	highways

Attest MORDECAI HOMAN town Clk

PAGE 200.

Be it Remembred that on the 2nd. day March 1824 Ebenezer Smith made application to the Trustees of the freeholders and commonalty of the town of Brook haven to Manumitt a certain slave of his named Joel and said Trustees being Satisfied that said slave is under forty five years and of Sufficient ability to provide for and maintain himself do hereby consent to his Manumition as the law of this State in such case directs

Nathaniel Smith } Trustees
Isaac Brewster }

Attest MORDECAI HOMAN town Ck

Be it remembred that on the fourth day of January 1825 —John Havens made application to the Trustees of the freeholders and commonalty of the town of Brook haven to manumitt a certain slave of his named Ira and said Trustees being satisfied that said slave is under forty five years and of sufficient ability to provide for and maintain himself do consent to his Manumtion as the law of this state in such case directs THOMAS S. STRONG President

Attest MORDECAI HOMAN town Clerk —

Be it remembred that on the fourth day of January 1825. John Woodhull made application to the Trustees of the freeholders and commonalty of the town of Brook haven to manumitt a Certain slave of his and said Trustees being satisfied that said slave is under forty five years and of sufficient ability to provide for and maintain himself do consent to the Manumition of said slave as the law of this state in such Case directs said Slave is named Benjamin Rafe

PAGE 201.

At a Meeting of the Inhabitants of the town of Brook haven held on the 6th. day of April 1824 the following persons were Elected town Officers for the ensueing Year Viz

Thomas S. Strong President

Isaac Brewster
Samuel Hopkins
Robert Hawkins
Briant Norton
Barnabas Wines
William Beale
} Trustees

Isaac Brewster } Overseers of the Poor
William Beale }

John Rose Supervisor
Mordecai Homan town Clerk
Nathan Post Collector

Lewis Rich }
Woodhull Smith }
Henry P. Osborn } Asessors
Nathan Post }
Timothy Miller }

Benjamin Hutchenson } Commissions
Nathaniel Smith } of highways
Timothy Davis }

Mordecai Homan } Commissioners
John R. Satterly } of Schools
Sineus C. Miller }

Robert Stivers }
James Robinson }
Henry Blydenburgh }
Jesse Hulse } Constables
Noadiah Carter }
George D Lee }
John B. Overton }
Charles A. Tooker }

PAGE 202.

Sereno Burnell } Inspectors
Ezra King } of common
William Beale } Schools

OVERSEERS OF HIGHWAYS

Timothy Davis   Nathaniel Miller Accepted
Nehemiah Hawkins   Capt Isaac Overton
Isaac Satterly   Nathaniel Smith Accepted
Stephen Edwards   Jonathan Burwell Acepte.
William Jayne Esq   Simmons Laws
Israel Davis Aceptd   James Dayton
Isaac Davis. Accepted Lewis Ritch Acceptd

John Davis. Accepted   William Randal Accepted
Samuel Davis Acepted   Joshua Overton
Henry C. Mathers Accptd Willard Rouland Accepted
James Woodhull Jur.   Davis Norton Acceptd
Henry Raynor   Elijah Terry
James Robinson Acepted Samuel Davis Jur Acepted
Jonathan Robinson   Geore Hawkins acept
William Smith   Richard Woodhull
Benjamin Raynor   Samuel Hammond
Silas Payne   Benjamin Hutchenson Acepted
Sineus C. Miller Acepted Jacob Hawkins Aceped

FENCE VIEWERS

Jedediah Williamson	William Beale
William Rudyard	Jonathan Burwell
Jesse Woodhull	Joseph Avery
Isaac Jayne	James Smith
Ebenezer Jones	Israel Smith
Zecheriah Hawkins	Messenger Overton
John Davis	Joshua Overton
Isaac Davis	Austin Rowe
Samuel Hopkins	Davis Norton
Joseph Miller	Azariah Hawkins
Timothy M. Woodhull	Samuel Hammond
James Woodhull Jur.	Davis Overton
Isaac Raynor	Willard Ruland
Joseph Raynor	Robert Hawkins
Elisha Raynor	Isaac Mills
Samuel Terry	William Randal
Nathan Post	John Laws
Timothy Rose	Daniel Overton
Justus Rowe	Briant Davis

PAGE 203.

Brook haven, ss.
To, Mordecai Homan Clerk of the town of Brook haven,

We the Commissioners of highways for said town have this day laid out a Road from the Road that leads from Coram to the Middle Island Mills at the East line of the late Joshua Smith Deceas,d through the land of Josiah Smith adjoining the land of said Joshua Smith deceas,d to be three Rods in width and to continue on Southerly by the land of said Joshua Smith until it meets the Patchogue Road for which Priviledge we agree to pay the said Josiah Smith the sum of twenty Dollars—to be paid out of the town Treasury said Road to be opened on or before the 10th. day of October next given under our hands at Brook haven this 19th. June 1824—

N. B. the old Road on the East side of said Josiah Smith,s land is to be given up to him—

      Nathaniel Smith   ) Commissioners
      Benjamin Hutchenson }   of
      Timothy Davis   ) highways

To. All to whome these presents shall come Whereas by certain Articles of agreement made and enterd into on the thirty first day of March one thousand six hundred and Eighty Between the town of Brookhaven of the one part and John Wade his Heirs and Assigns of the other part it is among other things promised and agreed by the said town of Brook haven that in consideration the said John Wade his Heirs and Assigns would Build maintain and keep in good order a Water Mill in the village of Setaket for grindin the Corn and other Grain of the Inhabitants they the said Inhabitants would keep and repair the dam appertaining to

PAGE 204.

the said Mill and if Occasion should require to make and construct a new dam—

Now therefore know ye that I Isaac Satterly of said town of Brook haven Owner and Occupier of the Mill in

Setauket and succeeding to all the Right title and priviledges of the said John Wade so far as regards the said Mill and dam, and entiteled of course to all benefits and advantages in law and equity secured or intended to be so, in and by the said Articles of agreement as well in consideration of one Dollar to me in hand paid as also on account that the Trustees of the freeholders and commonalty of the said town of Brook haven by an Instrument bearing date herewith have quitclaimed to me a certain piece or parcel of Land in the said village of Setauket called Laurel Hill and also all the right and title of the said town of Brook haven to the land and soil covered by the Waters of the old or new Mill pond—or upper Mill pond, do by these presents remise release and discharge the Trustees of the freeholders and commonalty of the said town of Brook haven and all and every of the Inhabitants of said town and their successors forever of and from all and every contract promise bargain, clause matter or thing contained expressed or declared in and by the articles of agreement above refer,d to so far as obliges the said Inhabitants of the said town of Brook haven and their Successors to repair the dam or dams appertaining to the said Mill and the constructing of a new one in Witness whereof I have hereunto set my hand and seal this sixth day of april one thousand eight hundred and twenty four— ISAAC SATTERLY L S

Sealed and delivered
in the presence of
MORDECAI HOMAN

Be it remembered that on the 4th. day of Nov. 1824 the undersigned commissioners of common schools formd a School District partly in Brook haven and partly in Riverhead by taking a part of the thiteenth District in Brook haven and uniting it with the 4th Dist in Riverhead and bounded East by Southampton line South by a line parallell with peaconic River one Mile south of it and west by the west line of David Hulses land which will be part No three of Brook haven

the other part described in Riverhead Sineus C. Miller } Commissioners
Mordecai Homan of Brookhaven

Page 205.

To all to whome these presence shall come the Trustees of the freeholders and commonalty of the town of Brook haven send Greeting. Whereas Thomas S. Strong Esquire has by his petition presented to the said Trustees requested permission to construct a dam and bridge over and across the westerly branch of Setauket harbour commencing at the southermost point of the peninsula formd by Setauket harbour and Conscience Bay known by the name of little neck or st Georges Manor and running from thence over and across the said harbour Southerly to the most convenient point at high water mark on the opposite shore and to construct a wharf on the easterly side of said dam and bridge, and whereas it appears to the said Trustees that it will be proper to grant the prayer of the said petitioner inasmuch as notice has been duly given and published and no opposition has been made thereto as it cannot be productive of injury to any individual and as the construction of a wharf as proposed will be beneficial to the public Now therefore know ye that the said Trustees in consideration of the premises and also of one Dollar to them in hand paid at or before the ensealing and delivery of these presence by the said Thomas S. Strong the receipt whereof is hereby acknowledged, do by these presence grant Bargain sell alien convey and confirm to the said Thomas s. Strong and to his Heirs and Assigns forever so much and such land covered with water as it will be necessary to have use and take occupy possess and enjoy for the construction and continuance of such dam bridge and wharf and they do hereby authorize the said Thomas S. Strong his Heirs and

Page 206.

Assigns to construct Build finish keep in repair and continue a dam Bridge and wharf over and across the said harbour at the place herein before specified and to charge demand sue for recover and receive a reasonable compensation and wharfage from all persons useing the said wharf the rates of wharfage however to be subject to the controul of the Trustees of the said town provided that they shall not be reduced by the said Trustees below the average wharfage chargd for the use of the wharfs in the said town on the North side of the Island and provided that the Trustees for the time being may load and unload goods Chattels belonging to the Corporation of the said town free of wharfage in witness whereof the said Trustees have caused the seal of the said Corporation to be affixed thereto and these presence to be signed by two of the said Trustees and countersigned by the Clerk of the said town the fourth day of January in the year one thousand eight hundred and twenty five reserving that there shall be forty feet space left for the ebbing and flowing of the water

in presence of Brewster Hawkins } Bryan Norton, Robert Hawkins, Samuel Hopkins } Trustees in the absence of the president

Attest MORDECAI HOMAN Town Clerk

Page 207.

Be it remembred that on the 4th. day of January 1825 John Havens made application to the Trustees of the freeholders and commonalty to Manumit a certain Slave of his named Ira and said Trustees being satisfied that sd slave is under forty five years and of sufficient ability to provide for and maintain himself do hereby consent to said Manumition according to the Law of this state in such made and provided   THOMAS S. STRONG President

Attest MORDECAI HOMAN Town Clerk

Suffolk County } ss.
town of Brookhaven }

A true Canvas and estimate of the Votes taken at an Election at the town of Brook haven in the town of Brookhaven in the County of Suffolk on the first day of November in the year one thousand eight hundred and twenty four and the two Succeeding days inclusive for the Office of governor Lieutenant Gov. and Senator—

two hundred and five Votes were given for Dewitt Clinton for the office of Governor—

one hundred and fifty eight votes were given for Samuel Younge for the office of Governor—

two hundred and ten votes were given for James Tallmadge for the Office of Lieutenant Governor

one hundred and fifty Seven votes were given for Erastus Root for the Office of Lieutenant Governor—

two hundred and Eleven votes were given for Cadwellader D. Colden for the Office of Senator—

one hundred and fifty five votes were given for Walter Bown for the Office of Senator—

Given under our hands at said town of Brook haven this third day of Novr. 1824—

       Timothy Miller
       Henry P. Osborn
       Nathan Post
       Woodhull Smith

    Page 208.

Suffolk County } ss.
town of Brook haven }

A true canvas and estimate of the votes taken at an Election held in the town of Brook haven in the County of Suffolk on the first day of November one thousand eight hundred and twenty four and on the two Succeeding days inclusive for one Representative to the Congress of the United States of America two hundred and twenty one Votes were given for Silas Wood for the Office of Congress—

one hundred and forty Nine votes were given for James Lent for the Office Congress—

Given under our hands at Brook haven this third day of November 1824—

Inspectors { Timothy Miller
Henry P. Osborn
Nathan Post
Woodhull Smith

Suffolk County } ss.
town of Brook haven

A true Canvas and estimate of the votes taken at an Election held in the town of Brook haven in the County of Suffolk on the first day of November one thousand eight hundred and twenty four and on the two succeeding days inclusive for two Members of Assembly for the County of Suffolk—

two hundred and six votes were given for Josiah Smith for the Office of Assembly—

one hundred and Ninty two votes were given for Abraham T. Rose for the Office of Assembly

one hundred and Seventy two votes were given for Joshua Smith for the Office of Assembly

one hundred and Sixty six votes were given for David Hedges Jur. for the Office of Assembly

Given under our hands at Brookhaven this third day of November 1824—

Attest
MORDECAI HOMAN
Clerk

Timothy Miller
Henry P. Osborn } Inspectors
Nathan Post
Woodhull Smith

PAGE 209.

Be it remembered that on the first day of March one thousand eight hundred and twenty five Israel Davis of the town of Brook haven obligated and agreed with the Trustees of the freeholders and commonalty of the town of Brook haven and their Successors in Office that he his Heirs and Assigns would repair and keep in good repair the Dock now owned by him at drown meadow so at that said Dock shall be sufficient for four Vessels to load to at one time at common tides that is to say two Vessels of eight feet one of six and one of five feet water and also the sufficiency and repairs of said Dock are to be left to a committee of three men to be Chosen by said Trustees for that purpose who are to decide on the sufficiency of said Dock and Zecheriah Hawkins William Jonenes and William H. Brewster are chosen as an examining Committee in the premises who are to be the said committee until the first day of March 1826 and until others are Chosen in their stead and in case of failure on the part of said Davis his Heirs or assigns he or they sall be liable to an Action of Damage to any person agriev,d or interested—

witness my hand   ISRAEL DAVIS—
  in presence of
MORDECAI HOMAN town Clerk

PAGE 210.

At a Meeting of the freeholders and Inhabitants of the town of Brook haven held at the house of Daniel Davis in Coram on the fifth day of April 1825 the followin persons we Elected as town Officers

        Thomas S. Strong President of Trustees

                Henry P. Osborn
                Nathaniel Smith
                William Phillips   } Trustees
                Davis Norton
                Samuel L. Thompson
                Wm. H. Helme

Thomas S. Strong Supervisor
Mordecai Homan town Clerk and treasurer
Nathan Post Collector

Barnabas Wines
Nathan Post
Timothy Miller } Assessors
Woodhull Smith
Isaac Hammond

Timothy Davis—
Benjamin Hutchenson } Commissioners of highways—
Nathaniel Smith

Selah B. Strong
Mordecai Homan } Commissioners of common Schools—
Sineus C. Miller

Constables

James Robinson   Charles A. Tooker
Henry bliydenburgh   Daniel Woodhull
George D. Lee   John Buckingham
Robert Stivers   Rumsey Rose
Jesse Hulse   James Smith
            Noadiah D. Carter

PAGE 211.

John R Satterly
Rev. Ezra King } Inspectors of Schools
Jonathan Burwell

OVERSEERS OF HIGHWAYS

Henry Smith   Nathaniel Smith
Thomas Baylis   Thomas R. Smith
Daniel Smith   Epenetus Mills—Acpt.
John Elderkin Acpt.   Josiah Corwin Acpt.
Floyd Smith   William Phillips
William Taylor Acptd.   Horace Randal
Charles Woodhull Acptd.   Daniel Overton Acpt.
Josiah Lupton Acptd.   Wm. S. Smith Acpt.

James Woodhull Jur. Acpt.   Richard Norton Acpt.
Henry Raynor   Samuel Hammond Acpt.
Gideon Robinson   James Smith
John Raynor   Richard W. Smith
Jeremiah Culver   Willard Ruland
John Howell Acpt.d.   Samuel Davis Jur Acpt.
Joseph Hawkins Jur.   Isaac N. Gould Acpt.
Barnabas Rider   Richard Woodhull
Nathaniel Miller   Ezra Guildersleve Acpt.
William Tooker   Israel Bennitt

FENCE VIEWERS

Jedediah Williamson   William Beale
William Rudyard   Jonathan Burrwell
Jesse Woodhull   Joseph Avery
Amos Smith   James Smith
Ebenezer Jones   Israel Smith
Zecheriah Hawkins   Richard W. Smith
John Davis   Noah Overton
Isaac Davis   Davis Norton
Samuel Davis   Henry Longbothon
Charles Woodhull   Ezrah Hawkins
Timothy M. Woodhull   Samuel Hammond
James Woodhull Jur   Davis Overton Jr
William Terry Jr   Scudder Terry
Joseph Raynor Jr.   Robert Hawkins
Elisha Raynor   Isaac Mills—
Samuel Terry   William Randal
Nathan Post   John Laws—
Timothy Rose   Briant Davis
Justus Rowe   Ezra Guildersleve

Page 212.

Be it remembered that on the fifth day of April 1825 Mills Brewster Made application to the Trustees of the freeholders and commonalty of the town of Brook haven to

Manumitt a certain Slave of his Named Peter and said Trustees being satisfied that said Slave is under forty five years and of Sufficient ability to provide for and maintain himself do hereby consent that he should be Manumitted as the Law of this State directs

THOMAS S. STRONG president

Attest
MORDECAI HOMAN town Clerk

We the commissioners of highways for the town of Brook haven being calld by the petition of Albert B. David and others to grant liberty to the said albert B. Davis to put two or more good easy swinging gates on the Road calld the Granny Road leading Southerly from the house of James Barnaby throug the land of said Davis, we the said commissioners after duly considering the premises find said Road to be of little use to public in general do therefore grant the request of the aforesaid petition and direct it to be recorded as Witness our hands this 13th. March 1825

Benjamin Hutchenson } Commissioners
Nathl. Smith } of highways.
Timothy Davis }

PAGE 213.

Be it remembered that on the 14th. day of June 1825 Henry P. Osborn made application to the Trustees of the freeholders and commonalty of the town of Brook Haven to manumitt a certain Slave of his named Reuben and said Trustees being Satisfied that said Slave is under forty five years and of sufficient ability to provide for and maintain himself do hereby consent to the manumition of said Reuben according to the law of this state in such case provided

THOMAS S. STRONG president

Attest
MORDECAI HOMAN town Clerk

Be it remembered that on the 14th. day of June 1825

Henry P. Osborn made application to the Trustees of the freeholders and commonalty of the town of Brook haven to Manumitt a certain slave of his named Judas and said Trustees being satisfied that said slave is under forty five years and of Sufficient ability to provide for and maintain himself do hereby consent to the manumition of said Judas according to the law of this state in such case provided

THOMAS S. STRONG President

Attest
MORDECAI HOMAN town Clerk

4th Sept. 1823 the Overseers of the Poor agreed to rase 1200 Dollars for the town expences—

5th. Sept. 1824 the Overseers of the poor agreed to raise 1000. Dollars for the town expences—

6 Sept 1825 the Overseers of the poor agreed to raise 850 Dollars for the support of the poor

PAGE 214.

A true Canvas and estimate of the Votes taken at an Election held in the town of Brook haven in the County of Suffolk on the Seventh day of Nov. one thousand eight hundred and twenty five and on the two succeeding days inclusive for one Senator for the first District of this State two Members of Assembly one Clerk one Sheriff and four Coroners for the County of Suffolk and for the purpose also of taking the sense of the Electors of the town of Brook haven as to the Manner of Choosing Electors of President and vice president of the United States given under our hands at the said town of Brook haven this Ninth day of March 1825

Senators

One hundred and ninety one votes were given for Joshua Smith for the Office of Senator

One hundred and forty three votes were given for Nicholas Wyckoff for the Office of Senator

Assembly

One hundred an fifty four votes were given for Isaac Conklin for the Office of Assembly—

One hundred and Seventy three votes were for Abraham T. Rose for the Office of Assembly—

One hundred and Seventy four votes were given for John M. Williamson for the Office Assembly

One hundred and fifty two votes were given for Usher H. Moore for the Office of Assembly

Clerk

One hundred and Sixty five votes were given for Charles A. Floyd for the office of Clerk—

one hundred and Sixty two votes were given for Charles H. Havens for the Office of Clerk

Sheriff

Two hundred votes were given for Nathan Post for the Office of Sheriff

one hundred and thirty votes were given for Samuel Smith for the Office of Sheriff—

PAGE 215.

three hundred and twenty one votes were given for Levi H. Hildreth for the Office of Coroner

One hundred and sixty four votes were given for Elijah Terry for the Office of Coroner

one hundred and sixty five votes were given for Mordecai Homan for the Office of Coroner

One hundred sixty four votes were given for David Carll for the Office of Coroner—

One hundred and fifty four votes were given for Selah Carll for the Office of Coroner

one hundred and fifty four votes were given for Samuel Davis Jur. for the Office of Coroner one hundred and fifty four votes were given for Joseph C. Conklin for the Office of Coroner

Eighty votes were given for Districts } on the Election
Eight votes were given for general ticket } Law for
Plurality ———— } President

Timothy Miller }
Isaac Hammond }
Woodhull Smith } Inspectors
Barnabas Wines }

At a Meeting of the Trustees of the freeholders and commonalty of the town of Brook haven held in said town on the seventh day of December one thousand eight hundred and twenty five Brewster Hawkins made application to said Trustees for liberty to Build a dock or wharf at a place call,d Robbins,s point in Setauket harbour and said Trustees after due consideration had in the premises did Grant unto the said Brewster Hawkins and to his Heirs and Assigns forever the priviledge of Building constructing and keeping

PAGE 216.

in repair a Dock or wharf at the aforesaid point against his own land to be fifty feet in width on the the shore and two hundred and fifty feet in length from common high water mark reserving to said Trustees and their successors in Office the right of regulating the rate of wharfage and the priviledge of landing and sending off all articles belonging to the Corporation of said town free of wharfage and the said Brewster Hawkins his Hiers and Assigns is to furnish a reasonable pathway for teams and Carriages to pass and repass to and from said Dock through his own land on the shore above high water mark or where the pathway now runs and the said Brewster Hawkins his Heirs and Assigns are to be allowed one cent per foot for loading cordwood from said Dock and for all light vessels lying alongside of said Dock when not loading twelve and half cents pr day and always to give way for Vessels to load for taking in or out Cattle fifteen Cents pr head Calves sheep or lambs two Cents pr head for every hogshead fifteen Cents every Barrell of liquor or pork six cents every Barrell of flour four Cents for every thousand long shingle twenty five cents— for every thousand feet of short shingle four Cents for every thousand feet of plank twenty five Cents, for every thousand feet of boards eighteen cents ; for every ten gallon keg of liquor three Cents for five Gallon do two Cents for every Hundred Bushel of Ashes nine Cents all other manure two Cents pr waggon load and every other article not enumerated three Cents pr load in that proportion

in presence of   Thomas S. Strong President L S
Mordecai Homan town Clerk

Page 217.

At a public town Meeting of the Inhabitants of the town of Brook haven held on the 4th. day of April 1826 the following persons were Elected town Officers for the ensueing year

Viz.

Thomas S. Strong president of Trustees

Barnabas Wines ⎫
Merritt Learned ⎪
Daniel Overton ⎬ Trustees
Davis Norton ⎪
Isaac Brewster ⎪
William H. Helme ⎭

Thomas S. Strong Supervisor

Mordecai Homan town Clerk and treasurer

James Robinson Collector

Henry P. Osborn ⎫
Nathan Post ⎪
Timothy Miller ⎬ Assessors
Samuel Hammond ⎪
Woodhull Smith ⎭

Timothy Davis \
Benjamin Hutchenson } Commissioners of highways \
William Tooker

Selah B. Strong \
Mordecai Homan } Commissioners of common Schools \
William Beale

Charles A. Tooker \
George D. Lee \
James Smith \
James Robinson } Constables \
Jesse Hulse \
Jacob Hawkins Jur

at the aforesaid meeting a vote was taken to prevent Rams and swine from runing in the commons and carried in the affirmative

PAGE 218.

John R. Satterly \
Josiah Smith } Inspectors of Schools \
Nathaniel Smith

OVERSEERS OF HIGHWAYS

Richard Smith
Thomas Bailes
Daniel Smith Aceptd
Ebenezer Smith
Samuel Satterly Acceptd
Israel Davis Accepted
Wm. H. Helme Accepted
Josiah Lupton Acepted
James Woodhull Acepted
Henry Raynor
Gideon Robinson
Jehiel Raynor
John Penny Jr.
James Fanning Aceped
William Robert

Daniel G. Gillett Acepted
Epenetus Mills Accepted
Appollos Mills Accepted
Horace Randal Acepted
Sylvanus Overton Acepted
William S. Smith.
Richard Norton
Samuel Hammond Acepted
James Smith
Richard W. Smith Acepted
Manly Ruland
Benjamin Clerk
Zophar Hallock
Richard Woodhull
Briant Davis

BROOKHAVEN TOWN RECORDS. 275

Silas Homan Accepted
Nathaniel Miller
William Tooker

Israel Bennett
Isaac Davis Accepted
Daniel Davis old mans Aceptd
Jeremiah Gourden—

*

Jedediah Williamson
William Rudyard
Charles Jayne
Amos Smith
Ebenezer Jones
Zecheriah Hawkins
John Davis
Isaac Davis
Samuel Davis
Charles Woodhull
James Woodhull Jur.
Miller I. Woodhull
Jerrus Wines
Christopher Robinson
Elisha Raynor
Samuel Terry
Nathan Post
Timothy Rose

Justus Rowe
Wm Beale
Joseph Avery
William Arthur
Noah Overton
Richard W. Smith
Davis Norton
Henry Longbotham
Azariah Hawkins
Samuel Hammond
Davis Overton Jur.
Scudder Terry
Robert Hawkins
Isaac Mills
William Randal
John Laws
Briant Davis
Ezra Guildersleve

*Note.—No title given, but probably the names in this column indicate *fence viewers.*—COM.

PAGE 219.

Be it rembered that on the 4th. day of April 1826 William Tooker made application to the Trustees of the freeholders and commonalty of the town of Brook haven to Manumitt a certain Slave of his Named Aaron and said Trustees being Satisfied that said Slave is under forty five years and of Sufficient ability to provide for and maintain himself do hereby consent to his Manumission as the law of this State in such directs—

Thomas S. Strong President

Attest

Mordecai Homan town Clerk

Be it remembered that we the undersigned commissioners of common Schools of the Town of Brookhaven by and with the consent of the Commissioners of the town of southampton have set off a part of School District No. 15 to be Annexed to School District No. one in Southampton embracing the families of Joel Hawkins Silas Edwards Matthew Roders Robert Gourden Jonah Hallock and Henry Raynor—to be part No—two of Brook haven this fourth day of April 1826

Selah B. Strong } Commissioners
Mordecai Homan } of common Schools

5th. September 1826. the Trustees of this town ordered that there should be one thousand dollars raised in said town for the support of the poor and othr contingent Charges in said town for the ensueing year

Attest Mordecai Homan Clerk

4th. September 1827—the Trustees of the town of Brook haven agreed to raise eight hundred Dollars for the support of the poor and other contingent charges for the ensueing year Attest Mordecai Homan Clerk

Page 220.

To All to whome these presents shall come the Trustees of the freeholders and commonalty of the town of Brook haven send Greeting. Whereas the Trustees of the freeholders and commonalty of said town did on the fifth day of December one thousand eight hundred and Nine by their certain deed bearing date on that day Grant to George Hallock of said town the liberty priviledge and Right to build a dock or wharf at a place call,d the deep hole in Stoney brook harbour against his own land one hundred feet in length on the shore and fifty feet in width from common hight water mark for the consideration and under the restrictions and regulations therein mentioned and did thereby Authorise him to receive for the use thereof certain rates of wharfage therein specified and Whereas the Trustees of the freeholders and commonalty of the said town of Brook haven did on the second day of february one thousand eight hundred and thirteen by their certain other deed bearing date on that day Grant and allow the said George Hallock the liberty priviledge and right to extend the said dock two hundred feet in length to the Northward and to be equal in width as the first mentioned dock that is to say fifty feet in width from common high water mark for the further consideration and under the restrictions and regulations therein mentioned and did thereby authorise him to receive for the use of the said wharf the compensation therein specified, And whereas the said George Hallock by his petition presented to us the said Trustees that at the time when the said deeds were executed and delivered to him it was the intention of the said Trustees by whome the said Deeds were executed and deliverd to him to grant and convey to him the said George Hallock his Heirs and Assigns forever the right Interest

PAGE 221.

and priviledge therein mentioned subject however always to the restrictions therein mentioned and under a full belief that such their Intention was well Sufficiently expressed in the said Deeds, he had constructed a wharf of the dimentions therein mentioned and at a very great expense and had conformed in all things to the provisions contained in the said Deeds but that he had been advised that the said Deeds only Granted and conveyed to him a life estate in the said wharf and has also prayed us the said Trustees to extend the right interest and priviledge mentioned in the said Deeds subject to the restrictions and reservations therein contained to him his Hiers and Assigns forever as was originally intended. Now therefore know ye that we the said Trustees in consideration of the premises of the provision herein after contained and also of one Dollar to us in hand paid by the said George Hallock before the Ensealing and delivery of these presents the receipt whereof is hereby Acknowledged have granted and conveyd and by these presents do Grand and convey to the said George Hallock and to his hiers and Assigns forever the right and priviledge to continue and keep in repair the said dock or wharf as located in and by the said deeds and if necessary at any time to rebuild the same and to Ask demand sue for recover and receive for the use thereof wharfage at the rates and in the manner specified in the said two former deeds and such other or further wharfage as shall or may be allowed to him or them by the said Trustees of the free holders and commonalty of the said town for the time being Provided howevr that the said George Hallock his Heirs or Assigns shall agreeable to an offer which he has voluntarily made widen the road to the width of three rods to start from Zepheniah Hallocks corner until it comes to the corner in said

PAGE 222.

George Hallock Land from thence four rods wide to the new made ground to be laid out and regulated by a committe to be appointed for that purpose from said Board of Trustees, the express purpose of said Road is for the public to lay wood on but not so as to hinder or obstruct people from passing and repassing to and from said Dock nor to lay any wood within four Rods of the new made ground, And also reserving a right for people to pass and repass to the southward of said Dock through the land of the said George Hallock that he or they also keep said Dock free from incumbrances so as that people may pass and repass to the northward with teams and carriages to and from the west meadow also reserving the priviledge of landing on said Dock (free from wharfage) all articles belonging to the corporation of said town. And a right for the said Trustees or their successors for the time being to regulate the said rates of wharfage in future, And also reserving a right for all light vessels to lay along side of said Dock twenty four hours free from wharfage but always to give way for vessels to load or unload, And also he the said George Hallock his Heirs or Assigns pay unto the said Trustees or their Successors in Office yearly and once in every year on the first tuesday in April forever an Annuity of fifteen Dollars for the use of said town the first payment to be made in the year one thousand eight hundred and twenty seven, And the said George Hallock shall be allowed to him and to his heirs and Assigns forever wharfage for shipping every Ox steer heifer or Cow twelve and an half cents for every Cask of flaxseed shipped four Cents, for shipping or landing full hogsheads six Cents for every Barrell of liquor or provision,s or flour two Cents for every Cask of Rice four Cents for every Crate of

PAGE 223.

Earthan three Cents for every load of Stone or lumber drawn by one pair of horses or Oxen two Cents for all foreign vessels unloading Ashes or other Manure six Cents for every hundred Bushels, And for putting on Board Cord wood one Cent pr foot to be Jointly paid by the Master and Owner of such vessel—done at Brook haven and sealed with the seal of said town this seventh day of March one thousand eight hundred and twenty six—1826

in presence of   THOMAS S. STRONG President L S
MORDECAI HOMAN town Clerk

Be it Ordained by the Trustees of the freeholders and commonalty of the town of Brook haven that if any Ram shall be found running on the commons in said town between the first day of June and the fifteenth day of November in any year such Ram shall be forfeited the one half to any person that will take up and secure such Ram and give information to the Trustees of said town and the other half to the use of said town and if any Ram shall be found running on the aforesaid commons within said term without being sufficiently hoppled the Owener thereof shall in addition to the aforesaid forfeiture pay a penalty of two Dollars to be sued for by said Trustees before any Court having cognisance thereof and applied as aforesaid.—And be it further Ordained

PAGE 224.

that if any person shall wilfully suffer any hog to run on the commons of said town at any time of the year after the first day of June ensueing except it be to drive such hog to market or to some field or a reasonable time to water shall for each offence pay the sum of fifty cents to be sued for by said Trustees as aforesaid and applied the one half to the person complaining and the other half to the use of said town. done at brookhaven this 2nd. day of May 1826—

Attest
MORDECAI HOMAN   THOS S. STRONG President   Seal
town clerk

The Subscribers a committee of the Trustees of the freeholders and commonalty of the town of Brook haven have laid the highway mentioned in the renewal of the Grant to George Hallock of his wharf at Stoney Brook dated the seventh day of March 1826 as follows commencing at the Northeast corner of the road at a Cedar post in the fence on the west side of Zepheniah Hallocks Garden marked with three Cuts and running from thence in a direct line southerly to the fence thence by and with the fence to the Northwest corner of the square lott so called to which place the Road is three Rods wide and the northerly side is designated by stakes which they have set up from thence the sotherly side winds around the said Corner to a Stake marked in the fence from thence it runs westerly to a Ceder tree Marked from thence to a Chesnut Marked Stake in the fence from thence westerly with the fence to a marked Post and from thence with the fence to a marked Stake and from thence westwardly to a stake

PAGE 225.

near the fence from thence Crossing eastwardly to a Stake and from thence Northeasterly four Rods wide from the southerly side as the stakes are set up to the three Rod,s Road just above mentioned

Dated 16th. May 1826

Thomas S. Strong } Committee
Isaac Brewster

Be it remembred that on the fifth day of September 1826 Samuel L. Thompson made application to manumitt a certain Slave of his named Hannah and said Trustees of the freeholders and commonalty of the town of Brook haven being Satisfied that said Slave is under forty five years and of sufficient ability to provide for and maintain herself do hereby consent that she shall be manumitted as the law of this State in such case provides

THOMAS S. STRONG President

Attest MORDECAI HOMAN town Clerk

Suffolk County } ss.
town of Brook haven

A true Canvas and Estimate of the votes taken at an Election held in the town of Brook haven in the County of Suffolk on the Sixth day of November one thousand eight hundred and twenty six and on the two succeeding days inclusive for the Office of one Governor one Lieutenant

Governor for this State one Senator for the first Senatorial District in this State one Representative to Congress for the first Congressional District in Said State and two Members of Assembly for the County of Suffolk viz—

one hundred and thirty Nine votes were given for William Rochester for the Office of Governor.

One hundred and Sixty one votes were given for Dewitt Clinton for the Office of Governor

one hundred and thirty Nine votes were given for Nathaniel Pitcher for the Office of Lieutenant Governor—

PAGE 226.

One hundred and Sixty two votes were given for Henry Huntington for the Office Lieutenant Governor

One hundred and forty two votes were given for Stephen Allen for the Office Senator—

One hundred and fifty five votes were given for Robert Bogardus for the Office of Senator—

One hundred and Sixty one votes were given for Silas Wood for the Office of Representative to Congress

One hundred and fifty votes were given for Samuel Strong for the Office of Assemblyman

One hundred and fifty votes were given for George L. Conklin for the Office of Assemblyman

One hundred and forty eight votes were given for Charles I. Deering for the Office of Assemblyman

One hundred and forty four votes were given for Isaac Conklin for the Office of Assemblyman

Given under our hands at Brook haven this eighth day of Nov. 1826

        Thomas S. Strong
        Timothy Miller
        Woodhull Smith   } Inspectors
        Samuel Hammond
        Henry P. Osborn

Suffolk County } ss.
Town of Brook haven }

A true Canvas and estimate of the votes taken at the annual Election held on the first Monday in November one thousand eight hundred and and twenty six and on the two succeeding days inclusive in pursuance of an Act to Submit to the people of this State certain Amendments to the Constitution passed April the seventeenth one thousand Eight hundred and twenty six—

PAGE 227.

one hundred and fifty seven votes were given for Electing Justices of the peace by the People

One hundred and fifty Nine votes were given for extending the Elective franchise

Seven votes were given against Electing Justices of the peace by the people—

One vote were given against extending the Elective franchise—

Given under our hands at the town of Brookhaven this eighth day of November 1826

Thomas S. Strong
Timothy Miller
Henry P. Osborn } Assessors
Samuel Hammond
Woodhull Smith

This doth certify that we the commissioners of common Schools for the town of Brook haven being called by the Inhabitants of the 21st. school district in said town to divide said District and after viewing said district do consider it necessary that said district should be divided and have set off all the westward part of said District from Islip line as far east as to include all the Houses and Inhabitants living on the Road call,d Smith,s Road Viz the Road that Joseph Homan and the Rev. Mr. Tuthill now lives on as witness our hands this 6th. day of June 1827. which said District is no thirty one—

Mordecai Homan ⎞ Commissioners
Selah B. Strong ⎠ of Common Schools

Page 228.

At an annual town Meeting of the freeholders and Inhabitants of the town of Brook haven held in said town on the third day of April 1827—the following persons were unanimously Elected for town Officers for the ensueing Year Vis

Isaac Brewster President of trustees

Silas Reeve ⎫
Smith Rider ⎪
William Phillips ⎬ Trustees
Isaac Hammond ⎪
Timothy Miller ⎪
Samuel Carman ⎭

Isaac Brewster ⎫
Smith Rider ⎬ Overseers of the poor

Thomas S. Strong Supervisor

Mordecai Homan town Clerk and treasurer

Isaac Davis Collector

Barnabas Wines ⎫
William H. Helme ⎪
Davis Norton ⎬ Assessors
Timothy Davis ⎪
Nathan Post ⎭

Timothy Davis— ⎫
Benjamin Hutchenson ⎬ Commissioners of highways
William Tooker ⎭

Mordecai Homan cept ⎫
Selah B. Strong cept ⎬ Commissioners of common Schools
James M. Fanning ⎭

Jacob Hawkins
Abel Bennett
Samuel Davis Jur.
Clerk Longbothom } Constables
Charles A Tooker
William Hulse

PAGE 229.

John R. Satterly
William S. Smith } Inspectors of common Schools
Nathaniel Smith

OVERSEERS OF HIGHWAYS

Richard Smith Acept.   Daniel Haff Acpt.
Thomas Bailes   Joseph Avery Acpt.
Isaac Satterly   Simmons Laws Acpt.
Daniel Smith Acpt   George Davis Acpt.
Samuel Satterly Acpt.   Lewis Ritch Acpt.
Lewis Hulse Acpt.   John Randal
Samuel Davis   Davis Norton
Phillip Hallock Jur. Acpt. Samuel Hammond Acpt.
Miller I. Woodhull Acpt. Bithar Hawkins Acpt.
Henry Raynor   Noah Overton Acpt
Gideon Robinson   Willard Ruland
Jehiel Raynor   Daniel Davis
Henry Raynor   Zophar Hallock
John Hallock   Elijah Terry Acpt
William Robert Acept.   Briant Davis
Samuel Carman Acpt.   Israel Bennitt Setauket
Nathaniel Miller Acpt.   Nathaniel Davis old mans
William Howell   Henry Hawkins old mans
        Isaac Howell Middle island

*

William Rudyard   Justus Rowe
Jedediah Williamson   William Beale
Archabald Jayne   Joseph Avery

Amos Smith	William Arthur
Ebenezer Jones	Mathusela Overton
Zecheriah Hawkins	Joshua Overton
John Davis	Austin Roe
Elisha Davis	Henry Longbothom
Samuel Davis	Azariah Hawkins
Charles Woodhull	Samuel Hammond
Jonathan Worth	Willard Ruland
Miller I. Woodhull	Daniel Terry Jur
Jerrus Wines	Robert Hawkins
Christopher Robinson	Isaac Mills
Elisha Raynor	William Randal
Samuel Terry	John Laws
Nathan Post	Briant Davis
Timothy Rose	Ezra Guildersleve

* Note.—No title, but probably fence viewers.—Com.

PAGE 230.

Suffolk County } ss.
town of Brook haven }

A true Canvas and Estimate of the votes taken at an Election held in the town of Brook haven in the County aforesaid on the fifth day of November in the year one thousand eight hundred and twenty seven and on the two succeeding days inclusive for two Senators for the first District in this State two Members of Assembly for the County of Suffolk and four Justices of the peace for the said town of Brook haven Viz

171 { one hundred and Seventy one votes were given for John I. Schenck for the Office of Senator—

171 { One hundred and Seventy one votes were given for Jacob Tyson for the Office of Senator—

167 { One hundred and sixty seven votes were given for Peter Sharp for the Office of Senator—

165 { one hundred Sixty five votes were given for
John D. Ditmas for the Office of Senator—

175 { one hundred and Seventy votes were given for
Tredwell Scudder for the Office of Assembly

173 { one hundred and Seventy three votes were given for
Abraham H. Gardiner for the Office of Assembly

168 { one hundred and Sixty eight votes were given for
Nathaniel Miller for the Office of Assembly—

165 { one hundred and sixty five votes were given for
Isaac Conklin for the Office of Assembly

317 { three hundred and seventeen votes were given for
John S. Mount for the Office of Justice of the peace

177 { one hundred and Seventy seven votes were given
for Samuel Davis Jur. for the Office of Justice of the
peace

169 { one hundred and sixty nine votes were given for
William H. Helme for the Office of Justice of the
peace

PAGE 231.

168 { one hundred and sixty eight votes were given
for William Beale for the Office of Justice of the
peace

157 { one hundred and fifty seven votes were given for
Smith Rider for the Office of Justice of the peace

153 { one hundred and fifty three votes were given for
Barnabas Wines for the Office of Justice of the
peace

136 { one hundred and thirty six votes were given for
James M. Fanning for the Office of Justice of the
peace

Given under our hands at Brook haven this 8th. day of November 1827—

    Thomas S. Strong ⎫
    Barnabas Wines |
    William H. Helme ⎬ Inspectors
    Timothy Davis |
    Davis Norton— ⎭

This doth Certify that on the 30th. day of November one thousand eight hundred and twenty seven agreeable to the Statute of this State the Supervisor of the town of Brook haven met with the Justices of the peace that were elected at the foregoing Election for the purpose of Ballotting for the term the said Justices are elected for and after the said Ballots were duly drawn they stood as follows Viz

Justices { John S. Mount—four Years
William Beale—three Years
Samuel Davis Jur.—two Years
William H. Helme—One Year

Attest Thomas S. Strong Supervisor.

Page 232.

We the Commissioners of highways for the town of Brook haven being call by a number of the freeholders of the town of Brook haven to alter a Road that leads down the fireplace neck and after viewing the same do think an alteration would be proper and have Accordingly alterd said Road runing through John Roses land from the lower fence to run in a Strait line or Course to the Bay Joining Richard Corwins meadow agreeable to a petition presented to said commissioners by the Inhabitats of this place and the said John Rose is to work twenty days on said Road and also to allow the Inhabitants to take dirt for the repairs of said Road on his land off from the highway where it will be convinient which we order to be recorded this 5th. March 1828

Benjamin Hutchenson } Commissioners of
William Tooker   }   highways

Page 233.

At an annual town Meeting held on the first tuesday Viz the first day of april 1828 the following persons were Elected town Officers for the ensueing Year Viz—

Isaac Brewster President of Trustees

Samuel Carman
Smith Rider
Barnabas Wines } Trustees
Daniel Overton
Davis Norton
John Davis

Thomas S. Strong } Overseers of poor
Samuel Carman

Thomas S. Strong Supervisor

Mordecai Homan town Clerk

Isaac Davis Collector

William H. Helme
Nathan Post
Henry P. Osborn } Assessors
William Phillips
John R. Satterly

John S. Mount
Lewis Ritch } Commissioners of highways
Wm S. Robert,

Selah B. Strong,
Mordecai Homan } Commissioners of Common Schools
James M. Fanning

Charles A. Tooker
James Robinson
Noah Overton
Wm. H. Buckingham } Constables
Rumsey Rose
Abel Bennitt
James Smith
William Hulse

PAGE 234.

John R Satterly
William S. Smith } Inspectors of Common Schools
Nathaniel Smith

Overseers of Highways

Phillip Longbothom
Thomas Bailes
Isaac Satterly
Stephen Jayne
John Brewster
Samuel L. Thompson
Zecheriah Hawkins
Charles A. Tooker Accept,d
Isaac Davis Acceptd
Daniel R. Miller
Phillip Hallock Jur. Acptd
Timothy M. Woodhull Acpt.
Henry Raynor
Gideon Robinson Acceptd
Lewis Gourden Jur. Acceptd
Moott Raynor Accept.
William S. Robert
Samuel Carman
Selah Hawkins

William Howell
Justus Roe
Epenetus Mills
Simmons Laws
William C. Booth
Isaac Howell
James Dayton
Lewis Ritch
Daniel Petty Jur.
John Randal Acept
Samuel Hammond Acpt
Davis Norton Aceptd
Bither M. Hawkins
Richard W. Smith
Manly Ruland
Brewster Terry
Daniel Davis Acept
Davis Overton Jur.
Solomon Bishop Aceptd

George Hawkins Acptd

Fence Viewers

Nathaniel Hawkins
Jedediah Williamson
John Elderkin
Amos Smith
Azel Roe
Zecheriah Hawkins
David Robbins
Robert Stivers
Samuel Davis
Charles Woodhull
Phillip Hallock Jr
Hiram Tuthill

Justus Roe
Jacob Bell
Joseph Avery Acp.
William Arthur
Mathusela Overton
Noah Overton
Davis Norton
Henry Longbothom
James Howell
Samuel Hammond
Charles Swezey Acpt.
Daniel Terry Jur.

Christopher Robinson
Jerrus Wines
Mott Raynor Act
Samuel Terry
Nathan Post
John Hallock

Robert Hawkins
Isaac Mills
Briant Davis
Ezra Guildersleve
William Randal
John Laws

Page 235.

Be it Ordained by the Trustees of the freeholders and commonalty of the town of Brookhaven that if any person or persons shall take or catch any Oysters or shells of Oysters in the South Bay belonging to said town and William S. Smith between the tenth day of May and the first day of October in any year shall for every such offence forfeit and pay to said Trustees or their order the sum of twelve Dollars and fifty cents to be sued for and recoverd in the name of said Trustees before any Court havin cognisance thereof—
done at Brook haven this 6th. May 1828—

Isaac Brewster | President
Attest Mordecai Homan town Clerk | Seal

We the Board of Inspectors of Election for the town of Brook haven in the County of Suffolk do certify that the following is a correct statement of the result of a General Election held in said town on the third fourth and fifth days of November in the year one thousand eight hundred and twenty eight—

Six hundred and eighty seven votes were given for the office of Governor Six hundred and eighty six votes were given for the office of Lieutenant Governor. Six hundred and eighty six votes were given for the Office of Senator. Seven hundred and four votes were given for the Office of Congress Seven hundred votes were given for the office of Elector for President and vice President of the United States thirteen hundred and ninety four votes were given for the Office of Assembly six hundred Ninety three votes were given for the office of Sherriff six hundred and ninety votes were given for the Office of Clerk

PAGE 236.

two thousand seven hundred and fifty five votes were given for the Office of Coroner four hundred and twenty votes were given for the office Justice of the Peace. Of the votes given for the office of Governor Martin Vanburen received four hundred and five votes Smith Thompson received for the same Office two hundred and eighty two votes of the votes received for the Office of Lieutenant Governor Enos T. Throop receivd four hundred and fifteen votes Francis Granger receivd for the same office two hundred and seventy one votes of the votes received for the office of Senator

Stephen Allen received four hundred and fifteen votes Daniel Gardined receiv,d for the same Office two hundred and seventy one votes. of the votes given for the office of Congress James Lent receivd four hundred and ten votes

Silas wood received for the same office two hundred and Ninety four votes. of the votes receiv,d for the Office of Elector for president and vice president of the United States.

Moses Rolph Receivd four hundred and ten votes Elbert H. Jones received for the same Office two hundred and ninety votes of the votes received for the Office of Member of Assembly John M. Williamson received four hundred and twenty votes

David Hedges received for the same Office four hundred and twelve votes.

Samuel S. Gardiner received for the same office two hundred and eighty two votes.

William P. Buffett receiv,d for the same Office two hundred and eighty votes of the votes given for the Office of

Sheriff Abraham H. Gardiner received four hundred and five votes Nathan Post receiv,d for the same Office two hundred and eighty eight votes of the votes given for the Office of Clerk Joseph R. Hunting received three hundred and ninety three votes George Miller Receid for the same office two hundred and Ninety seven votes of the votes given for the office of Coroner Selah Carll received four hundred and Nine votes

PAGE 237.

Samuel F. Norton recievd for the same Office four hundred and two votes.

Jonah Halsey recd for the same Office four hundred and five votes

Nathaniel Topping received for the same Office four hundred and seven votes.

Josiah Smith received for the same Office two hundred and eighty nine votes

Levi H. Hildreth receivd for the same office two hundred and eighty two votes

Renssellear Horton receivd for the same Office two hundred and eighty four votes

Daniel Wheeler receivd for the same Office two hundred and Seventy seven votes, of the votes given for Justice of the peace

Barnabas Wines receivd three hundred and thirty votes

Spencer Dayton receivd for the same Office Ninety votes in witness whereof we have subscribed our hands this 5th day of November 1828—

Nathan Post
Henry P. Osborn
William H. Helme
William Phillips
} Assessors

on the 2nd. September 1828 the Overseers of the poor of the town of Brook haven agreed to raise eight hundred

Dollars for the support of the poor and contingent charges of said town—

Be it remembred that on the third day of March one thousand eight hundred and twenty Nine the Trustees of the freeholders and commonalty of the town of Brook haven Granted unto William Tooker Esq and to his hiers and Assigns for the term of fourteen years and no longer the exclusive or entire priviledge of Laying down and taking up Oysters in the south Bay on a space of ground containing ten Acres to be located about one half Mile Southward of the neck of land now Owned by said Tooker in a square plot given under our hands and seal of Office this day aforesaid   Isaac Brewster President L S
in presence of
Mordecai Homan Clerk

Page 238.

At an Annual town Meeting held in the town of Brook haven on the first tuesday being the 7th. day of April 1829 the following persons were Elected town Officers for the Ensueing year Viz.

Isaac Brewster President

John Penny
Isaac N. Gould
John Davis
John Havens
Austin Roe
Daniel Overton
} Trustees

William S. Smith Supervisor

Mordecai Homan town Clerk

Isaac Davis Collector.

William H. Helme
David Brown
Barnabas Wines
Davis Norton
Timothy Davis
} Assessors

John S. Mount \
Samuel Davis } Commissioners of highways \
Smith Rider

Mordecai Homan \
Sereno Burnell } Commissioners of Schools \
William S. Smith

Isaac Brewster \
John Havens } Overseers of Poor

Joseph C. Hammond \
John Roseman \
Noah Overton \
Charles W. Darling } Constables \
James Robinson \
John B. Overton \
Smith Rider

John R. Satterly \
James M. Faning } Inspectors of Schools \
Nathaniel Smith

OVERSEERS OF HIGHWAYS

Phillip Longbothom	Samuel Carman
Thomas Bailes	William Howell Acpt.
Wm Dickenson Acpt.	Daniel Haff.
James Vanbrunt.	Epenetus Mills
John Brewster	Simmons Laws
Israel Bennitt Acpt	Wm. C. Booth
Israel Davis Acpt	Davis Overton Acpt.
Daniel Davis Acpt	Sylvanus Overton
Charles Phillips Acpt	Lewis Ritch
Daniel R. Miller Acpd.	Daniel Petty Jur.
Samuel B. Hallock Acpt	John Randal
James Woodhull Jur.	Samuel Hammond Acpt
William Terry Acpt.	Davis Norton
Henry Turner Jur.	George Hawkins Acpt
David Peterson	David Fordham Acpt
Mott Raynor Acpt.	Manly Ruland
Charles F. Smith	Brewster Terry

Wm. S. Robert Dea Daniel Davis
Selah Hawkins Davis Overton Jr. Acpt
      Joseph Newton Acpt.

Fence Viewers

Nathaniel Hawkins Charles Homan
Jedediah Williamson Martin Mott
John Elderkin Joseph Avery
Amos Smith William Arthur
Azel Roe Methusela Overton
Zecheriah Hawkins Noah Overton
David Robbins Davis Norton
Robert Stivers Henry Longbothom
Samuel Davis James Howell
Charles Woodhull Samuel Hammond
Hiram Tuthill William J. Swezey
Phillip Hallock Jr Daniel Terry
Christopher Robinson Robert Hawkins
Abel Raynor Isaac Mills
Mott Raynor Briant Davis
Samuel Terry Ezra Guildersleve
Nathan Post Wm Randal
John Hallock John Laws

Page 239.

At a Meeting of the Trustees of the freeholders and commonalty of the town of Brook haven held this third day of March 1829 Coll William Howell Thomas Bell and John Bell made application for the priviledg of Building a Dock in the South Bay at or near the North line of the land belonging to the said Howell and said Trustees after due Notice having been given and not considering said dock to be injurous to the public in general do by these presents grant unto the said William Howell Thomas Bell and John Bell and to their heirs and assigns forever the priviledge of

Building constructing and keeping in repair a Dock at the aforesaid place to extend into the Bay to six and half feet water at common highwater and for which the said William Howell Thomas Bell and John Bell their heirs or Assigns shall pay unto the said Trustees or their Successors in Office Annually the sum of two Dollars on the first tuesday in April forever the first payment to commence on the first tuesday in April 1832, in Witness whereof we have subscribed our hands and affixed our seal of Office this 7th. April 1829—

| Seal |

Isaac Brewster President L. S.
Attest Mordecai Homan Clerk

Be it remembered that on that 7th. April 1829 the Trustees of School District No. 20 and 21. Made application to us the undersigned Commissioners of common Schools to have a part of the District No. 20 annexed to District No 21. and after due consideration had in the premises have set off all that part of School District No. 20 to extend as far east as Between the house of Hiram Gerard and Jacob Bell on the South side of the Road and to the Road between the house of Justus Roe and Brewster Woodhulls store on the North side of the road all to the west of said Bounds is annexed

Page 240.

to the 21 School District which is done by the request and consent of both Districts—

Selah B. Strong ⎫ Commissioner
Mordecai Homan ⎬ of common Schools

An Act for the preservation of Oysters—

Be it Ordained by the Trustees of the freeholders and commonalty of the town of Brook haven that if any person or persons shall take or Catch any Oysters in the South Bay belonging to said town and William S. Smith between the

tenth day of May and the first day of October in any year shall for every such offence forfiet and pay unto said Trustees the sum of twelve Dollars and fifty cents—And be it further Ordained that if any person or persons shall take and carry away any shells of Oysters from the Oyster Beds in said Bay at any time of the year shall for every such offence forfiet and pay unto said Trustees the like sum of twelve Dollars and fifty cents to be sued for and recoverd in any Court having cognisance of the same and applied to the use of said town done at Brook haven this 5th May 1829   Isaac Brewster President L S
    Attest Mordecai Homan town Clerk

Be it remembered that on 2nd. day of June 1829 the Trustees of the freeholders and commonalty of the town of Brook haven Granted unto William Smith of Patchogue the entire priviledge of laying down and taking up Oysters to him and to his Hiers and Assigns for the term of fourteen Years from this date on a space of Ground in the south Bay on a space of Ground containing ten acres to be located South South West from the mouth of Mud Creek on the north side of the Channel to be forty Rods square given under our hand and seal of Office this 2nd. June 1829—

| Seal | Isaac Brewster President L S |

    Attest Mordecai Homan }
            town Clerk   }

Page 241.

We Samuel Davis Junr. John S. Mount and Smith Rider commissioners of highways of the town of Brook haven do hereby certify that on this day we have inspected a certain road leading from the highway between Setauket and Drown meadow to the land of Brewster hawkins commencing nearly opposite the store of Charles Tyler in Setauket and runing from thence Northerly by the Land in the possession of harvey hulse and Eliza his Wife Daniel Robbins and Walter Jones on the East side thereof and David Cleves on the west side thereof about Seventy Rods until it reaches the land of the said Brewster Hawkins about seven rods to the Northward of the house of the said David Cleves. And we have also made due enquiry relative to the said Road and find that no record thereof has been made in the office of the Clerk of the County of Suffolk or of the town of Brook haven but we are Satisfied and do adjudge that the said Road has been used as a public highway for twenty years and more next preceding the twenty first day of March one thousand Seven hundred and ninety seven and from thence to this date and it appearing to us on inspection of the said road that the same is less than three Rods wide we proceeded to mark and designate by stakes where the respective owners of the land adjacent to the said road shall or may set their respective fences making the road three rods wide; And we do hereby order and direct that the Overseer of the highways in whose District it is situated to open the said Road to the width and places which we have thus designated in pursuance of the Act in such case made and provided—

And we do further Judge that the said Walter Jones as it respects the land in his possession which we have thus taken the said Harvey Hulse and Eliza his wife and her Daughter Eliza Hulse the younger as it respects the land in

Page 242.

the possession of the said Harvey Hulse and Eliza his wife which we have thus taken the Said Daniel Robbins and Phillip Longbothom as his Mortgage as it respects the land in the possession of the said Daniel Robbins which we have thus taken and the said David Cleves as it respects the land in his possession which we have thus taken (so far as it relates to the several portions of the said several tracts of land now actually within fence and have been within fence within the last twenty years precedeing this date) are respectively entiteled to the value thereof with such damages as they shall respectively sustain by our taking the same for a highway dated this Seventh day of July in the year one thousand eight hundred and twenty nine

      John S. Mount ⎫
      Samuel Davis Jur ⎬ Commissioners
 Enterd by Smith Rider   ⎭ of highways
M. Homan town Clerk

We the board of Inspectors of Election for the town of Brook haven in the County of Suffolk do certify that the following is a correct Statement of the result of a Election held in Said town on the 2nd. 3rd. and 4th. days of November in the year one thousand eight hundred and twenty nine Viz Six hundred and Seventy eight votes were given for the office of Senator ; Six hundred and eighty two votes were given for the Office of Member of Assembly ; Two hundred and sixty four Votes were given for the office of Justice of the Peace—Of the votes given for the Office of Senator Alpheus Sherman received two hundred and fifty Nine Votes Jonathan S. Conklin recieved for the same Office two hundred and Sixty three votes ; Peter A. Jay Received for the same Office Seventy Eight votes Jeremiah Johnson Received for the Same Office Seventy eight votes Silas Wood received for the same Office one vote—

Page 243.

Of the votes given for the Office of Member of Assembly Samuel Strong recievd two hundred and sixty votes Noah Youngs Recievd for the same Office two hundred and Sixty one votes ; Josiah Smith Reciev,d for the same Office eighty votes George Miller Reciev,d for the same Office eighty one votes. Of the votes given for the Office of Justice of the Peace Samuel Davis Jur. Reciev,d two hundred and fifty four Votes Silvanus Overton receiv,d for the same Office ten Votes—

In witness whereof we have hereunto subscribed our names this fourth day of November one thousand eight hundred an twenty Nine

William S. Smith
Barnabas Wines } Inspectors
Timothy Davis } of Election
Davis Norton

Mordecai Homan } Clerks
David Brown

We the commissioners of common Schools for the town of Brook haven having met at the house of Gideon Robinson in said town in pursuance of previous Notice to each of the said commissioners do hereby adopt the following resolution relative to extending School District No. fourteen Resolved unanimously that School District No. 14. shall be extended as far East as Moses Robinson,s house including his house and Lands and also all the Inhabitants who live west of a North and South line to be run from the Eastward extremity of said Moses Robinsons land that is to say by adding the following Inhabitants hereafter named to District No. 14. Moses Robinson Benjamin Gould Giles Bradley Isaac Carter Stephen Turner Daniel Terry Calvin King Moses Gould Gideon Robinson Nathaniel Tyler Reeves Davis Joseph Turner Jasper Griffing James Robinson the Consent of the Trustees of Both District is given except one Trustees from the 13th. School District *

Dated Brook haven 23rd. December 1829—

Mordecai Homan } Commissioners
Wm Sidney Smith } of
Sereno Burnell } Schools

* Note.—This alteration was set aside by the Superintendent. Page 248.—Com.

PAGE 244.

At an annual town Meeting of the freeholders and inhabitants of the town of Brook haven held on the 6th. day of April 1830 the following persons were duly elected town officers for the ensueing year viz

Daniel Overton president

Barnabas Wines }
Austin Roe
Samuel Davis
Timothy Davis } Trustees
Smith Rider
Samuel Satterly }

William S. Smith Supervisor

Mordecai Homan Clerk and treas

Isaac Davis Collector

Phillip Hallock }
Isaac N. Gould
Barnabas Wines } Assessors
Smith Rider
Timothy Davis }

Samuel Davis Jur } Commissioner
Smith Rider } of
John S. Mount } highways

Mordecai Homan } Commissioner
Selah B. Strong } of
Samuel F. Norton } Schools

Barnabas Wines } Overseers of the poor
Samuel Satterly }

William Beale Justice of the peace

Noah Overton }
John W. Yarington
Joel Robinson } Constables
Joseph C. Hammond
Samuel Tooker }

Page 245.

Overseers of highways for the year 1830.

Thomas Wiggins	Nelson Smith
Thomas Bailes	Daniel Haff.
William Dickenson	Epenetus Mills
Brewster Hawkins	Wm. H. Buckingham
Floyd Smith	Wm. C. Booth
Israel Bennitt	Isaac Overton Hills
Israel Davis	James Dayton
John Hutchenson	Franklin Overton
Parshall Davis	Ezra Guildersleve
Charles Woodhull	John B. Laws
James Hallock	Davis Norton
James Woodhull Jur	Samuel Hammond
John Carter	George Hawkins
Joel Robinson	Noah Overton
Jonathan Robinson	Manly Ruland
William Hawkins	Davis Overton Jr
David Terry	Richard Woodhull
William S. Robert	John Rose
Samuel Carman	William Howell

at the same time a vote was taken as to the propriety of dividing the town and the vote were about five to one against dividing said town

Mordecai Homan town clerk

Page 246.

Town of Brook haven

We Samuel Davis Junr. and John S. Mount two of the Commissioners of highways now fence viewers for the town of Brook haven on application of Azariah Hawkins and after due Notice being given to Alexander S. Ruland do hereby certify that we have this day divided a division fence between the lands of the said Azariah Hawkins and the said Alexander S. Ruland leading from the Middle

Country road and extending North by the side and on the east side of a lane about one hundred and fifty rods to a short ditch across said lane setting off to the said Azariah Hawkins the south half of the said fence from a certain stake and mark on a bush by the side of said fence to be by him maintained and kept in repair the other part of the said fence we leave for the said Alexander S. Ruland from the said stake and mark to the before mentioned Ditch across said lane to be by him maintained and the said Azariah Hawking paying to the said Alexander S Ruland eighteen Dollars and seventy five Cents for the said fence so set off to the said Azariah Hawkins, the said Alexander S. Ruland being the owner of the whole of the fence so divided given under our hands at Brook haven this 20th. day of April 1830—

enterd this 29th April 1830   Samuel Davis Jur } fence
John S. Mount } viewers
Mordecai Homan town Clerk

Page 247.

Be it remembered that whereas there has been much complaint to us the Trustees of the freeholders and commonalty of the town of Brookhaven respecting the rate of wharfage at the Dock at Stoney Brook harbour formerly granted by said Trustees to George Hallock and now owned by Charles D Hallock and after hearing the proofs and allegations of both parties and also appointing a committee to inspect into the premises do make the following alterations and restrictions viz. vessels lying next to the Dock to pay as usual all other vessels lying second third or fourth from said Dock to pay six cents a day after lying twenty four hours. All Barrels of flour or other provisions landed on said Dock one Cent pr. Barrel. for landing Stone one Cent pr load for a common team for putting on Board Cordwood four Cents for every five feet cord or in that

proportion. Any person letting stone or lumber lie on said Dock for more than twelve days to pay one Cent pr day on every load for every day thereafter. Neither Mr. Hallock nor any other person to lay wood in the road within four rods of the new made ground or to take pay therefor.
Done at Brook haven this first day of June 1830. under our hands and seal of office—

DANIEL OVERTON President L S

On the 7th. September 1830 the Overseers of the Poor of the town of Brook haven Directed that a tax of seven hundred and fifty Dollars should be raised in said town for the support of the poor and other expences—

M. HOMAN town Clerk

PAGE 248.

State of New York }
Secretaries. Office } Albany 15th. June 1830

In the Case of the appeal of Christopher Robinson and others Inhabitants of District No. 13 in the town of Brook haven it appears that on the 23rd. Dec. 1829. the commissioners attached a portion of said District to an adjoining District No. 14. and established the line so as to leave the School House No. 13. in District No. 14 it is said the school House was of little value was near one line of District No. 13. and was built by proprietors but it seems to have been the District School House and was used as such, before the alteration 13 had many more Scholars than 14. since the change 14. has much the greater number as to the precise number is is not easy to acertain from a contradiction in the statements if District No 14 was too small the two should have been consolidated and not divided so as to leave reason to complain after the alteration as 14 had before after reading all the paper in this case I am induced to think that No. 13. ought to have her school house poor as it is therefore decided that the alteration made between

Districts No. 13. and 14. on the 23 Dec 1829. in setting a part of No. 13. including the school house to No. 14. be and the same is hereby set aside and the two districts are restored to their original boundaries

Given under my hand and seal of Office 15th. June 1830.

A. C. Flagg—
Superintenant of common Schools

Page 249.

We the board of Inspectors of Elections for the town of Brook haven in the County of suffolk do certify that the following is a correct statement of the result of a general Election held in said town on the first second and third days of November in the year one thousand eight hundred and thirty

Five hundred and thirty eight Votes were given for the Office of Governor

Five hundred and thirty four votes were given for the Office of Lieutenant Governor

Five hundred and thirty eight votes were given for the Office of Senator

Five hundred and forty two votes were given for the office of Representatives to congress

one thousand and seventy five votes were given for the Office of Members of Assembly. Of these votes given for the Office of Governor Enos T. Throop recieved three hundred and sixty Nine votes; Francis Granger recieved for the same Office one hundred and sixty eight votes Samuel L. Thompson received for the same office one vote. Of the votes given for the Office of Lieutenant Governor Edward P. Livingston recieved three hundred and sixty seven votes Samuel Stevens recieved for the same office one hundred and Sixty seven votes Of the votes given for the office of Senator Jonathan S. Conklin recieved three hundred and seventy one votes, Harmanus Guyon reciev,d for the same Office one hundred and sixty seven votes Of the votes given for the Office of representative to Congress James Lent recieved three hundred and seventy three votes John A. King recieved for the same Office one hundred and Sixty six votes. Of the votes given for the Office of Member of Assembly George S. Phillips recieved three hundred and seventy six votes—

PAGE 250.

George L. Conklin recieved for the same office three hundred and seventy five votes

Josiah Smith recieved for the same Office one hundred and sixty two votes

Josiah P. Howell recieved for the same Office one hundred and sixty two votes. in Witness whereof we have hereunto subscribed our names this third day of November in the year one thousand eight hundred and thirty

Wm. Sidney Smith ⎫
Smith Rider ⎬ Inspectors
Timothy Davis ⎪ of
Isaac N. Gould ⎭ Election

Be it remembered that on the fifth day of April one thousand eight hundred and thirty one Nethaniel Miller made application to the Trustees of the freeholders and commonalty of the town of Brook haven to Manumit a certain slave that belong,d to the Estate of Timothy Miller deceas,d and said Trustees being Satisfied that said slave was under forty five years and of Sufficient ability to provide for and Maintain himself do therefore Manumitt the said slave according to the Statute of this state said Slave is named Jeremiah   DANIEL OVERTON President

Attest MORDECAI HOMAN town clerk

PAGE 251.

List of Road districts No.ed and set off by the Commissioners of highways in the year 1830

No. 1. is to embrace the inhabitants of Stoney brook in part
No. 2 Stoney Brook
do. 3, Setauket
do. 4, Nasakeage
do. 5, east side of Setauket
do. 6, east side of setauket
do. 7, Drowned Meadow
do. 8, lower part of oldmans
do. 9, uper part of oldmans
do. 10, Millers place
do. 11, Rocky point
do. 12, Wading River
do. 13, Manor North part of Manor
do. 14, Manor South part
do. 15, east part Moriches
do. 16, West part of Moriches
do. 17, Mastick—
do. 18, fireplace Mills
do. 19, fireplace
do. 20, Jew street
do. 21, west part of do
do. 22, Swan Creek
do. 23, Patchogue
do. 24, West part of do
do. 25 Blue point
do. 26, Mooney ponds
do. 27, West middle Island
do. 28, North part of do
do. 29, Westfields
do. 30, Coram
do. 31, East part of do
do. 32, Balldhills
do. 33, West part of do
do. 34, Coram Hills

No. 35, East Middle Island
do. 36, North part of do
do. 37, Middle part of do
do. 38, uper Mills in do
do. 39, lower Mills in do
do. 40, Ridgefield—

5th. March 1832 the Commissioners of highways erected two New districts viz. No. 42 to be Between the district of Manny Ruland and David Overtons—
No. 41 to embrace all that part between James Robinsons West line east to David Robinsons West line—
Also the District No 2. in Setauket is disolved and Set over to No. 3.

43. is Swezey town
44. is the Middle part of Moriches—

John S. Mount
Barnabas Wines
Samuel Hammond
} Commissioners

PAGE 252.

At an Annual town Meeting held in the town of Brookhaven this 5th. day of April 1831 the following town Officers were elected—

William Sidney Smith Supervisor Acpt

Daniel Overton President of Trustees Acpt

acpt
acpt
acpt,d

Samuel Davis
Samuel Satterly
John Penny Jur
Davis Norton
Smith Rider
James H. Weeks
} Trustees

Mordecai Homan Clerk and treasurer acpt

Isaac Davis Collector

acpt.
acpt

Samuel Satterly
Smith Rider
} Overseers of the poor

Barnabas Wines
Smith Rider
Isaac Davis } Assessors
Isaac Brewster
Davis Norton

acpt John S. Mount
acpt Samuel Hammond } Commissioners of highways
Barnabas Wines

acpt. Mordecai Homan
acpt. Selah B. Strong } Commissioners of common Schools
acpt. Samuel F. Norton

John S. Mount Justice of the peace

Daniel Tooker—
Noah Overton
John W. Yarington } Constables
Jacob Hawkins Jr.

PAGE 253.

acpt John R. Satterly
acpt William Beale } Inspectors of common Schools
acpt Joel Robinson

OVERSEERS OF HIGHWAYS

District No. 1, Richard Garrett acpt
do. 2, Thomas Bailes acpt
do. 3, Isaac Satterly acpt
do. 4, Israel Bennitt
do. 5, Floyd Smith acpt
do. 6, James Hulse acpt.
do. 7, James R. Davis—
do. 8, Henry Hawkins
do. 9, Charles Phillips acpt.
do. 10, Thomas Helme acpt
do. 11, Charles Robinson acpt.
do. 12, Hiram Tuthill acpt.

	District No.	13,	John Carter
	do	14,	Joel Robinson acpt.
	do	15,	David Terry
	do	16,	William Hawkins Jr acpt.
	do	17,	William S. Robert
	do	18,	David W. Homan acpt
	do	19,	Azel Hawkins acpt
	do.	20,	William Howell
	do.	21,	Barnabas Smith
	do.	22,	Ananias Smith Jr
	do.	23,	Clerk Smith. acpt.
	do.	24,	James Smith acpt.
	do.	25,	Epenetus Mills—acpt
	do.	26,	Mills Hawkins acpt.
	do.	27,	Albert L. Homediewe
	do	28,	Isaac Hammond acpt
	do	29,	Richard Norton acpt
	do.	30,	Richard W. Smith acpt
	do.	31,	Benjamin Clerk acpt
	do.	32	Scudder Terry acpt.
	do.	33	Manly Ruland acpt
	do	34,	David Overton acpt
	do	35	Franklin Overton
36	do.		Henry P. Hutchinson acpt
37	do.		John Ruland acpt
38	do.		Nathaniel Tuthill acpt
39	do.		Apollos A. Mills acpt
		40,	Jeremiah Randal acpt.
		41,	Lewis Gourden acpt—

At the aforesaid Meeting a vote was taken on the question of a County poor house and the vote was unanomously opposed to it—And also on the proposed division of the town and the vote was unanomously opposed to such division—

MORDECAI HOMAN town clrk

Page 254.

To all to whome these presents shall come the Trustees of the freeholders and commonalty of the town of Brook haven send Greeting. Whereas Jonas Smith of the town of Brook haven in the County of Suffolk and State of New York did on the fifth day of April one thousand eight hundred and thirty one petition to said Trustees for liberty to build a dock or wharf at a place called the west meadow creek at stoney brook harbour against his own land and said Trustees having appointed a committee to view said premises and having received a report from said committee that said Dock will not be injurous but necessary for the public in general. Do by these presents grant unto the said Jonas Smith and to his Hiers and assigns forever liberty to Build construct and keep in repair and if need be to rebuild a Dock or wharf at the aforesaid place according to the following description and dementions Viz. commencing at the Northeasterly corner at a certain Stake near a small Ceder tree at the bottom of the bank or cliff from thence runing south fifty nine degrees west one Chain and eighty two Links, thence south thirty four degrees west one Chain and fifty seven Links thence south forty one and half degrees West one Chain and forty links thence North eighty five degrees West one Chain and eighty seven links thence south seven and an half degrees east two Chain and thirty links thence south fifty degrees east one chain and ninety two links to the bottom of the bank or cliff to be in range with the line of Charles D. Hallock—subject however to the following Annuity restrictions regulations and compensation, that is to say the said Jonas Smith his Heirs executors Administrators or assigns for and in consideration of the above said Grant shall well and truly pay or Cause to be paid unto the said Trustees or their Successors in Office for the use of the said town on the first tuesday in April Anually forever the yearly rent or Annuity of four Dollars and to be at the expence of the surveying and laying out said Dock and also to give the public the privilege of a passway with teams Waggons andsofourth from the School House

PAGE 255.

throug his land to said Dock so long as he shall receive wharfage for the use of Said Dock, and shall also allow the public to pass and repass on said Dock to and from the west meadow without any let or hindrance with teams Carts andsofourth and the said Jonas Smith his heirs or Assigns shall be allowed to ask for demand and sue for and recover for the use of said Dock wharfage at the following rate, Viz. for putting on board Cord wood at the rate of four Cents for every five feet cord for shipping every ox Steer Cow or heifer twelve and an half cents pr head for every cask of flaxseed four cents for shipping or landing full hogsheads six cents for every Barrel of liquor two Cents for every Cask of Rice four cents for every crate of earthan three Cents for every Barrel of flour or other provisions one cent for every load of Stone lumber or other such article one cent pr load for a common team for all foreign vessels unloading ashes or other Manure six Cents for every hundred Bushels all light vessels making fast to said Dock and laying over twenty four hours the vessel lying next to the Dock to pay twelve and an half cents pr day after laying twenty four hours and the vessels lying second third or fourth from the Dock to pay six cents pr day over twenty four hours and all light vessels to make way for vessels to load or unload the aforesaid wharfage to be paid by the master or owner of such vessel and also reserving a right for all articles belonging to the town of Brook haven viz. the Corporation of Brook haven to be landed on said dock free from wharfage and a right for the Trustees of said town to regulate the rate of wharfage for said Dock in future and the said Jonas Smith doth hereby bind himself his Hiers Executors Administrators or Assigns to pay unto the said Trustees or to their Successors in Office the aforesaid sum of four Dollars Annually and also to keep said Dock in good repair so long as he or they shall hold the grant for said Dock the first Annual payment to be made on the first tuesday in april one thousand eight hundred and thirty two but in case the aforesaid Jonas Smith his Hiers

PAGE 256.

or Assigns shall neglect to pay the aforesaid sum of four Dollars Annually at the time above specified or when demanded or to keep said Dock in good repair when reasonably requested then the aforesaid grant shall be nul and void or otherwise in force and virtue the aforesaid Smith shall be allowed to build his dock in a sweep or curve from the second Station to the fifth so as for the outer part not to extend more than ten feet beyond the fourth corner into the harbour in witness whereof the aforesaid parties have set their hands and seals this third day of May one thousand eight hundred and thirty one.

DANIEL OVERTON President L S
JONAS SMITH—L S

in presence of
MORDECAI HOMAN town Clerk

At a Meeting of the Trustees of the freeholders and Commonalty of the town of Brook haven held on the 7th day of June 1831. the said Trustees agreed to raise the rates of wharfage for Charles D. Hallocks Dock at Stoney brook to what they were before the deduction or alteration made in said rates of wharfage by the Trustees of said town of the first day of June 1831. DANIEL OVERTON, President

Attest
MORDECAI HOMAN town Clerk

and that the said Charles D. Hallock his hiers or Assigns pay the said Trustees four Dollars annually from the first day of April last for the use of the excess in length of his dock beyond the limits of his Grant

DANIEL OVERTON President

Attest MORDECAI HOMAN
town Clerk

PAGE 257.

We the Subscribers being a committee of the Trustees of the freeholders and commonalty of the town of Brook haven to whom was referred the subject in relation to George Hallock wharf at Stoney Brook do hereby make the following report that after a due examination of the grant relative to the said wharf and of the premises in question, we are fully satisfied that a part of the road which was given by George Hallock for the use of the public (upon the renewal of the grant for the said wharf) to wit the four rods square adjoining to the new made ground is to be kept entirely free from all incumbrances and that the Owner of the said wharf nor any other person have any right to use it as a depository for wood Ashes or any other article but that the same is to be kept free and clear for the purpose of driving to and from or turning Wagons and carriages at said wharf

Brook haven 8th. May 1831.

Samuel Satterly
Davis Norton } Committee
James H. Weeks

Attest M. HOMAN town clerk

We the Board of Inspectors of Election for the town of Brook haven in the County of Suffolk do certify that the following is a correct Statement of the result of a General Election held in the said town on the 7th. 8th and 9th. days of November one thousand eight Hundred and thirty one Viz. five hundred and twenty one votes were given for the Office of Senator one thousand and twenty seven votes were given for the Office of Member of Assembly Five hundred and Eleven votes were given for the Office of clerk two thousand and forty one votes were given for the Office of Coroners—

Of the votes given for the office of Senator Harman B. Cropsey recieved three hundred and Sixty four votes Jacob Tyson recieved for the same office one vote Silas Wood recievd for the same office one hundred and fifty six votes—

PAGE 258.

of the votes given for the Office of Member of Assembly John M. Williamson reciev,d three hundred and ninety six votes Samuel L. Homedieue reciev,d for the same Office three hundred and Ninety two votes Henry P. Osborn reciev'd for the same Office one hundred and twenty votes James Halliock recievd for the same Office one hundred and Nineteen votes of the votes given for the Office of Sherriff Richard W. Smith recievd three hundred and eighty seven votes Nathan Post recievd for the same Office one hundred and twenty five votes Jeffrey Randal recievd for the same Office two votes Of the votes given for the Office of Clerk Joseph R. Hunting recievd three hundred and Ninety one votes James M. Fanning recievd for the same Office one hundred and nineteen votes Mordecai Homan recievd for the same office one vote—

Of the votes recievd for the Office of Coroner Selah Carll recievd three hundred and Ninety votes Samuel F. Norton recievd for the same Office three hundred and eighty nine votes Jonah Halsey recievd for the same Office three hundred and Ninety votes Nathaniel Topping recievd for the same Office three hundred and Ninety votes David Hand recievd for the same Office one hundred and twenty votes Joseph Moore recievd for the same Office one hundred and nineteen votes Mordecai Homan recievd for the same Office one hundred and twenty two votes

Edward Dodd recievd for the same Office one hundred and twenty one votes—

In witness whereof we have hereunto subscribed our hands at Brook haven this ninth day of November one thousand eight hundred and thirty one—

Wm Sidney Smith
Isaac Brewster
Davis Norton } Inspectors of Election
Isaac Davis
Smith Rider

On the 2nd. Day of Sept. 1831. the Trustees of Brook Haven agreed to raise one thousand dollars for the support of the poor of said town

M. HOMAN town Clerk

PAGE 259.

At a Meeting of the freeholders and Inhabitants of the town of Brook held on the 3d. day of April 1832 the following persons were Elected town Officers it being town Meeting day—viz

Barnabas Wines Justice of the Peace

Davis Norton president of the Trustees

Smith Rider
William H. Brewster
Samuel Davis
Henry P. Hutchenson } Trustees
James H. Weeks
Joel Robinson

William S. Smith Supervisor

Mordecai Homan Clerk and treasurer

Smith Rider
William H. Brewster } Overseers of the poor.

Isaac Davis Collector

John Penny Jur
John Havens
John R. Satterly } Assessors
Isaac Davis
Davis Norton

Samuel Davis Jur
James H. Weeks } Commissioners of highways
John S. Mount

Selah B. Strong
Mordecai Homan } Commissioners of common Schools
Samuel F. Norton

Jesse J. Porter Sealer of weights and measures

John W. Yarington
Briant Hawkins
Noah Overton } Constables
James Robinson

PAGE 260.

John R. Satterly
William Beale } Inspectors of Common Schools
Joel Robinson

OVERSEERS OF HIGHWAYS

No. 1, William S. Williamson acpt.
do. 2, dissolved
do. 3, Isaac Satterly
do. 4, Israel Bennitt
do. 5, Stephen Edwards
do. 6, Walter Jones
do. 7 William T. Robbins
do. 8, Jehiel Norton
do. 9, Isaac Davis accept.
do. 10, Daniel Hawkins
do. 11, Joel Brown
do. 12 Hendrickson Hallock acept.
do. 13, Noadiah D. Carter—acpt.
do. 14, Nathaniel Robinson

No. 15, John Penny acept
do. 16 John Ross
do. 17 William Smith point
do. 18 David Homan Jur
do. 19—Smith Mott
do. 20 Charles Osborn
do. 21, John Havens
do. 22 Joseph Marvin
do. 23, Sillick Wicks
do. 24, James Smith
do. 25, William Arthur
do. 26 Mills Hawkins acept.
do. 27, Isaac L Homedieue
do. 28, Wickham Ruland accept
do. 29, Henry Longbothom acept
do. 30, Clerk Longbothom acept
do. 31, Benjamin Clerk acept.
32, Scudder Terry acept
33, Daniel Terry
34, Jeremiah Gourden
35, Isaac Hulse accept
36, Ezra Guildersleve
37, John Ruland
38, D. D. Swezey.
39, Lewis G. Davis accept.
40, Jeremiah Randal
41, Lewis Gourden Jur.
42, Brewster Terry Jur.

PAGE 261.

We Samuel Davis Jur. and James H. Weeks two of the Commissioners of highways for the town of Brook haven having by request of a Number of the freeholders and Inhabitants of the said town taken a view of Part of the highway (call,d the south Country Road) leading from the paper

Mill in Moriches to the Maple Hallow, do deem it necessary and expedient to regulate and establish the Bounds of the said highway agreeable to the following Survey viz. Commencing at a certain Stake Standing N. $82\frac{1}{2}°$ East from the North east Corner of the Paper Mill distant 58 Links and thence running N. $28°\frac{1}{4}$ East 50 Links to the Middle of the highway thence running as follows 1st. N. $52°\frac{1}{2}$ East 3 Chain 77. Links to a point in the road or Middle of the highway whence the Northwest Corner of John Leeks house bears S. 39° E. distant 74 Links 2nd. N. 54° E. eight Chain 27 links 3rd. N. 86° E. 4.87 links 4th. S. 85° E. 10.40 links to the east side of James Fannings land 5th. S. 86° E. 2.70 links 6th. S. 69° E. 13.00 links whence the South east corner of Charles Hulses house bears N. $2\frac{1}{4}°$ W. distant 62 links 7th. S. $72\frac{3}{4}°$ E. 4.61 links to a point in the highway whence to a certain Stone in the Northeast corner of Joseph Hawkins land bears S. $12\frac{1}{4}°$ W. distant 50 links 8th. S. 68° E. 3.50 links 9th. S. $51\frac{1}{2}°$ E. 12.80 to a point in the highway where a Certain white Oak tree marked with three Notches bears S. $13\frac{1}{4}°$ W. distant 59 links; the width of the highway from the beginning to the termination of the four first Courses is four Rods that is to say two rods on each side of the line run for the middle

PAGE 262.

from thence to the termination of the five last Courses three and a half rods wide being two rods on the south and one and a half rods on the North side of the said Courses Dated at Brook haven this 13th. Sept. 1832

     James H. Weeks } Commissioners
     Samuel Davis Jur. } of highways
MORDECAI HOMAN town clerk

This doth certify that we the undersigned commisioners of common Schools being call,d by the Inhabitants of school Districts No. 18. and 19. to form a new District on the Western and Eastern parts of said Districts and after having met for that purpose and hearing the reasons given and fully believing that the said Districts were too large, have accordingly set off a New District to commence at Daytons creek on the east and to extend westward to the west line of Samuel Tookers land which said District is No. thirty two Dated at Brook haven this 10th. day of Jan. 1833—

at the same time the school houses were valued and the 18 District is to pay to No. 32 the sum of $47.81. and the 19 the sum of $36.60 being their respective proportions Samuel F. Norton } Commissioners
Mordecai Homan— } of common Schools

To all to whom the presents shall come the Trustees of the freeholders and commonalty of the town of Brook haven send Greeting Whereas Charles Osborn of the town of Brook haven in the County of Suffolk and State of New York did on the fifth day of March last petition to said Trustees for liberty to Build a dock or wharf in the South bay against his own land and adjoining thereto and Said Trustees after due consideration had in the premises and believing

PAGE 263.

that it will be a benefit to the publick in General (and for and in consideration of the Yearly rent or Annuity of the sum of ten Dollars Annually to be paid to said Trustees or their Successors in Office on the first tuesday in May Yearly during the term of this Grant) do by these presents Grant unto the said Charles Osborn his heirs Executors Administrators and Assigns the liberty to Build construct and keep in repair a dock or wharf in the south Bay against his own

Land and to extend in length into the Bay seven hundred feet from common high water mark and to be one hundred feet in width on the shore the aforesaid Grant or lease is for the Space or term of one hundred years from the date of these presents at the expiration of which said term or in case default shall be made in the payment of the aforesaid Annuity, by the said Charles Osborn his Hiers Executors Administrators or Assigns when reasonably demanded then the aforesaid Grant shall cease and be void and the right thereof return again to said town the first Annual payment for the use or priviledge of the aforesaid Grant shall be paid by the said Charles Osborn his Hiers Executors Administrators or Assigns on the first tuesday in May one thousand eight hundred and thirty four in Witness whereof the aforesaid Trustees have Set their hands and caused the said of said town to be affixed this second day of April one thousand eight hundred and thirty three

         DAVIS NORTON President L. S
signed sealed and
 delivered in the presence
  of MORDECAI HOMAN town clerk

PAGE 264.

At an Annual town Meeting of the freeholders and Inhabitants of the town of Brook haven held on the 2nd. day of April 1833 the following town Officers were unanomously Elected viz.

    Samuel Davis Jur. Justice of the Peace
    Davis Norton President of Trustees

William H. Brewster	
Miller Woodhull	
Henry P. Hutchenson	Trustees
James H. Weeks	
Abraham Osborn	
Almerin Barns	

BROOKHAVEN TOWN RECORDS. 323

William Sidney Smith Supervisor
Mordecai Homan town clerk and treasurer
William H. Brewster } Overseer of the Poor
Almerin Barns

Isaac Davis Collector

Assessors	Constables
Joel Robinson	Noah Overton
Joseph Avery	Samuel Overton
John R. Satterly	Spencer Dayton
Isaac Davis	Briant Hawkins
Davis Norton	Rumsey Rose
	James T. Clayton

Samuel Hammond } Commissioners of
John S. Mount— } highways
David Worth—

Selah B. Strong } Commissioners of
Mordecai Homan } Common Schools
Samuel F. Norton

John R Satterly, }
Daniel G. Gillet } Inspectors of Schools
Lester H. Davis

Lester H. Davis Sealer of weights and Measures

PAGE 265.

We the Commissioner of highways for the town of Brook haven have laid out a public Road or highway from Bells Dock as follows viz—

No. 1. Commencing at the North end of said Dock where the post on the Northeast corner of the Same bears N. 54°. E. from said post—

No. 2. N. 38° 00' West three Chains where Thomas Bells store on the southwest Corner bears N. 45°. 00' E.
C L
0.51. from thence running the same Course until it reaches

the South Country Road distance 29 Ch. 38 Links four Rods wide—

No. 3 N. 20°. 00′ W. 1 Chain 31. links where the southwest Corner of Charles Osborns Store bears N. 64°. 00′ E distance 0 Chain 68 Links—

No. 4. N. 0°. 45′ E. 6 Chains 54 Links where the Southwest Corner of Aarons* House bears N. 84° E distance 37½ Links

(Note.—* Aaron, a colored man.)

No. 5 N. 0°—30′ E. Distance 47 Chains near the North end of Gardiners Land—

No. 6 N. 14°. 00′ E. distance 7 Chains to Gardiners Road

No. 7 N. 7° E. distance 3 Chains 20 Links to Robinsons Road—

No. 8. N. 0°. 30′ E. Distance 215 Ch. 92 Links until it reaches a large pine tree Marked Ex on the South side Standing on the South of the horsblock distance three Chains 38 Links

No. 9—N. 10°. 30′ East distance 12 Chains.

No. 10. N. 9°. 30′ E. distance 95 Ch. 75 until it intersects the road that leads from fire place to Coram and the road that leads from Swezeys Mills to Patchogue three rods wide Dated this 17th. Sept. 1833—

John S. Mount.
Samuel Hammond } Commissioners of highways
David Worth—

M. Homan town Clerk

Page 266.

We the Subscribers do hereby consent to the laying out and opening of a public highway through our Lands as discribed in the Survey taken by Richard W. Smith Esq. under the commissioners of highways from Bellville* Dock to Swezeys Mills Middle Island in the fall of 1832 and we also agree to relinquish all claims or demands for Damages that we may Sustain in consequence of the laying out and opening the said Road Brook haven 1st. Sept 1833

                        Henry Gardiner
                        John Bell
                        Thos. Bell
                        Chs. Osborn

Attest
MORDECAI HOMAN town Clerk

* Note.—now Bellport.—COM.

This doth certify that I Sillick Wicks of the town of Brook Haven in the County of Suffolk and State of New York for and in Consideration of the sum of ten Dollars to me in hand paid do release to the town of Brook Haven a certain piece of land on the East side of the Lane that leads from Justus Roes to the Bay beginning at a Locust Stake near my house from thence to the Bay leaving said * Road thirty feet wide this 15th. day of March 1834.

                                      SILLICK WICKS

David Worth } Commissioners of highways
Samuel Hammond }

MORDECAI HOMAN town clerk

* Road in Patchogue laid out in 1812, now Ocean Avenue.—COM.

PAGE 267.

LIST OF OVERSEERS OF HIGHWAYS FOR 1833

District No. 1, Timothy Davis
do   2, Dissolved
do.   3, John C. Bailis
do   4, Israel Bennitt
do.   5, John Roseman
do.   6, Walter Jones
do.   7, Israel Davis
do.   8, Charles A. Tooker Acpt

District No. 9, Parshall W. Davis
do. 10, Nathaniel Miller Acept
do. 11, James Hallock
do. 12, Moses Swezey
do. 13, John Carter
do. 14, Nathaniel Robinson
do. 15, Nelson Terry.
do 16, James Fanning
do. 17, Silas Payne
do 18, Thomas Jenings
do. 19, William Rose
do. 20, Isaac Overton Jur
do. 21, Joseph C. Hedges
do. 22, William Swezey
do. 23, William Smith
do. 24, Daniel G. Gillett
do. 25, Epenetus Mills cceptd
do. 26, Mills Hawkins
do. 27, Isaac N. Gould
do. 28, Wickham Ruland Acpt
do. 29, Nelson Norton.
do. 30, Noah Overton
do. 31, Benjamin Clerk Acpt
do 32, Richard Smith Pond
do. 33, Willard Ruland Aceptd
.34, David Overton
.35, Isaac Hulse
.36, Ezra Guildersleve acpt
.37, George Davis
.38, Daniel D. Swezey
.39, James H. Weeks acpt
.40, Jeremiah Randal
41, Lewis Gourden
.42, Brewster Terry Jur
.43, Oscar F. Swezey

at the aforesaid Meeting a vote was take to raise a Bounty for the distuction of foxes and carried unanamously

PAGE 268.

Be it Ordained by the Trustees of the freeholders and commonalty of the town of Brook haven that if any person or persons—(except the lessee of said town) shall take or catch any shell fish in any of the Bays waters or harbours on the North side of the Island belonging to said town of Brook haven except it be on tuesday and friday in each week he she or they shall for every such offence forfeit and pay the sum of twelve Dollars and fifty cents for every such offence given under our hands and Seal Dated at Brook haven this 11th. day of June 1833—

       James H. Weeks. } Trustees
in presence   H. P. Hutchinson }

MORDECAI HOMAN town clerk

| Seal |

At a Meeting of the Trustees and freeholders and commonalty of the town of Brook haven held on the 17th. day of Sept. 1833 said trustees agreed to allow Charles D. Hallock wharfage for putting on Board or landing any Horse 12½ cents. for every thousand Brick six cents. for every Cask of lime three cents done at Brook haven this day aforesaid   DAVIS NORTON President

| Seal |

PAGE 269.

Whereas application has been Made to Barnabas Wines Samuel Hammond and John S. Mount Commissioners of highways for the town of Brook haven by Nathaniel Smith and Daniel G. Gillett for permission to Make and construct a dam across little Patchogue Stream whear it crosses the

South country road for the purpose of obtaining water Power to be applied to Milling or Manufacturing purposes and we the undersigned having examined the premises and believing that the public Interest will not Suffer but rather be promoted by the proposed measure permission is hereby given to the said Nathaniel Smith and Daniel G. Gillett and who ever else may be associated with them in the premises to build and raise said Dam on the Site above designated as high as may be necessary for the purpose above mentioned provided that they the said Nathaniel Smith and Daniel G. Gillett and whoever else may occupy or own said premises shall make and construct a good and Sufficient Road across said Dam and also make as many bridges as may be necessary across the flues and wast gates connected with the same for the purpose of passing and repassing with carriages or otherwise and also clear out and open a pathway below said dam for the convenience of passing through said brook and further the said Nathaniel Smith and Daniel G. Gillett or their legal representatives shall ever after at their own expence and cost make and keep in repair all bridges more than one over or on said Dam so long as they shall use or occupy the premises for Milling or Manufacturing purposes and also the said Dam

PAGE 270.

Dated April 1832

John S. Mount ⎱ Commissioners
Samuel Hammond ⎰ of highways

At a Meeting of the Trustees of the freeholders of the commonalty of the town of Brook haven on the 6th. day of May 1834 Messrs Isaac Robbins and Charles T. Jones made application for liberty to build a rail way at Drown meadow for the purpose of hauling out vessels to repair &. C. and said Trustees after having duly considered the premises (and for and in consideration of the yearly rent or

Annuity of the sum of eight Dollars annually to be paid to said Trustees or their Successors in Office on the first tuesday in May hereafter) Do by these presents grant unto the said Isaac Robbins and Charles T Jones their hiers or Assigns for the term of twenty one years the right to build and construct a Railway for the aforesaid term on a certain tract or space of ground on Drownmeadow shore the first Bound to set sixty feet to the westward of the west side of the Dock at Drownmeadow now Owned by James R. Davis at high water mark and from thence to extend westward on the shore Seventy feet and to extend southward to the highway and Northward into the harbour one hundred and thirty feet from highwater mark. for which said priviledg the aforesaid Isaac Robbins and Charles Jones their Hiers or Assigns shall pay unto the said Trustees or their successors in Office the yearly rent of eight Dollars on the day aforesaid. Provided however that the said Isaac Robbins and Charles Jones their hiers or Assigns shall have a right to relinquish and give up this grant at any time hereafter within said term with their paying up all arrearages to said town and removeing all obstructions (if any there be) that shall remain in the way of the public all of which is Granted accordingly this day aforesaid
in presence of   DANIEL OVERTON President
MORDECAI HOMAN town clerk

On the 1st. Nov. 1836 the first Bound sixty feet on the shore was extended to seventy feet that being the first intent   Attest M. HOMAN clerk

PAGE 271.

At a Meeting of the Trustees of the freeholders and commonalty of the town of Brook haven held on the 17th. Sept. 1833 the Act pased on the 11th. day of June 1833 to prevent the taking of any shell fish in the Bays harbours or Waters on the North side of the Island are hereby repealed.

but Nothing herein contained shall revive any former law as to the taking of any shell fish on the North side of the Island done under the hand of the president of said Trustees and seal of said town—

Attest   DAVIS NORTON President

MORDECAI HOMAN town clerk

|Seal|

Town of Brook haven

The undersigned Commissioners of highways of Said town being calld by Samuel Woodhull to Stake of the tract of land or meadow formerly belonging to George King of said town deceased Situate in Setauket discribed and staked as follows viz begining at the North east corner of said tract at a Stake thirty eight feet west from the Northwest corner of John C. Baileys Store then runing Southwardly one Rod from Walter Jones fence as it now Stands until it comes to the road that leads from the house of Isaac Brewster to William Smiths Black Smith shop then runing Northwestwardly until it comes to a Stake thirty feet east from said William Smiths Shop leaving said road three rods wide from the said Walter Jones,s fence and Stone wall above said shop then runing east from said Stake across the runs to the first mentioned Stake declaring the road leading across said runs four rods wide from the North bounds of said land

given under our hands this 26 day of february 1834

John S. Mount
David Worth   } Commissioners.
Samuel Hammond

PAGE 272.

At a public town meeting held in the town of Brook haven on the first day of April 1834 the following town Officers were duly Elected—viz

Smith Rider Justice of the Peace

John M. Williamson Supervisor

Daniel Overton President of Trustees

Timothy Davis
Isaac N. Gould
Almerand Barns
Barnabas Wines
William H. Brewster
James H. Weeks
} Trustees

Mordecai Homan town clerk & treasurer

William H. Brewster
Almerand Barns
} Overseers of the Poor—

Almerand Barns Collector

Isaac Davis
David Worth
Daniel G. Gillett
William H. Brewster
Lester H. Davis
} Assessors

James R. Davis
Samuel Davis Jur
Smith Rider
} Commissioners of Highways

Selah B. Strong
Mordecai Homan
Samuel F. Norton
} Commissioners of Schools—

John R. Satterly
James M. Fanning
Daniel G. Gillett
} Inspectors of Schools

James H. Weeks. Inspector of weights & measures

Noah Overton
Albert A. Overton
James T. Clayton
Spencer Dayton
Charles a Tooker
} Constables

Page 273.
Overseers of highway for 1834

District
No. 1, Charles Seabury
do. 2, dissolved
do. 3, John C. Bailes
do. 4, Israel Bennitt
do. 5, Floyd Smith
do. 6, Walter Jones
do. 7, William L. Jones
do. 8, Charles A. Tooker
do. 9, Isaac Davis
do. 10, Shelden Roe
do. 11, Phillip Hallock Jur
do. 12, Moses Swezey
do. 13, John Carter
do. 14, Nathaniel Robinson
do. 15, Nelson Terry
do. 16, James Fanning
do. 17, Silas Payne
do. 18, Thomas Jennings
do. 19, William Rose
do. 20, William Howell
do. 21, Joseph C. Hedges

District
do. 22, William Swezey
do. 23, William O. Smith
do. 24, Daniel G. Gillett
do. 25, Epenetus Mills
do. 26, Joseph Newton
do. 27, John F. Hallock
do. 28, Samuel A. Hawkins
do. 29, George W. Ruland
do 30, Clerk Longbothom
No 31 Lester H. Davis
do. 32 Richard Smith Jur
do. 33, Scudder Terry
do 34, Lewis Gourden
do 35, John Swezey
do. 36, Jesse Aldrich
do. 37, Joshua Terry
do. 38 Simmons Laws
do. 39 James H. Weeks
do. 40, Horace Randal
do. 41, Henry A. Gourden
do. 42, Samuel Overton

do. 43, Oscar F. Swezey

Page 274.

Be it remembered that on the second day of September one thousand eight hundred and thirty four Messrs. Smith and Darling made application to the Trustees of the freeholders and commonalty of the town of Brook haven for liberty to construct and build a Dock or wharf on the west side of Drownmeadow Bay against their own land and said Trustees after due consideration had in the premises and for and in consideration of the yearly rent or an Annuity

of two Dollars annually to be paid on the first tuesday in September during said term have by these presence Granted unto the said Smith and Darling and to their hiers and Assigns for the term of forty years and no longer the right and priviledge to construct Build and keep in repair a Dock or wharf on the west side of Drownmeadow Bay and to commence at a certain Bound to be set due east from the dwelling house of the said Smith and Darling at highwater mark and from thence to extend Northwardly on the shore one hundred feet and from each Bound on the shore to extend into the Bay one hundred and twenty five feet from common high water mark for the use of said Smith and Darling and the public in general in witness whereof we have caused the seal of our said town to be affixed this day aforesaid   DANIEL OVERTON President L. S.
in presence of
MORDECAI HOMAN town clerk

The Trustees of Brook Haven on the 2d. day of September 1834 directed a tax to raised in said town for the support of the poor and other contingent expences in said town the sum of $800. for the ensueing year

Attest MORDECAI HOMAN town clerk

Also on the 10th. day of November 1835. the Trustees of Brook Haven Granted that the above Smith and Darling might construct a Rail Road or way on the limits of the above grant for the sum of five Dollars annually from the first of Sept last for the above term or grant—

PAGE 275.

The Commissioners of highways for the town of Brook haven have laid out a highway commencing at the place where the road leading from Setauket by the Store of Nathaniel Hallock thence extending along the shore adjoining the upland of Nathaniel Hallock and Charles D. Hallock four rods wide from the Bottom of the slope of the bank of said upland to the dock of Charles D. Hallock and Jonas Smith the eastern side a part of said road to extend quite on to the new mad ground of said Charles D. Hallocks dock in a direction with the general course of the said bottom of the slope of said bank thence along the said new made ground to the shore thence along the shore four rods in width from the bottom of the slope of the bank commonly calld deep hole bank to Jonas Smiths lower dock and from said dock to the west meadow which we return to be recorded this 13th. Sept 1834

      Smith Rider) Commissiones
      Samuel Davis Jur } of
      James R. Davis) highways
MORDECAI HOMAN town clerk

The commissioners of common Schools of the town of Brook Haven having met at the house of D. D. and V. R. Swezey in said town in pursusance of previous Notice to each of the said commissioners do hereby adopt the following resolution in relation to the division of School Districts No. 11. and 12 and forming a new District from the eastern part of the District No. 11. and the Northern part of District No 12. viz. first by setting off all that part of District No. 11. Bounded on the West by the West line of Daniel Pettys land extending south to include the land of Henry P. Hutchenson North to include the house and lands of Jonathan Edwards east to include the house and land of Joel Turner and to extend South into the 12. District so as include the houses of Zecheriah and that of James Dayton to the North line of the land of Sylvanus Overton including all the Inhabitants within said Bounds which new District will be No. 33. Dated at Brook Haven this 6th. day of March 1835

      Selah B. Strong)
      Samuel F. Norton } Commisioners

Attest MORDECAI HOMAN clerk

PAGE 276.

At an Annual town Meeting of the freeholders and inhabitants of the town of Brook Haven held in said town on the 7th. day of April 1835 the following town Officers were duled Elected viz.

John M. Williamson Supervisor

Brewster Woodhull Justice of the peace for the term of three years in the place of Smith Rider

Charles Phillips Justice of the peace for the term of four years in the place of John S. Mount

Davis Norton president of Trustees

William H. Brewster ⎫
Phillip Hallock Jur ⎪
Isaac N. Gould ⎬ Trustees
John Penny Jur ⎪
John Havens ⎪
Henry P. Hutchenson ⎭

Mordecai Homan town clerk and treasurer qualfi

Almerin Barnes Collector

William H. Brewster ⎱ Overseers of the poor
John Havens ⎰

ASSESSORS

Isaac Davis
John R. Satterly
Lester H. Davis qualifid
John Havens
Joel Robinson qualifd

CONSTABLES

Oscar F. Swezey
Albert A. Overton
Joel Davis
Spencer Dayton
Noah Overton

Isaac Davis ⎫ Commissioners ⎫
Samuel Davis Jur ⎬ of ⎬ qualifd
Smith Rider ⎭ highways ⎭

Selah B. Strong }
Wm. Sidney Smith } Commissioners } qualfid
Samuel F. Norton } of Schools

Benjamin T. Hutchenson acpt }
John R. Satterly Aceptd } Inspectors of
James M. Fanning } Schools

PAGE 277.

LIST OF OVERSEER OF HIGHWAYS FOR 1835

District
No. 1 Charles A. Seabury
do. 2, Dissolved
do. 3, John C. Bailey
do. 4, Samuel L. Thompson
do. 5, Joseph Danton
do. 6 Walter Jones
do. 7, William L. Jones
do. 8, Smith Davis acept.
do. 9, Isaac Davis
do. 10, Conklin Davis
do. 11, Amos Hallock acept
do. 12, Hiram Noyes accept
do. 13, John Carter
do. 14, Nathaniel Robinson
do. 15, James Stanshough
do. 16, Spencer Dayton
do. 17, Nicol Overton
do 18, Samuel Carman
do. 19, Isaac Ketcham
do. 20, William Howell acceptd
do. 21, Charles Smith acceptd
do. 22, Daniel Overton aceptd
do. 23, Lewis Wicks acceptd
do. 24, James Smith
do. 25, John Corey

District
No. 26, Samuel Newton
do. 27, John F. Hallock
do. 28, Samuel A. Hawkins acceptd
do. 29, Nelson Norton
do. 30, Richard W. Smith acceptd
do. 31, Lester H. Davis acept
do. 32, Richard Smith pond
do. 33, Daniel Terry Jur
do 34, Jeremiah Gourden
do. 35, Isaac Hulse
do. 36, Daniel Petty Jur
do. 37, Briant N. Overton
do. 38, Daniel D. Swezey acceptd
do. 39, Edmund Hawkins acpt
do. 40, Horace Randal
do. 41, Henry A. Gourdon
do. 42, Elisha Overton accptd
do. 43, Joshua Swezey Jur
do. 44, Albert Terrill

We certify the foregoing to be a tru Statement of the foregoing Election at the annual town Meeting held in Brook Haven on the 7th. day of April 1835

SAMUEL DAVIS Justice
MORDECAI HOMAN town Clerk
present Justices of the peace

Barnabas Wines ⎫
Samuel Davis   ⎪
Brewster Woodhull ⎬ 1835
Charles Phillips   ⎭

PAGE 278.

The Commissioners of Common Schools having met at the house of Harvey Hulse in said town in pursuance of previous Notice to each of the said commissioners do hereby adopt the following resolution in relation to the Division of the third School District in said town (viz) that the said District number three be and the sames is hereby bounded as follows the division line commencing at Setauket harbour at the division line of John Oaks and Joseph Jaynes land following the line of Joseph Jaynes property southwardly and westwardly until it strikes the property of Stephen Hulse Deceas,d thence by the property of said Hulse westwardly until it strikes the lane thence southwardly with the lane and Road between William Smith and Walter Jones,s property until it Strikes the lands of Isaac Brewster thence Eastwardly and southwardly by the land of said Isaac Brewster until it Strikes the road leading from said Isaac Brewster to Carlton Jaynes. (late William Jayne,s) thence Eastwardly along said road until it Strikes the division line between the land of the late charles Tooker deceasd, and the lands of James Hulse thence Southwardly and eastwardly by the land of the said James Hulse to the Road from John Dentons to cumsewague thence Eastwardly along said Road to the east end of said District all of said District No. 3. lying westwardly and Southwardly of said line to remain in said District No. 3. and all that part of said District lying to the eastward and Northward of said line is hereby set off and form,d as a New District being No. 34 and having examined the School House in said District do appraise the same at the sum of one hundred Dollars and that the part of said District No 3 retaining the old School House pay to the New District No. 34 the sum of forty five Dollars eighty seven cents dated at Brook Haven this 30th. day of March 1835

Attest	Selah B. Strong	Commissioners of common Schools
Mordecai Homan	Mordecai Homan	
Clerk	Samuel F. Norton	

Page 279.

Memorandam of an alteration made in the road leading from the farm now occupied by Samuel Glover to the Mills of Robert Hawkins by Samuel Davis Jur and Smith Rider two of the Commissioners of Highways for the town of Brook haven—The alteration above mentioned commences at a Stone marked W and placed in the ground on the south side of the highway thence running westwardly to a Stone marked 3. thence North 75°. West to another Stone marked S. thence North 66°. 30' west to a Stone Marked A lying in Yamphank line thence running the last mentioned course to a Stone Marked M. placed in the ground at the foot of a Bar post on the west side of the Road leading into Robert Hawkins,s Woods and in the Margin of the highway the whole road to be North of the line above described and to be three rods wide in Witness whereof we have hereunto Subscribed our names this 7th. day of April 1835

      Smith Rider   } Commissioners
      Samuel Davis Jur } of highways
Mordecai Homan town clerk

To all to whom these presents shall come the subscribers commissioners of the towns of Brook Haven Huntington and Islip in the County of Suffolk send greeting

Whereas we have been duly authorised by our respective towns to determine and fix the western Boundary line of the fisheries of the said Town of Brook Haven in the south Bay and also to settle a Suit relative to the said fisheries wherein Joseph Homan Jur. and Benjamin Wicks are plaintifs and Phinehas Smith Alexander Smith and Samuel Birch are Defendants which suit is now pending in the court of common pleas in the said County and is prosecuted by the

Page 280.

said town of Brook Haven and defended by the said towns of Huntington and Islip Now therefore know ye that we the said commissioners after a full examination of the said matter do agree of and concerning the same as follows that is to say the western Boundary line of the fisheries of the said town of Brok Haven under the two patents of that town and the Patent of Coll William Smith or by any other title shall be as follows that is to say it shall commence at the Northermost range pole on the south Beach and shall run from thence a due North Course polar direction across the South Bay to the Main shore of the Island—it is further agreed that a permanent monument shall be erected at the above said range pole and also on the Island on the North shore of the Bay—the said Suit is hereby discontinued the Cost of Each Party shall be duly taxed and the one half of the taxable Cost shall be paid by the town of Brook Haven and the other half shall be paid by the towns of Huntington and Islip

In Witness whereof we have hereunto set our hands and seals this fifteenth day of December one thousand eight hundred and thirty four

Nathaniel Potter }
Joel Jervis } of Huntington
Selah Carll }

Mordecai Homan }
Davis Norton } of Brook Haven
James M Fanning }

Eliphalet Smith }
Tredwell Scudder } of Islip
Richard A. Udall }

Recorded in the town clerks office of the town of Huntington   Moses Rolph town clerk

Recorded in the town clerks office of the town of Islip—this 16th. Sept. 1835.   Eliphalet Smith
     town clerk

Recorded in the town Clerks office of the town of Brook Haven. this 17th. Sept. 1835—
     Mordecai Homan town clerk

This may certify that we the subscribers have set up monuments of Stone at the two places designated in the above award (viz) One at the Northermost range pole on the Beach from which Jones,s House on the Beach bears N. 85° W. distant 45. Chains 90 Links to the Northwest

PAGE 281.*

Corner thereof also one on the North shore of the Bay due North (N. 5°. E. pr. compass) from that at the range pole on the Beach from the monument on the Bay shore the House of or occupied by Daniel Whitman Bears N. 24° 45' W. and Jacob Morris House bears N. 37°. 45' E. these are the Courses pr Compass the variation is now 5°. Westerly

Dated this 15th. day of Sept. 1835

Mordecai Homan.
Dav is Norton
James M. Fanning } Commissioners
Selah Carll
Eliphalet Smith

* Note.—This page and the next page are each numbered 281.—COM.

This Indenture Made the 29th. day of December one thousand eight hundred and thirty five between the Trustees of the freeholders and commonalty of the town of Brook Haven of the first part and Charles D. Halloc of same place of the second part. Whereas the said Charles D. Hallock has by his certain petition presented to the said Trustees requested of them a lease of certain premises situate at Stony brook in the said town adjoining the land described and intended in two former grants made by the said Trustees to George Hallock of and for the priviledge and right of constructing and continuing a Dock or Wharf thereon hereinafter particularly described for the sole purpose of continuing an addition to the said Dock or wharf which he has heretofore constructed or built thereon, and whereas the said Trustees has deemed it proper to grant such lease with the provisions conditions restrictions and reservations hereinafter contained. Now therefore this Indenture Witnesseth that the said Trustees in consideration of the rent covenants and conditions herein after contained on the part of the said Charles D. Hallock his Heirs Executors administrators and assigns to be paid kept and performed have Bargained demised and leased and by these presents do bargain demise and lease unto the said Charles D. Hallock his heirs Executors administrators and assigns all that certain piece of Land commencing at the Southwest corner of his present wharf and running

Page 281. 2d

from thence with the front of the said wharf North fifty two Degrees East thirty feet and running from the said Southwest corner and also from the termination of the said thirty feet front South twenty seven and an half degrees East fifty feet the Southeastern Boundary being parallel with the front of the wharf, And also all that certain piece of land commencing at the Northeast corner of the wharf and running from thence with the front of the said wharf sixty feet being South fifty two degrees West then south twenty nine and an half degrees East fifty feet then commencing again at the said Northeastern corner and running from thence North Seventy two and an half degrees East Sixty four feet and from thence running a Straight line to the Southeastern termination of the said Second Boundary line of this last mentioned pice leaving the West meadow Road unincumbered, for the sole purpose of continuing Building or constructing thereon a dock or wharf in connection with that part of the said dock or wharf constructed on the land covered by the said two former Grants the whole to constitute one dock or wharf and to be subject to the same regulations to have and to hold the said premises hereinbefore described unto the said Charles D. Hallock his Heirs Executors administrators and assigns from the day of the date hereof for and during the term of fifty years fully to be complete and ended yielding and paying therefor during the continuation of the said term unto the said Trustees and thier Successors the Annual rent of five Dollars on the first tuesday of April in each and every year, and the said Trustees do hereby Authorise and empower the said Charles D. Hallock his Executors administrators and assigns to continue and if necessary to rebuild a dock or wharf on the said premises and to recieve dockage or wharfage for the use of the same the rates of which shall be until some future regulation shall be made by the said Trustees or their Successors the same as those which have been established by the said Trustees and are at present subsisting and the rates of which said dockage or wharfage shall at all times be regulated by the said Trustees or their Successors for the time being and it is hereby mutually declared agreed and covenanted that the said Dock or

PAGE 282.

wharf shall at all times hereafter be Subject to the controul directions and regulations of the Trustees of the freeholders and commonalty of the Town of Brook Haven for the time being as to the incumbrances which may be placed thereon and that no incumbrance shall be placed or deposited on the road or highway leading from Stoney brook to the west meadow,s and it is also hereby mutually agreed that the Trustees of the freeholders and commonalty of the town of Brook Haven for the time being shall have the priviledg of landing or putting on board of vessels at the said Dock or wharf any articles belonging to the said Corporation free from any wharfage or charge whatever and the said Charles D. Hallock for himself his Executors Administrators and assigns hereby covenants to and with the said Trustees and their Successors to pay to the said Trustees or thier Successors the said rent at the time hereinbefore mentioned for the payment thereof and also to submit to and abide by the order directions and regulations of the said Trustees and their successors concerning the rates of wharfage and the incumbrances on the said Dock or wharf and road or highway and it is hereby mutually understood agreed and covenanted that if a default shall be made in the payment of the said rent for forty days after the times above specified for the payment thereof or if the said Charles D. Hallock his Executors Administrators or Assigns shall fail to comply with and fulfil the orders directions or regulations of the said Trustees or their successors for fourteen days after having been Served with a Copy of the same or at any time after the expiration of the said fourteen days relative to the rates of wharfage or such incumbrances or shall use the said premises or any part of them in any other manner or for any other purpose than a Dock or wharf without the Written consent of the said Trustees or thier Successors that then and from thencefourth and in either of the said cases it shall and may be lawful to and for the said Trustees and their successors into and upon the said demised premises to reenter and the same to have again repossess and

Page 283.

enjoy as in their former State and right these presents or any part thereof to the contrary notwithstanding—and it is hereby mutually agreed that if the said Charles D. Hallock his Executors administrators or assigns shall and do in all things perform fulfil and keep the covenants hereinbefore mentioned on their part during the whole of the said term this lease shall at the expiration of said term be renewed on reasonable terms with a similar clause of renewal or that the said Trustees shall and will pay to him or them the value of the Dock or wharf which shall then be on the said premises or that the said Charles D. Hallock his heirs Executors Administrators or Assigns may remove the material of which the same shall then consist at the option of the said

Trustees or their Successors in witness whereof the parties to these presents have hereunto set their hands and Seals this day and year first above Written

    DAVIS NORTON President of Trustees L. S.
in presence of   CHARLES D. HALLOCK—L. S.
MORDECAI HOMAN town clerk

A true copy of a lease given to Charles D. Hallock and acknowledged before S. B. Strong Commissioner
Attest
MORDECAI HOMAN town clerk

The undersigned commissioners of common Schools in the town of Brook Haven having been calld to define and designate the Boundaries of School district No. 4. in said town which has heretofore been left vague and uncertain and having been attended by the Trustees of that District and by a Trustee of each of the adjoining Districts do hereby direct that the following shall be the boundaries of said District No. 4 Viz. commencing at the bridge crossing Drowmeadow runs and running from thence westwardly on the highway leading to Setauket to the Brickkiln Road at the foot of Drownmeadow hill from thence with said Brickkiln Road to the road leading from Setauket

PAGE 284.

to Zecheriah Hawkins's thence Eastwardly on said last mentioned Road to the road at the foot of the hill thence Southwardly with said last mentioned Road up Dark Hallow to the sheep pasture Road from thence a due South line half the length of the long lotts from thence on a due East line to the Road leading from the house of Thomas S. Strong through Christial Brook Hallow to Coram thence Northwardly with said Road to the division line between the lands of Thomas S. Strong and the lands late of Nathaniel Tooker dece,sd at the Springs from thence with the brook to the old mans Harbour thence Northward with the Western shore of said old mans Harbour to the Sound thence Westwardly with the sound to Drown meadow Bay and Southwardly with the Eastern Shore of said Bay to the place of begining

Drown Meadow

12 March 1836   Selah B. Strong ⎫ Commissioners
                   Samuel F. Norton ⎬ of common
                Wm Sidney Smith ⎭ Schools

Attest MORDECAI HOMAN
         Clerk

We the commissioners of highways for the town of Brook Haven have laid out a highway through the land of Lester H. Davis three rods wide commencing in the hallow near the Meeting House in the old Mans running a Northwesterly course to the southeast corner of titus Silles House thence along through the hallow a Westerly direction to a certain Locust tree on the North side of the aforesaid highway and thence along westwardly until it intersects the Road that leads from Richard Davis,es to Kinners shore

Given under our hands this twenty Ninth day of December 1835.

                        Samuel Davis ⎫ Commissioners
                        Smith Rider ⎬ of
Enterd by   Isaac Davis ⎭ highways

MORDECAI HOMAN town clerk

PAGE 285.

This Indenture made this 29th. day of December 1825 Between the Trustees of the freeholders and commonalty of the town of Brook Haven in the County of Suffolk and State of New York of the first part and Lewis Hulse of the same place of the Second part Witnesseth. that the said Trustees of the first part for and in consideration of the Rents Annuities and covenants herein after contained and to be paid kept and performed on the part of the second part his Heirs Executors Administrators or Assigns they the said Trustees have Bargained demised and to farm let and by these presents doth bargain demise and to farm let unto the said party of the second part his Heirs Executors Administrators or Assigns all that certain piece of common land or shore belonging to said town of Brook Haven lying at the head of Drownmeadow Bay and Bounded on the east by the land or shore granted by said Trustees to Isaac Robbins and Charles I Jones for the purpose of Building a Railway from thence extending westwardly on the shore one hundred feet and to extend Southward to the highway and Northward into the harbour one hundred and Ninety feet from common highwater mark leaving the highway entirely unincumbered for the sole purpose of Building thereon constructing laying down and keeping in repair Railways for the purpose of hauling out vessels to repair and so fourth and also for the purpose of laying on wood and other lumber or materials for said dock. To have and To hold the said premises hereinbefore described unto the said party of the second part his Heirs Executors Administrators or Assigns from the day of the date hereof for and during the term of Nineteen years from the first tuesday in May next fully to be complete and ended they the said party of the second part yielding and paying therefor unto the said party of the first part or thier Successors in Office during said term the Yearly rent or annuity of fifteen Dollars

Page 286.

on the first tuesday in May once in every year and the said party of the Second part for himself and his Heirs Executors Administrators and Assigns doth hereby covenant and agree to and with the said Trustees and their Successors in Office to pay to the said party of the first part or their Successors in Office the aforesaid Rent or Annuity at the several times above specified for the payment thereof And it is hereby mutually understood covenanted and agreed by each party to these presents that if a default shall be made by the said party of the second part his Heirs Executors Administrators or Assigns in the payment of the said yearly rent for forty days at any time after such payment shall have become due or shall use the said premises for any other use or purpose other than is before mentioned without the Written consent of the said Trustees or their Successors in Office that then and in such case this present grant at the option of the said Trustees or their Successors in Office shall cease be null and void and the said Trustees or their successors in Office into and upon the said demised premises may reenter and the same to have hold possess and enjoy again as in their former State and right any thing in this present grant to the contrary Notwithstanding AND it is further mutually understood covenanted and agreed by either party to these presents they the said Trustees as well for themselves and their successors in office as also the said party of the second part his Heirs Executors Administrators and Assigns that at the expiration of this present lease it shall and may be lawful for the then said parties to enter into a new contract for the abovesaid premises on such terms as may then appear Just and equal and in case the aforesaid parties cannot agree as to a further extension of said lease or any other contract in the premises that then and in such case the improvements then existing on said premises for the above said purpose shall be appraised by three indifferent men for the benefit of the said second part his Heirs Executors Administrators or Assigns—

PAGE 287.

and the primitive right return to said Trustees or their Successors in office for the use of the town aforesaid in Witness whereof the said parties to these presents have set their hands and seals this day above written

     DAVIS NORTON president of Trustees L. S.
in presence of   LEWIS HULSE— L. S.
 MORDECAI HOMAN town clerk

At an Annual town Meeting held in the town of Brook Haven on the 5th. day of April 1836 the following town Officers were Elected for the ensuing year

John M. Williamson Supervisor

Daniel Overton President of trustees

Timothy Davis ⎫
Conklin Davis ⎪
Richard Smith ⎬ Trustees
Lewis G. Davis ⎪
John Penny Jur ⎪
Barnabas Wines ⎭

Lewis G. Davis ⎱ Overseers of
Conklin Davis ⎰ the poor

Mordecai Homan clerk and treasurer

Floyd Smith Collector

William H. Brewster ⎫
Phillip Hallock Jur ⎪
Davis Norton ⎬ Assessors
John Havens ⎪
Joel Robinson ⎭

Charles I. Jones ⎫
John Havens ⎬ Commissioners
Samuel Davis Jur ⎭ of highways

Selah B. Strong ⎫
Wm. Sidney Smith ⎬ Commissioners of Schools
Samuel F. Norton ⎭

Benjamin T. Hutchenson ⎫
James M. Fanning ⎬ Inspectors of Schools
John R. Satterly ⎭

Lester H. Davis Sealer of weights and measures

Walter Jones ⎫
Noah Overton ⎪
Albert A. Overton ⎬ Constables
David Terry ⎪
Charles A. Tooker ⎭

David Worth Justice of the peace

Charles Phillips Justice of the peace to fill a vacancy occasioned by said Phillips not qualifying in January last—

Page 288.

List of Overseers of highways for 1836

District
No. 1, Charles A. Seabury
do. 2, Dissolved
do. 3, Ebenezer Bailes Jur
do. 4, Samuel L. Thompson
do. 5, John Roseman
do. 6, Walter Jones
do. 7, William L. Jones
do. 8, Smith Davis
do. 9, Isaac Davis
do. 10, Charles Woodhull
do. 11, Isaac Brown
do. 12, Jonathan W. Mapes
do. 13, John Carter
do. 14, Joel Robinson
do. 15, Enoch Miller
do. 16, Rogers Robinson
do. 17, Joseph Hawkins Jur
do. 18, Samuel Carman
do. 19, George W. Ruland
do. 20, William Howell
do. 21, David Hedges
do. 22, John Havens
do. 23, Clerk Smith
do. 24, Edward N. Douglas
do. 25, John Corey
do. 26 Sylvanus Newton
do. 27, John F. Hallock
do. 28, Samuel Hammond

District
No. 29, Isaac A. L Homedieue
do. 30, Richard W. Smith
do. 31, Lester H. Davis
do. 32, Israel Smith
do. 33, Davis Overton Jur
.34, William Barnaby
.35, John Buckingham
.36, Ezra Guildersleve
.37, Zecheriah Dayton
.38, D. D. Swezey
.39, Apollos A. Mills
.40, Luther Topping
.41, Nathaniel Tyler
.42, Samuel Overton
.43, William Swezey
.44, David Worth.

on the 19th. May 1836 the commissioners of Highways appointed the following persons to fill Vacancies in Overseers of Highways viz

District
No. 6, Carlton Jayne
do 9, Isaac Davis
do. 20, William Howell
do. 25, John Corey
do. 29, Isaac A. L,Homedieue
do. 27, John F. Hallock
do. 40, John Randall
do. 43, William Swezey

Enterd this 31st. May 1836

M. HOMAN town clerk

PAGE 289.

At a Meeting of two of the Commissioners of highways of the town of Brook Haven in the County of Suffolk all of the said commissioners having been duly Notified to Attend said Meeting for the purpose of deliberating on the subject of this order upon the application of Isaac Overton for the laying out of a private Road hereafter discribed and on the certificate of twelve Reputable freeholders of said town that it is proper and necessary for the use of the said Isaac Overton pursuant to his application to lay a private Road through the land of William Hawkins (now Occupied by Benjamin Hawkins) it is therefore ordered and determined by the said commissioners that a private road be laid out for the use of the said Isaac Overton pursuant to his application commencing at the East line of the saaid Isaac Overtons Land at a certain Stake drove in the Ground near the Middle of a certain pair of Bars which open into the said Hawkins, land and running South ten Minutes west six chains seventy five links to another stake Standing Just beyond the Bars in second lot and from thence running south three degrees thirty five minutes West eight Chains sixty seven links parallel to a post and Rail fence and ten feet distant til it comes to another stake and to the fence at the south end of said lot according to a Survey which has been made thereof and it is further ordered that the line above discribed shall be the center of said road and that the said Road shall be on the width of twenty feet in Witness whereof the said Commissioners have hereunto discribed their Names the 15th. day of September 1836

Recorded this   John Havens   } Commissioners
   19th Sept. 1836.   Samuel Davis Jur. } of Highways
     MORDECAI HOMAN town clerk

the above order was reversed by the Judges of this County on the 18th. day of October 1836.
                 Attest MORDECAI HOMAN town clerk

PAGE 290.

At a Meeting of the Inhabitants of the town of Brook Haven held in Coram the 4th. day of April 1837. being the

Annual town Meeting the following town Officers were Choses—

Samuel Davis Esq. Justice of the peace

John M. Williamson Supervisor.

Daniel Overton President of Trustees

Lewis G. Davis
Conklin Davis
William H. Brewster
Joel Robinson
William C. Booth
Manly Ruland
} Trustees

Lewis G. Davis
William H. Brewster
} Overseer of the poor

Isaac N. Gould
William L. Jones
Phillip Hallock Jur
John Havens
Joel Robinson
} Assessors

Charles Phillips
John Havens
Samuel Davis
} Commissioners of Highways

Selah B. Strong
William S. Smith
Samuel Lafaette Norton
} Commissioners of common Schools

Benjamin T. Hutchenson
John R. Satterly
James M. Fanning
} Inspectors of school

Lester H. Davis Sealer of Weights and measures

Noah Overton
Charles A. Tooker
Oscar F. Swezey
Albert A. Overton
Spencer Dayton
} Constables

PAGE 291.

OVERSEER OF HIGHWAYS—

District No. 1, Nathaniel Hawkins
do 2 dissolved
3, Samuel L. Thompson. ac
4, Obediah D. Wells
5, John Roseman
6, William Satterly
7, Lewis Hulse
8, Jonathan Pike ac
9, Joel Davis ac
10, Thomas Helme ac
11, William Horton
12, James Woodhull
13, John Carter
14, Joel Robinson
15, David Terry
16, Rogers Robinson
17, Joseph Hawkins ac
18, Samuel Carman ac
19, Azel Hawkins ac
20, William Howell ac
21, John Avery ac
22, Nathaniel Conklin ac
23 William Clerk Smith—
24, Daniel G. Gillett. ac
25, John Corey
26, Sylvester Newton
27, Isaac A. L Homedieue
28, Samuel Hammond
29, Nelson Norton
30, Richard W. Smith ac
31, Lester H. Davis ac
32, Israel Smith ac

District No. 33, Phinehas Smith
34, Whitman Overton
35, Simeon H. Ritch
36 Ezra Guildersleve ac
37, Zecheriah Dayton ac
38, Simmons Laws ac
39, Edmund T. Hawkins ac
40, Matthew Randal ac
41, Nathaniel Tyler
42, Brewster Terry ac
43, William Swezey
44, Josiah W. Bishop ac
45, Joseph Penny ac

* Note.—No collector is recorded for this year, but probably Floyd Smith was collector.—Com.

Page 292.

We the Commissioners of highways for the town of Brook Haven being all Notified and called by Caleb Kinner and others to alter the Highway leading from Setauket across the runs at the head of Drown meadow Bay to Thomas S. Strongs the said Highway being recorded four rods wide and on the petition of twelve freeholders of said town we the said Commissioners have narrowed a part of the aforesaid Highway to three rods wide beginning at the bridge at the head of Drownmeadow Bay and running easterly along the beach the North side of Israel Davis House and so on by the Store of Charles I. Jones and Lewis Hulse to the foot of the Gully about forty rods East of William Tylers House dated the 4th. day of April 1837

Samuel Davis Jur. } Commissioners
Charles I. Jones } of highways

At a meeting of the Commissioners of highways of the town of Brook Haven in the County of Suffolk at the house of Joseph Avery in the said town on the 19th. day of february 1838 for the purpose of deciding on the application and petition of Daniel G. Gillett and other twelve reputable freeholders of said town Verified by their Oaths that a Highway is proper and necessary to be laid out through the lands of Joseph Avery William Avery and Epenetus Mills from the Eastern extremity of a certain new Road lately laid out and opened in the Eastern part of the town of Islip to the Road leading from the Country road by William Arthurs to the Bay at Blue point all the said Commissioners of the town being only two surviving ones having met and deliberated on the subject embraced in this order. it is ordered and determined by the said Commissioners that a highway be laid out pursuant to said application and petition

PAGE 293.

and that the same has been laid out by us on actual Survey the Course and Distance whereof are as follows by the Compas No allowance being made for variation beginning at the Eastern extremity of the Road aforesaid in Islip at a certain Cherry tree on or near the line of Brook Haven and Islip and running across the land of Joseph Avery first Course North 57° 45′ East seven Chains and Sixty nine links to the Southwest Corner of his shed or Cart house thence North 72°. 30′ East five Chains by and with the fence and near by the front of his House thence North 64°—30′ East two Chains thirty seven links to a Certain post marked in the fence being the third from the Corner between Joseph and William Avery thence Across William Averys land first turning across the Corner of his lot North 24°. East sixty eight links to another marked Post. (being the third North of the Corner) thence North 9°. 15′ west ten Chains sixty five links thence North 15°. 30′ West four Chains thirty five links thence North 65° 15′ East five Chains to the Creek and line between him and Epenetus Mills,s thence across Epenetus Mills, land first North 72°.

30' East seventeen chains thence North 53° East fifty links to the Road aforesaid leading from the Country Road to Blue point and it is further ordered that the line above discribed be the North and Westerly side of said Highway and that the said Highway be of the width of three Rods In witness whereof the Commissioners have hereunto subscribed their names the 19th. day of February 1838

                   John Havens) Commissioners
Enterd by   Charles Phillips) of highways
Mordecai Homan town clerk

Page 294.

At a Meeting of the Commissioners of Common Schools of the towns of Riverhead and Brook Haven on the 24th. day of february 1838 at the Inn of Peter skidmore for the purpose. of forming a New District by taking a part of district No 7. lying in Brook Haven and a part of of School District No. 1. lying partly in Riverhead and partly in Brook Haven Jonathan Horton Esq of Riverhead was Chosen President and William Sidney Smith of Brook Haven Secretary present all the Commissioners from Brook Haven. and two from Riverhead and Samuel Young one of the Commissioners from Riverhead was duly notified.—Resolved that so much of Joint District No 1 as lies west of a line commencing on the Sound at the Mouth of Wading River Creek and running Southwardly with said Creek until it strikes the land of Miller Woodhull at East Brook Creek then with that Creek and the Hallow leading from it to the main Country Road then Eastwardly with that road to the westerly Boundary line of Benjamin Woodhulls home place then Southerly with that line to the Butt line, be and the same is hereby seperated from the said Joint District No. 1 for the purpose of forming a new District in the town of Brook Haven the Inhabitants of such part of

District being willing to relinquish their claim under the Statuts to the School House in School District No 1.

Enterd by
M. HOMAN town clerk

Jonathan Horton } Commissioners
Sylvester Miller } of Riverhead

Selah B. Strong } Commissioners
Samuel F. Norton } of
Wm Sidney Smith } Brook Haven

PAGE 295.

At a Meeting of the Commissioners of common Schools of the town of Brook Haven on the 24th. day of February 1838 at the house of Peter Skidmore Commissioners all present.—On recieving the petition of Several of the Inhabitants of Joint District No. 1 and District No 7 for the formation of a new District from parts of those Districts together with the written consent of the Trustees of those Districts and it appearing that on a Joint Meeting of the Commissioners of Brook Haven and Riverhead held on this day so much of said District No. 1 as is comprised within the new District herein after discribed has been duly seperated from said District No. 1. and is comprised within the new District. It was Resolved and ordered that all that part of said town of Brook Haven Bounded Northwardly by the sound East by Wading River Creek until it reaches East Brook Creek thence by said Creek and the hallow leading from it to the North Country Road thence by that Road to the western Boundary line of Benjamin Woodhulls home place then by that line to the Butt line on the South by the Butt line on the west by the westerly bounds of Peter Skidmores Land be and the same is hereby formed into a New District which shall be called and known District No. 35

Enterd by
MORDECAI HOMAN clk

Selah B. Strong } Commissioners
Samuel F. Norton } of
Wm Sidney Smith } Schools

At a Meeting of the Commissioners of Common Schools

of the town of Brook Haven on the 26th. of February 1838 at the house of Henry P. Osborn Present all the Commissioners.—on recieving the application of School District No. 15 for the consent of the Commissioners to change the Site of the school House in said District after examination into and consideration of the matter the commissioners are of Opinion that a change of the Site and removal of the School House from its present location to a certain tract of Land lying on the South side of the South Country Road between the Barn of

PAGE 296.

Henry P. Osborn Esq. and the Black Smiths shop of Selah P. Parsons being on the East South and West by the Land of the said Henry P. Osborn being about four Rods square which has been designated by the Inhabitants of said District for that purpose as necessary and the said Commissioners consent to such change of said Site and removal of said School House

Selah B. Strong } Commissioners
Samuel F. Norton } of Common
Wm. Sidney Smith } Schools

At a Meeting of the Inhabitants of the town of Brook haven on the 3d. day of April 1838 being town Meeting day the following persons were elected town officers for the ensueing year viz—

John M. Williamson Supervisor

Brewster Woodhull Justice of the peace for four years

David Overton Justice of the peace to fill a vacancy of 3 years

Daniel Overton President

John Havens }
Silas Homan }
William Penny Jur } Trustees
William H. Brewster }
Philip Hallock Jur }
Richard Smith pond }

Mordecai Homan town clerk and treasurer

John Havens } overseers of the poor
William H. Brewster }

Floyd Smith collector

Isaac N. Gould }
John R. Satterly }
Isaac Davis } Assessors
John Havens }
John Penny Jur }

Charles Phillips } Commissioners of
John Havens } highways
Nathaniel Tuttle Jur }

Selah B. Strong }
Nathaniel Conklin } Commissioners of Schools
Simeon H Ritch }

John R. Satterly }
Benjamin T. Hutchenson } Inspectors of Schools
William S. Preston }

John Bunce Sealer of Weights and Measures

Noah Overton }
Charles A. Tooker }
John C. Smith } Constables
Albert A. Overton }
Samuel Overton }

PAGE 297.

OVERSEERS OF HIGHWAYS

District.
    No. 1, William S. Williamson
        2, dissolved
        3, Samuel L. Thompson
        4, Obediah D. Wells
        5, John Brewster
        6, Daniel Skidmore
        7, Lewis Hulse
        8, Jonathan Pike

District
No. 9, Joel Davis
10, Thomas Helme
11, Noah H. Jones
12, Jonathan W. Mapes
13, John Carter
14, Joel Robinson
15, Austin Culver
16, Rogers Robinson
17, Nicoll Floyd
18, Samuel Carman
19, Azel Hawkins
20, William Howell
21, Barnabas Smith Jur
22, Daniel Overton
23, William C. Smith
24, Daniel G. Gillett
25, John Corey
26, Mills Hawkins
27, John F. Hallock
28, Samuel Hammond
29, Davis Norton
30, Joshua Overton
31, Lester H. Davis
32, Israel Smith pond
33, Scudder Terry
34, Hampton Overton
35, Franklin Overton
36, Samuel Overton
37, Briant Davis
38, Simmons Laws
39, James H. Weeks
40, Sylvester Randal
41, Nathaniel Tyler
42, Caleb H. Hammond

District
No. 43, Thomas King
44, John Duryea
45, Joseph Penny

Page 298.

At a Meeting of the Trustees of the freeholders and commonalty of the town of Brook Haven held at the Inn of Richard W. Smith in the said town on the first day of November 1836—Ordered that Charles D. Hallock remove a certain log now lying on the westerly side of his wharf at Stony Brook and which is hereby declared to be an obstruction thereon within fourteen days next after his being served with a notice of this order and that in default thereof the attorney of this board commence an action of Ejectment against him.

MORDECAI HOMAN town clerk

To Charles D. Hallock

Pursuant to an order of which the foregoing is a copy you are hereby Notifyed to remove a certain log now lying on the westerly side of your wharf at stony Brook which is declared in the said order to be an obstruction thereon within fourteen days next after your being served with a Notice of the said order dated this 1st. day of November 1836.

MORDECAI HOMAN town clerk—

On the 2nd. day of April 1839 being town Meeting day a vote was taken whether this town would consent to erection of a County poor house and it was unanomously objected to—Also a vote was taken allowing the Inspectors of Common School fifty Cents a day for their Services

attest MORDECAI HOMAN town clerk

Page 299.

At a Meeting of the Inhabitants of the town of Brook Haven on the 2d. day of April 1839 being Annual town

Meeting the following persons were Elected town Officers for the ensueing year———(Viz)

John M. Williamson Supervisor
Charles Phillips Justice of the peace for four years.
Daniel Overton President of Trustees

Lewis G. Davis
Silas Homan
William Penny Jur
John Randal
William H. Brewster
Richard Smith pond
} Trustees

Lewis G. Davis
William H. Brewster
} Overseers of the poor

Mordecai Homan town clerk and Treasurer
Floyd Smith Collector

Isaac N. Gould
William S. Williamson
Phillip Hallock Jur
Moses Swezey
John Penny Jur
} Assessors

Charles Phillips
Nathaniel Tuttle
John H. Duryea
} Commissioner of Highways

Selah B. Strong
Simeon H. Ritch
Brewster Woodhull
} Commissioners of Common Schools

John R. Swezey
James Rice
Orlando Burnell
} Inspectors of Common Schools

John Bunce Sealer of Weights and measures

Noah Overton
Charles A. Tooker
Daniel Overton
Gershom R. Smith
} Constables

PAGE 300.

LIST OF OVERSEERS OF HIGHWAYS FOR 1839

Dis No. 1, William S. Williamson
do. 2, Dissolved
do 3, Youngs Howell
do 4, Obediah D. Wells
do 5, Samuel Woodhull
do 6, Daniel Smith
do 7, Benjamin T. Wiltsie
do 8, Henry Hawkins
do. 9, Parshall Davis
10, Charles Woodhull
11, Sylvester Hallock
12, Charles Hudson
13, John Carter
14, Isaac Raynor
15, Usher Benjamin
16, Rogers Robinson
17, David Floyd
18, Silas Homan
19, Azel Hawkins
20, Samuel Willetts
21, Jeremiah T. Bell
22, William H. Buckingham
23, Sillick Wicks
24, Daniel G. Gillett
25, Epenetus Mills
26, Mills Hawkins
27, Isaac A L, Homedieue
28, James Howell
29, Joel D. Norton
30, Richard W. Smith
31, Lester H. Davis
32, Israel Smith

Dis No. 33, Ebenezer Terry.
34, Jeremiah Gourdon
35, Franklin Overton
36, Gershom Hawkins
37, Abner Van Horn
38, James R. Laws
39, James H. Weeks
40, William Randall
41, Albert Hulse
42, Caleb Hammond
43, John Swezey
44 Joel Reeves
45, William Penny Jur
46, James Hallock

Page 301.

At a Meeting of the Trustees of the freeholders of the town of Brook Haven on the tenth day of November 1837. liberty was granted to William L. Jones to build and construct a Dock or wharf at the head of the Drown meadow Bay on the premises within the following limits or Bounds that is to say commencing at common high water mark Seventy feet west of Israel Davis Barn and running westwardly at common high water mark forty five feet and running from thence into the Bay the same width five hundred feet with a T across the end of one hundred and fifty feet in length the direction of the Dock into the Bay to be North west half North or thereabout the aforesaid grant to be for the term of thirty years from the first day of May 1838. And for and in consideration of which the said William L. Jones is to construct a Road or causeway across the Marsh or Slough leading from his house to said Dock sufficiently high to be out of the way of tide at common high water and to be of the width of eighteen feet to be Stoned up on each side and filled in with proper materials and to be made permanent for public use and the public is to take charge of said Road after it is completed and keep said Road in repair as other public Roads and also the said William L. Jones his heirs or Assigns are to pay unto the said Trustees or their Successors in office the yearly rent or Annuity of the sum of one Dollar annually to paid on the first tuesday in May the first Annuity to be paid on the first tuesday in May 1840. and the said Dock is to be completed within three years from May next the Rates of Wharfage to be regulated by the Board of Trustees or thier Successors in office, the rate of wharfage until so regulated to be the same as at the Dock granted to John Wilsie Deceasd, And at the expiration of said term of thirty years the said parties are to make a New contract or agreement as to the Annuity to be paid by the said William L. Jones or his Assigns

PAGE 302.

for the grant of said Dock and in case said parties cannot agree as to the price or Annuity to be paid for said grant Each party shall choose one arbitrator to decide in the premises and in case said arbitrators cannot agree they two shall choose one umpire or third Man and the decision of the two shall be final Sealed with our Seal and dated at Brook haven this day a foresaid

DANIEL OVERTON President L. S.

Attest MORDECAI HOMAN town clerk

At a Meeting of the undersigned Commissioners of Common Schools at the Inn of Justus Roes in patchogue in said town on the 17th. day of October 1839. it was resolved that District No. twenty in the said town be and the same is altered and a new District formed from the same as follows that is to say such new District shall consist of all that part of the said 20th. District which is Bounded West by number twenty one on the South by the South Bay on the East by a line commencing at the mouth of a Small creek forming the westerly bounds of Joshua Smiths farm and running from thence Northerly by the westerly bounds of the said Joshua Smiths farm until it Strikes the Southerly boundary of Smith Riders land then westerly by the Southerly Bounds of said Smith Rider Daniel Overton Smith Rider again Samuel Willett Justus Roe Ebenezer Roe Smith Rider again John Roe to Justus Roes Easterly Boundary line then Northerly with that line to the Country road then crossing that road Northwardly to the boundary line between the lands of the said John Roe and the said Justus Roe and then Northwardly with that boundary line and in the same direction until it strikes the road running from Justus roes Dwelling house to Coram and then Northwardly with that road to the North Bounds of said District Number twenty and on the North by the Northerly Boundary line of the District such New District shall be Number thirty six we have also Inspected the School House belonging to such District Number

PAGE 303.

twenty previous to its present Division which is retained by the old District and value it at one hundred and twenty three Dollars and the other District property and eighty seven and half cents and we acertain and determine the amount Justly due to the said New District as the proportion of such New District of the value of the said School House and other District property at the time of the division to be fifty Nine Dollars and eighty two Cents

M. HOMAN Clerk	Selah B. Strong Simeon H. Ritch Brewster Woodhull	Commissioners of Common Schools

This certifies that I have made the following Survey at the request of James Hurtin and others Inhabitants of the town of Brook Haven and proprietors in the lands called great and little Divisions we first traced a line called the west bounds of little division adjoining Winterups Patent and found it to run by the Compas as near as I could ascertain North 1. and ¾ degrees East—At a point on that line where the Horsblock road crosses it we turned to the eastward at right Angles with the aforesaid line and measured in a direct line across little Division and on to Great Division until we came to the old middle Island road (or Sills,s path) to a white Oak Sapling on the east side of the said road measures whole distance one hundred and five Chains Seventy two links

Dated April 1st. 1836   B. Woodhull Surveyor—

We Jeremiah T. Bell and Daniel Chichester of the town of Brook Haven being Sworn do Say that we were Chain bearers in the above Survey mad by B. Woodhull and that the measurment as Stated above is Correct according to the best of our belief   Jeremiah T. Bell
Sworn before me the   Daniel Chichester
28th May 1836
B. Woodhull Justice

N. B. the white oak tree above mentioned Stands five links from the east rut of Sills,s path and 63. Chs. 39 links from the North rut of the Horse block Road and 27 chs. 26 links from the west side of the Dock Road Measuring along Sills,s path

Page 304.

At an Annual town Meeting held in the town of Brook Haven on the 7th. day of April 1840. the following persons were duly Elected as town Officers—(viz)

John M. Williamson Supervisor

Barnabas Wines Justice of the peace for the term of four years

Daniel Overton president of Trustees

Silas Homan
William Penny Jur
Moses Swezey
Richard Smith pond } Trustees
Daniel Skidmore
Phillip Hallock Jur.

Daniel Skidmore
Moses Swezey— } Overseers of the poor

Mordecai Homan town clerk

Floyd Smith Collector

Isaac Davis
William S. Williamson
David Overton } Assessors
John H. Duryea
Joseph Avery

Charles Phillips
Nathaniel Tuttle } Commissioners of highways
Robert Smith

Selah B. Strong
Simeon H. Ritch } Commissioners of common Schools
Brewster Woodhull

Orlando Burnell
John R. Swezey } Inspectors of Common Schools
James Rice

John W. Bunce Sealer of Weights and Measures

Noah Overton
Daniel Overton 2d
Charles A. Tooker } Constables
Edward L. Conklin
John Hallock

PAGE 305.

OVERSEERS OF HIGHWAYS

Distct
No. 1— Charles D. Hallock
do. 2   dissolved

Distct
No. 3, Youngs Howell
 "   4   Benjamin Brewster
 "   5   Samuel Woodhull
 "   6   Briant Hawkins
 "   7   John Mather
 "   8   John Hutchenson
 "   9   Henry Robbins
 " 10   Charles Woodhull
 " 11   Amos Hallock
 " 12   Hiram Noyes
 " 13, John Carter
 " 14   Isaac Raynor
 " 15   Usher Benjamin
 " 16   Ebenezer Jayne
 " 17, David G. Floyd.
 " 18   Samuel Carman
    19, Briant N. Overton
    20, Thomas Bell   20, Jehiel Woodruff
    21, Jeremiah T. Bell
    22, Daniel Overton 2
    23, Micah Smith
    24, Brewster Woodhull
    25, Epenetus Mills
    26, Mills Hawkins
    27, William I. Gould
    28, Isaac Hammond Jur
    29, Joel D. Norton
    30, Richard W. Smith
    31, Lester H. Davis
    32, Richard Smith pond
 " 33   L. Homedieue Smith
 " 34   Jeremiah Gourden.
 " 35, Franklin Overton
 " 36, Benjamin T. Hutchenson

Distct
No. 37   Abner Venhorn
" 38   Nathaniel Homan
" 39   James H. Weeks
   40, John Randal
   41, Albert Hulse
" 42   Elisha Overton
   43, Oscar F. Swezey
   44, John Penny Jur
   45   William Penny Jur
   46, Phillip Hallock Jur
   47   Peter Skidmore

PAGE 306.

To all persons interested in the Great and little Divisions of land in the town of Brook Haven Transcript of a Survey taken by me on the 20th. of february and 4th. of March 1839. Started on the Rail Road line at a point 105. ch 72 Links South from Wintrups patent 1°. West from a certain Oak tree Marked near the Middle Island Road on the east side of which tree was the East end of a certain line ran by me in 1836 a transcript of which Survey has been already filed. and ran along said R. Road line* 67°. 50' East, 173 Chains 75 links to Yaphank line which is East of Connecticut River 17. Chains 25. links we next began on Yaphank line on the South Country Road and ran westerly along said Road to a Marked pine tree Standing on the west side of Ellisons Swamp said to be the Middle of the lot No. 15. in the Grat division Courses and distance as follows 1st. South 45°. 20' W. 3 C. 00. 2nd. 65°. 20 W. 18. C. 00. 3rd. 55° 30 W— 20. C. 00 this brought us to Priest Hawkins Corner being West side of lot No. 8— 4th. South 74°. 25' W. 7

* Note.—The Rail Road was not constructed upon this *line*, which was about half a mile north from Yaphank Station, and passed near the residence of the late James H. Weeks.—COM.

Chain 00 5th. S. 83°. W. 10 Chain 00 6th. 67°. 50′ W. 5.
Chain 00 this brought us to West side of lot No. 11 7th.
South 81°. W 7 Chain 8th. 77° West 3. Chain 9th. 53°. W.
6. 67. to the pine tree in Ellisons Swamp above named 4th.
March 1839 first 11. Lots. 20. Rods Each next 10 Lots. 18.
Rods Each next 14. Lots. 19. Rods Each next 20. Lots 13.
Rods Each little Division said to Contain 55 Lots of 4 Rods
and 13. feet Each in width—

We this day Started on the horsblock road on the East
line of Winterups Patent and ran 1°. 30′ East to the Middle
Island line then measured Easterly at right angles

Page 307.

ten lots and put up a Stake 6 lots and put up a Stake 6. do
and put up a Stake and then ran down between 33rd. and
34th. Lots parallel to Winterups Patent East line

B. Woodhull Surveyor

Distance from Winterups Patent to Yaphank line by
Measurment is 1065. Rods—14½ feet Distance Required
is 1051 5.½ feet.

excess in difference 14 — 9 feet—
from Yaphank line on the South end to Beaver dam Swamp
on a right Angle from said line is 285 Rods
from Beaver Dam Swamp to Daytons Swamp
 is on the right Angle 271—Rods
from Daytons Swamp to little Division 260—Rods
 Across little Division 263 Rods 5½ ft

1079 5½
Distance required is— 1051 5½

Excess of land in difference is—28 Rods
enterd this 6th. August 1840

M. Homan town clerk—

BROOKHAVEN TOWN RECORDS. 373

Field Notes of a Survey of a part of the Highway or Road Calld the South Post Road as laid out by Commissioners passing through Moriches Commencing in Moriches aforesaid at a certain Marked white Oak tree on the South side of the highway and near the west line of the land of Jonathan Hawkins being the tree at which other Commissioners Discontinued laying out said Highway in the year 1832. on the 13th. Sept. running on the south side of the highway as follows (viz) S. 52½°. E. 11.$\overset{C}{\ }$ 38$\overset{L}{\ }$ S. 68¼. E. 10. 00 S. 68°. E. 5. 10. S. 73½° E. 3. 00 S. 57½ E. 9. 36 S. 57¼° E. 9. 70. S. 66¼ E. 6. 00 S. 49°. E. 17. 21. S. 78½°. E. 1. 12 N. 88 ¾ E. 5. 25 N. 86 E. 4. 27 S. 89° E. 10. 52 S. 85½ E. 3. 47. S. 75¼° E. 7. 26 to the west line of land formerly of Elisha Raynor Deceased being the termination of this Road District said Road is four Rods wide.

PAGE 308.

the above or foregoing Courses are given as the needle now points the variation being near about 5°. 30′. W.
11th. June 1840—   J. M. FANNING Surveyor

Charles Phillips ⎫
Nathaniel Tuttle ⎬ Commissioners of highways.
Robert Smith*   ⎭

* Of Mastic

This Indenture Made this first day of December in the year one thousand eight hundred and forty Between the Trustees of the freeholders and commonalty of the town of Brook Haven in the County of Suffolk and State of New York of the first part and Lewis Hulse of the Same place of the second part Witnesseth that the said party of the first part for and in consideration of the yearly rent or annuity of the sum of one Dollar Annually to be paid on the first tuesday in May in each year during the continuance of this grant ; they the said party of the first part have

Granted farmed and to farm let, and by these presents doth grant demise and to farm let unto the said party of the second part and to his Heirs and Assigns for and during the term of fourteen years from the first tuesday in may next the use and improvement of all that common land or shore lying at the head of Drown meadow Bay lying on the North side of the highway that runs across the runs at the head of said Bay and Bounded North by the Bay East by the shore or land formerly Granted to said Hulse south by the said Road and to extend westward on the shore about twenty eight feet or to the West line of the land of said Hulse on the south side of said road thence extending square across said road to the Bay for the purpose of laying on wood lumber and othr articles and the launching of Vessels and

PAGE 309.

other Such uses leaving the said highway free and not incumbered by any such Articles and the said party of the Second part doth hereby covenant and agree to and with the said party of the first part and their Successors in office that he or they will pay or Cause to be paid unto the said Trustees or their Successors in Office at the times above Stated for the payment thereof the aforesaid rent or annuity of the sum of one Dollar Annually during the continuance of this grant and at the expiration of said term will remove all such incumbrances as may then be on said premises unles a new agreement be made between the said parties. In witness whereof the said parties have Set their hands and Seals the president of said Trustees his hand and Corporate seal of Brook H and the said Hulse his hand and seal this day aforesaid

in presence of   DANIEL OVERTON president L. S.
MORDECAI HOMAN
     town clerk   LEWIS HULSE— L. S.

This Indenture made this first day of December one

thousand eight hundred an forty Between the Trustees of the freeholders and Commonalty of the town of Brook Haven of the first part, and Silvester Randal of the same place of the Second part Witnesseth. that the said party of the first part for and in consideration of three Dollars and fifty Cents Annually to be paid on the first tuesday in May in each year by the said silvester Randal his Heirs or Assigns Have granted Bargained and let unto the said party of the second part his Heirs or Assigns the use and priviledge of a Certain piece of land or Shore belonging to said town for the purpose of Setting a blacksmith shop on for the term of twenty years from the first tuesday in May next. And Situated at the head of drown meadow Bay lying on the North side of the highway that leads

PAGE 310.

Across the runs at the head of said Bay and Bounded East by the land lately granted to Lewis Hulse. South by the said Road and to extend westward on the said road thirty five feet and North by the said Bay. for the express purpose of erecting a blacksmith s shop on and its accomodations and the said Silvester Randal for himself his Heirs and Assigns doth hereby covenant and agree to and with the said Trustees and their Successors in Office to pay unto the said party of the first part or their Successors in Office on the first tuesday in May Annually for the said term of twenty years the sum of three Dollars and fifty Cents the first payment to be made on the first tuesday in May 1841. In witness whereof the said parties have set their hands and seals the president of said Trustees his hand corporate seal of Brook Haven and the said Randal his hand and seal this day above Written in
presence of   DANIEL OVERTON President L. S.
  MORDECAI HOMAN   SYLVESTER RANDAL — L. S.
    town clerk
       the aforesaid annuity is reduced to $2. a year

This Indenture Made this first day of December one thousand eight hundred and forty Between the Trustees of the freeholders and commonalty of the town of Brook Haven in the County of Suffolk and State of New York of the first part and James R. Davis of the second part Witnesseth. that the said Trustees the party of the first part for and in consideration of the yearly rent or Annuity of the sum of one Dollar annually to be paid on the first tuesday in May in each year and also in consideration of other priviledges herein after mentioned they the said party of the first part have granted farmed and to farm let and by these presents doth grant rent and to farm let unto the said party of the second part and to his hiers and Assigns. the priviledges of using holding occupying building repairing and conveying

PAGE 311.

the Dock or wharf now owned by him the said James R. Davis for and during the term of twenty years from this date (which said Dock was formerly granted to John Wilsie) under the following regulations and restrictions viz, the said party of the first part shall be allowed and paid for putting on board of any vessel or craft from said Dock one cent for every foot of Cord wood and for every vessel laying alond side of said Dock when not loading twelve and an half Cents for every day for taking in or out Cattle such as Oxen Cows or horses fifteen Cents pr head for Calves or lambs two Cents pr head for every full hogshead of liquor Molasses or other liquid fifteen Cents for every barrel of pork liquor or other liquid six Cents for every Barrel of flour four cents. for every ten gallon keg of liquor three cents for five gallon kegs two Cents for every thousand long Shingle twenty five Cents for every Bundle of Short shingle four Cents for every thousand feet of plank twenty five Cents for every thousand feet of Boards eighteen and three quarter cents. reserving a right of landing or Sending off all articles belonging to the Corporation of said town of Brook Haven free from wharfage. and also that the said party of the second part keep said Dock in good repair for the accommodation of the public for the above said uses and at the expiration of said term of twenty years this present grant shall return to said town and the Dock appraised by indifferent men or further arrangment or agreement made between said parties or their Successors. and the said party of the second part doth hereby bind himself and and his Assigns that he or they will pay unto the said party of the first part or their Successors in Office at the times above Stated the said Annuity of one Dollar and keep said Dock in good repair for the accommodation of the public and in case any dispute shall arise in regard to the rate of wharfage such rate shall be fixed by the board of Trustees according to the true Intent and meaning of this instrument in Witness whereof the said partis have set their hands and Seals this day aforesaid

     Daniel Overton President L. S.
     James R. Davis   L. S.
in presence of
Mordecai Homan town clerk

Page 312.

Be it remembered that on the fourth day of September one thousand eight hundred and thirty eight Sylvester Smith and Mathew Darling made application to the board of Trustees of the freeholders and Commonalty of the town of Brook Haven for liberty to build and erect a Dock in Drown meadow Bay and to extend Southward from their Railway to the old Dock (so Called) and to extend into the Bay to Common low Water with one pier a few feet farther from low water mark for the purpose of landin plank timber lumber and other articles for the use of their shipyard, and said Trustees after due consideration had in the premises and for and in consideration of the yearly rent or annuity of the sum of four Dollars annually to be paid on the first tuesday in September during the continuance of this Grant the first annuity to be paid on the first tuesday in September 1840. did Grant unto the said Smith and Darling for the term of thirty six years from this date and to thier heirs and Assigns liberty to Construct build and keep in repair a Dock to extend Southwardly from thier Railway to the old Dock (so called) against thier own land and to extend into the Bay to common low water mark with one pier a few feet farther into the Bay for the purpose of landing plank timber lumber and other articles for thier accommodation in thier shipyard for Ship Building but not to hinder or obstruct people from passing and repassing on the Beach as usual above high water mark and the said Smith and darling doth hereby covenant and agree for themselves their heirs and Assigns to pay unto the said Trustees or their Successors in Office at the times above Stated the said yearly rent or annuity of four Dollars and in case default shall be made in any part thereof for the payment for the term of twenty days after such payment shall be demanded then this

PAGE 313.

present grant shall be void and of no effect and the premises revert back to the town again unless some further agreement be made between the tow said parties In witness whereof the said parties have Set their hands and Seals this day aforesaid

DANIEL OVERTON President L. S.

in presence
of MORDECAI HOMAN town clerk

At an annual town Meeting of the freeholders and Inhabitants of the town of Brook Haven held at the house of Lester H. Davis on the 6th. day of April 1841 the followin persons were elected town Officers for the ensueing year (viz)

Nathaniel Conklin supervisor

David Overton Justice of the peace

Silas Homan President of Trustees

William S. Williamson ⎫
John Randal ⎪
William C. Booth ⎬ Trustees
Joel Robinson ⎪
Thomas Jefferson Ellison ⎪
William J. Gould ⎭

William S. Williamson ⎫ Overseers of the poor
Silas Homan ⎭

Mordecai Homan town clerk

Floyd Smith Collector

Hiram S. Tuttle ⎫
Davis Norton ⎪
John R. Satterly ⎬ Assessors
James Ketcham ⎪
William Penny 2d. ⎭

Daniel Skidmore ⎫
Brewster Terry ⎬ Commissioners of highways
Robert Smith ⎭

Selah B. Strong ⎫
Brewster Woodhull ⎬ Commissioners of Com Schools
Simeon H. Ritch ⎭

Elias H. Luce ⎫
John R. Swezey ⎬ Inspectors of Com Schools
Orlando Burnell ⎭

Noah Overton ⎫
Charles A. Tooker ⎬ Constables
William Penny 4th. ⎪
Daniel Overton ⎭

John W. Bunce Sealer of weights and Measures

BROOKHAVEN TOWN RECORDS.

At said Meeting a vote was taken as to where the next town Meeting should be held and was voted to be held at The house of Richard W. Smith in Coram—

PAGE 314.

OVERSEERS OF HIGHWAYS ELECTED IN 1841.

District
No. 1, Charles D. Hallock
do. 2, extinct
do. 3, Youngs Howell
do 4, Benjamin Dickenson
do 5, Nicoll Smith
do. 6, Briant Hawkins
do. 7, Lewis Hulse
do. 8, Elisha Norton
do. 9, William Tillotson
do. 10, Thomas Helme
do. 11, William Horton
do. 12, James Woodhull
do. 13, John Carter
do 14, Nathan Davis
do 15, David Terry
do 16, Ebenezer Jayne
do. 17, David G. Floyd
do. 18, Samuel Carman
do. 19, John Downs
do. 20, Jehiel Woodruff
do. 21, Daniel Robinson
do. 22, Daniel Overton
do. 23, Micah Smith
do. 24, Brewster Woodhull
do. 25, John Corey
do. 26, Silvester Newton
do. 27, Daniel R. Hallock
do. 28, Isaac Hammond Jur

District
No. 29, Joel D. Norton
do. 30, David Fordham
do. 31, Lester Davis
do. 32, Richard Smith pond
do. 33, Thomas Terry
do. 34, Jeremiah Gourdon
do 35, Franklin Overton
do 36, Benjamin T. Hutchenson
do. 37, Abner Van Horn
do. 38, Vanrenselear Swezey
do. 39, James H. Weekes
do. 40, Wm. S. Smith
do. 41, Stephen Turner
do 42, Caleb H. Hammond
do 43, Oscar F. Swezey
do 44, Ketcham Chichester
do. 45, Mott Raynor
do. 46, Charles Robinson
do 47, Silvester Randal

At the aforesaid town Meeting a vote was taken whether there should be a vote taken for and against the division of said town and was Carried in the Affirmative

the said vote was given by Ballot. and there was 260. votes given against the division of said town and none in favor of said Division.

Also a vote taken and Carried allowing the Inspectors of Com Schools one Dollar a Day

Attest

MORDECAI HOMAN town Clerk total No. of votes—260

PAGE 315.

Be it Ordained by the Trustees of the freeholders and Commonalty of the town of Brook Haven that if any person or persons being an Inhabitant of said town shall take or

Catch any Oysters in the South Bay belonging to said town and William Sidney Smith for the purpose of Selling them to or for any foreign market or that shall be sold or carried out of said town of Brook Haven unless such person or persons shall first obtain permission from said Trustees or one of their Agents and also pay a tolleration of two Cents on every Bushell of Oysters so to be taken shall for every such offence forfeit and pay the sum of twelve Dollars and fifty Cents to be sued for and recovered in the name of the said Trustees before any Court having cognizance thereof And if any person or persons not being an Inhabitant of said town shall take or catch any Oysters in the aforesaid Bay without first obtaining permission as aforesaid and also pay the said tolleration of two cents on every Bushel so to be taken shall for every such offence pay the like sum of twelve Dollars and fifty cents to be sued for and recovered as aforesaid. the law respecting the tolleration of four cents on every Bushel passed the 4th. May 1841. is hereby repealed, but no dredges to be used in taking Oysters done at Brook Haven this first day of June 1841.

Silas Homan president L. S

Mordecai Homan town clerk

Barnabas Smith Jur	
Benjamin Wicks	Agents
Lewis Wicks	
Jonas Mills	

Page 316.

At an Annual Town Meeting held on the fifth day of April 1842 at the house of Richard W. Smith in Coram the following persons were duly Elected town Officers for the ensuing year (viz)

Nathaniel Conklin Supervisor
Brewster Woodhull Justice of the peace
Davis Norton President of Trustees

Silas Homan   ⎫
William S. Williamson ⎪
John H. Duryea   ⎬ Trustees
Nathaniel Tuttle   ⎪
Miller Woodhull   ⎪
David W. Case.   ⎭

Silas Homan   ⎫ Overseer of the poor
William S. Williamson ⎭

Mordecai Homan town clerk

Floyd Smith Collector

James Ketcham   ⎫
Joel Robinson   ⎪
John Davis   ⎬ Assessors
John R. Satterly ⎪
Davis Norton   ⎭

Charles Phillips ⎫
Nathaniel Tuttle ⎬ Commissioners of Highways
David Worth   ⎭

Selah B. Strong   ⎫
Simeon H. Ritch   ⎬ Commissioners of common Schools
Albert A. Overton ⎭

John R. Swezey ⎫ Inspectors of Schools—
Joel Robinson   ⎭

Noah Overton   ⎫
Daniel Overton   ⎪
William Penny 4th. ⎬ Constables
Charles A Tooker   ⎪
Jonathan Pike   ⎭

John W. Bunce Sealer of Weights and Measures

PAGE 317.

OVERSEERS OF HIGHWAYS FOR 1842

District
  No. 1, William S. Williamson
  " 2, Daniel S. Hawkins
     3, Youngs Howell

District
No. 4, Benjamin Dickerson
  5 John Brewster
  6—Henry Tyler
  7—Henry K. Townsend
  8—Jonathan Pike
  9—Parshall Davis
  10 Conklin Davis
  11 Amos Hallock
  12 Henry Tuttle
  13 John Carter
  14 Sylvester W. Wines
  15, David Terry Jur.
  16, Joseph Dayton
  17 David G. Floyd
  18 Samuel Carman
  19, Azel Hawkins
  20 Jehiel Woodruff
  21 Daniel Robinson
  22 Richard R. Davis
  23, Edward Mulford
  24, Isaac S. Douglass
  25, John Corey
  26 Silvester Newton
  27, John F. Hallock
  28, Isaac Hammond Jur
  29, Joel D. Norton
  30 Albert Terrell
  31, Lester Davis
  32 Richard Smith pond
  33, L Homedieue Smith
  34, Jeremiah Gourden
  35, Franklin Overton
  36, Benjamin T. Hutchenson
  37, Herman Petty

District
No. 38 William Phillips Esq
39, James H. Weeks
40, William Sidney Smith
41, Jonathan Robinson
42, Caleb H. Hammond
43, Oscar F. Swezey
44, John H. Duryea
45, John C. Smith
46, Charles Robinson.
47, Hendrickson Hallock.
48 James Fanning appointed

State of New York } this
Suffolk County

Certifies that we the undersigned Inspectors of town Election having canvassed and examined the tickets polled at a town Meeting held at the House of Richard W. Smith in Coram on the 5th. day of April 1842 in the town of Brook Haven—do State a certify that the foregoing persons were duly Elected for town officers for the ensueing year—

Brewster Woodhull } Justices
Charles Phillips   of the peace

PAGE 318.

on the 2nd. day of November 1840 a Monument or Stone was erected at Wading River Between the town of Brook Haven at the request of Each town By David Worth Esq. of Brook Haven and Noah Yound Esq. of Riverhead being a committee appointed for that purpose from each town (viz) a Stone Marked on the west side with the letter B— and on the East side with the letter R. to Stand and remain as a Monument between said towns being erected in the place where the old peperidge tree Stood as a dividing line between said towns in presence of

Jonathan W. Mapes⎫
Henry Hudson ⎬ of Brook Haven
Charles Hudson. ⎭
and Robert Woodhull ⎫
Vincent Mapes ⎬ of Riverhead
Gabriel Mills ⎭

David Worth ⎱ Committee
Noah Young ⎰

This Indenture made this Seventh day of June in the year of our Lord one thousand eight hundred and fourteen Between the Trustees of the freeholders and Commonalty of the town of Brook Haven in the County of Suffolk and State of New York of the first part and Robert Hawkins of the Same place of the second part Witnesseth that the said party of the first part for and in consideration of the sum of twenty Dollars to them in hand paid at or before the sealing and delivery of these the receipt whereof is hereby acknowledged they the said party of the first have granted bargained and Sold and by these presents do grant Bargain and Sell unto the said party of the second part and to his heirs and assigns forever a certain piece of Swamp and upland on the

PAGE 319.

west side of Beaver dam River it being a part of the land reserved for the use of the town in the Great Division of Land Between Connecticut River and the land formerly Mr. Winterups the aforesaid piece of land is Bounded South by the road that leads westward over the Brook opposide the house of Scudder Ketcham deceasd East by the aforesaid Beaver dam River West by the land of the said Robert Hawkins and to extend or run Northward as far as the Inclosed or cleared land of the said Robert Hawkins To have and To hold all and Singular the premises above mentioned with all and every of the hereditaments profits priviledges and appurtenances thereunto belonging or in

anywise appertaining unto the said party of the second part to the only proper use benefit and behoof of the said party of the second part and to his Hiers and assigns forever and the said party of the first part doth hereby declare that at the time of the ensealing and delivery of these presents they were lawfully siezed of the aforesaid premises and that they had lawful Authority to grant and dispose of the same in manner as aforesaid and the said party of the first part doth hereby bing themselves and thier successors in Office to warrant and defend the aforesaid premises unto the said party of the Second part and to his Hiers and Assigns forever against all the just and lawful claim or claims of any person or persons whatsoever in witness whereof the said party of the first part hath set their hands and caused the Seal of said town to be affixed
Signed Sealed and
delivered in the presents   JOHN ROSE President L S
of MORDECAI HOMAN town clerk   of Trustees
DAVID ROBINSON

PAGE 320.

Whereas a dispute has arisen between the towns of Brook Haven and Smith town County of Suffolk relative to the boundary line between them from the Mill dam at Stoney brook to Long Island Sound. And Selah B. Strong Davis Norton and Charles Phillips of Broo Haven and Joshua B. Smith William Wickham Mills and Joseph R. Hunting of Smith town were appointed by their respective towns to locate such line and in case of thier disagreement to Submit the matter in difference to arbitration with authority to bind thier respective towns to abide by and perform the award to be made by the arbitrator to be selected by them.—

And whereas the persons so appointed having examined and considered the said Matter in dispute and having disagreed as to the location of the said Boundary line and having thereupon appointed and selected the undersigned

Charles H. Ruggles of Poughkeipsie in the County of Dutches sole Arbitrator to locate fix and determine the said boundary line between the said two towns from the said Mill dam to the Sound and agreed each Committee for their own town that their respective towns should submit to abide by and perform the Award of the undersigned Arbitrator in the premises provided such Award should be made in Writing and subscribed by the said Arbitrator in duplicate on or before the first day of January 1842. as may more fully appear by the said Instrument of Submission in Writing duly executed and dated the sixth day of September 1842

AND whereas the undersigned Arbitrator did take upon himself the burden of such Award and upon the said sixth day of September being attended by both the parties had a view of the premises and then and there heard their allegations Writings and proofs on both sides but omitted to make his Award on or before the said first day of January in the year 1842

PAGE 321.

And whereas the said Selah B. Strong Charles Phillips and Davis Norton Commissioners appointed on the part of the town of Brook Haven aforesaid and the said William Wickham Mills Joshua B. Smith and Joseph R. Hunting appointed on the part of Smithtown agreed by an instrument under thier hands dated January 1st. 1842 to extend the time for making the award of the undersigned in the Matter herein before mentioned to the 22d. day of February then next and thereby agreed that if an award should be made concerning the premises by that day it should be binding and conclusive upon their respective towns.—NOW therefore I the said Charles H. Ruggles in pursuance of the Authority contain,d in the said Instrument in Writing and after having Viewed the premises and been attended by the parties and having heard their Witnesses proofs and allegations as aforesaid, Do by these presents Arbitrate Award order adjudge and determine of and concerning the premises as follows that is to say that the Boundary line between the town of Brook haven and the town of Smithtown from the Mill dam at Stoney Brook to long Island sound begins in the Middle of the main Channel of the Middle Branch of the said Stoney Brook at the said Mill dam and runs thence down the Middle of the said Main Channel of the aforesaid brook or Stream as the same now runs into the harbour and so along the Channel or deepest part thereof into Long Island sound, And the Middle of the main Channel of the said Stream until it comes to the harbour and thence the middle of the Channel of the harbour is hereby located fixed adjudged and awarded to be the boundary line between the two towns aforesaid from the Mill dam aforesaid to the Sound.

In witness whereof I have made this my award

PAGE 322.

in Writing in duplicate and subscribed the same this 14th. day of February in the year 1842

CHARLES H. RUGGLES

State of New York } ss.
Dutches County

on the fourteenth of february one thousand eight hundred and forty two before me came the honourable Charles H. Ruggles known to me as the person described in and who executed the foregoing Award and acknowledged that he had signed and executed the said Award for the uses and purposes therein expressed I find no alterations therein let it be recorded let it be made in evidence

JOHN BRUSH Supreme Court
Commissioner

We the Commissioners of Highways of the   of Brook Haven being call, d to istablish an ancient Section of a Road leading Westerly from the Beaver Dam in fireplace to the Country road which said Road although used as a publick Highway was not found to be recorded which is as follows (viz) commencing on the east side of Beaver Dam river at a Stake in the center of the road being the termination of a former Survey—surveying the centre track throughout to the center of the South country road the road to be three rods wide and four if necessary—Bearing as follows (viz) first North eighty seven and three quarter degrees West three chains and eighty eight links thence North Seventy nine West three chains thence North eighty six and and half West one chain and lastly South eighty five and one third West Seven chins and four links to the Centre of the South country road

as witness our hands this 29th. June 1843

    Smith Davis   Charles Phillips) Commissioners
         Surveyor John Havens   }   of
                    Nathaniel Tuttle) Highways

Page 323.

At an annual town Meeting held at the house of Richard W. Smith in Coram on the 4th. day of April 1843 the following persons were duly elected town officers for the ensueing year—(viz)

        Nathaniel Conklin Supervisor
     Charles Phillips Justice of the peace
     Davis Norton President of Trustees

          Simeon H. Ritch
          Hiram S. Tuttle
          Nathaniel Tuttle   } Trustees
          Joel Robinson
          Silas Homan
          William C. Smith

    Silas Homan   } Overseers of the poor
    Simeon H. Ritch

Mordecai Homan clerk and treasurer

Floyd Smith Collector

William Penny 4th Neck
Albert A. Overton
Davis Norton } Assessors
Isaac Davis
John R. Satterly

Charles Phillips
Nathaniel Tuttle } Commissioners of Highways
John Havens

Selah B. Strong
Benjamin T. Hutchenson } Commissioners of Schools
William Wickham Jur

John R. Swezey
Simeon H. Ritch } Inspectors of Schools

Noah Overton
Daniel Overton
William Penny 4th. } Constables
Elisha Norton

John W. Bunce Sealer of weights and measures

Inspectors of Elections

1st. District
  William S. Williamson
  Henry K. Townsend
  Zechariah Hawkins

2d. District
  Isaac Davis
  Hiram S. Tuttle
  Charles Woodhull

3d. District
  Joel Robinson
  David Worth
  James M. Fanning

4th. District
  Joseph Avery
  Nathaniel Conklin
  John Post

5th. District
  Lester H. Davis
  Elihu S. Overton
  William Phillips

PAGE 324.

OVERSEERS OF HIGHWAYS

District
No. 1, Joseph S. Hawkins
2, Charles D. Hallock
3, Charles Smith
4, John Dickerson
5 William M. Smith
6, John Oaks
7, Henry K. Townsend
8, Charles Hawkins
9, Selah Tooker
10, Charles Woodhull
11, William Horton
12 Henry Tuttle
13, John Carter
14, Silvester W. Wines
15, Usher Benjamin
16, Joseph Dayton
17, David G. Floyd
18, Samuel Carman
19, Wm Robbins
20, William Howell
21, Moses Swezey
22, Austin Roe
23, Daniel G. Gerard
24, Albert A. Overton
25, Joseph Homan
26, George S. Raynor
27, Joseph C. Hammond
28, Daniel A. Hawkins
29, Joel D. Norton
30, Richard W. Smith
31, Alfred Davis

District
No. 32, Israel Smith
    33, Daniel Terry Jur
    34, Jeremiah Gourden
    35, Franklin Overton
    36, Herrick Aldrich
    37, Abner Vanhorn
    38, William Phillips
    39, James H. Weeks
    40, Wm. Sidney Smith
    41, Jonathan Robinson
    42, Brewster Terry
    43, Jothom Swezey
    44, William Penny 4th.
    45, John C. Smith
    46, James Hallock
    47, Silvester Randal
    48, Edward L. Conklin

PAGE 325.

At an Annual town Meeting held in the town of Brook Haven on the 2nd. Day of April 1844—the following persons were duly elected town Officers for the ensueing year (viz)

Richard Robinson Justice of the peace
Thomas J. Ritch Supervisor
William S. William President of Trustees

John Hutchenson ⎫
Richard Smith pond ⎪
William C. Smith ⎪
Silas Homan ⎬ Trustees
Richard Robinson ⎪
Lester H. Davis ⎭

John Hutchenson ⎫
William C. Smith ⎬ Overseers of the poor

Mordecai Homan town clerk and treasurer
Floyd Smith Collector

Silas Homan
Lewis G. Davis
Brewster Terry } Assessors
John R. Satterly
Hiram S. Tuttle

Charles Phillips
Nathaniel Tuttle } Commissioners of highways
John S. Havens

William Sidney Smith { town Superentendent of Common Schools

Noah Overton
Daniel Overton
William Penny 2d. } Constables
Elisha Norton

Lester H. Davis Sealer of weights and measures

Inspectors of Elections

1st. District
- John M. Williamson
- Henry K. Townsend
- Zecheriah Hawkins

2d. Isaac Davis
- Hiram S. Tuttle
- Charles Miller

3d. William Penny 2nd.
- Joel Robinson
- John Stephens

4. John Roe
- Joseph Avery
- Nathaniel Miller Doctr

5 Benjamin T. Hutchinson
Davis Norton
William Phillips Esq

PAGE 326.

OVERSEERS OF HIGHWAYS FOR 1844—

District
No. 1, Richard M. Smith
2d. Daniel S Hawkins
3d Charles Smith

District
No. 4, Isaac Smith
5, Samuel Woodhull
6, James Hulse
7, Lewis Hulse
8, John Hutchenson
9, Timothy Davis
10, Conklin Davis
11, Joel Brown
12, Charles Hudson.
13, John Carter
14, Silvester Wines
15, Jacob Miller
16, Parker S. Robinson
17, Silas Hawkins
18, Samuel Carman
19, William Robbins
20, Isaac Overton
21, Smith Roe
22, John Havens
23, Epenetus Hendrickson
24, James Ketcham
25 Jonas Mills
26, Joseph Newton
27, Ansel Reeve
28, Samuel A. Hawkins
29, Samuel F. Norton
30, Lewis R. Overton
31, Benjamin Clerk
32, Israel Smith
33, Willard Ruland
34, Alfred Overton
35, John Buckingham
36, Ezra Guildersleve
37, Minor Davis

District
No. 38, Daniel D. Swezey
39, James H. Weeks
40, Wm. Sidney Smith
41, Sidney Griffin
42, Brewster Terry
43, Jothom Swezy
44, John H. Duryea
45, William Penny 2d
46 Phillip Hallock
47 Walter Dickinson
48, Edward L. Conklin

We certify the foregoing to be a true Statement of the Officers of Elected at the aforesaid Election

Charles Phillips ⎫ Justices
Brewster Woodhull ⎬ of the
David Overton ⎭ peace

Page 327.

At a Meeting of the Commissioners of highway of the town of Brook Haven in the County of Suffolk at Millville in said town on the 16th. day of April 1844. all the said commissioners having met and deliberated on the subject embraced in this order it is ordered and determined by the said Commissioners that a highway be laid out in the said town of the width of three rods on the application of twelve freeholders of the said town certified to on oath that such road was necessary and the said Commissioners having examined the premises do order and determin that the said road commence at the South Country road a little to the west of the dwelling of the Revd. Nathaniel Hawkins in fireplace in said town running Northwardly by the land of Stephen Bartoe and the land of Daniel Hawkins and Bounded on the east by the fence of the said Stephen Bartoe as it now Stands until it Comes to the horse block road thence running North 25. degrees East one chain and thirty five links then taking the Course of the line between the said Stephen Bartoe and Daniel Hawkings two rods on the land of the said Stephen Bartoe and one rod on the land of the said Daniel Hawkins until it comes to Gerards road and thence continuing Northwardly through the land of William Phillips Esq and the land of Daniel Homan deceased according to the line of Division one equal half on each until it intersects with the Patchogue road that leads from the fulling Mill at Millville in witness whereof the undersigned Commissioners of Highways of said town have hereunto subscribed thier names this 6th. day of May 1844

MORDECAI HOMAN town clerk

Charles Phillips
Nathaniel Tuttle } Commissioners of Highways
John S. Havens

Daniel Hawkins appeald to the Judges and was allowed the sum of twenty five Dollars which was paid

PAGE 328.

This doth certify that whereas there was a new Road laid out between the land of Samuel Carman and William Phillips on the 6th. day of May 1844 the Commissioners ordered that the road formerly laid from Daniel Homans Mill dam to Gerards road might be Stopped up whenever the new road was sufficiently cleared for traveling

Brook Haven   attest MORDECAI HOMAN town clerk
6th May 1844

It is agreed by and between Daniel Hawkins of the one part and the commissioners of Highways of the other part all of Brook Haven as follows that the damages sustained by reason of the laying out and opening a Highway trough his lands by the commissioners Dated the 6th. May 1844 be fixed and liquidated at the sum of twenty five Dollars. and the Said Daniel Hawkins doth hereby release to the

said town all further claim to damages by reason of the laying out and opening the said road Dated at Brook Haven this 11th. June 1844— DANIEL HAWKINS L. S.
in presence of
WM. P. BUFFETT

Charles Phillips } Commissioners
Nathaniel Tuttle } of Highways

Recd of the commissioners of Highways for the above said Damages the sum of twenty five Dollars—Daniel Hawkins

Be it remembered that on the 1st. day of April 1845 the Trustees of Brook Haven Granted liberty to Charles Phillips Esq. to set a fish House on Mogers shore in the old mans on the east side of the highway but not so as to interupt the public traveling—

attest MORDECAI HOMAN town clerk

PAGE 329.

At an annual town Meeting held in the town of Brook Haven on the 1st. day of April 1845 the following town Officers was duly elected viz

Thomas J. Ritch Supervis

Brewster Terry Justice of the peace

Nathaniel Tuttle president of Trustees

John Hutchenson
Benjamin Brewster
Lester H. Davis
Lorenzo D. Vail } Trrustees
Smith Rider
Silas Homan

John Hutchenson
Smith Rider } overseers of the poor

Mordecai Homan town clerk and treasurer

Floyd Smith Collector

BROOKHAVEN TOWN RECORDS. 399

John Symms Havens ⎫
Lewis G. Davis ⎪
Benjamin T. Hutchenson ⎬ Assessors
John R. Satterly ⎪
Hiram S. Tuttle ⎭

Lester H. Davis Sealer of Weights and measures

Charles Phillips ⎫
Nathaniel Tuttle ⎬ Commissioners of Highways
John Havens ⎭

William Wickham Jur Superintendent of Common Schools

Enos Freeman ⎫
Elisha Norton ⎪
Wm. Penny 4th ⎬ Constables
Briant N. Overton ⎪
Noah Overton ⎭

Inspectors of Elections

1st. District
   Zecheriah Hawkins   3d. John Stephens
   John M. Williamson   William Penny
   Henry K. townsend   Joel Robinson
2d. Charles Woodhull   4th. George P. Mills
   Isaac Davis   Nathaniel Conklin
   Hiram S. Tuttle   John L. Ireland
                 5th.
          Davis Norton
    Benjamin T. Hutchenson
     William Phillips Esq

1842   Brewster Woodhull ⎫
1843   Charles Phillips ⎬ Justices
1844   Richard Robinson ⎪
1845   Brewster Terry ⎭

PAGE 330.

OVERSEERS OF HIGHWAYS FOR 1845

District No   District No
   1, Richard N. Smith   25, James Smith
   2, Charles D. Hallock   26, Silvester Homan

District No
3, John Bennett
4, Isaac Smith
5, Samuel Woodhull
6, Charles Jayne.
7, John R. Mather
8, Charles Hawkins
9, Lorenzo G. Davis
10, Conklin Davis
11, Joel Brown
12, Hiram S. Tuttle
13 John Carter
14, Isaac Raynor
15, Henry P. Osborn
16, Parker S. Robinson
17, Silas Hawkins
18, Samuel Carman.
19, Azel Hawkins
20, Jehiel Woodruff
21, John Avery
22, Giltson Gillett
23, Wm. C. Smith
24, James Ketcham

District No
27, Ansel Reeve
28, Samuel A. Hawkins
29, Joel D. Norton
30, Albert Terrell
31, Alfred Davis
32, Richard Smith pond
33 L. Homedieue Smith
34, Silvester Homan
35, William M. Turner
36, Ezra Guildersleve
37, Joseph Davis
38 Van. Renselear Swezy
39, Apollos A. Mills
40, Wm. Sidney Smith
41, Elkana Robinson
42, Caleb Hammond
43, Joshua Swezey.
44, John S. Havens
45, William Penny 2d.
46, Charles Robinson
47, James Woodhull
48, Edward L. Conklin

the foregoing is a true statement of the result of the foregoing Election for town officers

Brewster Woodhull } Justices of
Charles Phillips } the peace

Page 331.

At a Meeting of the Trustees of the freeholders and commonalty of the town of Brook Haven held on the 4th. day of June 1844 It was voted and agreed that there be a tolleration of three cents on every bushel of hard clams that shall be taken in any of the Bays or harbours on the North side

of the Island and carried out of said town of Brook Haven. and if any person or persons shall take and carry or shall carry any clams out of said town without paying such tolleration shall for each and every such offence forfeit and pay to said Trustees or their Successors in office the sum of twelve Dollars and fifty cents to be sued for and recovered in the name of the said Trustees and applied to the use of said town done at Brook Haven this 4th. day of June 1844— WILLIAM S. WILLIAMSON President L. S.
Attest
MORDECAI HOMAN town clerk

At a Meeting of the Trustees of the freeholders and commonalty of the town of Brook Haven on the 3d. day of March 1846. said trustees agreed with Lewis Hulse to reduce the Annuity of his Grants for Railways and ground at Drownmeadow from $16. to $12 a year from the first tuesday in May last with a reservation to raise the said Annuity to $16. at any time by giving twenty days Notice previous to the expiration of any one years, grant to the said Hulse or his heirs or Assigns—the Annuity to remin a twelve Dollars a year until such notice shall be given—done at Brook Haven this day aforesaid
NATHANIEL TUTTLE President L. S.
Attest
MORDECAI HOMAN town clerk

PAGE 332.

at a Meeting of the Trustees of the freeholders and commonalty of the town of Brook Haven held on the 11th. day of November 1845. the said Trustees granted that Charles D. Hallock his Heirs or Assigns recieve six cents for every Hundred Bushel of Ashes Bone or other manure that may be landed or taken from his Dock from any vessel whether such vessel belong or be Owned in the town of Brook

Haven or elsewhere to be paid by the Master or Owner of such vessel—done at Brook Haven this day aforesaid

     NATHANIEL TUTTLE President L. S.

Attest
MORDECAI HOMAN town clerk

At an Annual town Meeting held in the town of Brook Haven on the 7th. April 1846 the following town officers were by Majority elected (viz)

    Thomas J. Ritch Supervisor
   Brewster Woodhull Justice of the peace
    Nathaniel Tuttle President

   Benjamin Guildersleve ⎫
   Wm. C. Smith |
   John S. Havens |
   Lester H. Davis   ⎬ Trustees
   Noah H. Jones |
   Henry K. Townsend ⎭

Wm. C. Smith   ⎫
Henry K. Townsend. ⎬ overseers of poor

Mordecai Homan town clerk and treasurer

    Lester Davis Collector

1 year— John Havens   ⎫
2 years— John R. Satterly ⎬ Assessors
3 years— Davis Norton   ⎭

1 year Nathaniel Tuttle ⎫
2 years John Havens   ⎬ Commissioners of highways
3 years Charles Phillips   ⎭

 William S. Preston town superintendent of common Schools

  Lester H. Davis Sealer of weights and measures

    Daniel Overton   ⎫
    Gershom R. Smith |
    Elish Norton   ⎬ Constables
    Alfred Davis |
    William Penny 4th. ⎭

Page 333.

Inspectors of Elections

1 District
  John M. Williamson
  Henry K. Townsend
  Carlton Jayne—

2d. District
  Isaac Davis
  Horace Hudson
  Charles Woodhull

3d. District
  Wm. Penny 2d.
  Joel Robinson
  James M. Fanning

4th. District
  George P. Mills
  Wm. Wickham Jur
  Wm. Raynor.

5th. District
  Richard W. Smith
  Nelson Norton
  Lewis Overton

Overseers of Highways

1st Distct Shepherd Smith
2—Charles D. Hallock
3—Samuel L. Thompson
4—Isaac Smith
5, Samuel Woodhull
6, Henry Tyler
7, Lewis Hulse act
8, Charles Hawkins act
9, Isaac Davis act
10, Caleb D. King act
11, Noah H. Jones
12, Hiram S. Tuttle
13, Seth Raynor
14, Isaac Raynor
15, George Terry.
16, Jesse Rogers
17, Daniel Lane
18, Samuel Carman

19, Azel Hawkins
20, George P. Mills act.
21, John Avery
22, Daniel Overton
23, Epenetus Hendrickson
24, Samuel S. Hammond
25, Joseph Homan.
26, Joseph Newton
27, Abraham W. Roseman
28, Samuel A. Hawkins
29, Joel D. Norton
30, David Fordham
31, Lester Davis ac
32, Richard Smith pond
33, Thomas Terry
34, Jeremiah Gourden
35, William M. Turner
36, Ezra Guildersleve
37, Joseph Davis
38, Vanrenselar Swezey
39, Apollos A. Mills
40, John Randal
41, Elkanah Robinson
42, Caleb Hammond
43, Joshua Swezey
44, Josiah H. Bishop
45, Jonah Turner
46, Henry C. Mather act
47, Albert Skidmore act
48, John Ross—

Page 334.

At a Special town Meeting held in the town of Brook Haven on the 19th. day of May 1846 to determine by Ballot whether there should be Licence or no Licence granted in said town to Sell Strong or Spirituous Liquors Six hundred and Seventeen votes were given of which four hundred and sixty seven votes were given for no licence and one hundred and fifty votes were given for Licence—

Dated at

Brook Haven
19th. May 1846

no Licence 467
Licence—150
———
total—617

Brewster Terry } Justices
Charles Phillips } of the peace

We certify the foregoing to be a true Statement of the result of the foregoing town Meeting

MORDECAI HOMAN
town clerk

Brewster Terry } Justices
Charles Phillips } of the peace

Be it ordained by the Trustees of the freeholders and commonalty of the town of Brook Haven that no person or persons shall Dredge or drag for Oysters in the waters of this town in the south Bay and that any person or persons offending against the provision of this ordinance shall forfiet the sum of twelve Dollars and fifty Cents for each and every offence to be recovered by and in the name of the said Trustees before any Court having Jurisdiction of the Matter done at Brook Haven this fourth day of May 1841. this act to take effect immediately

SILAS HOMAN President. of Trustees

L. S.

attest
MORDECAI HOMAN
town clerk

PAGE 335.

This Indenture made this tenth day of September in the year of our Lord one thousand eight hundred and forty four Between the Trustees of the freeholders and commonalty of the Town of Brook Haven County of Suffolk and State of New York of the first part and Jonas Smith of the Same place of the Second part Witnesseth. that the said party of the first part as well in consideration of the sum of one dollar to them paid at or before the Sealing and delivery of these presents by the said party of the Second part as well as also of the rents covenants and agreements herein after reserved and contained on the part and behalf of the said party of the second part his Executors admistrators and assigns to be paid kept and performed have demised granted and to farm let and by these presents do demise grant and to farm let unto the said party of the second part and to his Executors Administrators and Assigns forever a certain tract of sand flat lying at Stoney Brook beginning at a certain Rock which bears from another Rock on the Shore South fifty nine degrees East and distant one chain and forty two links and from thence North eleven degrees West four Chains thence North four and one half degrees West Six Chains and eighty four links thence South fifty five degrees West six chains thence South nineteen degrees East five Chains thence North seventy Six and one half degrees East seven Chains and fifty two links to the place of beginning for the purpose of Building Erecting and keeping in repair a Dock or wharf thereon and for making such other improvements thereon as the said party of the second part shall or may think proper to erect To have and to hold all and singular the said premisis with the appurtenances unto the said party of

the second part his Executors Administrators and Assigns forever he or they yielding and paying therefor from the first tuesday in april one thousand eight hundred and forty four annually unto the said parties of the first part or their successors in Office the sum of Nine Dollars yearly and every year on the first tuesday in April—And the said Jonas Smith doth for himself his Executors Administrators and

Assigns covenant grant and agree to and with the said parties of the first part and their Successors in Office that he or they will well and truly pay or cause to be paid unto the said parties of the first part and their Successors in Office the aforesaid yearly rent of Nine Dollars at the days and times above mentioned over and above all taxes and repairs thereon and it is hereby further covenanted and agreed by and between the parties to these presents that the said Jonas Smith his Executors Administrators and Assigns Shall be allowed to ask demand sue for recover and recieve for the use of said dock wharfage at the following rates (viz) for Shipping or putting on board Cordwood one cent pr foot to be paid equally between the owner of said wood and the Master or owners of the vessel but the Master or owners of the vessel to be responsable for the whole for shipping or landing full hogsheads six cents and for shipping or landing every tierce of salt rice flax seed (&.C) four Cents for Shipping or landing every crate of Earthan ware &.C. three cents for Shipping or landing every Barrel of liquor or provision one cent for shipping or landing every horse ox steer Cow hiefer or Bull twelve and an half cents pr head for shipping or landing 1.000 feet of Boards or plank four cents for every 1.000 feet board measure for shipping or landing every 1.000 Brick four Cents pr 1.000 for shipping or landing all other lumber not usually measurd

PAGE 337.

or bought by the foot two cents pr load to be drawn by two horses or Oxen for shipping or landing every load of Stone one Cent pr load all manures to be landed free of expence to the farmer from vessels that belong to Stoney Brook and Smithtown harbour but the vessel to pay the ordinary duties by the day all manures landed from transient or foreign vessels shall pay a sum not exceeding the following (viz) for every hundred bushel of Ashes six cents for every other kind of manure one cent pr load all vessels that belong to or are owned in Brook Haven shall be entiteled to lay along side of said dock or wharf twelve hours free of wharfage after that time the vessel that lays next to the wharf to pay twelve and an half cents pr day vessels that lay second third &.C. to pay six cents pr day all foreign or trancient vessels to pay twelve and half Cents pr day when they lay next to the wharf when second or third to pay six cents pr day the time to be computid from the arrival and making fast of such vessel to said Dock the aforesaid wharfage to be paid by the Master or Owner of Such vessel all light vessels to make way for vessels to load or unload all articles belonging to the Corporation of the town of Brook Haven for the use of the public poor to be landed free and it is hereby covenanted and mutually agreed by and between the said parties to these presents that in case the said party of the second part his Executors administrators or Assigns shall neglect or refuse to pay the aforesaid sum of Nine Dollars annually at the times above specified or when demanded after having reasonable notice for that purpose then and in such case these presents shall cease determine and be void otherwise to remain in force

PAGE 338.

in witness whereof the parties to these presents have set their hands and Seals this day above written the president of said Trustees his hand and Corporate seal of said town the second party his hand and Seal countersigned by the clerk of said town of Brook Haven
in presence of

    WM. S. WILLIAMSON president L S
    JONAS SMITH—L. S.

MORDECAI HOMAN
  town clerk

An Act for the preservation of Oysters.

 Be it ordained by the Trustees of the freeholders and

commonalty of the town of Brook Haven that if any person or persons shall take or catch any Oysters or Shells of Oysters in the South bay Belonging to said town and William Sidney Smith between the 15th. day of June and the 15th. day of September in any year shall for every offence forfiet and pay to said town the sum of twelve dollars and fifty Cents to be sued for and recovered in any Court having Cognizance thereof and applied to the use of said town done at Brook Haven this 2d. day of March 1847.

NATHANIEL TUTTLE president L. S.
attest MORDECAI HOMAN town clerk

PAGE 339.

At an Annual town Meeting held on the 6th. day of April 1847 at the house of Richard W. Smith the following town Officers were duly Elected (viz)

Thomas J Ritch Supervisor
Charles Phillips Justice of the peace
Nathaniel Tuttle President

Henry K. Townsend.
Joel Brown
Lester H. Davis
John S. Haven
Wm. C. Smith
Benjamin Guildersleve
} Trustees.

William C. Smith
Henry K. Townsend
} Overseers of the poor

Mordecai Homan town clerk
Lester Davis Collector
John Havens Assessor
William J. Weeks town superintendent of Common Schools
Nathaniel Tuttle Commissioner of highways
Lester H. Davis Sealer of weights and measures

Inspectors of Elections

1st. District
  John M. Williamson
  Henry K. townsend
  Carlton Jayne

2d. district
  John Hutchenson
  Horace Hudson
  Charles Woodhull

3d.
  William Penny 2d.
  Joel Robinson
  James M. Fanning

4th. District
  George P. Mills
  William Wickham
  William Raynor

5th.
  Nelson Norton
  Lester H. Davis
  Lewis R. Overton

Daniel Overton ⎫
William Penny 4th ⎪
Noah Overton ⎬ Constables
Elisha Norton ⎪
Briant N. Overton ⎭

George P. Mills was elected Supervisor on the 18th. May 1847 in the room of Thomas J. Ritch resigned. as a Special town Meeting
  attest M. HOMAN town clerk

PAGE 340.

OVERSEERS OF HIGHWAYS FOR 1847

District
  No. 1, Egbert Smith
  do. 2, Ebenezer Hallock
  do. 3, John Bennitt
      4, John S. Mount
      5, Floyd Smith
      6, Carlton Jayne
      7, Lewis Hulse
      8, Charles A. Hawkins ac
      9, Joel Davis

District
10, Thomas Helme
11, Noah H. Jones
12, Miller Woodhull
13, Seth Raynor
14, Mitchel Carter
15, Joshua Terrry
16, Rogers Robinson
17 Daniel Lane
18 Samuel Carman
19, John Downs ac.
20, George P. Mills a.c.
21, John Avery
22, James W. Sell appointed
23, Wm C. Smith
24, Samuel S. Hammond
25, Joseph Avery a.c.
26, Joseph Newton
27 Alfred Hawkins ac
28 Samuel A. Hawkins
29, Charles W. F. Dare
30, David Fordham ac
31, Lester H. Davis ac
32, Richard Smith pond
33, Thomas Terry
34, Jeremiah Gourden
35 Daniel L, Homedieue
36 Lester Ruland
37 Joseph Davis
38 VanRenselear Swezy
39 John Mills
40 Jehiel W. Randal
41 Job Raynor Jur
42 Caleb Hammond
43 Enos Cherry

District
44 John S. Havens
45 Jonah Turner
46 Herman Hallock
47 Elbert Woodhull
48 Elihu Hawkins

We certify the foregoing to be a true Statement of the result of the foregoing Election

M. HOMAN
town clerk

B. Woodhull ⎫ Justices
Brewster Terry ⎬ of the
Richard Robinson ⎭ peace

PAGE 341.

At a Special town Meeting held in the town of Brook Haven on the 27th. day of April 1847 for the purpose of determing by Ballot. whether there should be licence or no licence granted in this town to Sell Strong and Spirituous liquors—eight hundred and forty two vote were polled of which four hundred and fifty eight votes were given for Licence and three hundred and eighty four votes were given for no Licence

For Licence 458 ⎫ total 842
no Licence 384 ⎭

Majority for Licence -- 74

we certify the foregoing to be a true Statement and canvas of the foregoing or Special town Meeting

Attest
MORDECAI HOMAN
town clerk

Brewster Woodhull ⎫ Justices
Charles Phillips ⎭ of the peace

At a Special town Meeting held in said town of Brook Haven on the 18th day of May 1847—to Elect a Supervisor in the room of Thomas J. Ritch resignd two hundred and Seventy five votes were given of which George P. Mills received two hundred and Seventy one votes. Thomas J. Ritch received two votes Dick Smith received one vote and Dick W. Smith received one vote

George P. Mills 271. votes
Thos. J. Ritch 2. votes
Dick Smith 1. vote.
Dick W. Smith 1. vote.

total—275

We certify the foregoing to be a true Statement of the foregoing town Meeting

Attest

Charles Phillips } Justices
Brewster Terry } of the
Richard Robinson } peace

MORDECAI HOMAN town clerk

PAGE 342.

Be it Ordained by the Trustees of the freeholders and commonalty of the town of Brook Haven that the Act passed the 4th. day of May 1841. prohibiting people from dredging for Oysters in the waters of the South Bay be and is hereby repealed done at Brook Haven this 7th. day of March 1848   NATHANIEL TUTTLE President
in presence of   L. S.
MORDECAI HOMAN town clerk Copy

Be it remembered that on the 9th day of November 1847. the Trustees of the freeholders and Commonalty of the town of Brook Haven granted liberty to Charles S. Newey liberty to build and construct a Dock or railway into the south Bay against the strand of Wm. C. Smith by his consent for the term of ten years and to be 20 feet in width and to extend into the Bay six rods for and in consideration of the sum of one Dollar and fifty Cents Annually to be paid by said Charles S. Newey or hiers or assigns to the said Trustees or thier Successors in office on the first tuesday in april the first payment to be made the first tuesday in april 1848   NATHANIEL TUTTLE President
Attest MORDECAI HOMAN town clerk

PAGE 343.

At an Annual town Meeting held in the town of Brook Haven on the 4th day of April 1848. at the house of Lester H. Davis the following town officers were duly elected viz

George P. Mills Supervisor

Richard Robinson Justice of the peace

William S. Williamson President of Trustees

Isaac Davis
William Phillips
William Penny
Floyd Smith
William Hawkins
Richard Smith pond
} Trustees

Isaac Davis
Floyd Smith
} Overseer of the poor

Benjamin T. Hutchonson town clerk

Lester H. Davis Town treasurer

Lester Davis Collector

John R. Satterly Assessor

Isaac Overton Coll* commissioner of highways

William J. Weeks town Superintendent of Common Schools

Lewis R. Overton Sealer of Weights and Measures

Noah Overton
Daniel Overton
Elisha Norton
William Penny 3d.
Ebenezer Roe
} Constables

Note. * Colonel.—Com.

At said Meeting it was voted that the next Annual Town-meeting be held at the House of Lester H. Davis in Coram in this Town—

PAGE 344.

Inspectors of Elections

1st. District
John M. Williamson
Carlton Jayne
Orrin W. Rogers

2d. do
Phillip Hallock
Charles Miller
Isaac Davis

3d. do
William Penny
James M. Fanning
William Penny 3d.

4th do
Brewster Woodhull
William Beale
Albert A. Overton

5th.
Franklin Overton
Joel D. Norton
Lester Davis

Overseers of Highways

1st. District	Egbert Smith
2d.	Charles Mills
3d	Ebenezer Hawkins (ac)
4th.	William C. Tooker (ac)
5—	Floyd Smith (ac)
6—	Daniel H. Skidmore (ac)
7—	Lewis Hulse (appointed) (ac)
8—	Jonathan Pike (ac)
9	Lorenzo Davis (ac)
10	Alfred M. Davis (ac)
11	Noah H. Jones. (ac)
12	Hiram H. Noyes
13	George C. Raynor
14	Isaac Raynor
15	Edward D. Topping (ac)
16	Rogers Robinson (ac)
17	Daniel Lane

18th. District	Mordecai Overton (ac)
19	Lewis Hawkins (ac)
20,	George P. Mills (ac)
21,	Smith Roe
22	James Sell
23	Edward Mulford (ac)
24,	William Rowland (ac)
25,	Joseph Homan
26,	Joseph Newton
27,	Abram W. Roseman
28,	Samuel A. Hawkins (ac)
29,	Joel D. Norton
30,	Albert Terrell (ac)
31,	Lester H. Davis (ac)
32,	Richard Smith pond
33,	Noah T. Terry.
34,	Silvester Homan
35,	Daniel L. Homedieue
36,	Lester Ruland (ac)
37,	Gershom O. Overton (ac)
38,	Lester Homan (ac)
39,	John P. Mills
40,	Matthew Randal
41,	Job Raynor
42,	Caleb H. Hammond
43,	Edward Swezey
44,	John S. Havens
45,	Sidney Penny
46,	James Hallock
47,	Hendrickson. Hallock (ac)
48,	Elihu Hawkins.

we certify the foregoing to be the result of the said Election

Brewster Woodhull } Justices
Charles Phillips

PAGE 345.

Release of Roads at Manor Station—1848

We the subscribers do hereby release to the Town of Brookhaven all claim to damages arising from the use by the public of a private way to all persons who may travel, ride or drive thereon, which private way shall commence at the Highway north of the Manor Station and running Southerly to the Rail Road track, which said private way shall be two rods wide, that is one rod on each of us the said subscribers—Given under our hands the 24th day of June 1848—   J. G. WILBUR
In presence of   SETH RAYNOR
CHARLES PHILLIPS

Aso I the said Seth Raynor do also release to the Town of Brookhaven all claim to damages from the use by the public of a private road Commencing at the Highway adjoining the land of J. G. Wilbur, South of L. I. Rail road running westerly across the land of the said Seth Raynor—Given under my hand the 24th day of June 1848—
In presence of   SETH RAYNOR
CHARLES PHILLIPS

Recorded on the 26th day of June 1848 by me
BENJAMIN T. HUTCHINSON
Town Clerk

PAGE 346.

Highway from Manor Station Easterly—

At a meeting of the Commissioners of Highways of the Town of Brookhaven in the County of Suffolk at the house of J. G. Wilbur in said Town on the 24th day of June 1848 all the said Commissioners having met and deliberated on the subject matter of this order for the laying-out of a Highway hereafter described, and on the Certificate of twelve reputable freeholders of said Town convened and duly sworn certifying that such Highway is necessary and proper, and previous notice having been given that the Commissioners would meet at this time and place to hear all reasons offered for and against laying out such highway, and the undersigned having heard all reasons for and against the same, It is Ordered, determined and certified that a public Highway shall be and the same hereby is laid out, whereof a Survey hath been made and is as follows to wit Beginning at the Manor Station at the Rail-road passing through the lands of Seth Raynor, J. G. Wilbur, Samuel Lane, Thomas Osborn, William Terry, Stephen Turner, Gideon Robinson, George Corwin, David Robinson, Freeman & Daniel Lane, David Robinson and Lewis Gordon to the Highway near said Lewis Gordon's barn which survey shall be the centre of said highway which highway shall be three rods wide—In witness whereof we have hereunto subscribed our names this the 24th day of June 1848 —

     Chas Phillips   Commissioners
     Nathl Tuttle   of
     Isaac Overton   Highways

Recorded on the 26th June 1848
 by me
   BENJ T. HUTCHINSON
    Town Clerk

PAGE 347.

At a Meeting of the Board of Trustees of the Town of Brookhaven on the 5th day of September 1848 present Wm. S. Williamson, Floyd Smith, Wm. Phillips, William Penny, & Wm. Hawkins it was unanimously voted that the sum of fourteen hundred dollars be raised by tax for the support of the Town-poor during the coming year—

        WM. S. WILLIAMSON
Attest—   President
 B. T. HUTCHINSON
  Town Clerk—

At a Special Town-meeting held pursuant to publick Notice at the House of Lester H. Davis in the Town of Brookhaven on the 4th day of January 1849 to choose a person to fill the vacancy in the office of Trustee and Overseer of the poor caused by the death of Isaac Davis on the 20th Ult. Brewster Woodhull & Charles Phillips Justices of the peace being present presided, and Benj. T. Hutchinson Town-Clerk, acted as Clerk whereupon after canvassing the votes it was decided that Samuel Carman was chosen to fill said vacancies—

BREWSTER WOODHULL
Justice of the Peace

BENJN T. HUTCHINSON
Town-Clerk—.

PAGE 348.

At an Annual Town meeting held on the 3d day of April 1849 in the Town of Brookhaven and at the house of L. H. Davis in Coram the following officers were duly chosen viz.

Supervisor
George P. Mills

Justice
Franklin Overton—4 years

President of Trustees
Samuel Carman

Trustees

Benjamin Brewster   Horace Hudson
William Phillips   Isaac N. Gould
William Hawkins   Samuel A. Hawkins

Overseers of the Poor
Benjamin Brewster   William C. Smith

Town Clerk & Treasurer
Benjamin T. Hutchinson

Assessor
William Phillips—3 years

Collector
Floyd Smith

Town Superintendent of Schools
Lewis R. Overton

Town Sealer
Lewis R. Overton

Constables
Noah Overton   Daniel Overton
Briant N. Overton   Elisha Norton
William Penny 3d

Page 349.

Inspectors of Elections
District No. 1—
John M. Wiliamson   Floyd Smith
Carlton Jayne—apptd.

No. 2—
Smith Davis   James Hallock
Lewis Davis apptd.

No. 3
Egbert T. Smith   Joel Robinson
James M. Fanning appd

No. 4—
Isaac Overton   Brewster Terry
Moses Swezey appd—

No. 5—
William Swezey   Apollos A. Mills
Lester Davis appd

Commissioner of Highways
Phillip Hallock 3 years—

PAGE 350.

Overseers of Highways 1849—

Dis. no.	Names—	no. Dis	Names
1	Egbert Smith	25	Joseph Homan
2	Lewis Hallock	26	James Russel
3	John Bennet	27	A. Woodhull Roseman
4	Alexander Hamilton	28	Samuel A. Hawkins
5	Floyd Smith	29	James Mott
6	Amasa T. Sturtevant	30	William Fordham
7	Israel I. Davis	31	Lester H Davis
8	Charles Hawkins	32	Richard Smith
9	Parshall W Davis	33	Bradford Ruland
10	John M Brown	34	Jeremiah Gordon
11	William Horton	35	Daniel L'Hommedieu
12	Jeremiah Hummister	36	Lester Ruland
13	Jeremiah S. Wilbur	37	Joseph Davis
14	David Davis	38	Samuel F Norton
15	Solon Culver	39	John P. Mills
16	Parker S Robinson	40	Hiram Edwards
17	Jeremiah Glover	41	Stephen Turner
18	Samuel Carman	42	—Dissolved—
19	Azel Hawkins	43	Thomas J. King
20	Geo. P. Mills	44	Franklin Reeve
21	David Hedges	45	Sidney Penny
22	Daniel Overton	46	Henry C. Marther.
23	Walter Howell	47	John I. Woodhull
24	Edward Jayne	48	Elihu Hawkins

We the board of canvassers certify that the foregoing report of the result of the election at the said annual Town meeting is correct—

Brewster Woodhull } Justices
Brewster Terry

BENJN T. HUTCHINSON Clerk
Brook Haven 3d april 1849—

Page 351.

This Indenture made this third day of April One thousand eight hundred and forty nine between the Trustees of the freeholders and commonality of the Town of Brookhaven of the first part, and Willet Griffing of the same Town of the second part Witnesseth that in consideration of the hereinafter mentioned annuity the said parties of the first part have granted and do hereby grant unto the said party of the second part his heirs and assigns for the term of ten years the privilege of building and keeping a Dock for the purpose of raising and repairing vessels, on the South side of said Town at the West side of Walter Howells land in Patchogue to extend into the South Bay one hundred and fifty feet and thirty feet in width, to have until the first day of August next to build the same, and the said party of the second part hereby agrees to pay annually for the above privilege to the said Trustees or their successors the sum of two dollars per year commencing from said first day of august—In fulfillment of which covenants the parties hereby bind themselves their heirs and successors and have hereunto affixed their hands and seals the day and date above written

WM. S. WILLIAMSON President	Seal
WILLET GRIFFIN	Seal

Signed and Executed
on the part of Mr. Griffin
on the 4 day of June 1850
attest SAML. A HAWKINS Clerk

Page 352.

This Indenture made the third day of april One thousand eight hundred and forty nine between the Trustees of the freeholders and commonality of the Town of Brookhaven of the first part and William C. Smith and Walter Howell of the same Town of the second part Witnesseth that the said parties of the first part for and in Consideration of the annuities hereinafter mentioned have granted and by these presents do grant to the said parties of the second part their heirs and assigns for the term of twenty five years the privilege of building, repairing, holding and conveying a Dock on the South side of said Town, near the East side of the lane or road leading from the south country road at Patchogue to the Bay, said Dock to be fifty feet wide with the privilege to extend the same into the South Bay five hundred feet, paying for the first one hundred feet one dollar annually, for the second one hundred feet three dollars annually, and for every one hundred feet after the said two hundred feet two dollars, or in that proportion annually to have until the first day of April one thousand eight hundred and fifty to build the first part of said dock, and to pay on the 1st Tuesday in april one thousand eight hundred and fifty one for so much as may be then built and annually thereafter on said day for the same and for as much more as may be at that time added thereto, the said Trustees and their successors to have the privilege of regulating the rates and rules of wharfage and usages thereof

Page 353.

which rates and usages are at this present granting allowed to be the same as those docks on the north side of the Town so far as they agree and where they differ to be allowed the lowest rate, and all articles belonging to the Corporation of the Town of Brookhaven for the use of the public poor to be landed free, and the said parties to be allowed to charge wharfage on all articles to all other parties without exception; and the said parties of the second part do hereby agree to pay to the said Trustees or their successors the said annuity or annuities at the times they may be due according to the condition and intent of this grant, and keep said Dock in good repair for the accommodation of the public and in case any dispute shall arise in regard to the rate of wharfage, such rate shall be fixed by the Trustees according to the meaning and intent of this instrument ; and it is hereby agreed that at the expiration of said term of twenty five years, this present grant shall return to said Town and the Dock appraised by indifferent men or further arrangement or agreement made between the said parties or their successors of the first part and the said parties or their heirs or assigns of the second part—

In witness whereof the said parties have hereunto affixed their hands and seals of office binding themselves & successors on the one part and themselves, heirs and assigns on the other part the day and date above written

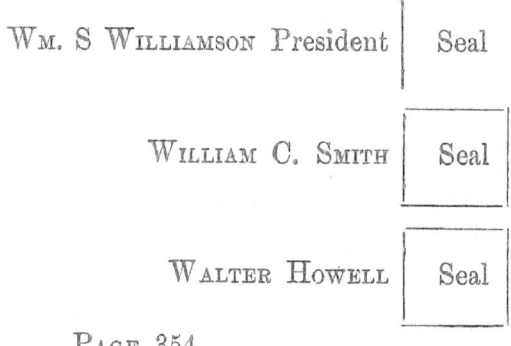

W<small>M</small>. S W<small>ILLIAMSON</small> President | Seal

W<small>ILLIAM</small> C. S<small>MITH</small> | Seal

W<small>ALTER</small> H<small>OWELL</small> | Seal

P<small>AGE</small> 354.

This Indenture made this seventh day of August 1849 between the Trustees of the Freeholders and commonalty of the Town of Brookhaven of the first part and Charles L. and James M. Bayles of the same Town of the second part, Witnesseth that whereas the said parties of the second are in lawful possession of the privileges of a rail-way at Port Jefferson granted to Robbins & Jones and recorded in this Book at page 270 which grant will expire on the 6th of

May 1855 and whereas the said parties of the second part wish to lay down new and costly ways have petitioned for a renewal to them of said lease, now then by these presents it is hereby covenanted and agreed that the said grant as above recorded with the additional privilege of extending it into the water two hundred feet instead of 130 as in the former grant, shall be and hereby is renewed or extended to the said parties of the second part for the term of Twenty years after the said 6th may 1855 to the 6th May 1875, and the said parties of the second part hereby covenant and agree to pay to the parties of the first part or their successors in office the yearly rent of Eight dollars according to the conditions of the said recorded former grant.

In witness whereof the parties have hereunto affixed their hands and seals binding the first parties and successors and the second parties and their heirs & assigns

SAMUEL CARMAN President	Seal
CHARLES L BAYLES	Seal
JAMES M BAYLES	Seal

PAGE 355.

At a meeting of the Board of Trustees of the Town of Brookhaven on the 4th day of Sept. 1849 Present Samuel Carman, Isaac Gould, Samuel A. Hawkins Benjamin Brewster, and Horace Hudson, it was resolved that whereas no vote was taken at the Town meeting to raise funds, therefore by virtue of the authority given us by our charter and in accordance with all former custom, we unanimously order that the sum of Sixteen hundred dollars be raised by

tax for the support of the Poor of this Town during the ensuing year— SAMUEL CARMAN President
BENJN T. HUTCHINSON Clerk

North Street at Patchogue

At a meeting of the Commissioners of Highways of the Town of Brook haven in the County of Suffolk it is ordered and determined by the said Commissioners that a Highway be laid out in the said Town of the width of Three rods on the application and consent of Robert Jayne Edmund Jayne, Eunice Jennings, and Mary E. Huggins, through whose improved land the said Highway is to pass—Such Highway to commence at the road leading from Patchogue to Canaan and to run thence Westerly to Patchogue Millpond, a Diagram or Survey of which is as follows—Distance from Country road 5 Ch. 75 L course N. 11° E then the Highway laid out by the Commissioners runs N. 80° W. the courses magnetic without noticing the declination— In witness whereof the undersigned Commissioners of Highways of the said Town of Brook Haven have hereto subscribed their names this 7th day of September in the year 1849—

                Nathl Tuttle } Commissioners of
                Isaac Overton }   Highways
Thomas J De Verell Surveyor

PAGE 356.

Release of the foregoing North Street, Patchogue.

We do hereby release to the Town of Brookhaven all claim to damages by reason of the laying out and opening of a Highway through our lands commencing at the Road leading from Patchogue to Canaan and running Westerly to Patchogue mill-pond, by order of the commissioners of Highways of the said Town dated the 7th day of September 1849.

In witness whereof we have hereunto set our hands and

seals this Twenty sixth day of September one thousand eight Hundred and forty nine—

Witness present
E. JOHN HUGGINS

Edmund Jayne L S
Eunice Jennings L S
Mary E. Huggins L S
Robert Jayne L S

This and the foregoing recorded by me

BENJ. T. HUTCHINSON
Clerk

This Indenture made this Fifth day of March 1850 between the Trustees of the Freeholders and Commonality of the Town of Brookhaven of the first part and Charles Homan of the Town of Islip in the County of Suffolk of the second part witnesseth that the Said party of the first part for and in consideration of the annuities hereinafter mentioned have granted and by these presents do grant to the said partie of the second part his heirs and assigns for the term of twenty years the privelage of building reparing holding and Constucting a Dock opposit his land about ten rods East of the road which starts near the house of the said Charles Homan and runs down to the Bay

PAGE 357.

Such wharf or dock to extend out into said Bay two hundred feet paying for the privelage two dollars annually to have until the first day of April One thousand Eight hundred and fifty one to pay the first annuity and annually thereafter on said day for the Same the said Trustees and their Successors to have the privilage of regulating the rates and rules of wharfage and usages thereof which rates and usages ar at this presant Granted allowed to be the same as those docks on the north side of the Town—and all articals belonging to the Corporation of the Town of Brookhaven for the use of the public poor to be landed free and the parties to be alowed to charge warfage on all articals to all other parties without Exception—and the said partie of the second part do hereby agree to pay to the said Trustees or their successors the said annuity or annuitys at the times they may be due according to the Condition and intent of this grant and keep said Dock in good repair for the accommodation of the public and in case any dispute shall arise in regard to the wharfage such rate shall be Fixed by the Trustees according to the meaning and intent of this instrument and it is hereby agreed that at the expiration of said term of twenty years this presant grant shall return to said Town and the Dock appraised by indifferant men—or further arrangement or agreement made between the said parties or their successors of the first part and the said partie or his heirs or assigns of the second part—In witness whereof the said parties have hereunto affixed their hands and seales of Office binding themselves & successors on the one part and he and his hares and assignes on the other part the day and date above written

WM. C. BOOTH	Seal
CHARLES HOMAN	Seal

Signed sealed & delivered this 4 day of June 1850
    SAMUEL A HAWKINS T. Clerk

PAGE 358.

At an annual Town meeting held on the 2nd. day of April 1850 in the Town of Brookhaven and at the house L. H. Davis in Coram the following officers were duly chosen viz

    Supervisor
    George P. Mills
   Justice of the Peace
   Brewster Woodhull

President of Trustees
William C. Booth

Trustees
Benjamin Bruster
Horace Hudson
Isaac N. Gould
Nathaniel Tuthill
Thomas J. Elison
Joel Robinson

Overseers of the Poor
William C. Booth
Horace Hudson

Town Clerk
Samuel A. Hawkins

Collector
William S. Williamson

Assessor
Moses Swezey 3 years

Commissioner of Highways
Nathaniel Tuthill 3 years

Constables
Noah Overton   Charles Hopkins
John Hawkins   William Penny 3rd.
Briant N Overton

Sealer of Weights and measures
Lewis R. Overton

PAGE 359.

Inspectors of Election
1 Dist 1 Floyd Smith
2 John M Williamson
3 John R Satterly

BROOKHAVEN TOWN RECORDS.

  2 Dist 1 James Hallock
    2 Smith Davis
    3 Walter Dickerson
  3 Dist 1 Joel Robinson
    2 John S Havens
    3 James Stephens
  4 Dist 1 James Ketchum
    2 Bruster Terry
    3 William Raynor
  5 Dist 1 Davis Norton
    2 Lester H. Davis
    3 Franklin Overton

OVERSEERS OF HIGHWAYS CHOSEN 2ND. APRIL 1850

No Dist	No
1 Edward Seabury	25 John Corey
2 Lewis Hallock	26 James Russel
3 Sylvester Hawkins	27 Joseph C Hammond
4 William C Tooker	28 William E Gould
5 Floyd Smith	29 Davis Norton
6 Amesy Sturdevan	30 John E Smith
7 Charles Jayne	31 Ham Smith
8 Henry Hawkins	32 Richerd Smith Pond
9 Lewis G Davis	33 Lhomadue Smith
10 George P Hellem	34 Hiram Overton
11 Joel Brown	35 Daniel Lhommadue
12 Henry Tuthill	36 Lester Rowland
13 Jeramiah G Wilbur	37 Joseph Davis
14 Nathan Raynor	38 Samuel F Norton
15 Solon Culver	39 Richard W Hawkins
16 Parker S Robinson	40 Jehial Randal
17 Nicol Overton	41 Lewis Gordon
18 Samuel Carman	42 —Disolved
19 Azel Hawkins	43 Thomas J King
20 Henry W Titus	44 Jefry S Hutchinson

No Dist	No
21 David Hedges	45 Jonah Turner
22 William S Preston	46 Hurman Hallock
23 Walter Howell	47 Nicolas Terril
24 William Rowland	48 Elihu Hawkins

LESTER DAVIS Town Clerk

PAGE 360.

At a meeting of the Board of Trustees of The Town of Brookhaven on the 7th day of May 1850 present Wm. C. Booth president Nathl Tuthill Isaac N Gould Horace Hudson Benjamin Brewster Thomas J. Ellison it was resolved and voted that The Overseers of Poor keep their accts Seperate from the Board of Trustees and that a Book be procured at the expence of the Town for that purpose For the ensuing year. W. C. BOOTH Prsd.

adjourned to June 4th
SAMUEL A. HAWKINS—Clerk

To the Commissioners of Highways of the Town of Brookhaven—

Your petitioner respectful represents to your Board that He is desirous of Having a private Road District set off to him for the term of three years commencg at the Harbour and running southeastly till it comes to the road leading from Millers place to Mount Sinai thence south till it comes to the road leading from Mount Sinai to Coram distance about two and three quarter Miles

Dated at Brookhaven
April 16th 1850   SAMUEL HOPKINS

We the Commissioners of Highways do grant the above application

Isaac Overton ⎱ Commissioners
Philip Hallock ⎰ of
Nathaniel Tuthill ⎱ Highways

Recorded May 7th 1850

SAML. A HAWKINS—Clerk

Page 361.

At a Meeting of the Commissioners of Highways of the Town of Brookhaven in the County of Suffolk at Patchogue in the Said Town on the 9th day of March 1850 all the said commissioners having been duly notified to attend the said Meeting for the purpose of deliberating on the subject Matter of this order I it ordered and determined by the said Commissioners upon the application and by the consent of John G. Westervelt and Epenetus Mills through whose hands the alteration hereafter described is to be made that the south country road or Highway west of little Patchogue stream in said Town be altered according to the following survey which the Commissioners Have caused to be made thereof as follows (viz) The centre line of the alteration is to begin at the centre of the present Highway opposite the northwest corner of the Land of Richerd Woodhull and to run thence south fifty five Degrees fifteen minutes West seventeen chains and Eighty links until it comes again to the centre of the present Highway opposite Homans Lane And that the Said alteration be of the width of four Rods

In Witness Whereof we have hereunto subscribed our names this 9th day of March 1850

        Isaac Overton   ) Commissioners
        Philip Hallock }   of
        Nathaniel Tuthill) Highways

Recorded 7th May 1850

                S. A HAWKINS Clerk

Page 362.

I John Wood a Justice of the Peace of the Town of Islip do certify that Henry Smith a Colored Boy the Child of Rachel Ceasar an Indian woman was in my presence and with my consent bound by Indenture dated the 28th day of March 1850 and this day duly Executed in the Town of Islip as an Apprentice to William Hawkins of the Town of

Brook-Haven and to which Indenture I Subscribed my name as a Witness
Dated the 24th day of April 1850
      JOHN WOOD Justice of the Peace

At a meeting of the Board of Trustees of the Town of Brookhaven on tuesday the 4th of June 1850 Present Wm. C. Booth President Horace Hudson Benjamin Brewster Nathaniel Tuttle Isaac N. Gould Thomas J Ellison & Joel Robinson. Voted and agreed that Dr. Brown be employed as Alms House Physician to be allowed five Shillings per. Visit—On application of Mr. H. Marvin for the priviledge of making a Break Water on his own land Nathl. Tuttle and Thomas J. Ellison was chosen a committee to view the premises and report at next Meeting at the Expense of Mr. Marvin adjourned to 6th Aug. next—
          W. C. BOOTH Prest.
SAMUEL A. HAWKINS Clerk

PAGE 363.

At a meeting of the Commissioners of Highways of the Town of Brook haven in the county of Suffolk at the village of Patchogue in the said Town on the Eighteenth day of May 1849 upon the application of William Hawkins and Joseph C. Chadeayne of the Said Town for the alteration of the road or Highway in the said village called South Street adjoining the lands of the said William Hawkins and Joseph C. Chadeayne The said Commissioners having examined the same and a diagram &c thereof being made It is ordered and determined by the said commissioners that all that part of the Said street opposite the dwelling House of the said Joseph C. Chadeayne measuring the distance of Four Rods westerly from the west boundary line of the land of Hiram Gerard be and the same is hereby discontinued and that the land included therein belong to the said William Hawkins and it is further ordered that in lieu thereof the said Street shall turn nearly at a right angle the easterly margin thereof running southerly four rods distant from and parallel with the said westerly boundary line of the land of Hiram Gerard about one Hundred and Seventy feet then turning at nearly a right angle and uniting with the north margin of the continuation of South street aforesaid between the lands of Hiram Gerard and Daniel G Gerard the said new road being three rods wide and is laid out over land of the said William Hawkins with his consent

Nathaniel Tuttle } Commissioners
Isaac Overton } of Highways

Page 364.

We William Hawkins and Joseph C. Chadeayne do hereby consent to the alteration of the road as mentioned in the annexed order of the Commissioners of Highways and Diagram endorsed thereon and We do respectively release all right and Claim for damages arising from such alteration and from laying out the new road as therein mentioned Dated May 18th day 1849 Witness present William Hawkins Wm. Wickham Jun Joseph C. Chadeayne

At a meeting of the Trustees of the freeholders and commonalty of the Town of Brookhaven held the 6th day of August 1850 Austin Roe made application for the privilege of Building a Dock in the south Bay on his own land after due consideration had in the premises did grant to said Austin Roe the right and privilege to build a Dock as aforesaid—On application also of Mary Smith for the right and privilege of extension of limits of the dock granted to Smith and Darling A D 1834 She claiming lawful possession of the same after due consideration did Grant her the privilege to extend the same as in the indenture will more fully appear the Board agreed also that public notice be given enforceing the Oyster act passed 1847 Voted and agreed

unanimously that Sixteen hundred Dollars be raised for the poor of this Town the ensuing Year
adjourned to 2d. tuesday in Oct. next

SAMUEL A. HAWKINS Clerk

W. C. BOOTH Prest.

PAGE 365.

Whereas differences have arisen betwixt the Trustees of the Town of Brookhaven the party of the one part and Raynor & Post & Hammond Marvin the parties of the Second part respecting the Southern boundary of the lanes of the said party of the second part lying on the south bay between Bellport Lane and George Brown,s Lane and whereas on or about the 4th of June 1850 the said Trustees for adjusting and settling said Differences did appoint and depute Thomas J. Ellison and Nathaniel Tuttle two of the members of the Board to meet with the said party of the second part for the purpose of peaceably and amicably settling and adjusting all differences and disputes respecting said boundary & Whereas the said Thomas J. Ellison and Nathaniel Tuttle accepted said appointment Now know all men that the said Thomas J Ellison and Nathaniel Tuttle appointees as aforesaid of the one part & the said Raynor & post and Hammond Marvin of the other part have agreed decided and determined and by these presents do agree decide and Determine that from the north side of the twenty foot lane or road leading from Bellport lane said George Brown's lane the Lands of Raynor & Post adjoint to Bellport lane shall extend south 240 feet and that the said raynor and Post,s lands on the east side and adjoining the land of Hammond Marvin shall extend south 179 feet and that Hammond Marvin land on the east and adjoining the lane called G. Brown's lane shall extend south 124 feet & that all to the south of those three several points shall be and remain as the South Bay & property of the Town of

Brookhaven. signed & sealed by the s,d parties in the Town of Brookhaven June 8th 1850

In presence of

Thomas J. Ellison
Nathaniel Tuttle
Raynor & Post
Hammond Marvin

Recorded the 7th Aug. 1850
by me S. A. HAWKINS. T. Clerk

PAGE 366.

This Indenture made this sixth day of August in the year of Our Lord one thousand eight hundred and fifty. Between the Trustees of the freeholders and commonalty of the Town of Brookhaven and Mary Smith of the same Town of the second part Witnesseth that Whereas the said party of the second part is in lawful possession of the privilege of a Dock or wharf on the west side of Drown Meadow Bay (now called Port Jefferson) granted to Smith and Darling on the 4th day of September one thousand eight hundred and thirty eight and recorded in Liber D. page 312—And whereas the said party of the second part desirous to enlarge said Dock has made application for Liberty to enlarge and extend the same. Now then by these presents it is hereby covenanted and agreed with the said party of the Second part that said dock or wharf be enlarged and extended forty feet farther into the Bay with the additional annuity of one Dollar a

PAGE 367.

year This grant of extension of limits to continue and expire with the said former grant and the said party of the second part does hereby covenant and agree to pay to the parties of the first part or their Successors in office the yearly rent of one dollar in addition to the sum specified and paid in the former grant—And also by request it is hereby covenanted and agreed that the said party of the second part have liberty to occupy and have the privilege of occupying one hundred feet on shore south of said former grant for laying timber lumber railways &c so as not to interfere and with this express provision that it does not interfere or obstruct the road or passway on shore for teams carriages &c In Witness whereof the parties have hereunto affixed their hands and seals binding the first parties and their successors and the second party and their heirs and assigns during the continuence of this grant

      WM. C. BOOTH President L S
      MARY SMITH   L S
   In presence of SAMUEL A. HAWKINS
           Town Clerk

PAGE 368.

At a meeting of the Board of Trustees of the freeholders and commonalty of the Town of Brookhaven on Tuesday the 8th day of October 1850 The Trustees all present—in the case of the Colored Boy George W. at Richard Corwins Mr Corwin claiming the right to the Boy by Indenture according to an agreement with the overseers of the poor at the time the Boy was a pauper for some cause it was defered The Boy has since been Indentured by the Mother to Austin Roe Mr Roe claiming the right to the said boy by Indenture on the ground that the boy was not a pauper at the time and therefore was not under the controle of the overseers

The Board concluded to defer the matter until next meeting to assertain the Legality of the Indenture &c adjourned until the first tuesday of Dec. next at 9 oclock A.M
          W C BOOTH Prest
SAMUEL A. HAWKINS Clerk

PAGE 369.

At a meeting of the Commissioners of Highways of the Town of Brookhaven in the County of Suffolk at Fireplace in said Town on the twenty Seventh day of May 1850 all the said Commissioners being present at said meeting for the purpose of deliberating on the subject matter of this order It is ordered and determined by the said Commissioners upon the application and consent of Silas Homan & Charles Homan through whose lands the alteration hereafter described is to be made that the South Country road or Highway leading from Carmans Mills to Fireplace neck be so altered from the southwest corner of the land of Silas Homan easterly till it comes opposite the northwest corner of the land of Gilbert Miller That the north side of said Highway shall be where and as the fence now stands In Witness whereof we have hereunto subscribed our names this 27th day of May 1850

      Isaac Overton) Commissioners
      Phillip Hallock   } of
      Nathaniel Tuttle) Highways

Recorded on the 7th Dec. 1850
 by me SAML. A. HAWKINS Town Clerk

PAGE 370.

At a meeting of the Board of Trustees of the Freeholders and Commonalty of the Town of Brookhaven on tuesday the day of Dec. 1850 the Board all present the Board decided that the Overseers of the poor had no right to interfere with the Colored boy George W. Indentured to Austin Roe by his Mother as he was not a pauper at the time. adjourned to the 14th day of Jan. next at 9 oclock A.M   WM. C. BOOTH President
 SAMUEL A. HAWKINS Clerk

A dispute having arisen between David Smalling and Uriah Smith concerning the proportion of the division fence to be maintained or made by them respectively between their adjoining lands which fence commences at the northeast corner of the land of Coleman N. Smith and runs thence northerly the distance of 4 Chains & 75 links and the undersigned Isaac Overton a Commissioner of Highways and Moses Swezey an Assessor of the Town of Brookhaven having been selected to act as fence viewers in the said matter and having examined the premises and heard the alligations of the parties do order and decide that the said Uriah Smith shall make & maintain the south half of the said fence commencing at the northeast corner of Coleman N. Smith's land and running thence northerly two chains and thirty seven and half links to a ceder tree marked and the said David Smalling shall make and maintain the north half of Said fence commencing at the said Cedar

PAGE 371.

tree and running thence northerly two chains and thirty seven and a half links—Dated June 14th 1850

Isaac Overton } Fence
Moses Swezey } Viewers

Pursuant to adjournment the Board of Trustees of the freeholders and commonalty of the Town of Brookhaven met at the house of Lester H. Davis on the 14th day Jan. 1851 all the Board present it was agreed and voted that the Oyster act passed the 2.d day of March 1847 be so amended as to read as follows viz. that if any person or persons shall take or catch any Oysters or Shells of Oysters in the South Bay belonging to Said Town and Wm. Sidney Smith between the 15th day of June and the 1st day of September in any year shall forfeit and pay the said Town the sum of twelve Dollars & fifty cent &c On the Petition of John C. Mather & Thomas B. Hawkins for a grant and the privilege of building a Stone wall opposite their land The Board voted and agreed that their request be granted commencing from the dock granted to Wm L. Jones Nov. 1837 and extending east or northeasterly on shore at low water mark 180 feet at the yearly rent of five Dollars a year.

on the petition of Ahirah Hawkins & Wm. Darling for a grant to erect or build a Dock or wharf at Port Jefferson opposite their own land The Board granted them the privilege to erect a Dock 40 feet in width on shore and 150 feet out into the Bay for the term of 20 years at 3 Dollars annuity per year &c. also on

Page 372.

the petition of a large and respectable number of Inhabitants on the south side of the Town asking for a law to be passed prohibiting the dredging or Draging for Oysters in the south Bay belonging to the Town and Wm Sidney Smith the Board unanimously determined and Enacted as follows viz. That no person or persons shall after the 1st day of Feb 1851 dredge or drag for Oysters in the waters of this Town under the penalty of 50 Dollars the complainer to be entitled to one half upon condition he be at one half the expence or cost of the suit also that six notices be posted up at different places on the south side of the Town to give notice thereof—also A petition was presented by a large number of Subscribers praying for an allotment of the north side of the Bay for laying down Oysters Viz from Bluepoint to Howell point from 3 feet to 6 feet water or outer Bar also the beach flatts viz in 2 acre lots for 10 years and that no Individual lease more than one lot each at a yearly rent to be paid in advance decided that this petition lay over to next meeting Board decided that Mr. Booth be orthorised to hire out the right and privilege of Oystering in the west Bay for the ensuing year at not less than 150 Dollars reserving the Beach

Page 373.

flatts and the north side of said Bay from Blue point to Howells point for the uses and purposes above mentioned and that the Clerk give notice by posting Notices at 6 or 7

public places on the South side of Town—Board decided that Mrs Horton be furnished with a sum of money sufficient to convey her to the city of new York—Adjourned to meet at Patchogue at the Inn of Austin Roe's on Saturday the 25th Jan. 1851   W C Booth. Prst Trustees
Sam. A. Hawkins T. Clerk.

This Indenture made the sixth day of August one thousand eight hundred and fifty Between the Trustees of the freeholders and commonalty of the town of Brookhaven of the first part and Austin Roe of the Same town of the second part Witnesseth that the said parties of the first part for and in consideration of the annuities hereinafter mentioned Have granted and by these presents do grant to the said party of the second part his heirs and Assigns for the term of Twenty five years the privilege of building repairing holding and conveying a Dock or wharf on the south side of said Town opposite his own land on the west side of the lane or road leading from the south country road at Patchogue to the Bay said dock to be thirty feet wide and to extend out into the Bay at right angles One hundred and fifty feet paying for the privilege two dollars annually the first payment in advance on the day of the date hereof and

Page 374.

annually and every year thereafter the like sum of two dollars during the term of time specified in this grant The Trustees and their successors to have the privilege of regulating the rates and rules of wharfage and usages thereof which rates and usages are at this present granting allowed to be the same as those Docks on the north side of the town and all articles belonging to the corporation of the town of Brookhaven for the use of the public poor to be landed free and the parties to be allowed to charge wharfage on all articles to all other parties without exception and the said party of the second part does hereby agree to pay to the said Trustees or their successors the said annuity at the times they may be due according to the conditions and intent of this Grant and keep said Dock in good repair for the accommodation of the public and in case any dispute shall arise in regard to the wharfage such rates shall be fixed or regulated by the Trustees according to the meaning and intent of this instrument and it is hereby agreed that at the expiration of said term of twenty five years this present grant shall return to said Town and the Dock appraised by indifferent men or further arrangements or agreement made between the said parties or their successors of the first part and the said party or his heirs and assigns of the second part—

In witness whereof the said parties have hereunto affixed their hands and seals of Office binding themselves and their successors on the one part and himself his heirs and assigns

PAGE 375.

on the other part the day and date above written

      W<small>M</small>. C. B<small>OOTH</small> President L S
       A<small>USTIN</small> R<small>OE</small>   L S

Signed sealed and Delivered this 6th. day of August 1850 in presence of

S<small>AMUEL</small> A. H<small>AWKINS</small> Town Clerk

at a special meeting of the Board of Trustees of the Town of Brookhaven held at the Inn of Austin Roe in Patchogue the Board took into consideration the Petition presented at the last meeting in relation to the allotment of a portion of the west Bay for planting oysters for a number of years and decided by vote that the north part of said Bay from 3 to 6 feet water or outer Bar extending from Blue point to Howells Point also the Beach flats be laid out in two acre lots for the above purpose and leased for five years at two Dollars per Year paid in advance if not paid in advance to revert Back to the Town and that no individual lease but one lot As the petitioners have formed themselves into associations the Board decided to lease to the foreman of Each association as many lots as will be sufficient to supply each member with one lot each The Trustees reserving to all the right and privilege of driving into the Bay for loading or unloading any vessel or vessels &c as formerly decided that Wm C. Booth and T. J. Ellison be a committee under the counsel of Mr.

PAGE 376.

Wm. Wickham to make a survey and an allotment of said leased premises The right and privilege of Oystering in the west Bay in Partnership with this Town and Wm. Sidney Smith for the ensuing year exclusive of the reservations was leased to Austin Roe for 210 Dollars commencing on the first of Feb. 1851

Adjourned to meet at Lester H. Davis in Coram on tuesday the 4th day of March next. This Jan. 25th 1851—

W. C. BOOTH Prst Trustees

SAMUEL A. HAWKINS Town Clerk

Pursuant to adjournment the Board of Trustees of the freeholders and commonalty of the Town of Brookhaven Met at the House of Lester H. Davis in Coram on the 4th March 1851 Present the whole Board viz Wm. C. Booth Horace Hudson I. N. Gould T. J. Ellison B. Brewster J. Robinson N Tuttle a Bill was presented by David Smalling in behalf of his son a Lunatic at Utica laid over to next meeting A petition was presented by Jeremiah Darling and Edward Bedell for a Dock at Port Jefferson 40 feet wide and 150 feet into the Bay together with an abutment Their request was granted at the yearly rent of Five Dollars

PAGE 377.

a year for the term of 25 years an account was presented by Richard Corwin for keeping a colored Boy G. W. laid on the Table until next meeting Adjourned until the first day of April next at 9 oclock A M at Lester H. Davis

        W. C. Booth Prst Trustees
Samuel A. Hawkins
 Town Clerk

Survey of Slipery lane by request of the Commissioners of Highways for the Town of Brookhaven made on the 26th day of June 1850

   Present—Isaac Overton ⎫
       Nathaniel Tuttle ⎬ Commissioners
       Phillip Hallock ⎭

Started at a locust stake on the south side of the Country road about the middle of the entrance of Slippery lane road called water Street and ran South 14° 15′ East (Magnetic) 33 Ch 90 Links till opposite a white oak tree near Edward Mulfords fence and a little to the north of Wm C. Smith House then South fourteen Degrees East 6 Ch 25 Links till opposite Wm. C Smith's Southwest corner adjoining John Priors north west corner then south 12° 45′ East 8 Ch 38 links till opposite Lewis Bakers southwest corner then continuing same course 10 ch 9 Links till opposite Austin Roe's Northwest corner then continuing same course 5 Ch till opposite the line between Abiathar Petty & John W Underwood and then south 10° East 2 chains till opposite Austin Roe's southeast corner—Let this be the centre of Slippery Lane and the Side lines to be parallel fifteen feet Each way of this centre line

       B. Woodhull. Surveyor

Page 378.

Pursuant to Adjournment the Board of Trustees of the freeholders and commonalty of the Town of Brookhaven met at Lester H. Davis on the first day of April A.D. 1851 Present Wm. C. Booth, Isaac N. Gould Horace Hudson Nathaniel Tuttle Benjamin Brewster The Bill of David

Smalling in Behalf of his son a Lunatic was reconsidered and the Board decided to refer the matter to the new board of Trustees for the ensuing year

The Bill presented by Richard Corwin was reconsidered & the Board decided that they should not pay the Bill the board decided that in case of further action of the Legislature of this state concerning the Oystering in Suffolk County that the President of the Board of Trustees be authorised to remonstrate against said action

W C. BOOTH Prest.

SAML. A HAWKINS
Town Clerk

PAGE 379.

At an annual Town Meeting held on the first day of April 1851 in the Town of Brookhaven at the House of Leste H. Davis in Coram the following officers were duly Elec t & chosen for Said Town Viz.

Supervisor
George P. Mills

Justices
Jesse W. Pelletreau To fill vacancy
Charles Phillips—4 years

President of Trustees
William C. Booth

Trustees
Lewis Davis
Benjamin Brewster
Richard Smith
Silas Carter
Thomas J. Ellison
John S. Havens

Overseers of Poor
Lewis Davis and Thomas J. Ellison

Town Clerk
Samuel A. Hawkins

Commissioner of Highways
Isaac Overton—3 years

Town Superintendent of common Schools
Lewis R. Overton—2 years

Assessor
John R. Satterly—3 years

Collector
William S. Williamson

Sealer of Weights & Measures
Jarvis Thurber

Constables
Noah Overton

PAGE 380.

John Hawkins
Wm Penny—3d
Briant N. Overton
Charles Hopkins

Inspectors of Elections

1st District { Carlton Jayne
John M. Williamson
Z. F. Hawkins

2d District { Phillip Hallock
Charles Woodhull
Noah H. Jones

3d District { Jacob H. Miller
Edward D. Topping
John S. Havens

4th District { Joseph B. Wilcox
William Wickham Jur
Smith L. Newins

5th District { Nathaniel Tuttle
Franklin Overton
Davis Norton

We the undersigned certify the foregoing is the true result of the annual Town Election held this 1st. day of April 1851 in the Town of Brookhaven

Brewster Woodhull } Justices
Franklin Overton } of Peace

PAGE 381.

OVERSEERS OF HIGHWAYS A.D 1851

District.
no.

1 Richard N. Smith
2 Charles Mills
3 Charles Smith
4 Wickham Wheeler
6 Alfred Darling
7 Buel Randall
8 Smith Davis
9 James W. Davis
10 James Brown
11 Isaac W. Brown
12 Henry Tuttle
13 Seth Raynor
14 David C. Davis
15 Solon Culver
16 Joseph Dayton
17 Nicol Overton
18 Samuel Carman
19 Timothy Ketcham
20 Henry W. Titus
21 David Hedges
22 Daniel Overton
23 John W. Underwood
24 Benjamin Wicks Sen.
25 Garret A. Westervelt
26 Richard Davis
27 John F. Hallock
28 Richard O. Howell
29 Joel D. Norton
30 Lewis R. Overton
31 Alfred Davis
32 Richard Smith
33 Ebenezer Terry
34 Hiram Overton
35 Franklin Overton
36 Lester Ruland
37 Joseph Davis
38 Saml. F. Norton
39 Edmund T. Hawkins
40 Hiram Edwards
41 Christopher Robinson
42 —Disolved—
43 James Swezey
44 Jeffrey S. Hutchinson
45 Jonah Turner
46 James Hallock
47 Nicolas Terrill
48 John Dolon

We certify that the above is a true result of the overseers of Highways chosen at an annual Election held the 1st day of April A D 1851

B. Woodhull } Justices
Franklin Overton

Page 382.

This Indenture made the fourth day of March one thousand Eight hundred and fifty one Between the Trustees of the freeholders and commonalty of the Town of Brookhaven of the first part and Jeremiah Darling and Edward Bedell of the same Town of the second part Witnesseth that the said parties of the first part for and in consideration of the annuities hereinafter mentioned have granted and by these presents do grant to the said parties of the second part their heirs and assigns for the term of Twenty five years the privilege of building repairing holding and conveying a Dock or wharf on the north side of said Town at the head of Port Jefferson Bay opposite their own land said Dock not to exceed forty feet in width with the privilege of extending the same into the Bay one hundred and fifty feet said Dock to extend out into the Bay the same course as Bayles Dock together with an Abuttment from said Dock westerly to meet the abuttment of Bayles Dock which is about 190 feet paying for the privilege five Dollars annually to have until the fourth day of Mar. 1852 to pay the first annuity and

Page 383.

annually thereafter on said day for the same the said Trustees and their successors to have the privilege of Regulating the rates and rules of wharfage and usages thereof which rates and usages are at this present granting allowed to be the same as those docks on the north side of the Town so far as they agree and where they differ to be allowed the lowest rate and all Articles belonging to the corporation of the Town of Brookhaven for the use of the public poor to be landed free and the said parties to be allowed to charge wharfage on all articles to all other parties without exception and the said parties of the second part do hereby agree to pay to the said Trustees or their successors the said annuity or annuities at the time they may be due according to the conditions and Intent of this Grant and keep said Dock in good repair for the accommodation of the public and in case any dispute shall arise in regard to the rates of wharfage such rates shall be fixed by the Trustees according to the meaning and Intent of this Instrument and it is

PAGE 384.

hereby agreed that at the expiration of said term of Twenty five years this present Grant shall return to said Town and the Dock appraised by Indifferent men or further arrangement or agreement made between the said parties or their successors of the first part and the said parties or their heirs or assigns of the second part—In witness whereof the said parties have hereunto affixed their hands and seals of office binding themselves and successors on the one part and themselves their heirs and assigns on other part the day and date above written

Signed sealed and Delivered
in presence of
SAMUEL A. HAWKINS
Town Clerk

W<small>M</small> C. BOOTH L S
President Trustees
JEREMIAH DARLING L S
EDWARD BEDELL L S

PAGE 385.

This Indenture made the fourteenth day of January one thousand Eight hundred and fifty one Between The Trustees of the Freeholders and commonalty of the Town of Brookhaven of the first part and Ahirah Hawkins and William Darling of the same Town of the second part Witnesseth that the said parties of the first part for and in consideration of the annuities hereinafter mentioned have granted and by these presents do grant to the said parties of the second part their heirs and assigns for the term of Twenty years the privilege of building constructing repairing holding and conveying a private Dock or wharf on the north side of said Town on the east side of Port Jefferson Bay opposite their own land said Dock not to exceed forty feet in width with the privilege of extending the same into the Bay one hundred and fifty feet from common high water mark paying for the privilege three Dollars annually to have until the fourteeneth day of Jan. 1852 to pay the first annuity and annually thereafter on said

PAGE 386.

day for the same. and all articles belonging to the corporation of the Town of Brookhaven for the use of the public poor to be landed thereon if necessary and the said parties of the second part do hereby agree to pay to the said Trustees or their successors the said annuity or annuities at the time they may be due according to the condition and Intent of this Grant and it is hereby agreed that at the expiration of said term of Twenty years this present Grant shall return to said Town and the Dock appraised by Indifferent men or further arrangment or agreement made between the said parties or their successors of the first part and the said parties or their heirs or assigns of the second part.

In Witness whereof the said parties have hereunto affixed their hands and seals of office binding themselves and successors on the one part and themselves their heirs and assigns on the other part the day and date above written

L. S
W_M C. BOOTH President
AHIRAH HAWKINS L S
W_M. DARLING L S

Signed sealed and Delivered in presence of
SAMUEL A HAWKINS
Town Clerk

PAGE 387.

Know all men by these presents that I Nelson Terry of the Town of Brookhaven County of Suffolk and State of New York of the first part for and in consideration of the sum of five hundred Dollars lawfull money of the United States to me paid by W. Carman Terry of said Town County and State aforesaid of the second part the receipt whereof is hereby acknowledged have Bargained and sold and by these presents do grant & convey unto the said party of the second part his heirs executors administrators and assigns four Acres of corn one and half acres potatoes 2 Acres of oats ten acres of English Grass five Beds and the Bedding two Doz Winsor and wood bottom chairs five Looking Glasses five wash and candle stands two Ingrain carpets one Rag carpet five window Shades bar fixtures and clock stove in Bar Room four dining Tables one Bureau two long tables and four Benches one Rocking chair now in my possession to have and to hold unto the said party of the second part his executors administrators and assigns and I do for my self. my heirs Executors administrators and assigns covenant and agree to and with the said party of the second part his executors administrators and assigns to Warrant and defend the sale of said property goods and chattels hereby made unto the party of the second part his executors administrators

PAGE 388.

and assigns against all and every person and persons whomsoever

In Witness whereof I have hereunto set my hand and Seal this 19th day of May 1851

NELSON TERRY L S

Signed sealed & delivered in presence of
J. W. PELLETREAU

Suffolk county SS }
Town of Brookhaven }

On the 19th day of May 1851 personally came before me Nelson Terry to me known to be the person who executed the within conveyance and acknowledged that he executed the same for the purposes therein mentioned

J. W. PELLETRAU Justice of the peace

Recorded 19th day of May 1851
per SAML. A. HAWKINS Town clerk

PAGE 389.

At a meeting of the Board of Trustees of the freeholders and commonalty of the Town of Brookhaven on the 6th May 1851 Present Wm C. Booth Benjn. Brewster Richd. Smith John S. Havens Lewis Davis Silas Carter In the case of David Smalling in relation to his Son a lunatic the Board decided that Mr Smalling,s proper course of proceeding would be to Make application to Judge Rose &c

on application of Edmund T. Darling to lease a piece of land at the head of Port Jefferson Bay for the Erection of a Boat Builders Shop resolved that Benjamin Brewster and Lewis Davis be a committee to view the premises and report at next Meeting By the request of Capt. Henry Tyler In relation to the shore at Setauket Harbor and privileges thereof Benjn. Brewster and Lewis Davis was appointed a committee to view the premises and report at next meeting

resolved that Dr. Brown be employed as almshouse Physician for the present year at the stipulated sum of 5 shilling per visit.

In consequence of the refusal of Austin Roe to Execute an Indenture and fulfill his engagements in relation to the Oystering Privileges of the West Bay the Board resolved that

PAGE 390.

two Individuals viz Smith L Newins and Nelson Daines be appointed as toleration men to take charge of the Oystering privileges of the west Bay as agents for the Town the present year ending on the last day of Jan. 1852 and that they be authorised and empowered to rent to all applicants entitled thereto the privilege of Oystering the present year at the following rates (viz) for each Individual one Dollar if paid by 15th June if not $1.25 for Spring or fall season .75 cts and that they as agents be allowed a reasonable compensation for their services The Trustees reserving to the Town all west of Blue point to the line Established by Commissioners of the Towns of Brookhaven and Huntington from low water mark to about 6 feet water or outer Bar and from Howells point east to Wm Smith line from low water mark also to 6 feet water or outer Bar for the purpose of Planting of Oysters and that a committe be appointed viz. Wm C. Booth to cause immediate Surveys of the premises for that pursose and that the Clerk notify the above named agents and cause public notice to be given of the above resolution adjourned to first Tuesday in June next at 9 oclock

Signed W. C. BOOTH Prest
   SAML A. HAWKINS
    Town Clerk—

PAGE 391.

Application to me having been made by the Trustees and Inhabitants of School District no 26 in the Town of Brookhaven for the better organization of School therein & the greater convenience of the Inhabitants of Said District to alter the same

It is hereby resolved and ordered that the south portion of Said District no. 26 be set off into a seperate district and shall embrace all that part of said District south of the line dividing the lands of Austin Roe from those of Edward Mulford on the west side of Patchogue lane and south of the northern line of Jacob Hortons land on the east side of

said lane which sd. new District shall hereafter be known as School District no. 35 in said Town It is also further resolved and directed that the northern portion of said district heretofore known as 26 be and is hereby set off into a new district to be known as district 36 and shall be bounded South by the south line of Austin Roes Akerly farm running from coram road to patchogue stream thence to Palace Brook (so called) thence running north from the head of said Brook to L. I. Railroad which shall constitute its north boundary thence running from Said Rail Road on the road leading from Medford station to Patchogue to south line of Austin Roe's said land but so varying as to include the whole farm of Jesse Haff the central dstrict lying between the two said new districts 35 and 36 shall As heretofore be known as dist. no. 26 L. R. Overton Town Supt
com. Schools for Brookhaven

Dated at coram
26 May 1851

Page 392.

To the Commissioners of Highways of the Town of Brookhaven in the County of Suffolk—

The subscribers owning lands in said Town and liable to be assessed for highway labor therein hereby apply to the said commissioners of highways to Lay out a new Road cammencing at the Bellport road where the same intersexts the head of the neck line and running northerly a distance of about four miles to Tookers turnout on the Long Island Rail Road which proposed road will pass through our wild unimproved lands

Now therefore in Consideration of the Laying out and opening said road or highway we the Subscribers do hereby release all claim to damages by reason thereof

Sealed with our seals and dated this Second day of May Eighteen hundred and fifty one 1851

                    Hiram Post   (L S)
                    Nathan Post.   (L S)
                    Charles Rider   (L S)
                    Saml. Tooker   (L S)
                    Geo. P. Mills   (L S)
                    Thomas Bell   (L S)
                    William Beale   (L S)
                    Walter Howell Executor (L S)
                for the Estate of Wm. Howell (L S)
                    Lester Roe   (L S)
                    Peter Daines   (L S)
                    William Smith   (L S)
Recorded by me.
    SAMUEL A. HAWKINS Town clerk

PAGE 393.

We the undersigned Commissioners of Highways of the Town of Brookhaven in the County of Suffolk having met at the Store of William Raynor's in Said Town to decide on the application of Samuel Tooker and others residents of Said Town liable to be assessed for highway Labor therein for the laying out of the road hereinafter described twelve reputable freeholders of Said Town having certified on oath that Such highway is necessary and proper. do order that a public Highway three Rods wide Shall be and the same is hereby laid out pursuant to the said application the centre whereof is the following described line Commencing where the Bellport Road Intersects the head of the neck line and from thence running north seven Degrees west the distance of about four Miles on a direct line to Tooker's turnout on the Long Island Rail Road
Dated at Brookhaven
    this 19th day of May 1851

            Isaac Overton   ) Commissioners
            Nathaniel Tuttle }   of
            Philip Hallock   ) highways.

Page 394.

Whereas application has been made to the Commissioners of Highways of the Town of Brookhaven in the county of Suffolk to lay out a highway in said Town beginning at the head of the neck on the Bellport Dock Road and running from thence north seven degrees west to Tookers turnout on the Long Island Rail Road which prosed highway will Pass through our unimproved lands—Now therefore in consideration of the sum of Forty three Dollars to us in hand paid We do hereby release all claim to damages by reason thereof

Sealed with our seals and dated this nineteenth day of May Eighteen hundred and fifty one 1851

In presence of   Selah Hawkins (L. S.)
Wm. Raynor.   Elias Floyd   (L. S.)
                        her
                     Julia × Floyd (L. S.)
                        mark

Page 395.

at a meeting of the Board of Trustees of the freeholders & commonalty of the Town of Brookhaven on the 3d June 1851 Present Wm. C. Booth John S Havens Benjamin Brewster Thomas J. Ellison Lewis Davis Silas Carter

on motion it was agreed and voted to assist George a colored man at Patchogue to 3 Shilling per week until next meeting of the Board

on motion it was agreed and voted that Wm. C. Booth be authorised to sell the Grass on the Islands in the west Bay—On application of Vincent Dickerson and Minor Dickerson for a grant for 150 feet of Old field Beach to be occupied by them as a ship yard or laying of timber &c for vessel building B. Brewster was appointed to contract with them for 2 Dollars a year &c on motion the Board decided that all lots Leased in the Great west Bay for the planting of Oysters hereafter be leased for the term of five years. In relation to the petition of Edmund T Darling for the privilege of Erecting a Boat Builders Shop at the head of Port Jefferson Bay the Board voted and agreed to lease to the said E. T Darling for the term of 25 years the following described piece or premises viz commencing at the west line of Wm. L Jones or 22 feet west of small Dock which is west of the Railways of T. B. Hawkins and running westerly 75 feet and northerly into the Bay 100 feet from a certain Stone wall at the yearly

Page 396.

annuity of 4 Dollars,—on motion Wm. C. Booth was appointed a committee to proceed to the Sale of the Grass on the Islands of Fiddleton &c as usual and with the assistance of T. J. Ellison to consult Counsel in relation to the points of Law respecting Islands where the tide Ebbs and flows &c on complaint of Isaac L. Jones in behalf of Mary Smith complaining of obstructions near and about her Dock Such as stones &c Wm. C. Booth was appointed a Committe to view premises and report at next meeting—In relation to the Complaint of Capt Henry Tylar the Board appointed William C. Booth and authorised him to cause personal notice to be served on all or any that may have obstructed the Shore in and about Setauket Harbor and have the obstructions removed—By request of Capt C. D Hallock for an addition to the wharfage of vessels lying at his Dock &c it was agreed and voted that the sd. C. D. Hallock shall charge for every vessel of 50 Tons or under $12\frac{1}{2}$ cts per day for all vessels over 50 T. and under 100—$18\frac{3}{4}$ cts and so at the rate of $6\frac{1}{4}$ cts for every additional 50 Tons and for all Steam Boats 50 cts per Day and the sd Steam Boats be allowed to load or unload all articles that may be necessary without any additional charge—this ordinance to take effect the 3d June 1851 Board decided that 1 S per. week be added to the pension of Polly Gould adjourned to 1st tuesday Aug. next   W. C Booth Pres. Trustees.
  S. A. Hawkins Town clerk

Benjamin Brewster was appointed a committe to view the condition limits & Bounds of Wm L. Jones Dock &c and report at next meeting

Page 397.

South country Road

Diagram of the highway laid out by the commissioners on the Seventh day of Nov. 1844 Commencing at the South Country Road adjoining the Parish Ground of the Union Church* on the west and running the following courses

	Deg.	Ch.	Links	
Viz.	N 10 E.	1.	50	
	N. 1. E	10.	30	* Presbyterian Church
	N. 5 W.	3.	74	in Moriches.
	N. 2½ E.	5.	00	

And so on northerly as the Road now Runs to Dungans Line

Charles Phillips ⎫ Commissioners
John S. Havens ⎬ of
Nathaniel Tuttle ⎭ Highways

Recorded Aug. 5th 1851 in Liber D page 397
In Town Clerks office by me

S. A. Hawkins Town clerk

Page 398.

At a meeting of the Board of Trustees of the Town of Brookhaven on the 5th Aug. 1851 Present William C. Booth Benjamin Brewster Lewis Davis John S. Havens Richard Smith Thomas J Ellison Silas Carter It being represented to the Board that a suit has been commenced against Jeffrey S. Hutchinson Road Master in 44th Road District in this Town and John S. Havens for taking and removing Earth from a certain Highway Running north of the Meeting House in Moriches and carrying and useing the same to mend the main Road being within the Bounds of said District Resolved that we the Trustees of this Town do Indemnify those Individuals against the expences of said Suit so far as the public Interest of the Town is concerned By request of Jason Brown & Edmund Woodruff for Lots for the planting of oysters the Board decided to grant to the above named Individuals lots of 2 Acres Each for the term of 5 years on the Beach flatts near Quanch upon condition they be at all the expence of surveying the same at 2 Dollars per lot annually Board resolved that Wm C Booth be empowered to give similar grants to any applicants wishing to take lots in the Great west Bay for the above named purpose upon the same conditions. On motion the Board resolved that Wm C. Booth be a committe to confer with Wm Smith and Wm Sidney Smith in relation to petitioning the Supervisor to regulate the Bye Laws pertaining to the penalties &c of Oystering and fishing

Page 399.

in the waters of the Town of Brookhaven on motion Lewis Davis was appointed to enquire into the condition and wants of Mitty Woodhull and ascertain the propriety of rendering her assistance. On motion the Board decided to lease to Henry F Osborne the Grass on the out shore Ridge in the south Bay for five years—Board decided and agreed to lease to V. and M. Dickerson 150 feet of old field Beach for ten years at 2 Dollars per year—

Board resolved that Henry Tylar commence a suit against Nehemiah Hand for obstructions placed Between High and low water mark in Setauket Harbor and to Indemnify him against the Expences necessary in prosecuting the suit. on motion the Board decided and agreed that the sum of twelve hundred Dollars be raised by tax for the use of the public poor of this Town the present year. the Board agreed to assist Miss Albin to 4 s. per week cammencing from Aug. 5th 1851 Adjourned to 2d. tuesday in Sept next

W. C. Booth Prest Trustees

Samuel A. Hawkins
    Town Clerk

Page 400.

At a meeting of the Commissioners of Highways of the Town of Brookhaven in the county of Suffolk held in the said Town at the house of Christopher Robinson on the 29th day of May 1851 all the said commissioners having met and deliberated on the subject of this order It appearing to the Said commissioners that the road in Said Town used as a highway from Seatuck Mills to Hot water Street in Halsey,s Manor has been used as a public highway for twenty years or more previous to the twenty first day of March 1797 and has been worked and used as such for the last six years and upwards but has not been recorded it is ordered by the said Commissioners that the said Road be entered of Record. and the said Commissioners do further order that the description courses distances and width of Said Road be as it is now fenced from or near the said Mills running northwesterly until it comes to Dongans line Such width being about two Rods and that the said road continue in a northwesterly direction from Dongans line the width of two Rods untill it comes to hot water street aforesaid near the House of Christopher Robinson—In witness whereof we have hereunto placed our hands this 30st day of May 1851

    Phillip Hallock
    Nathl Miller   } Commissioners
    Isaac Overton

Recorded 30th Oct. 1851 by me
  Saml. A. Hawkins
    Town Clerk

Page 401.

At a meeting of the commissioners of the Highways of the Town of Brookhaven in the County of Suffolk held in the said Town at the House of Mr Terry on the 29th day of May 1851 all the Said commissioners having met and deliberated on the Subject of this order it appearing to the said commissioners that the road in said Town used as a highway leading from the west line of the land of Josiah Smith to the South country Road in the Eastern part of the village of East Moriches has been used as a public highway for twenty years or more previous to the twenty first day of March 1797 and has been worked and used as Such for the last six years and upwards but has not been Recorded it is ordered by the Said commissioners that the said Road be entered of Record and the Said Commissioners do further order that the description courses and distances of the Said Road and the width of the same be as the said Road is now fenced Such width being about two Rods In witness whereof we have hereunto placed our names this 31st day of May 1851

      Phillip Hallock ⎫ Commissoners
      Nathl Tuttle   ⎬   of
      Isaac Overton ⎭ highways

Recorded this 30th day
of Oct. 1851 by me
SAMUEL A. HAWKINS
 Town Clerk.

PAGE 402.

At a meeting of the Board of Trustees of the Town of Brookhaven on tuesday the 9th day of Sept—1851 all the Trustees present
complaint being mad about and in behalf of David Smalling a Lunatic the Board resolved that the overseers of the poor go Immediately and Secure said Lunatic and convey him if possible to the Town Alms House and further resolved that an addition be made Immediately to the house for the purpose of accommodating Said Lunatic and others in like circumstances said addition to be made and constructed as hereinafter described viz 8 feet wide the length about 12 to

be coverd with short or Bunch Shingles sheathed with hemlock boards Sided with Albany Boards Sealed with Box Boards to be a door in East end and window in the west the floor to be laid with spruce plank window Shutter Iron Barred the whole to be done in a workman like manner— Resolved that Lewis Davis one of the overseers Superintend the Work

Resolved that Richd. Smith be a committe to view the dock and premises of Jonas Smiths and report at next meeting Resolved that Mr. Booth & Mr Ellison consult Lawyer Wickham in relation to the suit at Moriches and the propriety of carrying it up Adjourned to Second tuesday of Nov. next at 9 oclock

 Samuel A. Hawkins
  Town Clerk

Page 403.

This Indenture made the fourteenth day of Jan. one thousand Eight hundred and fifty one Between the Trustees of the freeholders and commonalty of the Town of Brookhaven of the first part and John R. Mather and Thomas B Hawkins of the same Town of the Second part Witnesseth that the Said parties of the first part for and in consideration of the annuities hereinafter mentioned have granted and by these presents do grant to the Said parties of the second part their heirs and assigns for the term of fifty years the right and privilege of Erecting and building repairing and holding a Stone wall at the head of Port Jefferson Bay in Said Town opposite their own land commencing Said wall at the Dock granted to Wm L. Jones Nov. 1837 and to extend on Shore an Easterly course at common low water Mark one hundred and Eighty feet with the privilege of filling in Back of Said wall sufficiently to answer the uses and purposes of a Private Dock or landing place for timber lumber stone and all articles of Produce for their own benefit and convenience paying for the privilege five

Dollars annually to have until the 14th day of Jan. 1852 to pay the first annuity and annually thereafter on Said Day for the same and all articles belonging to the corporation

PAGE 404.

of the said Town of Brookhaven for the use of the Public poor may be landed free of any expence to Sd Town And the Said parties of the Second part do hereby agree to pay to the Said Trustees or their Successors in office the Said annuity or annuities at the time they may be due according to the condition and intent of this Grant

In witness whereof the said parties have hereunto affixed their hands and seals of office binding themselves and successors on the one part and themselves their heirs and assigns on the other part the day and date above written

Signed Sealed in
Presence of
SAML. A. HAWKINS
Town Clerk.

WM. C. BOOTH President (L S)
JOHN R. MATHER (L S)
THOMAS B HAWKINS (L S)

This Indenture made this first day of June one thousand Eight hundred and forty one Between the Trustees of the freeholders and commonalty of the Town of Brookhaven of the first part and Wm L Jones of the same place of the Second part all of the County of Suffolk and State of New York Witnesseth that the Said Trustees for themselves and their Successors in office did grant unto the Said William L Jones and to his heirs

PAGE 405.

and assigns the privilege and Benefit of constructing and laying down two Railways at the head of Drown meadow Bay to be entirely within the Bounds and limits of the grant made to him the said Wm L. Jones by the Trustees of Said town on the thirteenth day of September 1836 for the purpose of Building a Dock or wharf this present grant shall be and continue until the expiration of the Said grant for a Dock which will expire on the first tuesday of May 1868 but the said Railway shall in no way or manner hinder or obstruct the highway that leads across or to the said Drown Meadow Bay—Done at Brookhaven the day aforesaid   SILAS HOMAN President (L S)

In presence of
 MORDECAI HOMAN
  Town Clerk

PAGE 406.

This Indenture Made this thirteenth day of September in the year one thousand Eight hundred and thirty Six Between the Trustees of the freeholders and commonalty of the Town of Brookhaven of the first part and William L. Jones of the same place of the second part all of the County of Suffolk and State of New york Witnesseth that whereas the said Wm L. Jones hath by his petition Signed by a respectable number of the Inhabitants of Brookhaven presented to the Board of Said Trustees for permission to Build a Dock or wharf at the head of Drown meadow Bay according to the boundaries and descriptions therein Set forth and Said Trustees after having appointed a committe to view said premises and due consideration having been had thereof and for and in consideration of the annuities rents performances and conditions hereinafter described to be paid done kept and performed by the Said party of the Second part his heirs or assigns they the Said Trustees for themselves and their successors in office do by these presents grant unto the said Wm L. Jones and to his heirs and assigns for the term of thirty years from the first tuesday in May next Liberty to build construct and keep in repair a Dock or wharf at the head of Drown Meadow Bay according to the following Boundaries that is to say commencing at common high water mark Seventy feet west of Israel

Page 407.

Davis Barn thence running westerly at common highwate mark two hundred feet and running from thence into the Bay five hundred feet if necessary and to be of the width of forty five feet in the Bay with a T across the end of one hundred and fifty feet in length the direction of the proposed Dock into the Bay being northwest half north or thereabout and the said Wm L Jones his heirs or assigns for and in consideration of the aforesaid grant and privilege is to Raise and build a Dam or causeway across the Marsh or Slough in the road leading to said premises Sufficiently high for people to pas and repass to and from Sd Dock at common highwater with a flew or passway for the tide to Ebb and flow through with a sufficient Bridge over the same the Sd road or causeway to be stoned up on each Side with good stones and filled in with Sand and other proper materials and to be of the width of Eighteen feet and also pay to the Said Trustees or their Successors in office the yearly rent or annuity of one Dollar annually on the first tuesday in May the first payment to become due on the first tuesday of May 1839 and whenever the said Dam or causeway is sufficiently finished across said Marsh or Slough

Page 408.

it shall belong to the public of Said Town and be supported as other highways and the said party of the Second part is to complete said Dock and causeway within three years from the first day of May next and the Said Wm. L Jones his heirs and assigns shall be allowed for the use of Sd Dock wharfage at the same rate as are now allowed for the Dock now owned by James R. Davis and formerly granted to John Wilsey subject however to be regulated by Said Board of Trustees or their Successors in office Reserving a right to land or send off from said Dock all articles belonging to the corporation of Said Town free from wharfage and at the

Expiration of said term of thirty years the aforesaid parties or their successors in office their heirs or assigns are to make new and further arrangement concerning the annual annuity to be paid for said Dock or otherwise and in case said parties cannot agree in the premises Each party is to choose one arbitrator to decide the same and provided Such arbitrators cannot agree on such annuity or otherwise they the said arbitrators Shall choose a third person whoose decision Shall be final—

    Done at Brookhaven the day aforesaid

                      DANIEL OVERTON President (L S)

In presence of
    MORDECAI HOMAN
        Town Clerk

                PAGE 409.

At a meeting of the Commissioners of highways of the Town of Brookhaven in the County of Suffolk at Short Neck in the Village of Patchogue in the Said Town of Brookhaven (all the Said commissioners having met and deliberated on the subject matter of this order) about the first of May 1851 upon the application and with the consent of Amos Rowland Benjamin Weeks Oliver P. Smith Roderick Phelps Henry Newens Hiram Gerard Lester Davis James W Davis Alfred Davis David Fordham and Francis A Weeks owners and occupants of the land through which the highway hereinafter described is laid out and on the petition of twelve Freeholders of the Said Town verified by their oath or affirmation it is ordered determined and certified that a public highway shall be and the same is hereby laid out pursuant to Said application whereof a Survey has been made and is as follows (to wit) Begining at the Bay at a landing laid out Six Rods Square bounded Southerly by the Bay on a line running South Seventy degrees East westerly by little Patchogue Creek on a line running South Twenty Degrees East northerly by Meadow on a line running South

Seventy Degrees East and Easterly by a line running across the Strand South Twenty Degrees East

The East line of the said highway Starts from the Centre of the north side of the said Landing and runs upon a curve west of a straight line bearing north one Degree and thirty minutes East seven chains and fifty links

PAGE 410.

its greatest departure from said line being Seventy five links then running north twelve degrees thirty minutes East Twenty one chains and Eighty two links then running north five Degrees thirty minutes East three chains Seventy five links then north one Degree East twenty chains and ninety links then north one degree west Seventeen Chains then north five Degrees and thirty minutes west forty one chains and forty links to the South Country road and the said highway is to be three Rods wide from the said Country Road to the South Bay.

In Witness whereof the said Commissioners of highways have hereunto Subscribed their names this fifteenth day of October 1851

    Nathaniel Tuttle ⎫ Commissioners
    Isaac Overton ⎬   of
    Phillip Hallock ⎭ highways

Know all men by these presents that we the undersigned in consideration of the benefits and advantages which will derive to us from a public highway on Short neck as of the consideration of Six cents to Each of us in hand the receipt whereof is hereby acknowledged have released and by these presence do release to the Commissioners of highways for the Town of Brookhaven so much of our and each of our land as may be necessary for the

PAGE 411.

purpose of opening a public highway from the Bay Shore near the mouth of little Patchogue Creek on the east side of the same to the now public highway or Country Road near the west end of Warren S. Conklin's Door Yard in Such manner as the said commissioners Shall lay the Same following as near as may be the direction set forth on a petition for the opening of Said Road

In witness whereof we have hereunto Set our hands and seals this 30th day of January one thousand Eight hundred and fifty one in presence of

    Amos Rowland Hiram Gerard
    Benjamin Weeks Lester Davis
    Oliver P Smith James W. Davis
    Roderick Phelps Alfred Davis
    Henry Newins David Fordham
      Francis A Weeks

Recorded the 27th Feb. 1851 by me
 SAML. A. HAWKINS
  Town Clerk

at a meeting of the Board of Trustees of the Town of Brookhaven Nov. 11th 1851 all the Board present Resolved that B. Brewster take Wm F. Ruland from the house to Setauket and if necessary render him some assistance

The propriety of Binding Ann Duick's Child to Joel Biggs was left to the discretion of the Overseers of the poor

adjourned until 2d tuesday in Dec. next at 9 Ocl A.M.
        WM C. BOOTH Prest
 S. A. HAWKINS
  Town Clerk

PAGE 412.

At a meeting of the Board of Trustees of the Town of Brookhaven Dec. 9th 1851 Resolved that Elihu Russell be allowed 1/. Extra per week or increase to 6/. also that Mrs. Marvin Receive 2/ per week from the 11th Nov. until 9th Dec. and from the last date to the first of March 3/ per week also Mr. Thompson of Swan Creek Receive 4/— a week from the 11th Nov. to 1st March next also Lester Overton to have $1.50 per week until next meeting of the Board

Resolved that Messrs Vinson and Minor Dickinson have the time Extended five years to their Grant for part of old field Beach also the privilege of Docking to low water mark

Resolved that James Akerly be allowed 1/ per week until 1st tuesday in April next for keeping his niece

Resolved that Messrs Brewster and Davis are hereby empowered to settle the difficulty Between Mrs Smith and Mrs Darling of port Jefferson

Resolved that Mrs Van Brunt have the privilege of taking her son to Board for 12/. per week at Alms house

adjourned to meet the 2d tuesday in Jan. 1852 at 9 oclock A M   Wm C. Booth—Prest
John S. Havens
   clerk pro. tem.

Page 413.

At a meeting of the Board of Trustees of the Town of Brookhaven on the 13th day of Jan. 1852 In relation to the renting of the Gunning priviledes of west Bay the Board choose Wm C. Booth to attend to the same and report at next meeting. Resolved that Mr Cherry have 25 cts weekly added to his pension from Dec. 9th and Mr Thompson's pension to increase 25 cts also from last meeting and that Mrs Terrill have 25 cts added weekly to her pension from last meeting to the next in March. Overseers decided to Indenture Ruth Duick child of Ann Duick to Joel A. Biggs of Islip until 18 years of age Resolved that Messrs Daines and Newins Bill of 25 Dollars be allowed for their trouble as agents of the Oystering privileges in west Bay

Resolved that all persons who refuse to pay for oystering privileges for Market in the waters of the west Bay be Subject to prosecution Wm C. Booth be authorised to attend to the matter Resolved that the same course be pursued the present year in relation to the oystering privileges of the Great west Bay (viz) that agents be appointed to take charge of the same that those agents be authorised to charge the sum of one Dollar each for the season if paid in advance if not $1.25 cts and 75 cts for fall and spring privilege Resolved that 110 feet of the shore in Setauket harbor be leased to Henry Tyler opposite his own land for two years at 2 Dollars annually from common high water to low water mark reserving to the public the right of landing and a passway &c Resolved to defend the same and indemnify Mr Tyler in any suit or suits and necessary expense in defending the same Mrs Smith case laid over to next meeting adjourned to the first tuesday in March next

Wm. C Booth Pres

Saml. A. Hawkins Town clerk

Page 414.

This Indenture made this third day of June one thousand Eight hundred and fifty one Between The Trustees of the freeholders and Commonalty of the Town of Brookhaven of the first part and Edmund T. Darling of the Same Town of the second part Witnesseth that the Said parties of the first part for and in consideration of four Dollars annually to be paid on the first tuesday in June in each year by the said Edmund T. Darling his heirs or assigns have granted Bargained and let (or leased) unto the Said party of the second part his heirs or assigns the use and privilege of a certain piece of land or shore belonging to Sd Town for the purpose of Erecting and Setting a Boat Builders Shop for the term of twenty five years from the first tuesday in June 1851 and Situate at the head of Port Jefferson Bay Commencing and Bounded on the east by Wm L Jone's west line and 22 feet west of his Small Dock (which is west of

Thomas B Hawkins Railway) and extending westerly by and with the Stone wall on shore Seventy five feet and northerly from Said Stone wall into the Bay one hundred feet and the said Edmund T. Darling for himself his heirs and assigns doth hereby covenant and agree to and with the Said Trustees and their successors in office to pay unto the Said

PAGE 415.

parties of the first part or their Successors in office on the first tuesday in June annually for the Said term of twenty five years the Sum of four Dollars the first payment to be made on the first tuesday in June 1852 and at the expiration of said term this present Grant shall return to Said Town and the improvement thereon appraised by indifferent men or further arrangment or agreement made between Sd parties of the first part or their Successors and the sd party of the second part his heirs or assigns

In witness whereof the Said parties have hereunto affixed their hands and Seals of office Binding themselves and Successors on the one part and himself his heirs and assigns on the other part the day and date above written

Signed and sealed WM C BOOTH L S
in presence of president of Trustees
SAMUEL A HAWKINS E. T. DARLING L S
    Town clerk

PAGE 416.

at a Meeting of the Board of Trustees of the Town of Brookhaven on tuesday the 2d day of March 1852 Present Wm C. Booth President also John S Havens Benjamin Brewster Thomas J. Ellison Lewis Davis Richard Smith and Silas Carter.

Board decided that Mrs Crow Receive 50 cts per week from last meeting to the present time amounting to $3.50 and that it be left discretionary with Mr Booth whether any thing be added to her pension Resolved that Nelson Daines and Smith L Newens be appointed as agents to take charge of the oystering privileges of West Bay for the ensuing year that the clerk post Notice to that effect at 7 Different places on the South Side of the Town Board decided to lease the Fishing privilege of West Bay to Alexander Smith for 3 years for $50— decided that Mrs Deborah Howell have 50 cts per week for keeping her son Davis Howell from last meeting to Town Meeting—Board decided to Quitclaim a certain piece of land about ten Square Rods belonging to the Town to Henry Hawkins for $10

* The Trustees at this meeting agreed to Lease the Gunning privileges of West Bay to John Homan for three years at $7.50 yearly

* Note.—On the margin of Page 416.—Com.

whereas Mrs Bowen has made application to the Trustees for liberty to build a house at or near oldfield Strand B. Brewster was chosen a committe to view the premises and decide on the propriety of Setting a

Page 417.

house there Board decided to accept of $100. of Daniel Carter provided Mr Wickham the attorney considers it best

Board decided that Frances Howell Grand Daughter of Peter Howell be Indentured to Hiram Robinson of Moriches from March 2d 1852 adjourned to first tuesday of April next at 9 oclock A M   Wm C. Booth President L S

S. A. Hawkins Town clerk

This Indenture made this fifth day of August one thousand Eight hundred and fifty one Between the Trustees of the freeholders and commonality of the Town of Brookhaven of the first part and Vincent Dickerson and Minor Dickerson of the same Town of the Second part Witnesseth that the Said parties of the first part for and in consideration of two Dollars annually to be paid on the first Tuesday in August in each year by the said Vincent and Minor

Dickerson their heirs or assigns have granted bargained and leased unto the said parties of the second part their heirs or assigns the use and privilege of one hundred and fifty feet of Old field Beach or Strand belonging to Said Town

PAGE 418.

near Setauket for the purpose of a Ship Yard with the privilege of Building a dock thereon to low water mark for the term of Fifteen years from the above date reserving to the Inhabitants of Said Town the right and privilege of a road or passway on Shore for teems carriages &c and the said Vincent Dickerson and Minor Dickerson for themselves their heirs and assigns do hereby covenant and agree to and with the Said Trustees and their Successors in office to pay them the sum of two Dollars on the first tuesday in August annually for the Said term of time for the use and privilege of the above described and leased premises the first payment to be made on the first tuesday in August 1852 and at the expiration of said term this present grant shall return to Said Town on further arrangment or agreement made between the Said parties of the first part or their Successors and the Said parties of the Second part their heirs or assigns In Witness whereof the said parties have hereunto affixed their hands & seals of office binding themselves & successors on the one part & themselves their heirs or assigns on the other part the day & date above written

        W<small>M</small> C. B<small>OOTH</small> Pres
        V<small>INCENT</small> D<small>ICKERSON</small>
        M<small>INOR</small> D<small>ICKERSON</small>

Signed and Sealed in presence of
    S<small>AML</small> A. H<small>AWKINS</small> Town Clerk

PAGE 419.

At a meeting of the commissioners of Highways of the Town of Brookhaven in the County of Suffolk at the village of Patchogue in the said Town of Brookhaven on the 24th day of February 1852 all the said commissioners having met and deliberated on the subject Embraced in this order It is ordered and determined that the centre of the Highway running northerly from the South Country Road near the Congregational Church in Patchogue between the Parish ground and the land now occupied by Oliver Jackson shall be and the same is hereby ordered to be and remain as follows viz. commencing at the north Margin of the South country Road at the distance of nine and a half Rods and three feet from the southwest corner of the land of Matthew Kirby thence running north twenty seven degrees west ten chains and sixty seven links until it comes opposite the south west corner of the land of Nathaniel Conkling thence continuing northerly as the said road now runs due notice of the said meeting having been given to all

Page 420.

parties interested therein—

In witness whereof we have hereunto set our hands this 23d. day of March 1852

    Nathaniel Tuttle Commissioners
    Phillip Hallock   of
    Isaac Overton   Highways

Recorded on the 23d March 1852
 by me   Samuel A. Hawkins
         Town Clerk

RECORDS OF BROOKHAVEN

BOOK E.

Page 1.

At an Annual Town Meeting held on the 6th day of April A.D. 1852 in the Town of Brookhaven at the house of L. H. Davis in Said Town the following named Individuals were duly Elected Town officers viz

For Supervisor
John M. Williamson

Justice of the Peace
Jesse W. Pelletreau for 4 years

President of Trustees
William Phillips

Trustees
Lewis Davis
William R. Satterly
Richard Smith pond
John R. Swezey
Sylvester W Wines
Thomas J. Ellison

Overseers of the poor
Lewis Davis
Thomas J. Ellison

Town clerk and Treasurer
Samuel A. Hawkins

Commissioner of Highways
Philip Hallock 3 years

Assessors
Isaac Overton for vacancy
Nathaniel Tuttle 3 years

Collector
William S. Williamson

Constables
Noah Overton   Briant N. Overton
John Ketcham   William Penny 3d
William C Overton

Inspectors of Election

1st. District   2d District
Carlton Jayne   Charles Woodhull
Charles S Seabury   Walter Dickerson
Zechariah F Hawkins   Phillip Hallock

PAGE 2.

3d District   4th District
James M Fanning   William Raynor
Edward D Topping   Isaac Overton
Peter Linnington   Lyman F Smith

5th District
Franklin Overton
Gersham O Overton
Alanson Overton

We the undersigned Justices of the peace certify that the foregoing is a true result of the annual Town Meeting held in the Town of Brookhaven on the 6 April 1852

B. Woodhull
J. W. Pelletreau
Chas. Phillips
Franklin Overton
} Justices

Overseers of highways

1st district		Richard N. Smith
2d	do	Alonzo Hawkins
3	"	Ebenezer Hawkins
4	"	Daniel Edwards
5	"	William R. Satterly
6	"	John Denton
7	"	William Fordham
8	"	Elisha Norton
9	"	Parshall W. Davis
10	"	Jeremiah Rowland
11	"	Sylvester Hallock
12	"	Nathaniel M. Tuttle
13	"	George C. Raynor
14	"	David C. Davis
15	"	Solon Culver
16	"	James Robinson
17	"	Nickols Overton
18	"	Samuel Carman
19.	"	De Witt C. Miller
20		Henry Hawkins
21		John Avery
22		Richard R. Davis
23		Walter Howell
24		Benjamin Wicks
25.	dis	Garret A. Westervelt
26	"	Richard Davis
27.	"	Isaac N. Gould
28.	"	William E. Gould
29	"	Joel D. Norton
30	"	Richard W. Smith
31	"	Thomas Bayles
32	"	Richard Smith pond
33	"	Sidney Terry
34	"	Hiram Overton

35	dis.	Franklin Overton
36	"	Lester Ruland
37	"	Samuel W. Randall
38	"	Samuel F. Norton
39	"	Edmund T. Hawkins
40	"	Orlando Randall
41	"	Henry A. Gordon
42	"	disolved
43	"	Orlando Edwards
44	"	Clinton Raynor
45	"	Jonah Turner
46	"	Phillip Hallock
47	"	Moses Akerly
48	"	John Dolon

The above named Individuals were duly chosen Road Masters

B. Woodhull
Jesse W. Pelletreau } Justices
Charles Phillips

PAGE 3.

At a meeting of the Board of Trustees of the Town of Brookhaven on tuesday the 6th April 1852 Present Wm C. Booth John S. Havens Thomas J Ellison Lewis Davis Benjamin Brewster Richard Smith Silas Carter Resolved that two Dollars be refunded to Smith Ruland member of the hope Flat Beach Co. for planting Oysters he having paid double or paid for a lot which proved worthless Resolved that all who have not paid in their annual rents to the respective Foremen of Oyster planting companies for the last year be requested to do so before the 1st tuesday in May next or forfeit their lots Resolved to Lease to Mrs Bowen a piece of Land adjoining old field strand

Resolved that Mr Wickham s Bill for the defending the road suit at Moriches in Justices Court and also at River-

head be allowed viz $25. 56 cts. Resolved that the Town make good to Lewis Davis what money has failed in his hands belonging to the Town during the past year adjourned Sine die   W<small>M</small> C. BOOTH Prest. Trustees.
SAMUEL A. HAWKINS
Town Clerk

At a Meeting of the Commissioners of highways of the Town of Brookhaven in the county of Suffolk held in the said Town at the house of William Daniels at Moriches on the fifth day of Nov. 1851 all the said Commissioners having met and deliberated on the subject of this order it appearing to the said Commissioners that the road in said Town used as a highway leading from the South Country Road near the Church at Moriches to the wading River Road has been used as a Public Highway for twenty years or more preceding the Twenty first day of March Seventeen hundred and ninety Seven but has not Been recorded :

It is ordered by the said Commissioners that the said road be ascertained described and entered of Record—

And the said Commissioners do further order that the description courses and distances of said Road be according to a survey which they have caused to be made of the same as follows. Starting at the north side of the Country Road in the middle of the travelled waggon Path Just west of the school house near said Church and running thence north seventeen and three quarter Deg. East two chains and ten links thence north two and a half Deg. East seven chains and sixty links thence north three and a half Deg. west five chains and thirty Seven links thence north two Deg. East sixteen Chains thence north five and a quarter Deg. East six Chains and sixty links thence north five Deg. west two chains and sixty three links thence north Eight Deg. East one chain and Seventy Eight links thence north twenty Eight and three quarter Deg. East six

PAGE 4.

Chains and Eighty one links thence north Thirty two and one half Deg. East one chain and fifty nine links and thence north Twenty two and a half Deg. East one chain to the said Wading River Road : And that the line of the said survey be the centre of the said Road or highway and that the Said highway be of the same width as it is now fenced used and travelled

In Witness whereof we have hereunto Set our hands this 24th day of January 1852

Isaac Overton   Commissioners
Nathaniel Tuttle   of
Phillip Hallock   Highways

At a meeting of the Board of Trustees of the Town of Brookhaven on tuesday the 4th day of May 1852 Present Wm Phillips Lewis Davis Thomas J Ellison Wm R. Satterly Richard Smith John R Swezey and Sylvester W. Wines. By request of Mr Walkman and Mr Millward for Information Respecting the Boundary line between Brookhaven and Islip the Board resolved that inquiry and search of record be made concerning thereof and acted upon at next Meeting On application of James Howell for compensation for keeping a grand child the Board decided that said child be brought to Alms House Board voted to allow Telem Smith 75 cts per week until next meeting adjourned to meet at the House of Horace G Randalls on tuesday the 1st day of June next at 9 o clock AM

Wm Phillips President

Samuel A Hawkins
    Town Clerk

At a meeting of the Board of Trustees of the Freeholders and commonalty of the Town of Brookhaven on tuesday the 1st day of June 1852 at the Inn of Horace G. Randal's Present Wm Phillips Thomas J Ellison Lewis Davis Richard Smith Wm R. Satterly and Sylvester W. Wines In Relation to the Boundary line between this Town and the Town of Islip Board decided that Information be given to the Supervisors of the two towns requesting them to cause a Just and true survey and legal settlement of said Boundary line. on application of Lewis Hulse Requesting a Reduction of his annuity for his Railway at P. Jefferson board decided to reduce sd annuity from 12 Dollars to 10. upon condition that all arrearages be paid up to the present time at the former Rate The Board decided that Brewster Hawkins be notified to remove all obstructions on shore west of his dock and that Mr. Wickham notify him to that effect. decided that Capt Charles D Hallock be Requested to remove all obstructions on the line between his Dock and Capt Jonas Smith Dock adjourned to 1st tuesday in August

PAGE 5.

next at 9 oclock A.M. at Horace G. Randals

WM PHILLIPS President

SAMUEL A HAWKINS
Town Clerk

For value Received we the Subscribers do hereby release to the Town of Brookhaven all claim to damages by reason of the laying out and opening of a highway through our lands by order of the Commissioners of highways
Dated this the 24th day of June 1848
In presence of
CHARLES PHILLIPS

David Robinson
Wm Terry
Lewis Gordon
Seth Raynor
J. G. Wilbur
Freeman Lane
Daniel Lane

Whereas application has been made to the Commissioners of highways of the Town of Brookhaven in the County of Suffolk to lay out a highway   rods wide in said Town

beginning at the Road leading from Fireplace neck to coram near Sylvester Homans house and running in a Southerly direction to Bellport Station on the Long Island Rail Road. Which proposed Road will run through our unimproved lands Now therefore in consideration of the laying out and opening said highway we the subscribers do hereby release all claim to damages by reason thereof.
Brookhaven February 14th 1852

       Charles Godfrey Gunthar O
       Samuel F Tooker   O
       Sylvester Homan   O

Whereas application has been made to the commissioners of highways of the Town of Brook haven to lay out a highway three Rods wide in said Town commencing at the south side of the Country Road at a point on the line between the lands of Daniel Robinson and William Avery Stephen Roe and the heirs of Lester Roe deceased to the Bay shore which proposed Road will run through my improved land Now therefore in consideration of the sum of one hundred and twenty five Dollars to me in hand paid I do hereby release all claim to damages by reason thereof.
Brookhaven Feb 26th 1852   Sarah Roe

Page 6.

The undersigned Commissioners of highways of the Town of Brookhaven do hereby order that Road district Number 21 in said Town be and the same is hereby divided as follows that is to say that all that part of said district lying Eastward of Robinson Mill Stream together with all cross Roads in said district that connect with the south country Road East of the said Mill Stream continue to be known and numbered as Road district Number 21 And that all the remainder of Said district lying west of the said Mill Stream including all cross Roads therein that connect with the south country Road to the west of Said Mill Stream be formed into a new Road district to be known and numbered as Road district number 42 and that the Inhabitants residing within the Boundaries above described and liable to work on the highways be and they are hereby assigned to work in the Road district in which they respectively reside dated the 25th day of June 1852

Isaac Overton ⎫ Commissioners
Nethaniel Tuttle ⎬ of
Phillip Hallock ⎭ highways

Recorded June 30th 1852
SAMUEL A. HAWKINS—
Town Clerk

At a meeting of the commissioners of highways of the Town of Brookhaven in the County of Suffolk at Bellport Station in said Town on the 27th day of February 1852 all the Said commissioners having met and deliberated on the Subject matter of this order upon the application and consent of C. Godfrey Gunther Samuel Tooker and Sylvester Homan the owners of the lands through which the highway hereafter described is to run the undersigned Commissioners of Highways of the said Town do hereby order determine and certify that a public Highway Shall be and the same is hereby laid out in the said Town pursuant to such application whereof a survey has been made out and is as follows (viz) Beginning on the Long Island Rail Road at Bellport Station at the termination of the Bellport road thence running (Compass course) north two Deg. E to the Middle Island line then running north one half of a Deg. East until it Intersects the old Road near Sylvester Homan's East line (formally owned by John Roe) then following the old road as it now Runs until it Intersects the Road Running

PAGE 7.

from Coram to Fireplace (near Sylvester Homans) the line of the said survey to be the centre of the said Highway which is to be three Rods in width

In witness whereof the Said commissioners have hereunto Subscribed their names this 30th day of April 1852

      Nathaniel Tuttle ⎫ Commissioners
      Isaac Overton ⎬ of
      Phillip Hallock ⎭ highways

Know all men by these presents that we the undersigned do hereby release to the Town of Brookhaven all claim to damages by reason of the laying out and opening of a Highway through our respective lands by order of the Commissioners of highways

Dated the 26th day of March 1852
In witness whereof we have hereunto set our hand and seals this 26th day of March 1852

In the presence of	W. E. Conkling	L S
W. E. Conkling	Brewster Terry	L S
Brewster Terry	John R. Swezey	L S
	Calvin Hait	L S
	Lester Glover mark ×	L S
	Daniel W. Case	L S
	Joshua Hammond	L S
	Albert Terrell	L S
	Rumsey Rose	L S

Whereas application has been made to the commissioners of Highways of the Town of Brookhaven in the county of Suffolk to lay out a highway three Rods wide in said Town beginning at the South side of the country road at a point on the line between the lands of Daniel Robinson and William Avery and running southerly over the several lands of Daniel Robinson William Avery Stephen S Roe and the heirs of Lester Roe deceased to the Bay shore which proposed road will Run through our improved lands

Now therefore in consideration of the laying out and opening Said Road we the subscribers do hereby release all claim to damages by Reason thereof—

Dated at Brookhaven this 23d. day of February 1852
DANIEL ROBINSON
STEPHEN S ROE
WILLIAM AVERY
PAGE 8.

Know all men by these presents that we the undersigned do hereby Release to the Town of Brookhaven all claim to damages by reason of the laying out and opening of a Highway through our respective lands by order of the commissioners of Highways
Dated the Twenty Sixth day of March 1852
In witness whereof we have hereunto set our hands and seals this 26 day of March 1852

In presence of
EDWARD N. DOUGLAS
BREWSTER TERRY

William H. Newens
Nancy E. Newens
Elizabeth Smalling
Uriah Smith
Richard R Davis
Sylvester Gordon
Allen Barnes
Hiram Swezey

At a meeting of the Commissioners of highways of the Town of Brookhaven in the county of Suffolk at the House of Richard R. Davis in Patchogue in the said Town on the 26th day of March 1852 all the said Commissioners having met and deliberated on the subject matter of this order upon the application and consent of William E. Conkling Brewster Terry John R Swezey Calvin Hait Lester Glover David W. Case Joshua Hammond Albert Terrell Rumsey Rose William H. Newens Nancy E. Newens Elizabeth Smalling Uriah Smith Richard R Davis Sylvester Gordon Allen Barnes and Hiram Swezey through whose lands the Highway hereafter described is to run It is ordered determined and certified by the Said Commissioners that a public Highway be and is hereby laid out in the said Town pursuant to the said application a survey whereof has been made and is as follows (viz) Commencing at the south side of the south country Road nearly opposite the dwelling House of the said Richard R. Davis at a stake on the East line of the said highway thence running (compass course) South Twelve and a half Degrees west seven chains and twenty seven links thence south fifteen degrees west Thirty four chains and ninety Eight links thence south Four and a half degrees West five chains thence south Two degrees East Ten chains Thence south Eight degrees West Twelve chains and seventy links thence continuing the same course two chains and twenty five links which last mentioned distance of two chains and twenty five links the said Road

PAGE 9.

is to be but two rods wide to avoid the House belonging to Hiram Swezey and Lester Glover the rod to be left from the west line of the said Highway Then running south three quarters of a degree East thirteen chains and seventy five links Thence south six and a half degrees west nineteen chains and five links to the South Bay The line of the said Survey to be the East line of the said Highway which is to be three Rods in width Except as herein before mentioned

And it is also ordered determined and certified by the said commissioners with the like consent that a highway be and the same is hereby laid on the beach or shore Commencing on the East line of the Highway above described at a certain Stake at the Edge of the Plowed land thence Running (compass course) south seventy nine Deg. East to the mouth of Swan creek the line of the said survey to be the north line of the said Highway which is to be three Rods in width—

In witness whereof the said commissioners have hereto Subscribed their names this 26th day of March 1852

Nathaniel Tuttle ⎫ Commissioners
Isaac Overton ⎬ of
Phillip Hallock ⎭ Highways

At a meeting of the Commissioners of Highways of the Town of Brookhaven in the County of Suffolk at the House of Stephen S. Roe at pine Neck near Swan creek in the said Town of Brookhaven on the 26th day of March 1852 All the said Commissioners having been notified and having met and deliberated on the subject matter of this order upon the application and consent of Daniel Robinson William Avery Stephen S. Roe. and Sarah Roe the owners and occupants of the land through which the said Highway hereafter described is to run and upon the petition of Twelve Freeholders of the said Town of Brookhaven verified by their Oath it is ordered determined and certified by the said Commissioners that a Public Highway be and the same is hereby laid out in the said Town pursuant to the said application a survey whereof has been made and is as follows (viz) Commencing at the south side of the south country Road at a certain stake a little East of the house of William Avery thence running (Compass course) South Thirteen and a half Deg. West Eighty chains thence south one and a half Deg. West four chains thence South Eleven and one quarter Deg. East thirteen chains to the south Bay the line of the said survey to be the centre of the said Highway which is to be three Rods in width

In witness whereof the said Commissioners have hereunto set their hands this 30th day of April 1852

PAGE 10.

Nathaniel Tuttle ⎫ Commissioners
Isaac Overton ⎬ of
Phillip Hallock ⎭ Highways

At a meeting of the Board of Trustees of the freeholders and commonalty of the Town of Brookhaven on the 4th day of August 1852 Present William Phillips President and L. Davis Thomas J Ellison Richard Smith Wm R Satterly Sylvester W. Wines and John R Swezey Board Resolved that under existing circumstances a suit be commenced against Brewster Hawkins in consequence of the several obstructions he has caused in and about Setauket Harbor and that Mr T. J Ellison be authorised to employ Mr Wickham Instructing him to write to Mr Hawkins before commencing a suit

    adjourned to 2d tuesday in Sept. next at nine O clock A M   W<small>M</small> P<small>HILLIPS</small>—President
  S. A. H<small>AWKINS</small>
     Town Clerk

At a Meeting of the Board of Trustees of the Town of Brookhaven on tuesday the 14th. September A.D. 1852 Present Wm Phillips Tho J. Ellison Lewis Davis Richard Smith John R Swezey Sylvester W. Wines on application of Mrs Elizabeth Darling the Board agreed and decided to grant her liberty to build a Pier of one hundred feet from the front of her dock north to prevent the sand from washing and collecting around her Dock this pier to be built opposite her own land—In relation to the difficulty with Brewster Hawkins the Board decided to commence a Suit in Supreme Court against him that Mr Ellison Instruct Mr Wickham to proceed in said Suit On motion the Board decided that the Sum of Sixteen hundred Dollars Be Raised By tax in this Town the Ensuing year for the use and Benefit of the poor thereof. on complaint being made Board decided that Mr J R Swezey be authorised in Behalf of the Town to prosecute any Individuals who may be found Tresspassing on the Laws of this Town in Relation to oystering priviledges thereof

    Adjourned to meet on 2d tuesday in Nov. next at 9 ock A.M.   W<small>M</small> P<small>HILLIPS</small> President
  S<small>AML</small>. A. H<small>AWKINS</small>
     Town Clerk

P<small>AGE</small> 11.

At a meeting of the commissioners of Highways of the Town of Brookhaven on the 23d. day of August 1852 called

for the purpose of tracing out the Highway at Millers place leading from the Rocky Point Road to Merritt S Woodhulls landing which Highway was laid out by an order bearing date the 15th. Day of June 1815 and is duly recorded &c We the said commissioners having examined the premises and heard the parties interested therein do certify and determine that the portion of Said Highway leading from the gate standing at the South line of land late of Merritt S Woodhull to the Sound adjoins the land of Lewis Davis and that the East line of the Said Highway is distant three rods from the land of the said Lewis Davis as the fence now stands until it comes near the Bank of the Sound and that the said Highway then turns North Easterly to low water mark and that we have designated the East line of the said Highway by stakes set up by us
Dated the 23d. day of August 1852

      Isaac Overton   )   commissioners
      Nathaniel Tuttle } of
      Philip Hallock   )   Highways

At a meeting of the Board of Trustees of the Town of Brookhaven on tuesday the 9th Nov. 1852 Present Wm Phillips President T. J Ellison John R. Swezey Wm R Satterly Sylvester W. Wines Lewis Davis in Relation to the matter of Difficulty with Brewster Hawkins the Board thought Best to have the commissioners of Highways called to see whether the obstructions complained of are in the Highway or not as complaint has been made that Charles D. Hallock has placed obstructions upon his Dock adjoining to Jonas Smith's Dock the Board decided that Mr Wickham be requested to Examine the grant to C. D. Hallock and serve a Written notice on Mr Hallock in behalf of the Trustees of the Town requesting him to remove the same as application has been made to lease certain premises at Port Jefferson by Henry Hallock and Harvy West Board concluded to act upon the matter at next meeting

Adjourned to the first tuesday in Jan. next at 9. oclock A. M.

        Wm Phillips President

 S. A. Hawkins
  Town Clerk

Page 12.

At a meeting of the Trustees of the Freeholders and commonalty of the Town of Brookhaven on the 4th Jan. 1853

Present
- Wm Phillips—President
- Wm R. Satterly
- Sylvester W Wines
- Lewis Davis
- Thomas J Ellison

on application the Board resolved and agreed to Lease to Henry Hallock a certain piece of land on Port Jefferson Beach commencing twenty five feet west of the Bridge north side of the Road for the term of forty years for the sum of three Dollars annually

On application the Board Resolved also to Lease to Harvy West another piece of said Beach west of the sd Henry Hallocks for the term of forty years for the sum of two Dollars annually

Board agreed to pay to Martha Horton one Dollar per week from the 16th Nov. last

On complaint of Capt Thomas Hallock Board Resolved that all obstructions be removed from the Docks at Port Jefferson

 adjourned to the first tuesday in Feb next

        Wm Phillips—President

Samuel A. Hawkins Town Clerk

At a Meeting of the Board of Trustees of the Town of Brookhaven on tuesday the 1st of Feb 1853 Present Wm Phillips Lewis Davis Thomas J Ellison John R Swezey Richard Smith Sylvester W. Wines on application of Edmund T. Darling to purchase a certain piece of Land already leased to him Board decided in negative. Then Mr Darling applied for an extension of limits of said leased premises the Board thought Best to defer the matter until next meeting and appointed Lewis Davis to view the premises and report at next meeting The Board voted and agreed that Notice be posted on the south side of the Town at the most public places giving information of the following Resolution viz Be it ordained that all persons who may wish to catch or take oysters the ensuing season in the waters of the Great South Bay belonging to said Town and Wm Sidney Smith for the purpose of Selling them to or for any foreign market or that shall be sold or carried out of the said Town of Brookhaven shall and are hereby required first to obtain liberty or licence from one of the said Trustees on or before the first tuesday of March next who will on the Receipt of one Dollar from

PAGE 13.

each applicant in advance give a written licence for the season and be it further ordained that if any person or persons are found takeing or catching oysters in said Bay during the ensuing season for any foreign market &c without first obtaining a written licence as aforesaid he or they will be liable to pay for every offence the sum of twelve Dollars and fifty cents to be sued for and recovered in the name of the said Trustees in any court having Cognizance thereof

adjourned to first tuesday in March next at 9 Oclock A.M.   WM PHILLIPS President of Trustees
SAMUEL A. HAWKINS Town Clerk—

at a meeting of the Trustees of the Town of Brookhaven on tuesday the first day of March A.D. 1853 Present William Phillips President Lewis Davis Tho J. Ellison Richerd Smith John R. Swezey and Sylvester W. Wines The Board decided to Lease to Edmund T. Darling about 50 feet of the Shore at the head of Port Jefferson Bay for the term of 23 years at 2 Dollars a year.

On motion it was Resolved that Nathaniel M. Terrill be appointed and authorised to superintend the oystering privileges of the great south Bay (in partnership with this Town and Wm Sidney Smith) for the ensuing year for which to Receive reasonable compensation and Resolved further that Mr Swezey one of the Board be authorised to procure printed licences for oystering and issue the same to all who pay over to him one Dollar in advance time extended to first tuesday in April

adjourned to meet on first tuesday in April next at 9 Oclock A.M.

Wm Phillips President of Trustees

Saml. A. Hawkins Town Clerk

Page 14.

At a meeting of the Commissioners of Highways of the Town of Brookhaven in the County of Suffolk at Medford Station on the 24th day of March 1853 all the said Commissioners having been duly notified to attend the said meeting for the purpose of deliberating on the Subject of this Order

It appearing to the said commissioners that the road in said Town used as a highway leading from the old Coram Road starting nearly opposite the House of Jesse Haff to Medford Station and so northerly from Medford Station until it again intersects the old Coram Road has been laid out but not sufficiently described of Record It is ordered by the said Commissioners that the Said Road be ascertained described and entered of Record And the said commissioners do further order that the description courses and distances of said Road be according to a survey which they have caused to be made of the same as follows (viz)

Commencing at the old Coram Road north of the Long Island Rail Road thence Running south Eleven and one third degrees west two chains being fifty five and a half links west from the northwest corner of the Kitchen part of the house lately built by John Smith thence south one and one third degree west five chains and Eighty two links (from the Northwest Corner of said Kitchen to the Rail Road track on said course being two chains and forty five links) thence south nineteen and two thirds degrees west Eighty chains thence south Twenty Degrees west Eighty four chains until it Intersects the old Coram Road near the said house of Jesse Haff and that the line of said survey be the Centre of Said Road and said Road be and the same is of the width of three Rods

In witness whereof we have hereunto placed our hands this 24th day of March 1853

     Isaac Overton   ) Commissioners
     Nathaniel Tuttle } of
     Phillip Hallock   ) Highways

Page 15.

This Indenture made this fourth day of January one thousand Eight hundred and fifty three Between the Trustees of the freeholders and commonalty of the Town of Brookhaven of the first part and Harvey West of the same Town of the second part Witnesseth that the said parties of the first part for and in consideration of two Dollars annually to be paid on the first tuesday in January in Each year by the said Harvey West his heirs or assigns Have granted Bargained let and leased unto the said party of the second part his heirs and assigns the use and privilege of a certain piece of Beach or Shore belonging to said Town situate and lying at the head of Port Jefferson Bay north side of the Road leading from Port Jefferson to Setauket for the term of forty years from the date hereof. Beginning at the west line of Henry Hallock and extending westerly two hundred and twenty five feet then northerly to common Low water mark then Easterly to the sd Hallocks line then southerly by said line to the place of Beginning And the said Harvey West for himself his heirs and assigns doth hereby covenant and agree to and with the said Trustees and their successors in office to commence Improvments on the above leased and described premises the ensuing season and to pay unto the said parties of the first part or their successors in office on the first tuesday in Jan annually for and during the said term of forty years the above said annuity of two Dollars. And at the expiration of the said term this present grant shall return to said Town and the improvments thereon appraised by indifferent men or further arrangment or agreement made between said parties of the first part or their successors and the said party of the second part his heirs or assigns

In witness whereof the said parties have hereunto affixed their hands and seals of office binding themselves and successors on the one part and himself his Heirs and assigns on the other part the day and year above written

     WILLIAM PHILLIPS (President L S)
     HARVEY WEST   L S

Signed and sealed in presence of
 SAMUEL A. HAWKINS Town Clerk

PAGE 16.

This Indenture made this third day of June one thousand Eight hundred and fifty three Between the Trustees of the Freeholders and commonalty of the Town of Brookhaven of the first part and Edmund T. Darling of the same Town of the Second part Witnesseth that the said parties of the first part for and in consideration of two Dollars annually to be paid on the first tuesday in June in Each year by the said Edmund T. Darling his heirs or assigns have Granted, Bargained Let and Leased unto the said party of the second part his heirs and assigns the use and privilege of a certain piece of Beach or shore belonging to said Town Situate and lying at the head of Port Jefferson Bay for the term of twenty three years from the date hereof and Bounded as follows (viz) Beginning at the Southwest corner of the premises already leased to the Said E. T. Darling By the trustees of said Town in June 1851 from thence westerly about forty or fifty feet to the bridge but not to interfere with the free passage through said Bridge then northerly to low water mark from thence Easterly by and with low water mark in rear of said E. T. Darling's leased premises to Wm Jone's west line then southerly to the bounds of the said first lease This lease is intended to Extend continue and terminate with the said former grant and the said Edmund T. Darling for himself his heirs and assigns doth hereby covenant and agree to and with the said Trustees and their successors in office to pay unto the said parties of the first part or their Successors in office on the first tuesday in June annually for and during the said term of twenty three years the sum of two Dollars the first payment to be made on the first tuesday in June 1854 and at the Expiration of the sd term this present grant shall return to said Town and the improvements thereon appraised by indifferent men or further arrangment or agreement made between said parties of the first part on their successors and the said party of the second part his heirs or assigns In witness whereof the said parties have hereunto affixed their hands and seals of office binding themselves and successors on the one part and himself his heirs and assigns on the other part the day and year above written

      WILLIAM PHILLIPS President L S
      EDMUND T. DARLING   L S
Signed Sealed and Delivered in presence of
SAMUEL A. HAWKINS Town Clerk

PAGE 17.

Be it remembered that I Isaac Satterly and Benjamin F. Thompson were duly appointed by the Trustees of the Town of Brookhaven in the year of Eighteen hundred and fifteen to lay out A negro burying Ground in the Village of Setauket known and called by the name of Laurel Hill the Bounds of Said Burying ground are as follows—beginning at a certain Cedar Tree standing in by the fence of Obediah Wells Deced. and thence running northerly in Range to a Rock in the second fence from the Road leading from Isaac Jayne's deceased to the west Meadows in Ruth Toby's Lot and then Southerly from the Road to the centre of the hollow till it strikes the fence of Ruth Toby now owned by Benjamin Dickerson and then East by the said fence of Benjamin Dickerson and Obediah Wells decd. to the place of Beginning being about one Acre more or less

             ISAAC SATTERLY

State of New York } ss.
County of Suffolk.

on the 11th day of April 1853 personally came before me Isaac Satterly and made Oath in due form of law that the facts contained in the above Statement are correct and true to the best of his knowledge and belief

      S. B. STRONG
        Justice of the Sepreme Court

Recorded on the 16th May 1853
 by me SAML. A. HAWKINS
     Clerk

PAGE 18.

At an annual Town Meeting held on the 5th day of April A.D. 1853 in the Town of Brookhaven at the House of Lester H. Davis in said Town the following named Individuals were duly Elected Town officers (viz)

    For Supervisor—
    John M. Williamson
   For Justices of the Peace
  Samuel F. Norton—for 4 years
  Jesse W. Pelletreau—for vacancy

President of Trustees
Davis Norton—

Trustees
Horace Hudson
Henry K. Townsend
John F Hallock
David Hedges
David W. Case
Joel Robinson

Overseers of Poor
Horace Hudson
David W. Case

Town Clerk
Samuel A. Hawkins

For Assessor
Isaac Overton for 3 years

Commissioner of Highways
Nelson Norton—for 3 years

For Collector
Daniel W. Davis

Superintendant of Com. Schools
Lewis R. Overton

Constables
Edward A. Swezey
Samuel Cooper
Cyrus Griffin
Lorenzo D. Vail
Daniel T. Overton

Inspectors of Election

1st District	2d District
Henry K. Townsend	John Davis
Floyd Smith	Phillip Hallock
Thomas J. Ritch	Charles Miller

3d District
Jeremiah G. Wilbur
Seth Raynor
Jacob H. Miller

PAGE 19.

4th District
William Wickham Jr.
John B. Terry
Smith L Newins

5th Dis
Lewis R. Overton
Daniel D. Swezey
Lester H. Davis

We the undersigned Justices of the Town of Brookhaven certify that the foregoing is a true Result of the annual Town Meeting held in Said Town on tuesday the 5th day of April A D 1853

Brewster Woodhull } Justices
Charles Phillips

SAMUEL A. HAWKINS Town Clerk

OVERSEERS OF HIGHWAYS OF THE TOWN OF BROOKHAVEN Chosen April 5th 1853 at an annual Town Meeting

District
No 1 William Davis
2 Charles D. Hallock
3 Sylvester Hawkins
4 Benjamin Brewster
5 Benjamin N. Smith
6 John L Denton
7 Cyrus Griffin
8 Charles A Hawkins
9 Charles Davis
10 Horace Hudson
11 Sylvester Hallock
12 Nathaniel M Tuttle
13 George C. Raynor.
14 Sylvester W. Wines
25 Nelson Daines
26 Joseph Newton
27 Isaac A. L Hommedieu
28 Horace Ruland
29 Joel D. Norton
30 Joshua Overton
31 Wm L. Lee
32 Richard Smith (pond
33 L Hommedieu Smith
34 Hiram Overton
35 Daniel L Hommedieu
36 Lester Ruland
37 James Dayton
38 Samuel L Homan

District
15 Usher Benjamin
16 Parker S. Robinson
17 Robert Smith
18 Samuel Carman.
19 William Snow
20 Henry Hawkins
21 David Hedges
22 John Davis
23 Floyd Smith
24 Israel Green
39 Apollos A. Mills
40 Orlando Randall
41 Lewis Gordon
42 John Avery
43 Orlando Edwards
44 Jeffrey S. Hutchinson
45 Jonah Turner
46 Sylvester D. Tuttle
47 Sylvester Woodhull
48 John Dolan
49 Wm C. Tooker.

We certify that the above is a correct List of Overseers chosen as above stated

Brewster Woodhull } Justices
Charles Phillips

SAMUEL A. HAWKINS T. Clerk

PAGE 20.

At a meeting of the Board of Trustees of the Freeholders and commonalty of the Town of Brookhaven on tuesday the 3d day of May 1853 Present Davis Norton—President— Henry K. Townsend Horace Hudson David W Case John F. Hallock David Hedges on motion Samuel A Hawkins was chosen Clerk of the Board for the ensuing year to Receive the Same compensation as Trustees per Day—application being made for the right and privilege to take or catch EEls in the waters of the great west Bay in partnership with this Town and Wm. Sidney Smith for one or more years—Board decided to advertise and Sell Said Right and privilege on tuesday the 7th June next—Some one presented a Bill for Dr. Jarvis for Medical aid Rendered F. Howells wife Board decided that Dr Jarvis present his Bill himself —It was decided by the Board that when any application is made for to lease any of the Shores or Beaches belonging to Said Town that public notice be given at least in three different places in Said village or vicinity on complaint of Capt Henry Tyler the Board decided to act upon at next meeting—Board appointed David W. Case and David Hedges to issue lisence for Oystering to all applicants who pay in advance during the Season—adjourned to first tuesday in June next at 9 Oclock A.M.

DAVIS NORTON—President
SAMUEL A. HAWKINS Town Clerk

At a Meeting of the Trustees of the Freeholders and commonalty of the Town of Brookhaven on tuesday the 7th day of June 1853 Present Davis Norton President Horace Hudson David W. Case John F. Hallock David Hedges Henry K. Townsend and Joel Robinson—Board decided to allow Alexander Hawkins 3/. per week—a Bill was presented by Robert Jayne for keeping or boarding Amanda Moger laid over till next meeting. the Bill presented by Dr. Preston to be Settled discretionary by Mr Hedges and Mr. Case— In relation to the highway or pass-way in or around Setauket Harbor (complaint being made at last Meeting) that said pass-way was obstructed by Stone &c. The commissioners having been called to view the premises have ordered the Overseer of Highways in that district to Remove Said obstructions—The Board decided to Indemnify said overseer against all damage he may sustain in Removing the same. Henry K. Townsend and Horace Hudson were appointed a committee to

PAGE 21.

view the negro Burying Ground in Setauket and Report at next meeting (Mr Satterly having entered a complaint concerning the Same) The Right and privilege of taking or catching EEls in South Bay was put up at auction but was Bid in by one of Trustees for about 21 Dollars Board appointed David Hedges to Sell the Grass on the Islands in

west Bay for the present Season Board decided that John Pinkard a county pauper be kept at the alms House in this Town for one Dollar per week. Board decided that a written notice be served on Captn C. D. Hallock Requiring him to Remove the obstructions complained of on his Dock adjourned to first tuesday in August next at nine oclock A. M.   Davis Norton—President
 Saml. A. Hawkins
  Town clerk

At a meeting of the Board of Trustees of the Town of Brookhaven on tuesday the 2d. day of Aug. 1853 Present Davis Norton President Horace Hudson David Hedges David W. Case Henry K. Townsend John F. Hallock Joel Robinson

It having been alledged that Captn Isaac Smith has trespassed upon the the negro Burying Ground in Setauket by cutting and carrying off trees of timber from sd ground which is considered belonging to the Town. Board decided that the clerk write to Mr Smith on the Subject before commencing a suit. Board authorised Mr. Hedges to collect from Mr Smith L Newens what money he may have Received as agent of the Oystering Privileges for last Season. Board decided to allow Sidney S Griffing 1 Dollar for conveying Margaret Robinson to the Alms House

The Bill presented by Robert Jayne for keeping Amanda Moger Board decided that Mr Case Settle according to his own discretion also the Expence of Mary Vail's confinement and Support of the Child Board appointed Joel Robinson to dispose of the Grass on the Islands in East Bay the present Season. Board Authorised Mr Case to take charge of the Oystering privileges for the present Season and appoint an agent &c Consult Mr Wickham on the Subject and proceed in the matter according to his discretion and advise of Mr Wickham commence a Suit in Justices court against those found Trespassing if thought advisable by his counsel

adjourned to the 2d Tuesday in Septr next at 9 Oclock
AM   Davis Norton President
  Saml. A. Hawkins Town Clerk

Page 22.

At a meeting of the board of Trustees of the Town of Brookhaven on tuesday the 13th day of Sept. 1853—

Present Davis Norton ⎫
         Horace Hudson ⎪
         David W Case   ⎪
         Henry K. Townsend ⎬ Trustees
         John F. Hallock ⎪
         Joel Robinson. ⎪
         David Hedges   ⎭

one motion the Board decided to Raise by Tax in the Town of Brookhaven the present year the Sum of Sixteen Hundred Dollars for the benefit of the poor of sd Town. The board agreed to accept and sanction the appointment of Nathaniel M. Terrill to Oversee and take charge of the Oystering privileges of the West Bay the present Season. Board decided that the Bill presented John R. Swezey be laid over to next meeting of the Board. On complaint Davis Norton and Henry K Townsend was appointed a committe to view the Dock and premises of Smith and Darling at Port Jefferson and report at next meeting

adjourned to the first tuesday in Nov. next at nine Oclock
A.M.   Davis Norton President
  Samuel A. Hawkins Town Clerk

At a meeting of the Board of Trustees of the Town of Brook Haven on tuesday the 1st. day of Nov. 1853 all the Trustees Present on motion the Board decided that the annuity or Rent of Lewis Hulse's Dock or Railway be Raised to twelve Dollars annually as it formerly was previous to the reduction in June 1852—
Wid Daines pension discontinued

Board adjourned to the first tuesday in Jan. next at nine O clock A M DAVIS NORTON President
SAMUEL A. HAWKINS Town Clerk

PAGE 23.

Brookhaven May 27th 1853

To the commissioners of Highways

We the undersigned Freeholders of the Town of Brookhaven Respectfully Petition the said commissioners of said Town of Brookhaven to lay out a Road from Waverly Station through A. Mc. Cotters East Avenue to the horse-Block Road and as much farther as the Said Commissioners Shall in their Judgment Deem it necessary for the convenience of the said Inhabitants and freeholders in the vicinity of Said Road and your petitioners will Ever Pray

  Joel D. Norton   Smith P. Gamage
  Daniel T. Overton   Thomas Terry
  W. C. Barrett   John Norton
  A. Mc. Cotter   Patrick Coleman
  John M. Fountain   Richard O. Howell
  John H. Gamage   Hiram E. Terry
  Davis Overton   Ebenezer Terry
  Daniel Terry   A. H. Smith
  Sidney Terry   Scudder Terry

Whereas application has been made to the Commissioners of Highways of the Town of Brookhaven in the County of Suffolk to lay out a Highway three Rods wide in Said Town beginning at the Horse-Block Road where it intersects A Mc. Cotters East avenue and running South by and with said Avanue to Waverly Station on the Long Island Rail Road and thence continuing South till it Intersects the old Road leading from Said Station to Patchogue. Now therefore in consideration of the laying out and opening the Said Highway we the undersigned do hereby Release all claim to damages by Reason thereof

Dated at Brookhaven June 4th 1853

Witness
  Daniel T. Overton

A. Mc. Cotter
Hugh Mc. Cotter } (L S)
by A. Mc. Cotter

John Gammage (L S)
W. C. Barrett (L S)
Wm Walkman (L. S)
Nelson Daines (L. S.)

Page 24.

At a meeting of the commissioners of Highways of the Town of Brookhaven in the county of Suffolk at Waverly in Said Town on the fifth day of June 1853 (all the Said commissioners Having been duly notified to attend the said meeting for the purpose of deliberating upon the Subject matter of this order) On the application of Daniel T Overton W. C. Barrett A Mc.Cotter and others and by the consent of the owners of the land through which the Highway Hereinafter described is to pass—

The said Highway being through lands not enclosed. The undersigned Commissioners of Highways of the Said Town of Brookhaven Do hereby order determine and certify that a Public Highway Shall be and the same is hereby laid out pursuant to such application a Survey whereof has been made and is as follows (viz. Commencing on the Horse-Block Road in the centre of Mc Cotters East Avanue and Running South one half of a degree East ninety nine chains thence due South twenty one chains to a Stone opposite the South East corner of the House late of Robert Hubbard deceased thence South four degrees west two chains and twenty nine links to a Stake on the South side of the L. I. Rail Road thence South one Degree East untill it intersects the old Road leading to Patchogue the line of the Sd. Survey to be the centre of the Said Highway which is to be three Rods in Width

In Witness whereof the Said commissioners have hereunto Subscribed their names this 5th day of June—one thousand Eight hundred and fifty three

Isaac Overton } Commrs
Nelson Norton }

Whereas application has been made to the commissioners of Highways of the Town of Brookhaven in the county of Suffolk to lay out a Highway on fireplace Neck in Said Town beginning on the Highway leading from Beaver Dam creek to carmans River at or near the west line of the lands of John L. Ireland and Running South by and with Said line to the South Bay or Shore. which proposed Road is to be three rods wide and will pass through our improved or cultivated lands.

Now therefore we the undersigned in consideration of the laying out and opening the sd Highway and discontinuing of the old road leading to Roses landing do hereby release all claim to damages by Reason thereof.

Youngs Moger. (L S)   Charles Swezey   L S
John C. Downs (L S)   Horace G. Randall L S
David H. Hulse (L S) Samuel W. Randall L S

Brookhaven
June 8th 1853

PAGE 25.

To the Commissioners of Highways of the Town of Brookhaven in the county of Suffolk. The Subscribers residents of said Town and liable to be assessed for Highway labor therein hereby apply to the said commissioners of Highways to lay out a new road three Rods wide commencing on the Highway leading from Beaver Dam creek to carmans River at or near the west line of the lands of John L. Ireland and running south by and with the said line to the South Bay or Shore which proposed Road will pass through the Enclosed or cultivated lands of David Hulse Charles Swezey Youngs Moger John Downs Samuel

W. Randall and Horace G Randall. who consent thereto. and further that the old Road leading to Roses landing be discontinued

Brookhaven May 30th 1853

Signers

Wm S. Swezey
Joseph Davis
Orlando Randall
Henry N. Moger
Youngs Moger
Richard Corwin
N. Miller Jur
N. Miller

Andrew M. Gildersleve
Charles H. Hulse
David B Reeve
Jacob B. Smith
Benjamin Gildersleve
Albert D. Randall
Charles Swezey
Saml. W. Randall

Horace G. Randall

At a meeting of the commissioners of Highways of the Town of Brookhaven in the county of Suffolk at Fireplace in the said Town on the 8th day of June 1853 (all the said commissioners having been duly notified to attend the Said Meeting for the purpose of deliberating upon the Subject matter of this order) on the application of Andrew M Gildersleve and Sixteen others and by the consent of David H. Hulse Charles Swezey Youngs Moger John Downs Samuel W. Randall and Horace G. Randall through whose improved land the Highway hereinafter described is to pass. The undersigned Commissioners of Highways of the said Town do hereby order determine and certify that a public Highway Shall be and the Same is hereby laid out pursuant to Such application three Rods wide on the East Side of the neck or tract of land formerly belonging to William Swezey at Fire place in the Said Town and county and the Said commissioners have caused a Survey thereof to be made as follows. The centre line of the said Highway is to begin at the South Side of the Beaver Dam or Fireplace neck Road at the distance of one Rod and a half from the north west corner of the land of John L. Ireland thence Running South three and a half degrees west twenty Eight chains and twelve links then South twelve and one quarter degrees West Eleven chains and twenty one links then South Six degrees west twenty Chains and Seventy five links Then South fourteen and a half degrees West Eleven chains or to the South Bay. And it is further ordered upon the like application and consent

PAGE 26.

that the old Road on the west side of the Said neck leading to Rose's landing be and the same is hereby discontinued the Road down Said neck having been Altered and the Highway hereby laid out being Substituted for the Said old Road by the Said commissioners with the consent of all persons Interested therein

In witness whereof the Said Commissioners have hereunto Subscribed their names this 8th day of June 1853

Isaac Overton } Commissrs
Nelson Norton }

We the commissioners of the Town of Brookhaven in the County of Suffolk for the year one thousand Eight hundred and forty two having been notified by the Inhabitants of the village of Stoney Brook to divide the Road district No. one in Said Town did by said notice propose to said village on the fifth day of March 1842

We the undersigned Brewster Terry and Daniel H. Skidmore Commissioners of the Town aforesaid appearing and Robert Smith the other Commissioner not appearing although legally notified by us to appear. did proceed to divide Said District into two Seperate districts as follows (viz) No. one to commence one hundred Rods on the Road that leads from Stony Brook to Goulds to the South of Richard Hawkin's house situate at the South end of Said village from thence northerly as far as the Square extends to the north including all the Inhabitants residing on Said Square excepting the Road to the west and north of Said Square taking all cross Roads as far as the aforesaid bounds extends to be included in said district No. one as aforesaid

District No 2 to commence at the southwest corner of the Square aforesaid and the Road north of Sd Square and so on to the Docks of Charles D Hallock's and Jonas Smith and all other Roads to the northeast and East excepting the Road to the east of the aforesaid Square and adjoining Said Square as were formerly worked within the bounds as aforesaid

In witness whereof we the Commissioners as aforesaid have Set our hands this twenty second day of March on thousand eight hundred and forty two

     Brewster Terry } Commissioners
     Daniel H. Skidmore }

PAGE 27.

At a meeting of the Board of Trustees of the Town of Brookhaven on tuesday the 3d day of Jan. 1854 Present at sd meeting

    Davis Norton President
  Horace Hudson David W. Case
  David Hedges John F Hallock
    Joel Robinson

At said meeting it was resolved that the timber standing on the land known as the negro Burying Ground at Setauket be sold at auction on thursday the 17th Feb 1854 adjourned to meet on tuesday the 7th day of Feb next at 9 oclock A.M.   DAVIS NORTON President

County of Suffolk }
 Town of } s s
 Brookhaven }

It is hereby ordered and determined by Isaac Overton Philip Hallock Nelson Norton Commissioners of Highways of Said Town that the Highway leading southerly through the village of Port Jefferson be altered from two Rods to three Rods in width commencing on the eastern Side of Said Highway at a point Six feet distant Southerly from the Stone wall near the House of John Roe in said village thence Running South thirty degrees and thirty minutes East Four Chains & eighty four links thence South Sixty two degrees East four chains to the Intersection of said highway with the Road Running on the north side of Z. Hawkins house in Said Village to Mount Sinai

In witness whereof We the Said Commissioners have hereunto Subscribed our names this 2d. day of Feb. 1854

Isaac Overton
Philip Hallock
Nelson Norton
} Commissioners of Highways of Brookhaven

PAGE 28.

At a meeting of the Trustees of the freeholders and commonalty of the Town of Brookhaven on tuesday the 7th day of Feb. 1854—Present

Davis Norton President

Horace Hudson
David W Case
John F. Hallock
Henry K. Townsend
David Hedges
Joel Robinson
} Trustees

The board being informed at this meeting that some person residing in Islip was constructing or about to construct a Dock or wharf in the waters of this Town opposite Islip without obtaining a grant from the Town David W. Case and David Hedges two of the Trustees were appointed a committe to go and enquire into the affair and report at next meeting. On motion the Board decided to lease to Jonas Mills of Blue point the Island in the South Bay called the inshore Ridge opposite Bell Port for five years at 3 Dollars per year—

The board decided to authorise Horace Hudson to advertise and Sell the timber standing on Laurel Hill or the negro Burying ground in Setauket belonging to the Town As Several applications were made for the priviledge and Right to take EEls in the waters of the great South Bay for foreign market the Board decided to give them an answer at next meeting of the Board

Adjourned to the first tuesday in March next at nine oclock A M Davis Norton President

Saml. A Hawkins Town Clerk

At a meeting of the Board of Trustees of the Town of Brookhaven on tuesday the 7th day of March 1854 Present the full Board By request the board decided and agreed to Renew the Lease to Capt Henry Tyler for the Shore at Setauket Harbor for two years longer at the same Rate of two Dollars per year on motion the Board decided that in case of any difficulty to defend to the purchaser the Sale of the timber Sold by said trustees on Laurel Hill in Setauket. Board decided to Lease to Individuals or companies the privilege of EEling for one year from the date hereof in the west Bay with nets and pots for foreign or any market who apply to the Trustees for a certificate each company to consist of not more than four persons each company or Individual So EEling to catch skin and prepare for market all such EEls taken in said Bay and out of the proceeds derived from the Same take one quarter of the Same for expenses and out of the remaining

Page 29.

three quarters to pay to Said Trustees or their Successors one tenth of that amount and present to Sd trustees all the Bills and accounts of EEls So taken or caught and disposed of under oath The committe appointed to enquire into the matter of Docking out into the west Bay opposite Islip without liberty reported that they Saw the Individual so trespassing and obtained his promise to meet the board at this meeting but being drawn on Jury at Riverhead will not be able to come

adjourned to the first tuesday in April next at 9 oclock A.M.   DAVIS NORTON President
SAMUEL A. HAWKINS
Town Clerk

The undersigned Commissioners of Highways of the Town of Brookhaven having met and deliberated on the subject embodied in this order do hereby order and determine

That Road district number Twenty two in said Town be and the same is hereby divided into two Districts as follows. All that part of Said District south of the South Country Road which is west of the west line of the land late of Joshua Smith decd. and all that part of Said district north of the south margin of said country Road which is west of the East margin of the Road leading past the House of Edward H Whiting from Patchogue to Medford Station including the said Road leading to Medford Station shall be known as Road District number Fifty. and all the Inhabitants residing in the present Road District west of the line above designated are hereby assigned to work in said Road District Number Fifty.

and all that part of Said District East of the line above designated shall be known as Road District number Twenty two and all the Inhabitants residing in the present Road District East of the line above designated are hereby assigned to work in said Road District Number twenty two—

That Road District Number twenty be altered so that all that part of Said District west of the east line of the farm of Wm Munsell including all that part of the Munsell Road until it intersects the Bellport Road shall be known as Road District Number Fifty one And all the Inhabitants residing therein West of the line above designated are hereby assigned to work in Said District Number Fifty one

That Road District Number Twenty shall include the Territory in said district between the East line of the land of William Munsell on the west and Osborn's Brook on the east That the Territory included between

PAGE 30.

Osborn's Brook on the west and Beaver Dam Creek or Brook on the East shall be a new Road District to be known as Road District Number Fifty two and the Inhabitants residing therein are hereby assigned to work on the Roads therein

That Road District Number Nineteen Shall include all the Territory in Said district East of Beaver Dam Creek or Brook

Given under our hands at the Town of Brookhaven in the County of Suffolk this 21st day of March one thousand Eight hundred and fifty four

Isaac Overton) Commissioners
Nelson Norton) of Highways

PAGE 31.

At an annual Town Meeting held on tuesday the 4 day of April A.D. 1854 in the Town of Brookhaven at the House of Lester H. Davis in Said Town the hereinafter named Individuals were duly Elected Town officers in sd Town for the Ensuing year viz.

For Supervisor
John S. Havens*

Note.—* John Syms Havens, of Moriches

For Justice of the Peace
Samuel C. Hawkins

President of Trustees
Davis Norton
For Trustees
Horace Hudson   Micah Jayne
David W. Case   Charles Rider
Joel Robinson   Daniel D. Swezey
For overseers of the Poor
David W. Case & Horace Hudson
For Commissioners of Highways
Isaac Overton
For assessor
Floyd Smith
Collector
Daniel W. Davis
For Constables
G. Osborn Overton   Daniel Overton
Gilbert K. Vail   George W. Overton
and Daniel W. Davis

Inspectors of Election—1st district
Thomas J. Ritch   Eden L. Roseman
and Wm S. Williamson

2d. district—
John Davis   Charles Miller
and Charles Phillips

3d district
John Hallock   Seth Raynor
and James M. Fanning

4th district
John B. Terry   Smith L. Newins
and Geo. P. Mills

5th district
Morgan L. Gould   Lester H. Davis
and Lester Davis

For additional Justices of the Peace
Joel Robinson—   Z. Franklin Hawkins
   Silas Homan & Richard O. Howell

Page 32.

For additional assessors
Conklin Davis   Isaac N. Gould
   and James M. Fanning

Said additional Justices and assessors are classified as follows—viz

Joel Robinson for one year   Z. Frankin Hawkins 2 years
Silas Homan for 3 years and Richard O. Howell 4 years

additional assessors
Conklin Davis   for one year
Isaac N. Gould   " two years
James M. Fanning. " three years

We the undersigned Justices of the Peace of the Town of Brookhaven do hereby certify that the foregoing is a true Statement of the Result of the annual town meeting held in Said Town on the 4th day of April 1854

Brewster Woodhull ⎫
Charles Phillips   ⎬ Justices
Jesse W. Pelletreau ⎪
Saml. F. Norton   ⎭

OVERSEERS OF HIGHWAYS OF THE TOWN OF BROOKHAVEN chosen April 4th 1854

1st. district—Charles Howe
2   do   Shepherd S. Jones
3   Sylvester Hawkins
4   Benjamin Brewster
5   Benjamin N. Smith
6   Wm B. Hawkins
7   William Fordham

8	Luther M. Satterly
9	James M. Hulse
10	Charles Woodhull
11	Sylvester Hallock
12	Nathaniel M. Tuttle
13	Ichabod G. Carter
14	Henry Carter
15	Solon Culver
16	John Iverson Raynor
17	Robert Smith
18	David T. Hawkins
19	John W. Petty
20	Edward Osborn
21	David Hedges
22	John Newton app'ted
23	Floyd Smith
24	Benjamin Hawkins
25	Nelson Daines
26	Joseph Newton
27	Ansel Reeve
28	Horace Ruland
29	Joel D. Norton
30	Richard W. Smith
31	Wm L. Lee
32	Richard Smith pond
33	LHommedieu Smith
34	Sylvester Homan
35	Holmes Swezey
36	Lester Ruland
37	James Dayton
38	Saml. L. Homan
39	Apollas A. Mills
40	Jehial Randall
41	Lewis Gordon
42	Humphrey Avery

43	Orlando Edwards
44	Gilbert K. Vail—appointed
45	Jonah Turner
46	Henry C. Mather
47	Sylvester Woodhull
48	John Dolon
49	Samuel Floyd

PAGE 33.

50 John Davis
51 Isaac Overton   52 Isaac Seaman—appointed

 I certify that the above or foregoing is a correct List of the overseers of Highways chosen and appointed in the Town of Brookhaven for the ensuing year
Brookhaven April 4th 1854
SAMUEL A. HAWKINS Town clerk

 The commissioners of Highways of the town of Brookhaven at their first meeting Subsequent to their Election do hereby assign to Wm Sidney Smith of sd. Town the following roads as a private Road district for the period of five years from this date (viz) commencing at a point on the Road leading from Middle Island to the Manor known as the new Road at the top of the Big hill and running from thence on sd new Road to the Hay Road a distance of about two and an half miles and from thence commencing north of the New Road on the Hay Road one mile and running from thence Southerly on the said Hay Road to the Rail Road a Distance of about 3 Miles

 Given under our hands this 18th day of April 1854 at Coram

Isaac Overton ⎫ commissioners
Nelson Norton ⎬   of
Phillip Hallock ⎭ Highways

 I hereby consent to take the above described roads for a

private Road district and keep in repair for five years next ensuing

Coram April 18th 1854   WILLIAM SIDNEY SMITH

To the Honorable the commissioners of Highways and public Roads in the Town of Brookhaven

The undersigned Respectfully solicit you so to alter the boundary line of path district No four and 49 so as to leave the district No. 4 all Roads in the vicinity of Grove place or lubber Street and to district No 49 the Road leading from the Mill pond to gipsey Square and all roads north of a westerly line from thence to the head of the meadows. All Roads South of sd westerly line to belong to district No 4 and your petitioners will ever pray &c Setauket April 3d 1854

Wm C. Tooker	Wickham Wheeler
Vincent Jones	Minor Dickerson
Vincent I Dickerson	Robert Jayne
Daniel Edwards	Samuel Floyd

PAGE 34.

William T. Wiltsie	Henry E Smith
Charles Dykes	Sidney W. Darling
James Howell	Henry Mulford
Charles Dickerson	John Dickerson
William Mitchell	Stephen Howell
Luther Darling	Benjamin Brewster
Elias Terrell	Stephen Swezey

at a meeting of the commissioners of Highways of the Town of Brookhaven in the county of Suffolk held at the House of Lester H. Davis in Said Town on the 18th day of April 1854 for the purpose of deliberating on the Subject matter of this order it was ordered and determined that the request of the within named Petitioners be granted and that the dividing line of Road Districts No. 4 and 49 be and the same is hereby altered accordingly

Brookhaven April 18th 1854

     Isaac Overton   ) Commissioners
     Phillip Hallock } of
     Nelson Norton   ) Highways

At a meeting of the Trustees of the Freeholders and commonalty of the Town of Brookhaven on tuesday the 2d. day of May 1854

    Present Davis Norton President
      Horace Hudson
      David W. Case
      Daniel D. Swezey } Trustees
      Charles Rider
      Micah Jayne
      Joel Robinson

The Board decided to pay Miller Woodhull 4 Dollars for keeping and transporting a colored women to the Alms House. Board agreed to help Hannah Smith to one Dollar as tempory aid. The Board decided that Notices be posted in at least four of the most public places on the South Side of the Town forbiding all persons EEling in the waters of the Great west Bay with pots nets or otherwise for any foreign market without first obtaining License of the Trustees of the Town

 adjourned until first tuesday in June Next.
  S. A. HAWKINS   DAVIS NORTON President
    Town Clerk

       PAGE 35.

At a meeting of the Trustees of the Freeholders and commonalty of the Town of Brookhaven on tuesday the 6th June 1854

    Present—Davis Norton President
      Horace Hudson
      David W Case
      Joel Robinson
      Daniel D Swezey } Trustees
      Charles Rider
      Micah Jayne

By Special Request the Board decided to lease to Charles L. Bayles the premises formerly leased to James M. & C. L. Bayles at Port Jefferson granting him liberty to Set a shop on Sd premises for which he is to pay five Dollars in addition to the former annuity

Board agreed to allow Mrs Norton 5 Dollars per month from and after the 3d day of June for Superintending the Alms House

Board decided to allow Mrs Gould 25 cent per week from June 6th 1854

Decided also to pay Bill presented by Parker S Robinson for keeping Nancy Lane

adjourned to first tuesday in Sept. next at 9 Oclock A M
S. A. HAWKINS   DAVIS NORTON Present
Town Clerk

At a meeting of the Trustees of the Freeholders and commonalty of the Town of Brookhaven held on tuesday the 5th day of September 1854

Present Davis Norton President

Horace Hudson ⎫
Micah Jayne ⎪
Daniel D Swezey ⎬ Trustees
Joel Robinson ⎪
Charles Rider ⎪
D. W. Case ⎭

at Said Meeting it was Resolved and voted that the sum of Eighteen Hundred Dollars be assessed and Raised for the benefit of the Poor of Said Town for the ensuing year.

Board decided on application to lease to John B Dan the gunning privileges in that part of the South Bay herein described viz from Fiddleton to Wm Smith line for the term of five years for 5 Dollars per year in advance yearly

Board agreed to assist Mary Raynor to 75 cts per week in stead of 50 cts from this date.

adjourned to meet the 2d tuesday in Nov. next at 9 oclock A.M.   Davis Norton President
S. A Hawkins
    Town Clerk

Page 36.

Whereas I Walter F. Smith of the Town of Brookhaven County of Suffolk and State of New York am Justly Indebted unto George W. Smith of town County and State aforesaid in the Sum of three Hundred and fifty Dollars being on a Note Said Geo. W. Smith holds against me to be paid on or before the 20th day of Sept. 1855 with Interest on the Same from the date thereof—Now therefore in consideration of Such Indebtedness and in order to secure the payment of the same as aforesaid I do hereby Sell assign and Set over unto the said George W. Smith the property consisting of goods wares and merchandise now in or which may be in the Store I now occupy at Moriches in aforesaid Town. Provided however that if the said debt and Interest be paid as above Specified this sale shall be void and this grant is also Subject to the following conditions The property hereby Sold is to remain in my possession untill default be made in the payment of the debt and Interest aforesaid or some part thereof unless I suffer Such property to depreciate to an unreasonable amount in which case the said Geo. W. Smith may take Said property or any part thereof into his own possession and proceed on the same as by law provided

Witness my hand and Seal this 20th day Sept 1854
Signed Sealed and   Walter F. Smith (L. S)
delivered in presence of
    J. W. Pelletreau

Suffolk County s s on the 20th day of Sep 1854 personally appeared before me Walter F. Smith to me known to be the Individual described in and who Executed the above

chattel mortgage and Acknowledged that he executed the
Same   JESSE W. PELLETREAU. Justice
                                              of the Peace

At a meeting of the Trustees of the Freeholders & commonalty of the Town of Brookhaven on tuesday the 14th day of Nov. 1854 Present all the Board Viz Davis Norton President Horace Hudson David W. Case Danl. D. Swezey Micah Jayne Charles Rider & Joel Robinson on application the Board decided to Lease to C. Green 10 lots in West Bay for planting Oysters, Board Resolved that Wm S. Williamson Ex collector be written to by Wm Wickham in relation to a Settlement. adjourned to meet first tuesday in Jan. next at 9 oclock A.M.
   S. A. HAWKINS   DAVIS NORTON President
     Town clerk

PAGE 37.

At a meeting of the Board of Trustees of the Town of Brookhaven on the 2d day of Jan. 1855 Present

                Davis Norton President
                Horace Hudson ⎫
                D. W. Case
                Daniel D. Swezey ⎬ Trustees
                Micah Jayne
                Joel Robinson.
                Charles Rider ⎭

Isaac Satterly made application to sd Trustees for an Exchange of some land adjoining the negro Burying ground for what timber may grow on sd Burying Ground* but the Trustees decided in the negative not to make the exchange

Board decided to add one Shilling per week to the pension of   from this date. the Board decided to add 2/ per week to the pension of Jacob & Rose from this date

adjourned to meet the first tuesday in Feb. next at 9 Oclock A.M
                        DAVIS NORTON President
S. A. HAWKINS
    Town Clerk

*Note. At Laurel Hill in Setauket

at a meeting of the Trustees of the Freeholders and commonalty of the Town of Brookhaven on tuesday the 6th of Feb 1855

Present—Davis Norton President.

Horace Hudson
David W. Case
Micah Jayne   } Trustees
Daniel D. Swezey
Charles Rider
Joel Robinson

Board decided to allow Brewster Woodhull Bills which he presented amounting to $17.67 cts.

adjourned to meet on tuesday the 6th day of March Next at 9 Oclock A.M. at the House of L. H. Davis

at the above meeting the Board decided to advertise the Oystering and EEling privileges of the West Bay and sell the same to the highest Bidder

                      DAVIS NORTON President

S. A. HAWKINS Town clerk

PAGE 38.

Trustees of School District No. 18 in the Town of Brookhaven
    versus.
Trustees of School District No 19 also versus Town Supt Supervisor and Town Clerk of Said Town
    } V. M. Rice Superintendent

From the statements presented in the two appeals Signified in the title of this paper it appears that on the 28th of Oct.

1854 The Town Superintendent of Brookhaven Suffolk County in concert with the Supervisor and Town Clerk of Said Town associated with him upon the application of the Trustees of District No 18 in said Town did determine & describe the boundaries of said district. In so doing they set off a portion of its admitted territory to District No. 17 which adjoins on the north They failed to find any Recorded boundary on the eastern side nor as it appears any boundary very clearly defined by occupation or actual exercise of Jurisdiction—They however established a line from which the Trustees of the conterminous dist. No 19 dissent regarding the order as an alteration of their district as well as of Dist—No 18

The appellants deny that the establishment forming the eastern boundary was an alteration because there has been no boundary previously established and insist that consequently the newly defined line became that boundary at once instead of remaining inchoate until the first day of May 1855 as must otherwise be the case

It is impossible under the circumstances to determine whether the line established between districts 18 and 19 was a new boundary the law presumes that there was an ascertainable boundary heretofore tho its precise location has been lost. The appellants state that some of the Inhabitants of district No. 19 claim that a line known as the Yaphank line constituted that boundary : an attempt to disprove this allegation by showing that Individuals Residing in houses east of that line have sent their children to school in district No. 18 which children have been for years included in their annual reports made by the Trustees of said district : moreover, that Samuel Glover while Inhabiting the house fartherest east of the Yaphank line and nearest the line established in Oct. last was elected Trustee of district No. 18 so long ago as 1829—The map accompanying the appeal shows that the land appertaining to and occupied with one of the houses above mentioned comes up to the eastern boundary as established in Oct. But that land does not extend the whole length of that

Page 39.

boundary and in opposition to the inference that might be drawn from it. stands the fact that the house of one Thos. Aldrich was recorded as the western boundary of a district which is now No. 19 This house stands northward of the old boundary of district No 18 but much nearer the Yaphank line than to a continuance of the new line

The evidence is not sufficient to enable Supert. to decide whether the line established in Oct. last is the veritable ancient boundary of the district tho probably it does not widely diverge therefrom :

Whereas it should be definite enough to enable a private Individual to recover in an action of ejecment. So long as it remains a matter of reasonable doubt whether the order in question amounts to an alteration. No 19 tho not affected by an actual alteration would be seriously affected by the division that such alteration has not been made & should therefore in equity be considered as entitled to the same delay before the order becomes operative—

In fact the commissioners have no jurisdiction in the matter except for the purpose of making an alteration and their declaration in respect to an old boundary is of no more legal force than that of the same number of other inteligent persons except that they can make it the boundary tho it was not before—

The order of Oct. 1854 due notice thereof having been given will take effect upon the first day of May next. so far as the eastern boundary of said district No 18 is concerned

No question relative to the other boundaries is properly before this department on the two appeals but if evidence is obtained of the assent of the trustees of the other districts affected this decision will not prevent said order from taking effect as to the alterations aforesaid immediately upon the day when it was granted by the officers named in this paper—

These appeals are therefore dismissed. The Town Clerk of the Town of Brookhaven and the clerks of districts No 18 and 19 are directed to record this decision—

Given under my hand and the Seal of Office of the department of public Instruction at the City of Albany this thirty first day of January 1855

| Seal |

(Copy)

V. M. RICE
Supt. of Public Instruction

PAGE 40.

School districts Renumbered 24th Oct 1842 by

Selah B. Strong } Com. of
Simeon H Ritch } Com. Schools
A. A. Overton }

Former No.	Present No.	
30	1	N. E. part of Stony Brook
2	2	W. Setauket
28	3	Nassakeag
3	4	E. Setauket
34	5	N. E. Setauket
4	6	Port Jefferson
5	7	Mt. Sinai
6	8	Millers Place
7	9	Rocky Point
35	10	Woodville
9	11	New Village
25	12	West fields
27	13	Bald Hills
10	14	Coram
23	15	Hills

Former No.	Present No.	
11	16	Middle Island church
33	17	Middle District
12	18	Millville
22	19	Ridge
24	20	Manor North
14	21	Manor W.
13	22	Manor E.
31	23	Bluepoint
21	24	Patchogue W.
20	25	Patchogue E.
36	26	Patchogue Lane
19	27	Union St
32	28	Bellport
18	29	Fireplace Neck
26	30	Fireplace Mills
17	31	Mastic
29	32	Moriches W.
16	33	Moriches Centrel
15	34	Moriches E.
Part No 1 Part districts	1	Stony Brook S.
No 8	2	Pond
part No 1	3	Wad. River
3	4	Conungum Mills
District	35	Patchogue S. Shore
	36	Canaan N. of Patchogue
	37	Seatuck

Part District No 6 organised 1847 West of J. F. Hallock.

Page 41.

Boundary Line between north Side and Middle Island Districts

Decision of Commissioners 1842—

Ordered that where School Districts on the north side of Brookhaven and those in or near the Middle of the Island adjoining each other and where no definite boundary has heretofore been made. The Butt line so called shall constitute the boundary lines and line of said districts Also that when districts on the south side of sd town and those in or near the middle of the Island lying west of Smith's patent line adjoining each other and where there has been no definite line between them Such definite line to the north shall be the Long Island Rail Road—

That the Long Island Rail Road shall also be the boundary line between districts No. 20—21— and 22 and that Dongans line be the south Boundary of No. 21 & 22 and the north boundaries of Nos. 33 and 34 And that No. 31 extend north to the boundary stone Between Wm Smith and Wm Sidney Smith District No. 17 formed from No 16 & 18 by Commissioners S. B. Strong and Saml. F. Norton on the 6th March 1835—

Resolved that a new district be formed from the eastern portion of No. 11 (now 16) and north part of No. 12 (now 18) 1st. by setting off all that part of district No. 11 bounded on the west by the West line of Daniel Pettys land extending south so as to include the land of H. P. Hutchinson north to include the house and land of Jonathan Edwards east to include the lands and house of Joel Turner and to Extend south into the 12 district so as to include the houses and lands of Zechariah and James Dayton into the north line of the lands of Silvanas Overton including all the Inhabitants within said bounds which new district will be No. 33 (now 17)

Removal of Site of School House in district 15th now 34 At a meeting of the commissioners at Henry P. Osborn's in sd district 26th Feb. 1838 on Receiving the application of School district 15 for consent of commissioners to change the Site of School house in sd district after examination into and consideration of the matter the Commissioners are of opinion that a change of the Site and removal of sd School

House from the present location to a certain tract of land lying on the South side of the South country Road between the barn of H. P. Osborn and the Black-Smith Shop of Selah B. Parsons being bounded on the east south and west by the land of Said H. P. Osborn being about 4 Rods Square which sd tract has been designated by the Inhabitants of Said district for that purpose as necessary and the Said

PAGE 42.

Commissioners consent to such change of site and removal of School-House

    Selah B. Strong
    Wm Sidney Smith ⎬ Commissioners
    Saml. F. Norton

Alteration of School district Part No. 2 so as to include a part of Islip—At a meeting of the Town Supert. of Brookhaven and Islip and Smith Town at John Newton 26 Feb. 1846 Resolved that Joint district No. 2 of Brookhaven 5 of Smith Town now composed of parts of Sd towns be and the same is hereby altered and enlarged so as to include all that part of Islip to be Part no. 10 in Sd town within the following boundaries (viz) commencing at the point where the Nicoll Road Intersects the S. and Islip line thence running Southerly along the Nicoll Road till it comes to the Oxhead Road & thence continuing Southerly along the sd Oxhead Road till it comes to the fire Road twenty Rods south of the L. I. R. Road Thence Running easterly along the sd fire Road & parrallel with the R. R to the Islip and Brookhaven line and continuing thence east along Sd fire Road as far as the present east bounds of sd district so as to include all that part of B. Haven which lies between the present S. boundary line and fire Road sd territory being mostly uninhabited those persons included in sd bounday having consented to Such alterations

H. Brewster. J. R. Hunting. Wm Wickham Superintendents

Alteration of Districts Nos. 30—31—32 by Wm Sidney Smith Supert. Nathl. Conkling Supervisor and M. Homan Town clerk 16 Sep. 1843

Resolved and ordered that School dist. no. 30 be altered by annexing thereto the House and triangular portion of ground now occupied by Jeremiah Glover bounded Southerly by the country Road easterly by the Road leading to the Middle of the Island northerly by the Road leading from sd last mentioned Road to Saml Carmans and that district No 32 be altered by annexing the former parcels of lands belonging to Silas Paine Wm. Paine Nicoll Overton Charles Murray John Thurston Daniel Paine to sd district No. 32 and that district no. 31 be altered in conformity to the above described alterations of districts 30 & 32 Petition of Trustees of No 31 and consent of those of 30 and 32 having been had

Formation of School dist. No. 10 formerly 33—At a meeting of the Com. of Com. Schools of Brookhaven at Peter Skidmores 24 Feb. 1838 On Recg the Petition of several of the Inhabitants of dis. no 6 now 8 and of part dis. no. 1 now 3 for the formation of a new dist. from parts of those dists. together with the written consent of the Trustees of those dists. and it appearing that on a Joint meeting of the Com. of Brookhaven and Riv. Head held on this day so much of sd dists. no 1 (3) as is comprised within the new district hereafter described has been duly Seperated from dist. no 1 it was Resolved and ordered that all that part of the Town of B—Haven bounded northerly by the Sound East by wading River creek until it Reaches east thence by said creek and the Hollow leading from it to the north country Road thence by that Road to the western boundary line of Benjamin Woodhull home place then by that line to the Butt line & on the west by the westerly bounds of P. Skidmore land be and is hereby formed into a new dist. known as dist. No 33 now 10 Woodville agreed to by the Com. of Brookhaven and Riverhead

Page 43.

Know all men by these presents that I Geo. Robinson of the Town of Brookhaven county of Suffolk and State of New York for and in consideration of the sum of Seventy five Dollars to me in hand paid by Oliver Robinson of the same place at and before the ensealing and delivery of these presents the Receipt whereof is hereby acknowledged have bargained, sold and delivered and by these presents do bargain sell and deliver unto the said Oliver Robinson a one mast Sail boat to have and to hold the said boat unto the said Oliver Robinson his Executors administrators heirs and assigns to his and their own proper use and benefit forever

and I the said Geo. Robinson for myself and my heirs Executors and administrators will warrant and defend the said bargained premises unto the sd Oliver Robinson his Executors administrators and assigns from and against all persons whomsoever In witness whereof I have hereunto set my hand and seal this Eighth day of Jan. one thousand Eight hundred and fifty five

In presence of   GEORGE W. ROBINSON (L. S.)
MATHEW E WOODRUFF

At a meeting of the Trustees of the Town of Brookhaven on the 6th day of March 1855

Present Davis Norton President
Horace Hudson ⎫
David W. Case ⎪
D. D. Swezey   ⎬ Trustees
Charles Rider   ⎪
Micah Jayne   ⎪
Joel Robinson ⎭

at said meeting the Board decided to lease the fishing privileges of the west Bay to Alexander Smith of Huntington for the term of three years from May next for fifty Dollars for the whole term— on complaint the Board decided that David Robinson be written to and Requested to take care of his son David who is unable to provide for himself

adjourned to the first tuesday in April next at 9 oclock A.M. DAVIS NORTON Prest.

SAML. A. HAWKINS Town Clerk

PAGE 44.

At a meeting of the Trustees of the freeholders and commonalty of the Town of Brookhaven on tuesday the 3d. day of April 1855

Present Davis Norton President

Horace Hudson
David W. Case
Micah Jayne
D. D. Swezey
Charles Rider
Joel Robinson
} Trustees

On application the Board decided to Lease to Capt. Charles Rider Pelican Island or the Grass growing on Said Island for the term of five years. at three Dollars—a petition was presented asking for liberty to dredge or drag Oysters or Shells in west Bay Bay decided that they had no power or authority to grant Such liberty Board decided that Danl. Overton a constable proceed to collect of Benjamin Homan the sum due from him to the town on a obligation adjourned Sine die— DAVIS NORTON Prest.

SAML. A. HAWKINS Town clerk

Suffolk County S s

Whereas on the 26th day of March 1855 David Robinson Jun appealed to the County Judge of Suffolk Co. from an order and determination of the Commissioners of Highways of the Town of Brookhaven made on or about the 10th day of March aforesaid laying out a highway in sd town from the south country Road nearly opposite the House of Andrew Ketcham (in the Village of Moriches) to the south Bay and whereas the said County Judge at a time and place for that purpose appointed has heard the proofs and allegations of the parties now the Said court have does hereby adjudge decide and determine that said order and determination of Said commissioners be and the same is in all things approved

In witness whereof I Wm P. Buffett County Judge of Suffolk County have hereunto set my hand the 14th day of June 1855 WILLIAM P. BUFFETT

PAGE 45.

At an annual Town Meeting held in and for the Town of Brookhaven on tuesday the 3d. day of April 1855 for the Election of Town officers the hereinafter named Individuals were duly Elected for the ensuing year (viz)

For Supervisor
John S. Havens

For Justices of the Peace
Richard W. Smith for Vacancy and also for the full term of 4 years
Samuel R. Davis for Vacancy and also for the full term o 4 years

President of Trustees
Davis Norton

For Trustees

Horace Hudson	George F. Carman
Micah Jayne	John Hallock
David Hedges	Daniel D. Swezey

For Overseers of Poor
Horace Hudson and George F. Carman

For Superintendent of Schools
Lewis R. Overton

For Town Clerk
Samuel A. Hawkins
For Commissioners of Highways
James Hallock
For Assessors
Conklin Davis William H. Clark and John S. Havens
For Collector
Daniel W. Davis
For Constables
Daniel W. Davis   G. Osborn Overton
Gilbert K Vail   George W. Overton
and Daniel Overton
For Inspectors of Election
1st district Thomas J. Ritch Nehemiah Hand and John M. Williamson
2d. district John Davis Charles Woodhull and Walter Dickerson
3d district Seth Raynor John C. Stephens and Egbert T. Smith
4th district Washington Wadsworth Brewster Terry and Jacob G. Horton
5th district Nelson Norton Orlando Randall and Hiram Overton

We the undersigned Justices of the peace in and for sd town do hereby certify that the foregoing is a true Statement of the result of sd annual town meeting

Saml. F. Norton   Charles Phillips   } Justices
Samuel C. Hawkins   Z Franklin Hawkins

PAGE 46.

LIST OF OVERSEERS OF HIGHWAYS OF THE TOWN OF BROOKHAVEN Chosen Apr. 3d 1855

district
1st William S. Williamson   27 Morgan L. Gould
2   Scudder S. Wells   28 Richard O. Howell

district

3	Ebenezer Hawkins	29	Davis Norton
4	Joseph Jayne—appointed	30	Smith Still
5	William Smith	31	Lester Davis
6	James Anderson	32	Richard Smith—pond
7	Tuttle Dayton	33	Martin V. B. Ruland
8	Jonathan Pike	34	Daniel T. Overton
9	Timothy Davis	35	George W. Ritch
10	John M. Brown	36	Floyd Edwards
11	Joel Brown	37	Joseph N. Hurton
12	Benjamin Tuttle	38	Edward Homan
13	Charles M. Petten	39	Apollas A. Mills
14	Nathan Davis	40	Hiram Edwards
15	Samuel S. Stansbrough	41	Henry A. Gordon
16	Ebenezer Jayne	42	Daniel Robinson
17	Silas Payne—appd	43	James Swezey
18	David T. Hawkins	44	David Robinson
19	Sylvester N. Corwin	45	Sidney Penny
20	Briant N. Overton	46	Herman Hallock
21	David Hedges	47	Elbert Woodhull
22	Wm E. Conkling	48	John Dolon
23	Wm J. Horton	49	Wm Clark Tooker
24	Wm Rowland—appd.	50	John Roe
25	Jonas Mills	51	Isaac Overton
26	Joseph Newton	52	Joel Hawkins

I certify that the foregoing is a correct List of Overseers of Highways chosen and appointed in and for the Town of Brookhaven for the ensuing year
Brookhaven
April 3d. 1855 SAMUEL A. HAWKINS Town clerk

At a meeting of the Trustees of the Freeholders and commonalty of the Town of Brookhaven on tuesday the 1st day of May 1855 Present Davis Norton Prest. Horace Hudson Geo. F. Carman D. D. Swezey Micah Jayne David Hedges & John Hallock Resolved to allow Deborah Howell 5/ a week from April 3d 1855 Resolved to reduce Mrs Cherry pension to 3/ per week Board paid Alfred Davis fifty Dollars in advance as overseer of poor house and engaged him to oversee for one year from this date. Board Resolved to petition or Recommend to Board of Supervisors to amend the law in relation to dredging for Oysters in the waters of this Town and that a petition be drafted to that effect—adjourned to the first tuesday of June next at 9 O clock A. M.

SAML. A. HAWKINS   DAVIS NORTON President
  Town clerk

PAGE 47.

In the matter of the appeal of Wm Sidney Smith from an order of the Town Supt. and Town clerk of Brook haven to establish the boundary between School districts Nos. 18 and 19 in sd town } Rice Superintendent

The facts presented upon this appeal were in great part before the Department upon an appeal in Jan. last It was then decided that the line established by the order appealed from was not so proven to be the ancient boundary as to Justify the department in regarding that order otherwise than as an alteration of the districts concerned.

The propriety of that conclusion is strengthened by the evidence now adduced. Though not entirely conclusive it goes far to prove that the "Yaphank Line" so called has been for many years claimed and regarded by the Inhabitants of district no. 19 as the boundary dividing them from district no. 18 Occasional acts of the Trustees of district No 18 in admitting Children as pupils whose residence was in dist. no. 19 if the Yaphank line was the true boundary, and in one case even electing as a trustee the Father of some of those children whose residence is closely adjoined to that boundary, have tended in some degree to obscure a question the solution of which has been left to depend upon oral tradition and acts of use, instead of documentary evidence. These acts are capable of explanation on the ground of indulgence to the children and mistake as to the proper place for their enumeration, arising from the fact that such indulgence has been suffered to grow into custom. If however the evidence in favor of the Yaphank Line as the former boundary is not so satisfactory as is desirable, there is on the other hand a total of all evidence in favor of the Hay Road the newly established boundary. The most that is proven is that the Yaphank Line was sometimes oversteped, but there is nothing to fix the hay Road as the limit. The order must therefore be regarded as an *alteration* of the districts; and regarded in this light there is no evidence of any such necessity or expediency as should Justify the transforment of a large amount of taxable proper from district no. 19 which is very weak and has very small population to district no 18 which already possesses a much greater amount of property. It is quite possible that an alteration ought to be made which would transfer to dist. No 18 that portion of the territory in the extreme southern part of district no. 19 the Inhabitants of which have been permitted to send pupils to the School in dist. no 18 for the purpose of promoting the convenient access of such pupils to the means of Instruction. The Supt. however has not the requisite information to define such Territory This appeal is sustained and the order appealed from, so far as it establishes the eastern boundary of School dist. no 18 is vacated. The Town clerk of Brookhaven is directed to record this decision

PAGE 48.

Given under my hand and the Seal of office of the Department of Public Instruction at the city of Albany this sixteenth day of April 1855

V. M. RICE
Superintendent of Public Instruction

At a Meeting of the Trustees of the Freeholders and commonalty of the Town of Brookhaven on tuesday the 5th day of June 1855—

Present—Davis Norton President
Horace Hudson }
George F. Carman
Daniel D. Swezey } Trustees
John Hallock
David Hedges
Micah Jaye

on application of Wm C. Tooker to purchase a piece of public land at old field the Board decided to defer action on the subject until next meeting. Mr Jones also applied for a piece of the Shore at Port Jefferson Board decided to defer the matter until next meeting also—

Resolved that Mrs Nicoll Receive 4/ instead of 3/ from this time

on application of Lewis Hulse for a renewal of his grant for Dock and Rail way the Board appointed Davis Norton & Micah Jaye a committe to View premises and report at next meeting

On application of Mr Spenola for liberty to lay down Oysters in Flax pond. The Board appointed Mr Jaye to View the premises and report at next meeting

adjourned until first tuesday in Sept. next at nine Oclock A.M.   Davis Norton Prest.

Samuel A. Hawkins
   Town Clerk

Page 49.

At a meeting of the Trustees of the Freeholders an commonalty of the Town of Brookhaven held Sept. 4th 1855

Present Davis Norton President
Horace Hudson }
Geo. F. Carman
John Hallock } Trustees
Micah Jayne
David Hedges

Board voted to reduce Mrs Terrells Pension to 5 S. per Week from this date—

William M. Jones made application for a piece of Meadow near the harbor of Port Jefferson Board voted and agreed to Quit Claim to sd Jones about $\frac{1}{4}$ part of an Acre for the Sum of 50 Dollars

on application Board voted and agreed to allow Mrs Gould 6/. per week from this date

On application the Board voted and agreed to lease to Edward T. Moore as President Martin Mott Alfred Mott John Ruland as Directors 50 or 60 Acres of land under water in the Great South Bay for the purpose of laying down or planting Oysters for the term of three years at a Dollar a year per Acre in advance with the privilege of the same for two years longer. at the Same Rate

On application the Board decided to Renew the lease to Lewis Hulse for liberty to Erect a Railway in Port Jefferson at 13 Dollars annuity to continue as long and to extend as far into the Bay as C. L. Bayles Lease

The Case of the Barnes Children who are now living with their Grand Father Joel Wicks be left discretionary with Mr Carman till next meeting

Davis Norton and Micah Jayne were appointed a committe to Stony Brook to view the School House Hill in relation to Setting an Acadamy thereon

adjourned to the 2d. tuesday in Oct. next

Davis Norton Prest.

S. A. Hawkins
   Town clerk

Page 50.

At a meeting of Trustees of the Freeholders and Commonalty of the Town of Brookhaven on tuesday the 9th day of Oct. 1855

Present Davis Norton Prest.

Geo F. Carman ⎫
Horace Hudson ⎪
David Hedges ⎬ Trustees
Daniel D. Swezey ⎪
Micah Jayne ⎪
John Hallock ⎭

at this Meeting it was voted and agreed to allow Joel Wicks 4/ per week for keeping the Eldest Boy of the Barnes Family also agreed to allow Carman Wicks 3/ for keeping the younger Boy of Sd family--per week Board agreed to Quit Claim to Saml. L. Thompson a narrow scrap or piece of Land at Old field

adjourned to the first tuesday in Dec. next at 9 Oclock A.M.
                                      DAVIS NORTON Prest

SAML. A. HAWKINS Town clerk

To the Commissioners of Highways of the Town of Brookhaven in the County of Suffolk

The undersigned freeholders of the Town of Brook Haven do hereby make application to you to lay out a new highway of the width of three Rods through the enclosed lands of John S. Bishop Isaac Bishop Robert Jones David Robinson Jun Andrew Ketcham and James Ruland Said Road to begin at the South Country Road opposite or nearly opposite the Protestant Methodist Meeting House and to extend in a southerly direction over or nearly over the Road now travelled and in as direct a line as may be practicable to the South Bay

Dated December 15th 1854

    Josiah H. Bishop   Cephus Rodgers
    David Terry   Silas Reeve
    E. P. Jarvis M.D.   John R. C. Smith
    John Bishop Sen   Henry P. Osborn
    John S. Bishop   Laban Raynor
    John T. Robinson   W. R Howell
    John Howell   Josiah Smith

S. S. Stansbrough
Edward D. Topping
J. C. Lamphier
Wm Smith
Epenetus Rodgers
Nelson Bishop
Lester Hulse

PAGE 51.

Suffolk County. ss Town of Brookhaven

Epenetus Rogers Wm Smith Josiah Smith John Bishop Sen David Terry Nelson Bishop John Howell John T. Robinson Silas Reeve John S. Bishop Lester Hulse and John R. C. Smith

The Subscribers to the within application being Severally duly Sworn each for himself says he has Read the within application by him Subscribed and he further Says that he verily believes the Highway therein applied for is required for the public good

Sworn before me this 18th
day of December 1854
    J. W. PELLETREAU Justice of the Peace

Freeholders.

Epenetus Rogers
Wm Smith
Josiah Smith
John Bishop Sen
David Terry
Nelson Bishop
John Howell
John T Robinson
Silas Reeve
John S. Bishop
Lester Hulse
John R. C. Smith

Suffolk County S s
Town of Brookhaven

We the subscribers the Jurors drawn, Summoned and Sworn to assess the damages for laying out the Highway Running from the South country Road to the South Bay in the Village of Moriches and nearly opposite the House of Andrew Ketcham according to a Survey made by Jesse W. Pelletreau Esq. Pursuant to the order of Isaac Overton Phillip Hallock and Nelson Norton Commissioners of Highways in and for the Town of Brookhaven aforesaid bearing date the 10th of March 1855 having viewed the premises and heard the parties and Such witnesses as were offered before us do hereby assess the damages aforesaid as follows. To pay David Robinson the Sum of one hundred and Twenty Dollars for the damages Sustained by him by Reason of the laying out the said Highway

In witness whereof we have hereunto Set our hands this Tenth day of March 1855

        Israel Howell
        John T. Pugsley.
        Richd A. Norton
        David W. Howell   } Jurors
        Nelson S. Woodhull
        Daniel G. Howell

PAGE 52.

Suffolk County S s }
Town of Brookhaven }

Jesse W. Pelletreau one of the Justices of the Peace of Said town do hereby Certify that the above is the verdict of the Jury Summoned by my Summons and drawn and Sworn by me to determine and assess the damages for the laying out the highway mentioned in the Said Verdict Given under my hand this 10th day of March 1855

        J. W. PELLETREAU Justice of the Peace

Suffolk County S s }
Town of Brookhaven }

Whereas upon the application of John Bishop and others residents in Said Town of Brookhaven and liable to be assessed to work on the Highway hereinafter described and on the certificate of twelve reputable freeholders of the Town convened and Sworn after due public notice, as required by the Statute certifying that such highway was necessary and proper. Now therefore in conformity to the Special Act provided in Such cases We the undersigned commissioners having met and after hearing all the reasons for and against the same, have ordered and determined and certified that a public highway shall be laid out pursuant to said application whereof a Survey has been made and is as follows to wit:—Running from the Bay to the South Country Road coming out nearly opposite the Protestant Methodist church in Moriches. Said highway running through the lands of Isaac Bishop John Bishop David Robinson Robert M. Jones John S. Bishop Nelson Bishop James Ruland and Andrew Ketcham courses and distances to wit: Commencing at the Bay from a certain Stake (all Stakes hereinafter mentioned are put down as the centre of said highway) and running north 5° E 18 Chains to a Stake thence north 5° E 4 chains to a Stake thence N. 5° E. 1 chain to a stake thence N. 24° E. 18 Chains to a stake thence N 18° E. 10 chains to a stake thence N. 15½° E. 6 Chains & 80 links to a Stake thence north 12° E 6 Chains and 20 links to a stake thence N. 18° E. 12 chains & 70 links to a stake Thence N. 12° E. 7 chains and 25 links to a stake thence N. 16° E 6 chains & 30 links to a stake thence north 13° E 4 Chains & 10 links to a Stake thence N. 13° E 3 Chains to a stake thence due N 4 chains & 40 links to a stake on the south side of the south Country Road said Road or highway to be of the width of three rods Dated this 10th day of March 1855

      Isaac Overton) Commissioners
      Phillip Hallock }   of
      Nelson Norton) Highways—

PAGE 53.

A Highway having been this day the 10th day of march 1855 laid out by Isaac Overton Phillip Hallock and Nelson Norton Commissioners of Highways of the Town of Brookhaven and County of Suffolk on the application of Epenetus Rogers William Smith Josiah Smith John Bishop Sen.

David Terry Nelson Bishop John Howell John T. Robinson Silas Reeve John S Bishop Lester Hulse John R. C. Smith through certain improved lands belonging to us commencing at the country Road and running to the South Bay agreeable to a Survey made by Jesse W. Pelletreau Esq on the 9th Jan. 1855

Now therefore know all men by these Presents that we Andrew Ketcham James Ruland John S. Bishop Nelson Bishop John Bishop and Isaac Bishop for value Received and in consideration of the benefits accruing from the privileges of Such and by Reason of the laying out and opening the Said Road do hereby release all claim to damages by having Such Road opened

Witness our hands and Seals this tenth day of March 1855

James Ruland (L S)
John Bishop (L S)
Andrew Ketcham (L S)
John S. Bishop (L S)
Nelson Bishop (L S)
Isaac Bishop (L S)

A highway having been this day the 10th of March 1855 laid out by Isaac Overton Phillip Hallock and Nelson Norton commissioners of Highways of the town of Brookhaven and county of Suffolk on the application of twelve freeholders of the Said Town through certain improved lands belonging to me commencing at the South Country Road and running to the South Bay in the Village of Moriches

Now therefore know all men by these presents that I Robert M. Jones for value Recd. and in consideration of the benefits accruing from the privileges of Such Road do hereby release all claim to damages by Reason of the laying out and opening such Road

Witness my hand and Seal this 14th day of March 1855

ROBERT M. JONES (L S)

J W. Teller no. 80. Second St. ⎤
City and County of N. York S s ⎦

On the 14th day of March 1855 personally appeared before me Robert M. Jones to me known to be the person within described and who in my presence Executed the within consent and he acknowledged he executed the Same for the purposes therein mentioned

T. W. TELLER. Commissioner of deeds

PAGE 54.

Quit Claim Deed.

Know all men by these presents that we whose names and Seals are hereunto Subscribed for and in consideration of the benefits of a public Highway from the centre of Moriches to the South Bay do hereby give and Quit-claim unto the town of Brookhaven in the county of Suffolk and State of New-York The land for Said Highway which is to be two rods wide and to run in accorance with a Survey taken by Jesse W. Pelletreau Esq as follows The Stakes are Set on the west side of Said road Commencing at a Stake on the Bay Shore and running North 30° W. 5 Chains and 86 links to a Stake thence N. 17° E. 11 Chains and 10 links to a Stake thence N. 17° E 6 chains to a stake thence N. 27° E. 12 Chains and 57 links to a Stake Thence N. 37° E. 5 Chains and 54 links to a Stake thence N. 37° E 5 Chains and 90 links to a Stake thence N. 37° E 10 Chains & 68 links to a Stake where it connects to and with the already laid out Road leading out of the Country Road at the Store of Wm Penny.

The above land to be used for a Public road and for no other purpose

In witness whereof we have hereunto Set our hands and Seals, this thirty first day of January in the year of our Lord one thousand eight hundred and fifty five

In presence of
L. D. Vail
D. E. Rhodes

Silas E. Topping (L. S)
Strong Terry (L. S)
Elias Topping (L. S)
Paul A. Cartwright (L. S)
John Baldwin (L. S)
Serepta Ellison (L. S)
Silas Topping (L. S)
John Bishop (L. S)
John T. Robinson (L. S)
Richard Robinson (L. S)
Daniel Brown (L. S)

We the undersigned commissioners of Highways of the Town of Brookhaven in the county of Suffolk do hereby Signify our acceptance of the foregoing Quit claim and order the Same to be filed in the office of the Town Clerk Dated Brookhaven April 17th 1855

Isaac Overton } Commissioners
Nelson Norton } of Highways

Entered by me

S. A. Hawkins
Town clerk

Page 55.

At a Meeting of the Trustees of the Freeholders and commonaty of the Town of Brookhaven on tuesday the 4th Decr. 1855 Present

Davis Norton Prest.
Horace Hudson ⎫
Geo. F. Carman ⎪
Micah Jayne ⎬ Trustees
D. D. Swezey ⎪
David Hedges ⎪
John Hallock ⎭

Application was made by several Gentlemen from Stony Brook for liberty to Set an Acadamy on the town land near the School House in sd village The board defered action in Said matter until next meeting

adjourned to meet the first tuesday in Jan. Next 1856

S. A Hawkins Town clerk   Davis Norton Prest.

at a meeting of the Trustees of the Freeholders and commonalty of the Town of Brookhaven on tuesday the first day of Jan. 1856

Present
Davis Norton President
Horace Hudson ⎫
Geo. F. Carman ⎪
Micah Jayne ⎬ Trustees
David Hedges ⎪
D. D. Swezey ⎭

Nothing of much importance was transacted at sd meeting the Bills were Settled and the Board adjourned to the first tuesday in Feb. 1856   D. Norton Prest

Saml. A. Hawkins
Town clerk

at a meeting of the Board of Trustees of the Town of Brookhaven on tuesday the 5th Feb. 1856—Present all the said Board of Trustees on application the Board decided to lease to James M. Fanning the new made Islands in the East Bay for five years at $6.50 per Year.

adjourned to meet on tuesday the 4th March next at 9 Oclock A.M.   D. Norton Prest.

S. A. Hawkins Town clerk

Page 56.

Whereas Charles L. and James M. Bayles are in lawful possession of the privilege of a Rail way at Port Jefferson granted to Robbins and Jones the 6th day of May 1834 and Recorded in Liber D. page 270 and to them renewed and extended August 7th 1849 and also recorded in Liber D. page 354 and as the said Charles L. and James M. Bayles have mutually agreed to disolve partnership James M. relinquishing all Right to said privilege Charles L. has petitioned for a new lease to him alone of Said premises with the additional privilege of setting a work Shop thereon for which he agrees to pay five Dollars additional annuity Now therefore This Indenture made this Sixth day of June in the year one thousand Eight hundred and fifty four Between the Trustees of the Freeholders and commonalty of the Town of Brookhaven of the first part and Charles L. Bayles of the same Town of the Second part Witnesseth that the Said parties of the first part for and in consideration of the yearly rent or annuity of thirteen Dollars to be paid annually to said Trustees or their Successors in office on the first tuesday in June in each year during the continuence of this Lease Have granted leased and to farm let and do by these presents grant lease and to farm let unto the said party of the second part and to his heirs and assigns for and during the term of twenty one years from the date hereof the Right and privilege to build construct and keep in repair a Rail way for hauling out Vessels to repair &c. on a certain tract or space of ground on Port Jefferson Shore belonging to said Town the first bound to set Sixty feet to the west-ward of the west side of the Dock at Port Jefferson owned by James R Davis at high-water mark and from thence to extend westward on the Shore Seventy feet and to extend Southward to the highway and northward into the Harbor two hundred feet from high water mark also the parties of the first part for and in consideration of the additional annuity (above refered to) do hereby further covenant and agree and grant unto the sd. party of the second part the Right and privilege of Erecting and setting on the above described and leased premises a work Shop or store house providing however that nothing be placed or stored therein that shall be offensive or be considered a nuisance to the Village

Page 57.

and the said Charles L. Bayles for himself his Heirs and assigns doth hereby covenant and agree to and with the Said Trustees and their Successors in office to pay unto the said parties of the first part on the first tuesday in June annually for the said term of twenty one years the sum of thirteen Dollars the first payment to be made the first tuesday in June 1855 and it is hereby agreed that at the expiration of said term of twenty one years this present grant Shall return to said town or further arrangment or agreement made between the Said parties or their Successors of the first part and the Said party of the second part or his heirs or assigns

In witness whereof the said parties have hereunto affixed their hands and Seals of office binding themselves and Successors on the one part and himself his heirs and assigns on the other part The day and year above written

Signed and Sealed   Davis Norton President (L S)
In the presence of   Charles L. Bayles   (L S)
   Samuel A. Hawkins
Entered Sep. 5th 1855
by me. S. A. Hawkins Town clerk

This Indenture made this fourteenth day of Sept. in the year of our Lord one thousand eight hundred and fifty two Between the Trustees of the freeholders and commonalty of the Town of Brookhaven of the first part and Elizabeth Darling of the same town of the Second part Witnesseth that the Said parties of the first part for and in consideration of the annuities hereinafter mentioned have granted and by these presents do grant to the Said party of the second part her heirs and assigns for the term of twenty two years (corresponding with and to continue and terminate with the grant given to Smith and Darling in 1834) The Right and privilege of constructing building repairing holding and conveying a Pier of one hundred feet in length from the front of the above mentioned Dock northerly to prevent the Sand from collecting around the said Dock this Pier to be constructed opposite her own land She paying for the privilege three Dollars annually and every year during said term of time the first payment to be made on the fourteenth day of Sep. 1853 and the Said party of the Second part doth hereby agree to pay or cause to be paid unto the said Trustees or their Successors the said annuity or annuities at the time they may be due according to the condition and Intent of this grant and it is hereby agreed that at the expiration of the Said term of twenty two years this present grant shall

PAGE 58.

return to Said Town and the dock appraised or further arrangment or agreement made between the Said parties or their Successors of the first part and the Said party or her heirs or assigns of the Second part

In witness whereof the Said parties have hereunto affixed their hands and Seals of office binding themselves and Successors on the one part and herself her heirs and assigns on the other part the day and year above written

Signed Sealed and   WM PHILLIPS President (L S)
Delivered in presence   ELIZABETH DARLING   (L S)
of SAML. A. HAWKINS
    Town clerk
Recorded Jan. 2d 1856
   S. A. HAWKINS Town clerk

Suffolk County S s. ⎤
Town of Brookhaven ⎦

Whereas a Road leading from the Village of Patchogue to Mott's Mills at a place called Canaan in said Town now used as a public highway was laid out by the commissioners of the said town on the 20th day of March 1822 but not sufficiently described of Record—now therefore we two of the said Commissioners of Highways of Said town all of the said Commissioners having been duly notified to attend and deliberate on the Subject matter of this order, Do hereby order that said Road be ascertained and described and entered of Record in the office of the town clerk of Said town according to a Survey which has been made under our direction as follows Beginning at the Junction of the said Road with the Coram Road at a point in line with a Stone proved to be the corner Stone of Oliver Russel's Barn as the same stood on the 20th of March 1822 and from thence running north six degrees thirty five minutes east to the northeast corner of the land of Eunice Jennings and William K. Thorn at the division line of the said land and the land of Austin Roe as the corner of the division fence now stands. and we do further order that the line of said Survey be the west line of Said Road and that the Said Road be of the width of three Rods

Given under our hands this 28th day of Dec. 1855

    Isaac Overton) Commissioners
    Nelson Norton (of Highways

Page 59.

At a meeting of the Trustees of the freeholders and commonalty of the town of Brookhaven on tuesday the 4th Mar. 1856

   Present Davis Norton President
    Horace Hudson
    John Hallock
    David Hedges
    Daniel D. Swezey } Trustees
    Micah Jayne
    Nelson Daines

On application the Board decided to assist Margaret Arch Colored to four Dollars as tempory Aid. on complaint the Board at sd meeting passed the following act viz. that no person or persons shall take or catch EEls with Seine or nets or pots in any of the waters on the north side of this town under the penalty hereinafter set forth Be it ordained by the Trustees of the freeholders and commonalty of the town of Brookhaven that if any person or persons shall take or catch EEls by or with seines or nets or pots from any of the Bays ponds creeks or harbors on the north side of the Town of Brookhaven to take to any foreign market or to Sell to any person or persons to be taken to any foreign market shall forfeit and pay to said town the sum of $12.50 cents to be sued for and Recovered in any court having cognizance thereof one half of the said sum of $12.50 so recovered to be paid to the person entering the complaint the other half to the use of the town poor Board decided to sell the oystering privileges of the South Bay for the ensuing year and that notices be posted at several public places on the south side offering sd privileges for sale at public Auction on the 15th March under the same restrictions that it was sold last year

adjourned to meet on tuesday the first day of April 1856 at 9 oclock A M.   DAVIS NORTON President
S. A. HAWKINS Town clerk

NOTE.—The Records continue from page 60, Book E.—COM.

www.ingramcontent.com/pod-product-compliance
Lightning Source LLC
Chambersburg PA
CBHW071712300426
44115CB00010B/1393